Yale Linguistic Series

A Manual of Japanese Writing

BOOK 1

by Hamako Ito Chaplin and

Samuel E. Martin

REVISED EDITION

New Haven and London, Yale University Press

Library of Congress catalog card number: 66-21510
ISBN: 0-300-00358-7 (cloth),
0-300-00040-5 (paper)

Published in Great Britain, Europe, and Africa by
Yale University Press, Ltd., London. Distributed
in Latin America by Kaiman & Polon, Inc.,
New York City; in Australasia and Southeast
Asia by John Wiley & Sons Australasia Pty. Ltd.,
Sydney; in India by UBS Publishers' Distributors
Pvt., Ltd., Delhi; in Japan by John Weatherhill,
Inc., Tokyo.

This work was developed pursuant to a contract
between the United States Office of Education
and Yale University and is published with the
permission of the United States Office of Education,
Department of Health, Education, and Welfare.

FOREWORD

We have written this book to teach the 881 essential or "education" characters (kyōiku-kanji) to English-speaking students of Japanese. Although kana reading exercises are provided, we assume that the student will have learned the hiragana and katakana syllabaries before beginning the book. We also assume that the student will have acquired a basic knowledge of Japanese grammar patterns equivalent to the coverage in Beginning Japanese by Jorden and Chaplin, in Spoken Japanese by Bloch and Jorden, or in Essential Japanese by Martin. Explanations are given for unusual expressions likely to be unfamiliar to the student, such as those common to writing but seldom heard in conversation.

Orthographic conventions throughout follow closely those suggested by the Language Board (Kokugo-shingikai) of the Ministry of Education (see Book 1, Part I). All kanji used are included among the 881, with the single addition of the hama of Yokohama, which is provided for reference. In general no attention is paid to the "radicals" under which the characters are traditionally classified, since that system of classification has become increasingly meaningless with the reduction in number of characters and the simplification of the shapes of many of them; but in the Kanji Lists we have noted, for reference purposes, the traditional radical number.

The Manual contains a number of sections, and each section is intended to aid the student in a particular way:

1. The Text Lessons (Book 2, Part I) introduce about 25 characters in each lesson and cover all 881 characters in 35 lessons. The new characters introduced in each lesson are listed at the bottom of the page, each with a number above to show the listing in Sakade's A Guide to Reading and Writing Japanese (Tokyo, 1959) and with a number below to show the listing in Seki and Toyama's Tōyō-Kanji Jiten (Tokyo, 1950). The text material is intended to serve the same function as that served by the "basic sentences" of textbooks devoted to the spoken language: the student must familiarize himself with the material in each lesson to the point where it becomes virtually memorized. That is, the student must be able to pronounce and understand the text without recourse to notes; he must be able to write out the Japanese text in characters from seeing the romanized version; and we hope that he will be able to re-create the entire Japanese text from the English translation.

2. The Drill Sentences (Book 2, Part III) are intended to give the student extensive familiarity with each character in its full range of uses, including the essential vocabulary of common compound words in which it occurs.

3. The Romanized Versions of the Text Lessons and the Romanized Versions of the Drill Sentences (Book 1, Parts II and V) give the student a ready check on the correct pronunciation and accent. They can also be used for practice in translating Japanese into English and in writing both kana and kanji.

4. The Vocabulary and Grammar Notes (Book 1, Part III) will help the student with puzzling constructions and new vocabulary items (see Book 1, page 44).

5. English Translations have been provided both for the text lessons (Book 1, Part IV) and for the drill sentences (Book 1, Part VI), but it will be better for the student to make his own translations first, and then check them against our translations (see Book 1, page 151).

6. The Kanji Lists (Book 3, Part I) give essential information about each

v

character, together with the order in which the strokes are to be written and the number of the character in the graded list established for elementary schools by the Ministry of Education (see Book 3, page 1).

Since extensive aids are provided, the book can be used with minimum access to a teacher. In university classes most of the material should be covered as homework. By studying the material at home, students will free the classroom hours for continued practice in conversation, help in calligraphy (using pen, chalk, or brush), and practice in rapid comprehension reading—with no use of English. The book can easily be used for self-instruction, and students who have already acquired some familiarity with the Japanese writing system will find the material a useful review to help consolidate their knowledge.

NOTE ON THE REVISED EDITION

Heartened by the warm reception accorded this book during its first year of publication, we have decided to issue a second edition with a number of corrections and improvements that should be of help to the student, who will find of particular convenience the addition of lesson references to the running heads and the inclusion of page references in the kanji index. We are grateful to the readers who made these suggestions and to those who called our attention to errors and inconsistencies in the text. The prompt appearance of this second edition was made possible by assistance provided by Far Eastern Publications, for which we express our thanks.

H.I.C.
S.E.M.

New Haven
December 1968

CONTENTS

Contents

Contents

Part I

MODERN JAPANESE ORTHOGRAPHY

There is no single Japanese orthographic system that can be termed "correct." Today, people usually write in a mixture of kanji, characters borrowed from the Chinese (→1), and the two varieties of kana symbols from the Japanese syllabaries (→2), namely hiragána (→2b) and katakána (→2a), with occasional admixtures of roman letters or rōmá-ji (→3a) and other symbols, such as arabic numerals. However, it is also possible to write in kana only, or even in rōmá-ji (romanization) only, although we find few cases of the latter. The extensive use of kanji alone has been limited to very special instances (→2e).

In general, Japanese is written in vertical columns, or tate-gaki, from top to bottom and the columns run from right to left. But scientific publications follow the Western practice of left-to-right horizontal lines running from top to bottom, and horizontal lines also appear in magazine and newspaper headings, picture captions, and so forth.

1. KANJI

The kanji are characters borrowed from the Chinese.

The Chinese characters were invented in Ancient China some three thousand years ago. It is believed that they started coming into Japan from China as early as the first century, as a way of writing Chinese words. Later, they were adapted to write native Japanese words as well, and they are still used for writing many such words today. Originally the characters sprang from a few hundred pictograms, but gradually ingenious methods were devised (1) to create new characters (zōji-hō), and (2) to divert old characters into other meanings (ten'yō-hō). The characters then so increased in number that Ueda's Dai-jíten includes nearly 15,000 characters, and the many volumes of Morohashi's dictionary contain nearly 50,000. But nowadays no more than 3,000 characters are used in everyday life by the ordinary person.

A single character consists of a SHAPE, one or more READINGS (= pronunciations, sounds), and one or more MEANINGS. That is to say, each character, by means of its shape, stands for a definite sound, and at the same time usually symbolizes some particular meaning. However, this does not mean that every character is independently used to convey meaning, for some characters occur only in combination with other characters.

a. The Shapes of Kanji

The shape of a kanji often differs from one text to another. For writing by hand there are three calligraphic styles: kaisho 'the square style,' which resembles the printed form; gyōsho 'the semi-cursive or "running" style,' which is generally used in ordinary letters and the like and is a somewhat simplified version of the square style; and sōsho 'the cursive or "grass-writing" style,' which is a further simplification of the semi-cursive style. Kanji are usually classified according to the structure of the printed form and are collected in a kanji dictionary. (→1c) Furthermore, new and simplified printed forms are now used for some kanji. (→1f)

1

b. The On and Kun

There are two main kinds of reading for a character. One of these is called the on or jion; this corresponds to the Chinese version transmitted with the character itself, though it has, to be sure, undergone a change from the original Chinese pronunciation. The on are further divided according to their assumed place of origin and time of transmission: (1) Go-on 'the Wu sound,' (2) Kán-on 'the Han sound,' and (3) Tō-on 'the Tang sound.' However, it is not important that students who learn the kanji as beginners remember these three classifications; it is sufficient for them to keep them all in mind as the on. The most commonly used of the three is the Kán-on.

In contrast to the on, the kun or jikun is the pronunciation which is appropriate for reading the character in native Japanese words. In dictionaries, on are usually indicated by katakána and kun by hiragána. In the kanji list of this book, for your convenience, on are printed in capital roman letters and kun in small roman letters.

An example of one character with three on and three kun:

$$
行 \quad
\begin{array}{ll}
\text{KŌ} & \text{[Kán-on]} \\
\text{GYŌ} & \text{[Go-on]} \\
\text{AN} & \text{[Tō-on]}
\end{array} \Bigg\} \text{ on}
$$

$$
\begin{array}{l}
\text{i(ku)} \\
\text{yu(ku)} \\
\text{oko(naᵘ)}
\end{array} \Bigg\} \text{ kun}
$$

Letters in parentheses indicate Okuri-gana (→2d).

But not every kanji has exactly three on and three kun; there are many characters that have one kun reading only, others with one on and no kun, one on and one kun, one on and two kun, two on and three kun, or two on and five kun, and so forth. There are even a few characters, made up in Japan and called kokuji, that have only a kun reading; for some of the kokuji made-in-Japan "Chinese" readings have also been created: 働 hatara(ku) 'works' has been given the pseudo-Chinese reading DŌ. It is extremely difficult to read characters with so many different on and kun. Multiple readings have of late been drastically curtailed for kanji in frequent use.

c. Kan-júkugo or Jukugo 'Character Compounds'

A compound of two or more characters bearing a single meaning is called jukugo or kan-jukugo 'character compound':

読 (DOKU 'to read')+ 書 (SHO 'to write, book')→ 読書 (DÓKUSHO 'reading').

Such character compounds are quite commonly used; authors make them up whenever the need arises. (But foreigners should be wary of making up compounds they have not heard or seen.)

There are a great variety of character compounds: but while there are some in which the meaning of the compound consists of the meaning of each character respectively, there are other cases where the characters have lost their original meanings and the whole compound has taken on an entirely different meaning. Hence, in studying compounds, one should capture the meaning of the entire compound. Remember that the characters are used to write WORDS and parts of words—not meanings directly.

Examples:

骨 (KOTSU 'bone')+ 肉 (NIKU 'meat')→ 骨肉 (KOTSUNIKU 'blood relations, one's own flesh and blood, and so forth').

自 (JI 'self')+ 動 (DŌ 'to move')+ 車 (SHA 'wheel')→ 自動車 (JIDŌSHA, 'automobile')

d. Classification by "Radicals"

In dictionaries of kanji, the characters are usually classified according to what are called "radicals." The ordinary way to compile a kanji dictionary is to list the characters under 214 key parts found in the structure of the characters, and then to arrange the characters belonging to each radical in the order of the number of the remaining strokes, from the fewest to the most. The traditional order of the radicals was set by the number of strokes in their original shapes. This means that (for example) the character 休 (KYŪ 'to rest') will be found under radical 9 (the 'man' radical) イ with a residual stroke-count of 4 in a section that may be headed "9,4." But nowadays, when the forms of often-used kanji or TŌYŌ-KÁNJI have been simplified, we do not always see the original radical in the new simple shapes.

Radicals are divided into the following general categories: (1) hen, (2) tsukurí, (3) kanmuri, (4) ashí, (5) taré, (6) kamaé, and (7) nyō. But these categories are not used for ordering the radicals, only for naming them and telling something about their shapes.

1. The hen is the left side of the kanji when it can be divided into left and right sides: 休

2. The tsukurí is the right side of the kanji when it can be divided into left and right sides: 休

3. The kanmuri is the upper part of the kanji when it can be divided into upper and lower parts: 花

4. The ashí is the lower part of the kanji when it can be divided into upper and lower parts: 点

5. The taré is a variation of (3), with the left side of the upper part hanging down: 厄

6. The kamaé is the outer side of the kanji when it encloses most of the character: 同 凶 国

7. The nyō is a kind of (4), which extends itself around from left to bottom, with a part of the kanji more or less on top of it: 遊

e. The Tōyō-kánji 'Characters for General Use'

The kanji are complicated in shapes and multiple in readings, with many compounds and an enormous number of characters, resulting in great inconvenience in education as well as in social life. As early as the Edo Period (the eighteenth century) some concern was shown. But it was not until 1866 that a scholar, Maejima Raisuke, suggested to the Shōgun that the people be educated in the kana (→2) so that the kanji could be gradually abolished; he advocated using the easiest possible letters in order to spread literacy.

There was no radical movement after this, but in the beginning of the Meiji Period (1868–1912) opinion began to support a gradual lessening of the number of kanji, with the idea that complete abolishment would be difficult to enforce all at once. This was the forerunner of the present-day campaigns for the exclusive use of kana (kana-moji-úndō) and roman letters (rōma-ji-úndō). In 1923 the Ministry of Education (Monbúshō) published, with the support of the newspaper firms and others, a list of 1,962 characters called Jōyō-kánji 'Everyday Characters'; but this system was rarely put to practical use.

Following the war, in 1946, the government officially published the list of 1,850 characters called Tōyō-kánji 'Characters for General Use' (also translated 'Current Characters,' 'Standard Characters'). These have come to be used in official government papers, laws and ordinances, and in the textbooks of the nine-year compulsory educational system. The leading newspapers and magazines also try to follow the various recommendations of the Ministry of Education.

Of the Tōyō-kánji, 881 characters have been chosen and designated as the Kyōiku-kánji 'Characters for Educational Use'; these have been published as a separate appendix (the Tōyō-kánji Beppyō) and are the characters which students must learn during the period of compulsory education. Besides this the government has also published a list of approved on and kun readings for the Tōyō-kánji (On-kun-hyō), a list of recommended character shapes (Jitai-hyō), and a special list of 92 additional characters to be used only in personal names (Jinmei-yō kanji-hyō). The Tōyō-kánji were selected on the basis of the frequency of each character, its usefulness in making character compounds, the shape of the character, and so on: the responsible scholars chose characters with the simplest forms and widest usage; at the same time they avoided homonymous near-synonyms (more than one character with the same sound and similar meanings), those with kun readings only, those used only in government offices, and the like. However, since the Japanese Constitution is considered required reading for the whole nation, the characters used therein are all included.

At the same time the on and kun were also restricted in number and systematized. In the writing of such things as laws, public documents, textbooks (for compulsory education), and the like, this system is carefully observed and only Tōyō-kánji are used. The major newspapers and magazines of the day are also trying to abide by the system as far as possible. But criticism and opposition have arisen in some quarters; opposition is especially strong among literary men. Widely felt problems arise from the fact that names of places and people cannot always be written within the confines of the list of approved characters. But despite this, the general trend favors the Tōyō-kánji.

In letters written by people at large, those who have received a higher education (to say nothing of those who had finished their education before the promulgation of the Tōyō-kánji) are apt to use more than the limited number of characters. Also, of course, knowledge of the Tōyō-kánji alone is not enough to read texts printed before 1946 or to read the classics. But it is best for the student to start with the 881 Kyōiku-kánji, for they are used most often, and then proceed to the remainder of the 1,850 that are most practical; students with special aims can then continue with the study of whatever additional characters they may need. To be sure, the entire system is, to some extent, still at a transitional and tentative stage. What do you do with words that cannot be written in Tōyō-kánji? In principle, those excluded from the Tōyō-kánji are written in kana. There are even some words that are coming to be regularly written in kana, though it is possible to write them with Tōyō-kánji (→ 2b). Compounds that might be confusing if written in kana are to be paraphrased in some other way; for example, 夭折する YŌSETSU suru → 若死に扡 waka-zíni suru, 'dies when young,' using a Japanese expression. Or, in some instances, they may be replaced with easier compounds that can be written in Tōyō-kánji: 宿痾 SHÚKUA → 持病 JIBYŌ 'chronic disease.' In some cases the word is replaced with an easy foreign word and written in katakana: 範疇 HANCHŪ → カテゴリー katégorī, 'category.' In other cases the word is rewritten with the use of a kanji of the same sound. 註文 CHŪMON → 注文 CHŪMON 'order.' Here is a list of pairs of kanji that are regarded as interchangeable so that the character on the right is substituted for the one on the left.

廻 → 回 (KAI)	礦 → 鉱 (KŌ)	歿 → 没 (BOTSU)
劃 → 画 (KAKU)	坐 → 座 (ZA)	熔鎔 → 溶 (YŌ)
廓 → 郭 (KAKU)	洲 → 州 (SHŪ)	慾 → 欲 (YOKU)
稀 → 希 (KI)	輯 → 集 (SHŪ)	輌 → 両 (RYŌ)
兇 → 凶 (KYŌ)	智 → 知 (CHI)	聯 → 連 (REN)
絃 → 弦 (GEN)	註 → 注 (CHŪ)	篇 → 編 (HEN)

f. The Kyōiku-kánji 'Characters for Educational Use'

Among the 1,850 Tōyō-kánji, 881 characters are called the Kyōiku-kánji. They are those which are the most frequently used, have fewer strokes, have simpler on and kun, are easy to apply in forming new compounds, and have common meanings. During the period of required education, students are taught both to read and to write all these characters.

However, this does not mean that only 881 characters are acquired during the nine years of compulsory education. The other Tōyō-kánji are also taught, but passively: the student learns to recognize them but he does not have to know how to write them.

g. The Shin-jítai 'New Character Shapes'

Shin-jítai are characters simplified in shape from the Tōyō-kánji for the sake of easier writing. Among the 1,850 characters, 600 fall into this category;

some are found in the Shin-jitai-hyō at the end of the third volume of this Manual.

The shapes of characters often differ according to the style of type used in printing. The new shapes are used when writing by hand in the kaisho 'square style,' but there are many people who still use the old characters. In letter writing, the old and new forms are often freely used side by side.

h. Hitsujun 'Stroke Order'

'Stroke order' refers to the way in which a character is built up, when writing, by adding dots and strokes one after the other in a set order. At one time everyone, from the professional calligrapher to the man in the street, had his own preferences with respect to minor points of stroke order, despite general agreement on major points; now, however, the Ministry of Education has tentatively standardized all this and made it possible even for one who cannot read the Japanese explanation to find out the preferred order by looking at a stroke order list, such as those in:

(1) Hitsujun shidō no tebiki Monbushō, Hakubundō, Tokyo, 1933.
(2) A guide to reading and writing Japanese, C. E. Tuttle, Rutland, Vermont, 1959.

The stroke order for gyōsho and sōsho are often different from that for kaisho, though the principles are much the same.

2. KANA

Kana are syllabaries that were made up in Japan by using for each syllable either some part of a kanji or an abbreviated ("shorthand") form of kanji. There are two varieties of kana: hiragána and katakána.

a. Katakána

Katakána are syllable symbols made up of some part of a kanji, often the hen or tsukurí radicals. Nowadays, katakána is used all by itself only in books for children, telegrams, and books put out by societies advocating the exclusive use of kana. Formerly, however, katakána and kanji were used together in official publications, scientific and literary essays, laws and ordinances, and so on. In the orthography in general use today, kanji and hiragána are used together; but we would like to point out briefly when and where katakána can be used within this general framework:

1. Modern foreign names of places or persons with the exception of the words for China (Chūgoku) 中国 and Korea (Chōsén) 朝鮮, and some well-known names from those countries. (→ 3a)

アメリカ 'America'   ロンドン 'London'   ニューヨーク 'New York'

フルシチョフ Khruschchev'   ペキン 'Peking'   シャンハイ 'Shanghai'

パリ 'Paris'   ソウル 'Seoul'

2. Foreign words or recent loanwords.

ラジオ 'radio'   ピアノ 'piano'   アイスクリーム 'ice cream'

マント 'manteau, Fr.'

3. Onomatopoeic words.

ガ゙タガ゙タ 'rattle-rattle'   ニャーニャー 'meow'   リンリン 'ting-a-ling'

4. Phonetic symbols, dialect words, baby talk, pidgin language.

天才 (テンサイ) [phonetic symbols]   シンネェー [dialect] 'I don't know'
          'genius'

              ウマウマ [baby talk] 'food'

5. Scientific words.

サビ止ペイント 'anticorrosive paint'

6. Animal and plant names.

サクラ 'cherry'   マメ 'soy bean'   マグロ 'tuna'

7. Names of tools and diseases.

ナベ 'pan'   カマ 'sickle, scythe' クワ 'hoe' ガン 'cancer'

8. Chinese words which cannot be written in Tōyō-kánji.

シュクア 'chronic disease'   チュウチョ 'hesitation'

9. Slang, neologisms, fashionable words, or words calling for special attention.

ヨロメキ 'illicit love affair' ニコヨン 'day-laborer'   ゾ゙ッとする 'shivers'

10. Telegrams.

アスアサユク 'Coming tomorrow morning.'

Note: Newspapers write Groups 6 and 7 in katakána, but in school textbooks they are frequently written in hiragána.

We are free to write names of cities and towns as well as personal names in katakána, if we like:

トヨタ町 (Toyotá-machi),   ハル子 (Háruko).

When a typewriter is used for business matters, katakána script is often used as a matter of convenience.

There is not yet complete uniformity with respect to the spelling of foreign loanwords, foreign words, or foreign place and personal names. There are many cases of transliteration into Japanese of the foreign words, with a faithful adherence to the spelling in the original language.

In general, it is agreed that ファ, フィ, フェ, フォ, ヴァ, ヴィ and so forth should be avoided as much as possible and replaced by ハ,ヒ,ヘ,ホ,バ,ビ and that チ, ジ should be used in place of ティ, ディ . But this is only a recommendation, and the rule admits exceptions.

The syllabic nasal n̄ (or 'ben') is written: ン as in: パン 'bread'; double consonants are indicated by a small ツ tsu as in: コップ 'glass'; palatalized sounds (syllables beginning with consonant plus y) are indicated by adding small ヤ ya, ユ yu, and ヨ yo as in: シャ sha, チュ chu, or キョ kyo. Long vowels are shown by using the dash-sign—as in: ボール 'ball,' カード 'card,' ショー 'show,' テーブル 'table.' Other conventions for lengthening vowels, such as ウ， ア， エイ, or オウ are as a general rule not used; there are, however, exceptions as in エイト 'eight.'

The English suffixes -er, -or are as a rule indicated by the long dash as in ランナー 'runner,' ライター 'lighter,' エレベーター 'elevator.' The spelling (i)a becomes ア as in: アジア Asia.' Final (y)a becomes ヤ as in: マラヤ 'Malaya'; however, if in English a consonant precedes final (y)a, we write ア as in: リビア 'Libya.' Outside newspapers and textbooks, such intricate rules are not strictly followed: アジヤ， リビヤ and similar transliterations are often found.

Besides this, occasional mixtures of rōmá-ji and kana may be seen in street signs or newspaper advertisements: Xマス 'Christmas,' Yシャツ 'shirt,'and so forth.

b. Hiragána

Hiragána are symbols in a syllabary derived from the sōsho form of the kanji. They were developed during the ninth century and used in writing letters and wáka (Japanese poetry of 31 syllables). Today, the method of writing used most commonly in society in general, as well as in the Japanese Constitution and laws, is a mixture of kanji and hiragána, called Kana-májiri. The cases in which hiragána is used are as follows:

1. PARTICLES: ni, o, wa, (に，を，は), etc.

2. COPULA: desu, da, de, na, ni, no, datta, etc. (です, だ, で, な, に, の, だった).

3. The inflected endings of VERBS and ADJECTIVES (including the final consonant of consonant-base VERBS):

   ká-ku 'writes,' (書く), ka-kimásu (書きます), ká-keba (書けば),
   ka-kitái (書きたい), ka-kánai (書かない), ka-kóo (書こう); hayá-i 'is early,' (早い), háya-ku (早く), háya-katta (早かった), háya-kereba (早ければ), etc.

4. PRE-NOUNS: ano 'that,' kono 'this,' sono 'that,' dónna 'what kind of,' anna 'that kind of' (あの, この, その, どんな, あんな), etc.

5. PRONOUNS: anáta 'you,' bóku 'I,' kimi 'you' (あなた, ぼく, きみ); INTERJECTIONS: hái 'yes,' iie 'no,' áa 'Oh' (はい, いいえ, ああ); ADVERBS: zéhi 'by all means,' sekkaku 'with trouble,' hotóndo 'almost' (ぜひ, せっかく, ほとんど); and certain other words: ómo-na 'main,' ómo-ni 'mainly' (おもな, おもに), etc.

6. The names of animals and plants:

   sakura (さくら) 'cherry,' take (たけ) 'bamboo.'

Note: The newspapers usually use katakána: サクラ, タケ.

7. In place of false substitute characters, or <u>ateji</u>, formerly used for a number of words:

<u>medetái</u> (めでたい) 'is auspicious,' <u>oshiroi</u> (おしろい) 'face powder,' <u>shigure</u> (しぐれ) 'shower in late fall,' <u>miyage</u> (みやげ) 'gift,' etc.

8. A part or the whole of a word which cannot be written with <u>Tōyō-kánji</u>.

<u>hón-dana</u> (本だな) 'bookshelf,' <u>ka-bin</u> (花びん) 'vase,' <u>kudámono</u> (くだもの) 'fruit,' etc.

c. The Kana Spelling Usage

By the kana spelling (<u>kana-zúkai</u>) we mean the rules which decide which spelling to choose as standard when there are more than two possibilities.

Until the mid-<u>Heian</u> Period (around A.D. 1000), the pronunciation of a word and its kana spelling were in agreement. In those days, かわ (川 'river') was pronounced かは (<u>kaha</u> [kaFa] 'river'), and チョウチョウ (蝶蝶 'butterfly') was pronounced テフテフ (<u>tehu tehu</u>). But the pronunciation gradually changed and came to differ from the kana spelling: kaha → kawa, tehu tehu → tyō tyō. Hence the system of one-to-one correspondence between kana symbol and spoken syllable deteriorated, and the spelling grew complex.

In 1695 the <u>kana-zúkai</u> was put in order and unified by <u>Kéichū</u> (契冲), on the basis of classical grammar and etymology. This is the basis underlying the so-called Historical Spelling, or <u>Rekishi-Kana-zúkai</u> (also called <u>Kyū-Kana-zúkai</u> 'Old Spelling'). But pronunciation and spelling were not identical in this system, either. For example, for the sound <u>o</u> at least four symbols (お , ほ , を , ふ ,) were used, and the kana ふ was pronounced some times <u>hu</u>, at other times <u>u</u>, and at still other times <u>o</u>.

For the people in general, apart from specialists in Japanese literature and classics, the Historical Spelling was recognized as too difficult; the system had been adopted by the government during the <u>Meiji</u> Period, but it was abolished in 1946. Since 1947, the New Spelling (<u>Shin-Kana-zúkai</u>) which uses kana in a manner more faithful to the pronunciation, has gradually spread, beginning with its use in state textbooks. Today, the main newspapers and magazines follow the New Spelling. And the average man has gradually begun to write his letters with it. Needless to say, there are some scholars in Japanese literature, novelists, poets, and so forth, who still oppose the new standard and observe only the Historical Spelling. And it is indispensable for those who study any publications dating before 1947, including the classics, to know the Historical Spelling.

What kind of spelling is the modern kana spelling commonly in use today? The first principle of the modern spelling is that kana stand for standard modern Japanese pronunciation so that each syllable has a corresponding kana symbol and that symbol is always pronounced the same way. What was written てふてふ 'butterfly' in the Historical Spelling is written now ちょうちょう or チョウチョウ according to the actual pronunciation.

1. Exceptionally, the spelling へ , を , and は , are used for the particles pronounced as <u>e</u>, <u>o</u>, and <u>wa</u> respectively. 田中さんは本を東京へ送りました.

   (Tanaka-san wa, hón o Tōkyō e okurimáshita. 'Mr. Tanaka sent the book to Tokyo.')

2. ぢ and づ, in principle, are avoided; instead じ and ず are used.   But

when ち or つ becomes voiced by the combination of two words, ぢ" and づ" are used: めし (meshi 'rice') + ちゃわん (chawan 'bowl') → めしぢゃわん (meshi-jáwan 'rice-bowl'). かな (kana) + つかい (tsukai 'usage') → かなづかい (kana-zúkai 'kana spelling usage')

3. In a few native words, when two identical syllables occur, with the second voiced, ぢ" and づ" are used: ちぢむ (chijimu 'shrinks'), つづみ (tsuzumi 'hand-drum'), つづく (tsuzuku 'continues').

4. The long sign is not used. The long sounds in the lines of a, i, u, and e, are indicated by adding あ, い, う, and え, respectively: おかあさん (okāsan 'mother'), にいさん (níisan 'elder brother'), ゆうがた (yūgata 'evening'), ねえ (nē 'You see!'), etc. But the long sound in the e-line which represents the on reading of a character uses い: えいが (éiga 'movie'), しつれい (shitsúrei 'rude'). And the long sound in the o-line is usually written with う: とうきょう (Tōkyō 'Tokyo'). Some words are exceptions where 'お' is used instead of 'う.' This was decided upon the basis of familiarity with the Historical Spelling and seems to be transitional. The beginner who does not learn the Historical Spelling had better memorize these words mechanically with the use of the following table.

5. As in the case of the katakána, the double consonants are indicated by the addition of a small っ, syllabic n̄ by ん, and palatalized sounds (syllables beginning with consonants plus y) by the addition of small や, ゆ, and よ.

6. "言う" 'speaks' is written "いう", not "ゆう."

おおやけ	公 (210)	ōyake	'public'
こおり	氷 (498)	kōri	'ice'
ほのお		honō	'flame, blaze'
おおせ		ōse	'statement, order'
おおきい	大きい (22)	ōkii	'is large'
とおい	遠い (160)	tōi	'is far'
おおい	多い (108)	ōi	'are many'
とおる	通る (281)	tōru	'passes'
こおる		kōru	'freezes'
とどこおる		todokōru	'stagnates'
もよおす		moyōsu	'holds (a meeting)'
いきどおる		ikidōru	'resents'
おおかみ		ōkami	'wolf'
ほお		hō	'cheek'
おおかた		ōkata	'probably'
おおよそ		ōyoso	'roughly'
とお		tō	'ten'

(*The numbers in parentheses are the numbers in the kanji list.)

d. The <u>Okuri-gana</u> 'Send-off Kana'

The <u>okuri-gana</u> is used in order to avoid misreading and misinterpretation when the modern spoken language is written in a mixture of kanji and kana. When a word is written with a kanji sometimes kana is added to make the reading clear; such kana is called <u>okuri-gana</u>. For example, 書く (KÁ-<u>ku</u> 'writes'), 書かない (KA-<u>kánai</u>), 書きます (KA-<u>kimásu</u>), 書こう (KA-<u>kóo</u>), 当てる (A-<u>teru</u> 'hits it'), 当たる (A-<u>taru</u> 'hits'), 大きい (Ō-<u>kii</u> 'is big'), 少ない (SUKU-<u>nái</u> 'is few'), 明るい (AKA-<u>rui</u> 'is light'), 半ば" (NAKÁ-<u>ba</u> 'half'), 後ろ (USHI-<u>ro</u> 'back'), 楽しみ (TANO-<u>shimi</u> 'delight'), 生き物 (I-<u>ki</u>-mono 'living thing'), etc.

The <u>okuri-gana</u> are used only with <u>kun</u> readings of the kanji. The principle types of use are these:

1. To inflected words (or parts of words that come from inflected words) the inflectional endings are added in kana. 読みます (YO-<u>mimásu</u> 'reads'), 落ちる (O-<u>chíru</u> 'drops down'), 落とす (O-<u>tósu</u> 'drops it'), 早い (HAYÁ-<u>i</u> 'is early'), 早く (HÁYA-<u>ku</u> 'quickly'), 乗り込む (NO-<u>ri</u>-KÓ-<u>mu</u> 'marches into'), etc.

2. For ADJECTIVES, the <u>okuri-gana</u> starts with い (-<u>i</u>), かった (-<u>katta</u>), く (-<u>ku</u>), ければ" (-<u>kereba</u>). But if those endings are preceded by <u>shi</u>, the <u>shi</u> starts the <u>okuri-gana</u>: 新しい (ATARA-<u>shii</u> 'is new'). Words like 大きい (Ō-<u>kii</u> 'is big'), 少ない (SUKU-<u>nai</u> 'is few'), 小さい (CHII-<u>sai</u> 'is small'), 明るい (AKA-<u>rui</u> 'is light'), etc. are special cases involving etymological suffixes.

3. ADJECTIVAL (or "COPULAR") nouns that end in -<u>ka(na)</u>, -<u>yaka(na)</u>, or -<u>raka(na)</u> write these suffixes in kana: 静かな (SHIZU-<u>ka na</u> 'is quiet').

4. The <u>okuri-gana</u> -<u>tsu</u> is added as an ending to some numbers: 一つ (HITO-<u>tsu</u> 'one thing'), 二つ (FUTA-<u>tsu</u> 'two things'), etc.

5. NOUNS that do not come from inflected words take no <u>okuri-gana</u>: 海 (úmi 'sea'), 山 (yamá 'mountain'), 春 (háru 'spring'), etc. But nouns that are derived from inflected words usually have <u>okuri-gana</u>: 休み (YASU-<u>mí</u> 'vacation'), 動き (UGO-<u>kí</u> 'movement'), 楽しみ (TANO-<u>shimi</u> 'delight'), 遠く (TŌ-<u>kú</u> 'far away'), etc.

There are other, more detailed rules, but they are part of a transitional system to which much opposition is heard. It is not necessary for the beginner to learn all the details.

When the Ministry of Education published the "Okuri-gana no tsukekáta" 'How to Attach Send-off Kana' in 1959, they said "Exceptions are allowed where usage is fixed." But, since each individual has a different feeling about "fixed usage," involving complicated exceptions, opinions vary on many words. The student is advised to follow the table of the <u>on</u> and <u>kun</u> for appropriate send-off kana. When doubt remains, it is best to add as many <u>okuri-gana</u> as possible, since the purpose of the <u>okuri-gana</u> is to avoid misreading.

e. The Man'yō-gana and Ateji

Sometimes the kanji are used, not for their meanings, but just to represent the sounds of native Japanese words, as if they were kana. This is called the Man'yō-gana. It is so called because it was used in the Man'yōshū (the oldest collection of Japanese poems). When the waka (Japanese poems of 31 syllables) were written in the Man'yō-gana, only kanji were used, without any kana. To-day we rarely see Man'yō-gana except in place names, such as Nára (奈良).

Besides this, there is a method of writing called ateji. It is often seen in shop names, and in a few common words. めでたい 'is auspicious' is written, for example, 目出度い; うらやましい 'is enviable' is written 浦山敷い, and おしろい 'face powder' is written 白粉. This way of writing is never used in official writings and textbooks, but we mention it as it is still seen here and there in the streets. There are two kinds of ateji: those using the characters for meaning alone (the last example above 白粉) and those using the characters for pronunciation (the earlier examples). Man'yō-gana can be regarded as a systematic exploitation of this type of ateji.

3. MISCELLANEOUS

a. Placenames of China, Korea, Sakhalin (Karafuto), and the Kuriles (Chishima)

As a rule, the standard pronunciation of foreign placenames is to be noted in katakána, but it is permissible, in exceptional cases, to use familiar characters and old readings. Since the kanji involved in these placenames are mostly beyond the limit of the Kyōiku-kánji, we do not give examples here. If interested, consult the following book: "Chimei no yobikata to kakikata" 'How to read and write placenames,' Ōsaka Kyoiku Tosho, 1959.

b. Special Marks (in Vertical Writing)

1. The Kurikaeshi-fúgō (Repeat-marks). When the same element is repeated, the sign used in place of the second element is called the kurikaeshi-fúgō. There are several kinds, and they are mostly used when writing vertically.

   (a) ヽ Used for kana, when a syllable within a word is repeated. あヽ (Áa 'Oh'), いヽえ (iie 'No'), たヽみ (tatami 'mat')

   (b) ゞ Used for kana, when the repeat in a word is voiced. かゞみ (kagámi 'mirror'), すゞむ (suzúmu 'cools oneself'), たゞ (táda 'free') いかゞ (ikága 'how'). Note that without the voicing mark, the syllable is repeated voiceless, even when the first syllable carries a voicing mark: がヽ (gaka 'artist')

   (c) 〱 Used when two or more kana are repeated. いろ〱 (iroiro 'various'), なか〱 (nakanaka 'quite') むかし〱 (mukashi-mukashi 'long long ago')

   (d) 〲 Used when two or more kana are repeated, with the repeat voiced: とき〲 (toki-doki 'sometimes'), ところ〲 (tokoro-dókoro 'here and there')

(e) 々 Used when a kanji is repeated regardless of the pronunciation. 人々 (hitó-bito 'people') 国々 (kuní-guni 'countries').

You may use these signs, but the Ministry of Education is of the opinion that it is better to avoid using them if possible, despite their popularity.

2. The Kutō-ten 'Punctuation Marks.' The kutō-ten, like the comma and period in English, are signs used to clarify the structure of the sentence or the context of the phrase.

   (a) 。 kuten 'period.' Commonly called maru. Used at the end of a sentence. 東京にいる。 (Tōkyō ni iru. 'He is in Tokyo.') It is not used for mottos, titles, or the names of things written in a row.

   (b) 、 tōten 'comma.' Commonly called just ten. This is used somewhat arbitrarily to show how the words break in a sentence. See the uses in this text.

   (c) ・ naka-ten 'middle-dot.' The naka-ten is used when nouns are written in a row; when dates, hours, etc. are written in abbreviation; and when separating foreign names or initials transcribed in Japanese, when separating parts of a foreign phrase; and so forth.

   1960・9・10 'Sept. 10, 1960'

   N・H・K Nihon Hōsō Kyōkai 'Japan Broadcasting Company'

   ドワイト・アイゼンハワー Dowaito Aizenháwaa 'Dwight Eisenhower'

   (d) 「 」 kákko 'quotations.' For quotations, "key" brackets (kagi-kákko) 「 」 are used. To indicate notes and abbreviations, parentheses ( ) are used. 「だめだ。」といった。 "Damé da" to itta. 'He said "Dame da".' 句点（まるともいう）。 Kuten (maru tó mo iu). 'period (also called maru).'

Besides these, the vertical hyphens tsunagi-ten (ǀ single and ǁ double) are also used. The question mark (?) and the exclamation mark (!) are not used much but they are not strictly prohibited.

c. Wakachi-gaki 'Word or Sentence Division'

When kana are used either alone or extensively, sentences are often separated into smaller units to make them easy to read and understand. This way of writing is called wakachi-gaki. Little need is felt for wakachi-gaki when one writes in the usual way with a mixture of kanji and kana accompanied by punctuation marks.

Wakachi-gaki is carried out in several ways: dividing by words, dividing by phrases, mixtures of both, and so forth. The division differs according to the individual's interpretation of the grammar.

d. Yoko-gaki Horizontal Writing from Left to Right'

The mixture of kanji and kana has long been written from top to bottom and from right to left i.e., migi - tate-gaki 'right-vertical.' But the hidari - yoko-gaki 'left-horizontal' style, is now increasing in textbooks (except those devoted to the Japanese language) and in official writings. Newspapers, magazines, novels, and so forth, continue the older vertical style as do letters and most personal notes.

In yoko-gaki, the repetition marks are not used except for 々 . The comma (,) may be used in the place of the tōten (、). The arabic numerals 1, 2, 3, 4, and so forth are used as in English, but you will sometimes see a combination of the Chinese numerals from one to nine with the arabic zero: 一九六〇'1960'.

e. The Roman Alphabet

   Though unusual, passages of Japanese written in the roman alphabet are occasionally seen. Romanized Japanese has been taught as a part of the compulsory education since 1947. There are various ways to romanize Japanese, but the spelling which was published in 1954 is considered official Kunrei-shiki. See Table 1. However, the several variations shown in Table 2 Hyōjun-shiki or Hebon-shiki 'Hepburn' and Nihon-shiki are also recognized as permissible, and inadvertent mixture of the two tables is not uncommon, though hardly to be recommended. (Note that there is no conflict between the tables. For a given spelling there can be only one interpretation.)

Table 1

a	i	u	e	o								
					ga	gi	gu	ge	go	kya	kyu	kyo
ka	ki	ku	ke	ko	za	zi	zu	ze	zo	sya	syu	syo
sa	si	su	se	so	da		de	do		tya	tyu	tyo
ta	ti	tu	te	to	ba	bi	bu	be	bo	nya	nyu	nyo
na	ni	nu	ne	no	pa	pi	pu	pe	po	hya	hyu	hyo
ha	hi	hu	he	ho						mya	myu	myo
ma	mi	mu	me	mo						rya	ryu	ryo
ya		yu		yo						gya	gyu	gyo
ra	ri	ru	re	ro						zya	zyu	zyo
wa										bya	byu	byo
										pya	pyu	pyo

Table 2

Nihon-shiki		Kunrei-shiki		Hyōjun-shiki	
hu	フ	hu	フ	fu	フ
n	ン	n	ン	n, m	ン
si	シ	si	シ	shi	シ
ti	チ	ti	チ	chi	チ
tu	ツ	tu	ツ	tsu	ツ
zi	ジ	zi	ジ	ji	ジ
sya	シャ	sya	シャ	sha	シャ
syu	シュ	syu	シュ	shu	シュ

Nihon-shiki		Kunrei-shiki		Hyōjun-shiki	
syo	シ゛ョ	syo	シ゛ョ	sho	シ゛ョ
tya	チャ	tya	チャ	cha	チャ
tyu	チュ	tyu	チュ	chu	チュ
tyo	チョ	tyo	チョ	cho	チョ
dya	ヂャ	zya	ジャ	ja	ジャ
dyu	ヂュ	zyu	ジュ	ju	ジュ
dyo	ヂョ	zyo	ジョ	jo	ジョ
kwa	クヮ	ka	カ	ka	カ
gwa	グヮ	ga	ガ	ga	ガ
di	ヂ	zi	ジ	ji	ジ
du	ヅ	zu	ズ	zu	ズ
wo	ヲ	o	ヲ, オ	o	ヲ, オ

Note:

1. The syllabic nasal n + Vowel or ya yu yo: n̄ or n'; teñiñ or ten'in 'clerk.'
2. Long Vowel: oo-sama or ō-sama 'king,' okáa-san or okā-san 'mother.'
3. Double consonant: yukkúri 'slowly,' zassō 'weed,' itte 'going,' happyaku '800'; before ti and chi: mátti or mátchi 'matches.'
4. Use capital letters for the first letters of sentences and proper nouns. A few romanization enthusiasts start all nouns with a capital letter, as in the old-fashioned way of writing German.

Part II

ROMANIZED VERSIONS OF THE TEXT LESSONS

INTRODUCTORY NOTE

1. The primary purpose of these romanized versions is to teach the pronunciation of the Japanese texts, that is, the proper way to read them aloud. That is why accent and juncture are marked.

2. At the same time, the romanization is intended to provide home dictation practice for the student to convert the material back into the kanji and kana of the original texts. For this reason a number of special devices are used.

3. The basic romanization used is a slightly revised form of the official Japanese system known as the kunrei-shiki romanization. Students should acquire a familiarity with this system, which is used in slightly different forms in the textbooks Spoken Japanese and Beginning Japanese, as well as with the Hepburn system which we have used for romanizing the Japanese words that appear in the English translations of the texts.

4. Capital letters are used where kanji appear in the original text; small letters are used where the original text has kana, including okuri-ğana ("send-off kana"). Where katakána appears in the original text, the romanized version has an underline. (Note how this differs from the section of English Translations where the underline is used for ANY Japanese word; in the romanized versions, only katakána words are underlined.) You will find that there the capital letters are used for ALL character readings, not just the Chinese readings; in the kanji lists, capital letters are used only for the Chinese readings. When a string of capital letters represents a sequence of more than one character, an on-the-line dot is used to separate the individual readings: SÁ.I 'difference' is written with two characters (SA and I), SÁI 'talent' is written with one character.

5. We have preserved the punctuation of the original text so far as possible, but space and hyphen are used in special ways (see below). The Japanese naka-ten (center dot) is represented by a raised dot with no space before or after: razio·térebi 'radio-television.' This is to be distinguished from the on-the-line dot (see preceding paragraph) and from the sentence-final period, which is always followed by space.

6. Word division and hyphenation cause many problems. In general, we have used spaces and hyphens in a generous way, so as to help the student grasp the structure of compound words. In written Japanese many long compounds of free NOUNS occur; to show the structure of these compounds, which are spoken as one word (with a single accent pattern), we use space-hyphen-space as in GI.KAI - SÉI.ZI 'Diet politics.' Bound elements, such as PREFIXES and SUFFIXES, are set off by the hyphen; but the element to which they are bound is set off from the hyphen by a space unless itself bound. Thus OO- ZÍ.NUSI consists of the PREFIX oo- 'great' attached to the free NOUN zinusi 'landowner,' and KEI.ZAI -TEKI consists of the free NOUN kéizai 'economics' with the suffix -teki '-ical' attached. (Frequently, as in these two examples, the accent of the compound will be different from the accent of the underlying free NOUN.) A number of special problems have been taken care of somewhat arbitrarily. You may wonder about such cases as the following:

(a) We have used hyphens (without space) to link words forming a NOUN that is derived from a phrase but differs in accent from the expected accent of the phrase:

su-nó-mono 'salad' from sú no|monó 'vinegar thing'
te-nó-hira 'palm of hand' from té no|hira 'flat of hand'
hi-no-mí 'firewatch' from hí no | mí 'watching of fire'
otokó-no-ko 'boy' from otoko no|ko 'a child who is a male' (in which
    otokó, like most non-monosyllables, drops its final accent before the
    word no) etc.

(b) Truncated PREFIXES are written with a hyphen followed by a comma with no subsequent space: SI-,ḠO-MAI '4 or 5 sheets'; GET-,SUI-,KIN-YÓO 'Monday-Wednesday-Friday.'

(c) Where it is difficult to make a decision about the immediate constituency, we have avoided using a hyphen altogether. Since we might want to consider 'Saturday' analogous either to NAN-YÓO.BI 'what day of the week' or to KI.NÉN -BI 'anniversary day,' we duck the issue by writing DO.YÓO.BI. Similar cases are SYOO.ḠÁK.KOO 'primary school' and DAI.ḠAKÚ.IN 'graduate school.'

(d) We have treated one-element NUMERALS (such as ití-, kyúu-, zyúu-; hito-, huta-) as essentially bound (though they are used as free NOUNS in counting and arithmetic), but two-part numerals are treated as free, following the usual Japanese juncture-phrasing. This leads us to write DÁI | HÁK-KA 'Lesson 8' but DÁI | ZYUU-HÁK -KA 'Lesson 18' (where zyuu-hatí '18' appears with altered shape). Counters (such as -ka 'lesson,' -mai 'flat object,' -hon 'long slender object') are treated as bound; they are hyphen-linked directly to a single-element NUMERAL (ní-mai, go-hon, etc.) but separated by a hyphen-followed space after a two-part NUMERAL (zyuu-sán -mai, ni-zyúp -pon). The counter -tu attaches only to single-element NUMERALS from '1' through '9,' but -ka 'day' occurs in two expressions that are more complex: zyúu-yok -ka '14 days' and ní-zyuu | yok-ka '24 days.'

(e) Although the first element of the reduplication is free, we have not spaced the hyphen in such cases as hitó-bito, soré-zore, toki-doki, etc. Nor have we used a space when the head NOUN of a simple native-Japanese compound undergoes niḡori (voicing of the initial consonant): uzí-ḡami, mamorí-ḡami, ko-zútumi, ao-zóra [rather than uzí -ḡami, mamorí -ḡami, ko- zútumi, ao -zora]. Compounds involving NOUN + ADJECTIVE or VERB are usually unspaced: ne-zuyói 'is deep-rooted,' na-dakái 'is famous.'

7. A bar over the letter g (ḡ) is used when the nasal velar is appropriate. The distinction between oral g and nasal ḡ is usually ignored both in kana and in romanization; we have followed the convention introduced in Beginning Japanese.

8. Unlike Spoken Japanese and Beginning Japanese, we indicate the syllabic nasal with a simple n (sinbun 'newspaper') except before VOWEL or y within a word, and there we follow the n with an apostrophe (ten'in 'clerk,' hón'ya 'bookshop'), unless some other mark intervenes: men- orí-mono 'cotton textiles,' TEN.IN, HÓN.YA.

9. The long VOWELS are written as double VOWELS (ookii 'is big'); but the long VOWEL ee is written as ei whenever the kana spelling has ei, as in heitai 'soldier,' eiḡo 'English'—cf. ée 'yes,' teeburu 'table.'

10. Unvoiced or dropped VOWELS are shown by using a slash symbol through the letter: s̸ta dés̸ 'it's below.' These unvoicings are largely predictable, you will discover, in terms of the surrounding sounds.

11. The letter -t is used for the glottal stop represented by the kana symbol "small tu" whenever typography makes it impossible or inconvenient to double a following CONSONANT.

12. To enable the student to practice a native-sounding version of the text, we provide three marks to help with accentuation and phrasing: an accent mark (´) and two juncture marks, a single bar to represent MINOR juncture (|) and a double bar to represent MAJOR juncture (||). The major juncture is automatic at the end of a sentence, but we have added it after the period (or other punctuation) to remind you that it is present. Between any two juncture marks there is one and only one ACCENT PHRASE. There may be no accent mark (kono kodomo wa ||); this means the phrase is spoken with no fall of pitch, the first syllable slightly lower than the rest. If there is an accent mark, there is only one (kono otokó wa ||) and it marks a fall of pitch; all syllables following the accent are low in pitch, while all syllables preceding it are high with the exception of the beginning syllable, which is always somewhat lower unless it carries the accent itself (as it does in sóo des̸ ka ||). When there is more than one accented phrase, each succeeding pitch plateau is slightly lower (atarasíi | zidóosya o| kaimásita || 'I bought a new car') unless a major juncture intervenes (zidóosya wa || dáre ḡa | kaimásita ka.|| 'Who bought a new car?'). After a major juncture the pitch pattern of an accent phrase is the same as it would be at the beginning of a sentence.

13. Other native-sounding versions of the text are possible; only one has been given here. If the reading is slowed down, more junctures will appear, and many minor junctures will be promoted to major junctures. Conversely, a faster version will demote some of the major junctures, and many of the minor junctures will drop out altogether, taking with them any accents whose suppression is mandatory when a prior accent joins the phrase.

14. The accent of a word in particular phrases often differs from its accent in isolation: you will notice that an expected accent is sometimes suppressed (e.g. yamá in yama no ue 'on top of the mountain') and an unexpected accent is sometimes induced (e.g. itte in itté kara 'after going'); some abbreviated expressions (e.g. that exemplified by neté 'ta 'was asleep') show an accent absent from the underlying model (nete ita). The accent of a compound is often different from that of the component words. A fuller description will be found in the various textbooks. (For a summary, see Appendix II of Essential Japanese.)

15. .. is used at the end of a sentence as an intonation symbol. It denotes incompleteness, and indicates that there is a gradual fading into silence.

DÁI | ÍK-KA ||

teeburu no UÉ ni || HÓN ḡa | SÁN-satu ari-masi̧. ||

IS-satú wa | ÓOki̧ki̧te || áto no | NÍ-satu wa || TIIsái | HÓN desi̧. || OOkíi | HÓN wa | AÓi desu ḡa || TIIsái no wa || ÁOku | ari-masén. || NI-sati̧ tomo || AKAi HÓN desi̧. ||

AÓi | HÓN no | SI̧TA ní wa || SIRÓi | KAMÍ ḡa | SI-,ḠO-mai ari-masi̧. || sóba ni || TIIsái TE.TYOO to || pén ḡa | ÍP-PON ari-masi̧. ||

muzukási̧ki̧te || wakaránai | tokoró o || sono KAMÍ ni | káite oite || áto de || SEN.SÉI ni | si̧tumon suru tumori dési̧. ||

DÁI | NÍ-KA ||

móto wa || GAI.KOKU -ḠO dátta | kéredomo || ÍMA wa || móo || NI.HON -ZÍN ḡa | MÁI.NITI̧ ti̧kau | NI.HON -ḠO ni nátte simatta | kotobá o || GAI.RAI -ḠO to ii-masi̧. || tatóeba || mátti̧ || pán || mánto || si̧kíi nado wa || EI.ḠO || porutogaru -ḠO || huransu -ḠO || doitu -ḠO kara Ki̧ta | GAI.RAI -ḠO dési̧. || taitei || konna kotobá wa || katakána de | KAki-masi̧. ||

mázu || MÉ de | MÍtari || MIMÍ de | kiitári | suru monó ni wa || térebi || ópera || báree || rázio || rekóodo nado ḡa ari-masi̧. || KU̧TI ni Ireru monó ni mo || koohíi || zyúusi̧ || bíiru || sandoítti̧ || kéeki o hazime || taki̧sán no | GAI.RAI -ḠO ḡa ari-masi̧. || náihi̧ || hwóoki̧ || si̧púun wa || TÉ de | ti̧kaú si̧ || ASÍ ni wa || sókki̧su ya | súrippa o haki-masi̧. ||

ÁME ḡa | húru to || rein- kóoto o | kirú si̧ || SAMÚi HI ni wa || óobaa o | ki-masi̧. ||

DOyóoBI ya | NITIyóoBI ya | YASUmi no HÍ ni wa || ténisu ya | góruhu o | si̧tári || doráibu o | si̧tári si-masi̧. || mata || háikingu ya | píkunikku ni | Iki̧ kotó mo | ari-masi̧. ||

kono yóo na GAI.RAI -ḠO wa || NI.HON -ZÍN no | SEI.KATU no NÁKA ni | toke-kónde simatte ite || wakái HI̧TO-BITO | bákari de | náki̧ || ROKU̧-,SI̧TI- ZYÚU no | tosi -yóri ni mo || yóku ti̧kawarete i-masi̧. ||

DÁI | SÁN-KA ||

wataki̧si̧ -tati wa || KYÓ.NEN no | KÚ.ḠATU ni | KI-mási̧ta kara || NI.HÓN e | Ki̧té kara || móo || HAK-káḠETU ni nari-masi̧. ||

kánai mo | musumé mo || daibu | NI.HON no SEI.KATU ni | nare-mási̧ta. ||

wataki̧si wa || MAI.SYUU || GET-,SUI-,KIN-YÓO ni wa || ISI̧.KAWA to iu TOMOdati ni | NI.HON -ḠO o narái || KA.YÓO to | MOKU.YÓO ni wa || tosyó -kan e Itte | BEN.KYOO si̧te i-masi̧. || musumé wa || MÁI.NITI̧ || TI̧KÁku no | NI.HON -ZÍN no | ONNÁ no KO to asonde i-masi̧. || kánai wa || o- syooḡati̧ kara || Iké-BANA o | narátte i-masi̧. ||

uti no MIḠI -dónari wa || YAMA.NAKA -san to iu zituḡyoo -ka de || HIDARI -dónari ni wa || MÓRI.TA -san to iu | benḡó -si ḡa | súnde i-masi̧. ||

minna sínsetu de ‖ ítu mo ‖ NI.HON no │ syuukan ya │ sáhoo o │ osiete kure-
masɥ́.

DÁI │ YÓN-KA ‖

YAMA.DA   "kyóo wa ‖ GAK.KOO │ o- YASUmi désɥ́ ka."

súmisɥ́   "ée. ‖ kinóo kara ‖ HARU - YÁSUmi na n desɥ́."

YAMA.DA   "íi desu ne. ‖ ítu made desɥ́ ka."

súmisɥ́   "IS-SYÚU.KAN desɥ́ kara ‖ RAI.SYUU no MOKU.YÓO made desu
            yo."

YAMA.DA   "urayamasíi desu ne. ‖ bókɥ́ -tati wa ‖ NATU - YASUmi daké de ‖
            HÁRU ya │ ÁKI ni wa ‖ YASUmí ḡa │ nái n desu yo. ‖ RYO.KOO
            dé mo │ surú n desɥ́ ka."

súmisɥ́   "ée. ‖ máda ‖ inaka no hóo e │ Itta kotó ḡa │ nái no de ‖ TOO.
            HOKɥ - TÍ.HOO no │ MURÁ o │ ARÚite │ miyóo ka to │ OMÓtte │
            irú n desu ḡa . ."

YAMA.DA   "TOO.HOKU désɥ́ ka. ‖ tokoro ni yotté wa ‖ máda ‖ YUKÍ ya
            KOORI ḡa │ áru ka mo │ siremasén yo. ‖ atti no HUYÚ wa │ NAḠÁi
            kara . . ‖ KƗ.SYÁ de │ Ikú n desɥ́ ka."

súmisɥ́   "ée. ‖ dé mo ‖ YUKÍ ḡa │ áru n zya . . ‖ TOO.HOKU - RYÓ.KOO
            wa ‖ NATU no hóo ḡa │ íi desyoo ne."

YAMA.DA   "ée. ‖ máda ‖ attí wa │ SAMÚi desu yo. ‖ KÁN.SAI wa │ dóo desɥ́
            ka."

súmisɥ́   "KÁN.SAI ni wa ‖ MI-tái │ tokoró ḡa │ YAMÁ hodo │ áru kara ‖
            SI-,ḠO-NITI no RYO.KOO zya . ."

YAMA.DA   "zya ‖ SIMO.DA no hóo e │ Itte mítara │ dóo desɥ́ ka. ‖ daibu
            MINAMI dá kara ‖ móo ‖ KÍ no ME ḡa │ kírei da to │ OMOi-másu
            yo. ‖ sono ue ‖ ATARAsíi sakana mo │ TAberare-másu yo."

súmisɥ́   "sore ḡa yo-sasóo desu ne."

DÁI │ GÓ-KA ‖

NI.HON -ḠO wa ‖ kana daké de mo ‖ roomá -ZI de mo │ KAke-másu ḡa ‖
hɥ́tuu wa ‖ KAN.ZI to katakána │ hiraḡána o │ mázete KAki-masɥ́. ‖

KAN.ZI wa ‖ SÉN │ SUU-HYAKÚ -NEN mo │ MÁE ni ‖ TYÚU.ḠOKɥ kara │
watatté kɨ́ta │ MÓ.ZI desɥ́. ‖ sono KÁZU wa ‖ taihen ÓOkɥ́ ‖ TYÚU.ḠOKU no │
HURÚi │ ZI.TEN ní wa ‖ YON-MÁN │ GO-HYAKU -ZI ƗꞋ.ZYOO │ áru soo desɥ́. ‖
NI.HON no "UE.DA DAI- ZꞋ.TEN" ni wa ‖ ITI-MÁN │ GO-SEN ḡúrai ari-masɥ́. ‖
kéredomo ‖ sono utɨ́ ‖ SAN-ZEN -ZI ḡúrai │ Sɨ́tte iréba ‖ hɥ́tuu no HƗ́TÓ ni
wa │ zyuubún desɥ́. ‖

SAN-ZEN -ZI dé mo ‖ oboéru no wa │ taihen desɥ́. ‖ to iú no wa ‖ KAN.ZI ní
wa ‖ KATATƗ to │ YOmi-KÁTA to │ ƗꞋ.MI ḡa │ áru kara desɥ́. ‖ YOmi-KÁTA
ni mo ‖ ON (on) to KUN (kun) ḡa ari-masɥ́. ‖ ON to iú no wa ‖ TYÚU.ḠOKU

no | YOmi-KÁTA ḡa tᴀtawatte || NI.HON -KA sᴀta monó desᴀ. || KUN to iú no
wa || KAN.ZI o KOKU.ḠO ni atete YÓmu | YOmi-KÁTA desᴀ. || tatóeba ||
"山" no ON wa | "<u>san</u>" || KUN wa | "yamá" desᴀ. || KAN.ZI ní wa || ITI-ON |
IK-KUN no monó mo | ari-másu ḡa || ITÍ-ZI ni | takᴀsán no | ON ya KUN ḡa
áru | monó mo ari-masᴀ. || "生" to iu ZÍ wa || "séi" || "syóo" to iu ON no
hoka ni || "u(mareru)" || "náma" || i(kíru)" || "kí" | nádo no | KUN ḡa ari-
masᴀ. ||

KAN.ZI o HᴀTA-tu Í.ZYOO | KUmi-Awáseta | monó de || betu no Í.MI o | mótu
zyukuḠO mo ari-masᴀ. || "学" to "生" o KUmi-Awáseta "学生" to iu zyukuḠO
wa || "DAI.ḠAKU nádo de | BEN.KYOO sᴀte iru HᴀTO" | to iu | Í.MI desᴀ. ||
"生命" (séimei) to iu zyukuḠO wa || "ínotᴀ" to mo | YOmi-másᴀta. || kono yóo
na || zyukuḠO no KUN mo KAZOéru to || "生" ni wa || HYAKU ROKU-ZYUU GÓ
no | tiḡatta YOmi-KÁTA ḡa | átta soo desᴀ. || konna ni takᴀsán no | ON ya
KUN || sore kara || zyukuḠO no YOmi-KÁTA ya | sono Í.MI wa || IS.SYOO
kakátte mo | oboe-kirénai ka mo | sire-masén. || sore de || ÍMA no | NI.HÓN
de wa || SÉN HAP-PYAKU | GO-ZYÚU -ZI o | TOO.YOO - KÁN.ZI to sᴀte ||
hᴀtuu no SIN.BUN ya zassi ya || SYOO.ḠÁKᴀ-SEI || TYUU.ḠÁKᴀ-SEI ḡa |
GAK.KOO de BEN.KYOO suru | HÓN nado ni tᴀkau | KAN.ZI to || sono | ON |
KUN ḡa | kimete ari-masᴀ. ||

mata || TOO.YOO - KÁN.ZI no uti de || SYOO.ḠÁK.KOO to | TYUU.ḠÁK.KOO
de || YÓmu koto mo | KÁKᴀ koto mo | dekíru yoo ni suru | KAN.ZI o || HAP-
PYAKᴀ HATI-ZYUU ITÍ -ZI | kime-másᴀta. ||

watakᴀsᴀ -tati wa || hazime ni || kono HAP-PYAKᴀ HATI-ZYUU ITÍ no KAN.ZI
o | BEN.KYOO suru kotó ni | si-masyóo.

DÁI | RÓK-KA ||

ATARAsíi | IÉ o | TÁteta TOMOdati ni | SYÓO.TAI sareta | <u>súmisᴀ</u> -san ga |
Ii-másᴀta. ||

"konna <u>kirai</u> na utí wa || Mᴀta koto ḡa | ari-masén." ||

Iwareta TOMOdati wa || mut to si-másᴀta ḡa || ZITᴀ wa || <u>súmisᴀ</u> -san ḡa |
Ii-tákatta no wa || "<u>kírei</u> na | utí" desᴀta. ||

TOMOdati o o- TYA ni yonda <u>zyóonzu</u> -san ḡa | Ii-másᴀta. ||

"kono o- kási wa | <u>gomí</u> ḡa | háitte ite || oisíi n desu yo. || hᴀtó-tu | dóozo." ||

"<u>gomí</u>" ḡa | háitte iru | monó o | TÁbetara || BYOO.KI ni nari-másu ne. ||
ZITÚ wa || "<u>goma</u>" désᴀta. ||

TYÓO.ON to | TÁN.ON ni mo | KI o tᴀkéte kudasai. || "oba -san" o | "o- báa-san"
nan te | yondára || MOOsi- wake ari-masén kara . . ||

<u>ákᴀ</u>sento ni mo | TYÚU.I si-masyoo. || "hana" mo | <u>ákᴀ</u>sento ni yotte || "HANÁ"
ni mo | "HANA" ní mo nari-masᴀ. || "<u>sᴀta</u> ni oku" mo || "SITA ni Okú" no ka ||
"SITÁ ni | Okú" no ka || hakkíri | wakáru yoo ni | HANÁsᴀte kudasai. ||

GAI.RAI -ḠO no NÁKA ni wa || hén na RYAKU.ḠO mo | Sᴀ̄KUnáku | ari-masén. ||
konna kotobá wa || obóete kudasai. || "térebi" wa || "terebízyon" no || "tóire"
wa || "toirétto" no | RYÁKU desᴀ. ||

"KANE -MOtí" wa || o-KANE ḡa takʉsan áru HɪTO de || "MOti-ḠANE" wa || MÓtte iru o- KANE desʉ. || "MONO -hósi" wa || MONÓ o | hósu BA.SYO de || GYAKU ni | "hosi- MONÓ" to iu to || hósɪte aru | MONÓ to ka || hósʉ | kotó ni nari-masʉ. ||

ISÍ.YA (isíya) to I.SYA (isya) mo || zúibun | tiḡai-másu ne.

DÁI | SɪTɪ-KA ||

"TOKORO KAwaréba | SINA KAwaru" || to Iu tóori || HANAsɪ- kótoba ya | ákʉsento mo | TOKORO ni yotte || zúibun tiḡai-masʉ. || hʉtuu wa || kono | Tɪ. HOO ni yotte | tiḡau kotobá o || HOO.ḠÉN to itte i-masʉ. || HOO.ḠÉN ni | TÁIsɪte || NI.HON - ZÉN.KOKʉ | KYOOTUU ni Tʉ́KAwareru kotobá o || KYOO. TUU -ḠO || matá wa || HYOO.ZYUN -ḠO to ii-masʉ. ||

KYOO.TUU -ḠO no | "o-hayoo gozai-másʉ" ni Ataru | áisatu no | kotobá o || ZÉN.KOKʉ kara | HIROtte míru to ||

o-hayo gansu. ||

hayai no mosi. ||

hayo me ga sameyasɪta. ||

kesa mada zyai mosɪta. ||

kyoo wa mekkari moosan. ||

o-hi n nari. ||

nádo || KAwatta Ii-KATA ḡa || SʉKUnáku | ari-masén. ||

TOKORO ni yori || HɪTO ni yotte || iroiro na Ii-KATA ḡa | ari-másu ḡa || ÍMA de wa || térebi ya | rázio mo | kánari | yuki-watátte | irú sɪ || GAK.KOO dé mo | KYOO.TUU -ḠO o OSIete irú no de || NI.HON -ZIN dóosi de || ZEN.ZEN kotobá ḡa | TUUzinai to iu kotó wa | ari-masén. || kéredomo || mósɪ || KYUU. SYUU -BEN to TOO.HOKU -BEN de | HANAsi-Áttara || o-taḡai ni || NÁNI ḡa | NÁN da ka | wakaránakattari || GO.KAI sɪtári sɪte || komáru koto ḡa | ÓOi desyoo. ||

HOO.ḠÉN wa || Tɪ.HOO -TEKI na SEI.KATU -ḠO de || TÚU.YOO suru | hán'i wa | semái no desu ḡa || kessɪte WARÚi | kotobá de wa | ari-masén. ||

mázu || KYOO.TUU -ḠO o | yóku BEN.KYOO sɪte || sore kara || KÁKʉ.TI no | HOO.ḠÉN o | KEN.KYUU suréba || NI.HON -ḠO no SEI.SɪTU ḡa | yóku | wakáru | bákari de | nákʉ || NI.HON -ZÍN no | KANḠAe-KÁTA ya || sono BÚN.KA mo | yóku | RI.KAI dekíru yoo ni | náru desyoo.

DÁI | HÁK-KA ||

IKE.DA　　"mósi mosɪ."

o　　　　"mósi mosɪ."

IKE.DA　　"USI.YAMA -san no o- taku désʉ ka."

o　　　　"iie || tiḡai-masʉ. || NÁN-BAN e | o-kake ni nari-másɪta ka."

IKE.DA   "BAN.GÓO desú ka. || NI || HATÍ || ITÍ no || YON-SÉN | SÁN-BYAKÚ | GO -BAN désu ḡa . ."

o   "kotira wa || YON-SÉN | SÁN-BYAKÚ || YÓN -BAN desu yo."

IKE.DA   "A! || dóo mo | SÍTÚ.REI simasíta. || sumi-masén."

o   "iie."

*   *   *

IKE.DA   "mósi mosí."

ZYO.TYUU   "mósi mosí."

IKE.DA   "USI.YAMA -san no o- taku désú ka."

ZYO.TYUU   "háa || sayoo de gozai-masú."

IKE.DA   "MÍTÍ.KO -san | irassyai-mású ka."

ZYO.TYUU   "o-zyóo-san wa || máda || ZIMÚ -SYO kara | o-KAEri ni nari-masén ḡa || dótira -sama de | irassyai-mású ka."

IKE.DA   "AKÁ.SAKA no | IKE.DA désu ḡa || NAN-ZI ḡóro | o-KAEri desyóo ka."

ZYO.TYUU   "kyóo wa | DO.YÓO.BI de gozai-masú kara || ITI-ZI HAN ḡóro | o-KAEri ni náru to | OMOi-másu ḡa || notí hodo || kotira kara || o- DÉN.WA | itasi-masyóo ka."

IKE.DA   "sóo desu ne . . zya || sumi-masén ḡa || o- kotozuke o-NEḠAi si-masú."

ZYO.TYUU   "dóozo."

IKE.DA   "asátte no | ÁSA | HÁYAkú || KYÓO.TO e | tati-mású kara || asíta no GÓḠO || mósí || o- hima dáttara || ITÁ.BASI no | bóku no | KEN.KYUU -ZYO no hóo e | ASObi ni Kíté kudasaru yoo ni | o-TÚTAe kudasái."

ZYO.TYUU   "háa || kasíkomari-másíta. || o-TÚTAe itasi-masú."

IKE.DA   "zya || o-NEḠAi si-masú. || sayonára."

ZYO.TYUU   "gomen kudasai-máse."

DÁI | KYÚU-KA ||

"ASA.HÍ - SÍN.BUN" || "MAI.NITÍ - SÍN.BUN" || "YOMI.URI - SÍN.BUN" no | MIT-tú wa || NI.HON no DAI.HYOO -TEKI na SIN.BUN désú. ||

SIN.BUN no NÁKA ni wa || senséesyonaru na MI.DAsi de || DÓKÚ.SYA o | odorokaséru yoo na | monó mo | SÚKUnáku | ari-masén ḡa || "ÁSA.HI" wa || KÍ.ZI ḡa | SEI.KAKU de || IN.SATU no AYAMÁri mo | SÚKUnái to | iú no de || nakanaka SIN.YOO ḡa ari-masú. ||

taitei no SIN.BUN ní wa || KÍ.ZI wa || SEI.ZI || KÉI.ZAI || SYÁ.KAI || GAKU. ḠEI.BÚN.KA || supóotú || razio·térebi nado ni | WÁkete || KÚnde ari-masú. ||

sono ue || SIN.BÚN -SYA no | Í.KEN o | nóbeta SYA.SETU ya || SYOO.SETÚ || manḡa nádo mo | ari-masú. ||

DÓKU̸.SYA kara no | TOO.SYO mo | kánari | NIN.KI ḡa ari-masu̸. ||

KÍ.ZI ya | SYA.SIN Í.ḠAI ni || SIN.BUN ní wa || HÓN || zassi̸ || depáato ||
éiḡa || ku̸suri || kesyoo -HIN | kámera nado no | KOO.KOKU ḡa | taku̸san
ari-masu̸. ||

SIN.BUN o | YÁSU̸ku | KAu kotó ḡa | dekíru no wa || KOO.KOKU ni yoru | SIN.
BÚN -SYA no SYUU.NYUU ḡa | ÓOi kara desu̸.

DÁI | ZYÚK-KA ||

DAI NI-ZI - TAI.SEN -ḠO no | NI.HON no KYOO.IKU̸ - SÉI.DO wa || iwayúru |
ROKU̸ | SAN | SAN -SEI ni | KAwari-mási̸ta. ||

HURÚi | SÉI.DO || sunáwati̸ | KYUU.SEI dé wa || SYOO.ḠÁK.KOO | ROKÚ-
NEN || TYUU.ḠÁK.KOO | GO-NEN || KOO.TOO - ḠÁK.KOO | SAN-NEN ||
DAI.ḠAKU̸ | SAN-NEN to nátte | i-mási̸ta. || TYÚU.ḠAKU wa || OTOKO no
SÉI.TO no GAK.KOO de | ZYO- SÉI.TO wa || ZYO-ḠÁK.KOO e | Iki-mási̸ta. ||
DÁN.ZYO - KYOO.ḠAKU wa || hotóndo | ari-masén desi̸ta. || KOO.TOO - ḠÁK.
KOO wa || DAI.ḠAKU e SIN.ḠAKU̸ suru | OTOKO no GAKU̸.SEI no GAK.KOO
de || DAI.ḠAKU e SU̸SUmanai MONÓ wa || TYÚU.ḠAKU | matá wa | ZYO- ḠÁK.
KOO kara | SEN.MON - ḠÁK.KOO e | Iki-mási̸ta. || SEN.ZEN wa || ZYO.SI -
ḠÁKU̸.SEI no NYUU.ḠAKU o | YURÚsi̸ta DAI.ḠAKU mo | SU̸KUnákatta si̸ ||
SI.ḠÁN -SYA mo | SU̸KUnákatta no de || ZYÓ.SI no | DAI.ḠÁKU̸ -SEI wa |
KAZOéru hodo si̸ka | i-masén desi̸ta. ||

KOKU.MIN ḡa | kanarazu Ukénakereba | naránai KYOO.IKU o | GI.MU - KYÓO.
IKU̸ to | ii-másu ḡa || SEN.ZEN no GI.MU - KYÓO.IKU wa || SYOO.ḠÁK.KOO
no | ROKU-NÉN -KAN | daké desi̸ta. || SEN.ḠO wa || SYOO.ḠÁK.KOO wa |
ROKÚ-NEN de | ONAzi désu ḡa || TYÚU.ḠAKU̸ to KOO.KOO ḡa | SAN-NEN
zútu̸ || DAI.ḠAKU ḡa | YO-NEN ni nari-mási̸ta. || mata || DÁN.ZYO no tiḡai
ḡa | naku nari || GI.MU - KYÓO.IKU wa || TYÚU.ḠAKU made no | KYÚU-NEN
ni | NObi-mási̸ta. ||

GAK.KOO ní wa || KOO.RITU no monó mo || SI.RITU no | monó mo ari-masu̸. ||

DAI.ḠAKU o SOTU.ḠYOO si̸te || sára ni | KEN.KYUU si̸tai GAKU̸.SEI no tamé
ni wa || DAI.ḠÁKU.IN ḡa ari-masu̸.

DÁI | ZYUU-ÍK -KA ||

NI.HÓN wa || SI.ZEN no BÍ ni | meḡumáreta | KUNI de áru. || sono ue || NÍK.
KOO ya | KYÓO.TO nado no | ZÍN.ZYA ya | TERÁ wa || sono TATÉ.MONO ya |
NIWA no | miḡoto na | ZIN.KOO no BÍ ni yotte || SÉ.KAI ni | YUU.MEI de áru.||

KANE o osímazu | TU̸KU̸tta MONO | daké ḡa || rippa de ári || neuti ḡa áru |
to | OMÓu HI̸TO mo | NÁi koto wa | nái ḡa || ware-ware ḡa || MÁI.NITI
TU̸KAtte iru | YASÚi sara ya TYAwan no | NÁKA ni mo || yosó no KUNI ni |
MÍru koto no | dekínai | DOKU̸.TOKU no UTU̸KU̸si̸-sa ḡa | áru koto mo |
wasureté wa | naru mái. ||

koré -ra no | yaki- MONO ní wa || MU.MEI no HI̸TÓ−BITO no | TE - SÍ.ḠOTO
ni yotte | TU̸KUráreta | MONÓ ḡa | SU̸KUnáku | nái. || motíron || DAI- KÓO.
ZYOO de | TU̸KUraréru | KI̸.KAI - SÉI.HIN no | NÁKA ni mo || UTU̸KU̸síi

MONO ḡa | áru koto wa || Iu máde mo | nái ḡa | hi̶tuu || KI̶.KÁI wa ||
MIZIKÁi ZI.KAN ni || dekiru dake TA.SÚU no | MONÓ o | YÁSu̶ki̶ | Tu̶KÚru
tame ni | Tu̶KAwarerú no de || Tu̶KUráreta | MONÓ ḡa || dóre mo | ONAzi
yóo de || mata || sómatu ni | Tu̶KUrare-yasúi. || sono ue || NIN.ḠEN ḡa |
KI̶.KÁI ni | Tu̶KAwarerú no de || HATARAku̶ HI̶TÓ-BITO kara || HATARAku
YOROKÓbi o | TÓtte simau. ||

TE - SÍ.ḠOTO ni wa || NIN.ḠEN no KAN.ZYOO || YOROKÓbi ya | KANAsími
ya | KURUsími ḡa | komótte iru. ||

KANE o kakénaku̶te mo || IS.SYOO - kénmei ni | Tu̶KÚtta | MONÓ ni wa ||
áru | UTu̶Ku̶si-sa ḡa | áru to | OMÓu.

DÁI | ZYUU-NÍ -KA ||

go-busata itasi-mási̶ta ḡa || _háwai_ no | miná -san || o- GÉN.KI desyoo ka. ||
kotira wa || o-kage -sama de || taihen GÉN.KI de || MÁI.NITi̶ || TOMOdati ni
Áttari || KAi- MONO ya KEN.BUTU ni Ittári si̶te || TANÓsi̶ku̶ | suḡósi̶te
i-masi̶. ||

TOO.KYOO wa || tuyu ḡa Owatte || KYUU ni ÁTu̶ku | nari-mási̶ta. || musi-
buro no yóo da to | iu tóori || musi-ATu̶ku̶te || YÓRU | yóku | nerarenai kotó
mo | ari-masi̶. ||

NATU no KI̶.SETu̶ -HUU ḡa || TAI.HÉI.YOO no | HÓO kara | húite || ÚMI no |
SUI- zyóoKI o | HAKOnde kúru no de || musi-ATÚi no da | sóo desu ḡa || kono
ÁME to | KI.ON wa || NÓO.ḠYOO || TÓKU ni | KOMÉ o | Tu̶KÚru no ni |
HI̶TU.YOO ná no de || gáman | sinákereba | nari-masén. || TAbe- MÓNO mo |
ku̶sari-yasúi si̶ || I.TYOO no BYOO.KI mo | huéru no de || háyaku̶ | suzúsi̶ku
nareba | íi to | OMÓtte i-masi̶. ||

ATÚi aida wa || inaka no | SIN.RUI no utí e Itte || YAMA -nóbori o | si̶tári ||
ÚMI de | NAMI -nóri o | si̶tári si̶te | ASObu tumori desi̶. ||

NI-HYAKu̶ TOO -KA ḡa súgite || NI.HON -bare ḡa TUZUku yóo ni | náttara ||
KÁN.SAI e | Iki-mási̶ kara || soko kara | mata | o- táyori | si-masyóo. ||

miná -san ni yorosi̶ki̶. ||

SI̶TI.ḠATu̶ | ITu̶.KA ||

TÚNO.DA | SAN.PEI -KUN ||

sayonára ||

TA.NAKA | KÓO.ZI ||

DÁI | ZYUU-SÁN -KA ||

KÉI.ZAI no | HAT.TEN no ué ni | ZYUU.YOO na mono no hi̶tó-tu ni || BOO.
EKI ḡa ari-masi̶. ||

BOO.EKI to iú no wa || GAI.KOKu̶ tó no | SYOO.ḠYOO - TÓri-Hi̶ki desi̶. ||
kore ní wa || YU.SYUTu̶ to | YU.NYUU ḡa ári || YU.SYUTU wa || GAI.KOKU
ni | SYOO.HIN o | Uru kotó de || YU.NYUU wa || GAI.KOKu̶ kara | SYOO.HIN
o | KAu kotó desi̶. ||

YU.SYUTu̶ -HIN ní wa || _amerika_ -MUke no MEN -SÉI.HIN o | hazime || ORI.

MÓNO ḡa | ÓOkṹ || sonó hoka | móto wa || setomono || omótya || ÁN.KA na |
ZAK.KA nádo ḡa || sono ómo na | monó desíta ḡa || KÍN.NEN wa || SI.DAI ni ||
kámera || toranzisṹtaa - rázio || KÍ.KÁI || HÚNE nado mo | ZOO.KA síte
i-masṹ. ||

YU.NYUU -HIN ní wa || MÉN.KA ya | KOO.ḠYOO - GÉN.RYOO ḡa | ÓOkṹ ||
kore wa || NI.HON no BOO.EKI ni || KA.KOO - BÓO.EKÍ || (GEN.RYÓO o |
YU.NYUU síte || SEI.HIN o | YU.SYUTṾ suru BOO.EKI) | no | ÓOi koto o |
simesíte i-masṹ. || mata || ZIN.KOO ḡa ÓOi no ni || TAbe- MÓNO ḡa |
TArinái no de || KOMÉ ya | MÚḠI mo | YU.NYUU síte i-masṹ. ||

BOO.EKI no AITÉ -KOKṾ to | síté wa || amerika ḡa | SAI.KÓO -I o | símete
i-masṹ. || SEN.ZEN wa || TYÚU.ḠOKU ḡa | ÓOki na | AITÉ -KOKU desíta
ḡa || ÍMA wa || TYUU.KYOO - BÓO.EKI | yóri mo || músiro || TOO.NAN -
azia - SYÓ.KOKṾ to no | BOO.EKI no hóo ḡa || YUU.BÓO - SÍ sarete iru |
yóo desṹ.

DÁI | ZYUU-YÓN -KA ||

KOO.KOO o SOTU.ḠYOO sítá no de || zéhí || TOO.KYOO de SYUU.SYOKṾ
sí-tái to | OMÓtte || TOO.KYOO no TOMOdati ni || NÁN-DO mo | TE.ḠAMI
o | KAki-másíta. || kéredomo || inaka ni Ite || TOMOdati ni | SI.ḠOTO o |
saḡasíte moraú no de wa || "NI.KAI kara ME.ḠÚSURI" de || TYOKṾ.SETṾ ||
ZI.BUN de saḡasú no ni | kosíta kotó wa | nái no de || OMOi-Kítte || ZYOO.
KYOO suru kotó ni || KIme-másíta. || sabisíi | TANI -MA no MURÁ de mo |
"SÚmeba MIYAKO" desṹ. || WAKAréru | TOKÍ ni wa || KANAsíku | nari-
másíta. ||

TOO.KYOO ni TÚite miru to || "KIite GOKU.RAKṾ || Míte ziḡokṹ" || no |
kotowaza no tóori de || "Iki- NMA no MÉ o nuku" | yóo na | DAI- TÓ.KAI
desíta. || ittai | dóo síte | SI.ḠOTO o saḡasítára | íi ka || KEN.TÓO mo |
tṹki-masén desíta. || kéredomo || "INÚ mo | ARÚkeba || boo ni Ataru" ||
to | Ii-másṹ kara || SIN.BUN no KOO.KOKU o Míte || katap-pasí kara |
tazúnete | mi-másíta. ||

IS-SYUU.KAN bákari || MÁI.NITI | MÁI.NITI | ARUki-MAWAri-másíta ḡa ||
dóre mo kore mo | "ÓBI ni | MIZIKÁsí || tasṹki ni | NÁḠAsi" de || TEKÍ. TOO
na SI.ḠOTO wa | ari-masén. || sono ue || yuubé wa || ZEN- ZÁI.SAN o Ireta
saihu o | Otósíte simau sí || MATTAkṹ || "nakí- tura ni hatí" tó wa || kono
kotó da to || nasakenáku nari-másíta. ||

késa || TÍTÍ kara | TE.ḠAMI de || MURA no YAKUBÁ ni | NÁNI ka | SI.
ḠOTO ḡa áru sí || inaka ni Í sae | suréba || TAbéru no ni wa | komaránai no
da kara || KÁEtte | Kítára | dóo ka to | Itte ki-másíta. || sore de || OYA no
Í.KEN ni | SíTAḠAtte || sassokṹ | KÁEru koto ni | si-másíta.

DÁI | ZYUU-GÓ -KA ||

wá ḡa KUNI wa || azia - TÁI.RIKṾ to | TAI.HÉI.YOO to no | AIDA ni áru |
SIMÁ.ḠUNI de || KÓKU.DO wa || KYÚU.SYUU || SÍ.KÓKṾ || HÓN.SYUU ||
HOK.KÁI.DOO no | YOT-tú no | SIMÁ to || sono HṾ.KÍN ni | áru | SAN-ZEN
-YÓ no | TIIsái | SIMÁ -ZIMA kara | NÁtte iru. ||

sono ZEN- MÉN.SEKI wa ‖ YÁKʋ ‖ SÁN-ZYUU SʲTI-MAN ‖ HEI.HOO
-kiroméetoru de aru. ‖

DAI NI-ZI - TAI.SEN máde wa ‖ konó hoka ni ‖ tyoosén ‖ (KʲTA - tyoosén ‖
kánKOKʋ) ‖ taiwán ‖ okinawa ‖ MINAMI - kárahʲto ‖ TÍ.SIMA mo ‖ NI.HON
no RYÓO.DO de atta. ‖

HAI.SEN no KEK.Kʌ ‖ koré -ra no ‖ RYÓO.DO o ‖ USINAtta ué ni ‖ GÁI.Tʲ
kara ‖ Hʲki-áḡeta MONO ‖ óyobi ‖ Kʲ.KOKʋ -HEI ḡa ‖ KUWAwátta no de ‖
ZIN.KOO ḡa ‖ HI.ZYOO ni ‖ ZOO.KA sʲta. ‖ mata ‖ SYUS.SYÓO -RITU
ḡa ‖ TAKÁi no de ‖ ZIN.KOO no ‖ SI.ZEN - ZÓO.KA mo ‖ SʋKUnáku ‖ nái
kara ‖ ZIN.KOO ITÍ-OKU ni ‖ náru HI mo ‖ TOOkú wa ‖ aru mái. ‖

wá ḡa KUNI no Tʲ.SEI wa ‖ KÓKU.DO no ‖ DAI- BÚBUN ḡa ‖ SAN.TI de áru
kara ‖ KOO.TI - MÉN.SEKI ni ‖ TAIsúru ‖ ZIN.KOO - mítuDO wa ‖ GÉN.ZAI ‖
SÉ.KAI de ‖ ITI.BAN TAKÁi. ‖

sʲtaḡatte ‖ SEI.KATʋ - SÚI.ZYUN o ‖ TAKAme-náḡara ‖ ÓOku no ZIN.KOO
o ‖ YASINAu tamé ni wa ‖ dóo sʲtara ‖ yói ka ‖ to iu TEN ḡa ‖ ZYUU.YOO
na MON.DAI de áru.

DÁI ‖ ZYUU-RÓK -KA ‖

NI.HÓN wa ‖ SÍ-MEN ‖ ÚMI ni ‖ KAKOmarete ite ‖ KATATI ḡa ‖ HOSO-
NÁḠAkʲ ‖ SAN.MYAKU ḡa ‖ ÓOi. ‖ sono tamé ni ‖ TÁI.ḠA ‖ TYOO.RYUU ‖
DAI- HÉI.YA ḡa ‖ hotóndo ‖ NÁi. ‖

KYUU.RYUU no ÓOi ‖ kotó wa ‖ SUI.RYOKʋ - HÁTU.DEN ni wa ‖ BÉN.RI de
aru ḡa ‖ SUI.ḠAI o Ukéru ‖ kotó mo ‖ ÓOkʲ ‖ ZIN.KOO ḡa ‖ ÓOi no ni ‖ HEI.
YA ḡa SʋKUnái ‖ kotó wa ‖ SYOKU.RYOO - SÉI.SAN no Hʋ.SOKU o ‖ Í.MI sʲ ‖
mata ‖ KOO.TUU ní mo ‖ HÚ.BEN de aru. ‖

NI.HÓN ni wa ‖ KÁ.ZAN ḡa ‖ ÓOkʲ ‖ sʲtaḡatte ‖ onsen mo ÓOkʲ ‖ HO.YOO
ni TEKʲsʲta TO.TI ḡa ‖ SʋKUnáku ‖ nái. ‖ sʲkásʲ ‖ sono HAN.MÉN ‖ zisin o
hazime ‖ KA.ZAN - KÁTU.DOO ni yoru ‖ GÁI mo ‖ kánari ‖ ÓOi. ‖

HAN.TOO ‖ MINATO ‖ MIZUÚMI ‖ MORI ‖ HAYASI wa ‖ itáru ‖ tokoró ni ‖
MIráre ‖ SYOKÚ.BUTU no ‖ SYÚ.RUI mo ‖ ÓOkʲ ‖ HÚU.KOO ni ‖ meḡumárete
iru. ‖
ON.TAI ni áru tame ni ‖ Kʲ.KOO ḡa ‖ ON.WA de ‖ Sʲ.Kʲ no ‖ KÚ.BETU ḡa ‖
hakkíri sʲte iru. ‖

yooróppa ya ‖ amerika - TÁI.RIKʋ kara ‖ hanárete iru ‖ kotó wa ‖ KÉI.ZAI
ya ‖ BÚNKA no KOO.RYUU ni ‖ HÚ.BEN da ḡa ‖ kono MON.DAI wa ‖ KOO.
KÚU -KI nado no ‖ KOO.TUU - Kʲ.KÁN no HAT.TATU ni yori ‖ SI.DAI ni ‖
KAI.KETʋ sare-tʲtu aru.

DÁI ‖ ZYUU-SʲTʲ -KA ‖

RYOO.RÍ -YA de. ‖ KYAKʋ to ZYO.TYUU no ‖ KAI.WA. ‖

ZYO.TYUU   "irassyai-máse. ‖ NÁN ni ‖ itasi-masyóo ka."

TÁMA.Kʲ   "moo hʲtó-ri ‖ KÚru kara ‖ tyótto ‖ MÁtte."

ZYO.TYUU "háa haa."

TÁMA.KĮ "osoi ne || HAYASĮ -KUN wa . ."

UE.DA "moo KŰru daroo. || NÁN ni suru?"

TÁMA.KĮ "kyóo wa | TORI ni siyóo ka."

UE.DA "ZITŰ wa || yuubé mo | TORI dátta n da yo."

TÁMA.KĮ "zya || tenpura wa dóo da i?"

UE.DA "íi ne. || dá kedo || íi ka i? || tenpura ni sĮté mo . ."

TÁMA.KĮ "íi tomo."

HAYASĮ "yáa || o-MAtidoo -sama. || ÚN | WÁRUkĮ || YUU.ḠATA máde | KAI.ḠĮ ḡa | átta mon de . ."

TÁMA.KĮ "bókĮ -tati mo | KĮta | bakkári da yo. || tenpura dé mo | TYUU.MON siyóo ka tte | Itté 'ta toko | ná n da kedo ne. || dóo da i?"

HAYASĮ "KÉK.KOO."

UE.DA "hoka ní wa? || koko wa | UO - ÍTI.BA no | sóba da kara || íi sakana ḡa | áru yo."

HAYASĮ "zya || SÍRO - MI no sakana no | SIO -YÁki o | tanómu ka."

TÁMA.KĮ "tyótto."

ZYO.TYUU "háa. || o-yobi de gozai-másĮ ka."

TÁMA.KĮ "ano ne. || tenpura to || SÍRO - MI no | SIO -YÁki o | SAN-NIN. MAE. || YA.SAI wa || KĮ.SÉTU no | MONÓ o | mitĮkurotte . ."

ZYO.TYUU "kasĮkomari-másĮta. || o- NOmí-MONO wa?"

TÁMA.KĮ "SAKE ni suru?"

UE.DA "SYOKU.YOKU - ZOO.SIN ní wa || TUMEtai bíiru no hoo ḡa | íi daroo."

HAYASĮ "SAN.SEI."

TÁMA.KĮ "zya | bíiru o. || bíiru to | issyo ní wa || KÁI no | su-nó-mono ḡa | íi daroo."

ZYO.TYUU "háa || kasĮkomari-másĮta. || o- bíiru ḡa | o-SUmi ni nátte kara || gó-HAN | o-MOti itasi-masyóo ka."

TÁMA.KĮ "áa || soo sĮte."

ZYO.TYUU "SYOO.TI itasi-másĮta. || SYÓO.SYOO | o-MAtĮ kudasai-máse."

    *   *   *

UE.DA "úmakatta ne."

HAYASĮ "OMÓwazu | TAbe-suḡityattá yo."

TÁMA.KĮ "kudámono de mo | dóo?"

HAYASĮ "móo | KÉK.KOO. || KIMI wa?"

UE.DA "bóku mo | ippai da. || ATÚi o- TYA dake | moo ÍP-PAI | NOmi-tái ne."

TÁMA.KÍ   "tyótto | tyótto. || ATÚi o- TYA."

ZYO.TYUU   "háa || tadá- IMA."

TÁMA.KÍ   "o- KAI.KEI mo."

ZYO.TYUU   "háa haa."

TÁMA.KÍ -san wa || ZYO.TYUU ḡa | MOtté KÍta | "KÍN || NI-SÉN ROP-
PYAKѶ | KYÚU-ZYUU | ITÍ -EN" to | KÁite aru | KAMÍ o | Míte || SAN-
ZEN -EN watasi-másíta.

ZYO.TYUU   "SAN-ZEN -EN o-AZUkari itasi-masѝ. || SYÓO.SYOO | o-MAtѝ
            kudasai-máse."

TÁMA.KÍ   "o- turi wa iranái kara . ."

ZYO.TYUU   "háa || aríḡatoo gozai-masѝ. || MAI.DO | aríḡatoo zonzi-masѝ. ||
            mata dóozo."

DÁI | ZYUU-HÁK -KA ||

"ÓOki na | NÍ.MOTU o | RYOO.TE de kakaéru to | Iu tóki no | TÉ wa || káta
kara | YUBI.SAKI máde no | kotó desu ḡa || "TÉ ni | tóru" toki no | TÉ wa ||
TÉ.KUBI kara | SAKI no kotó desѝ. || mata || "TÉ o | Awásete | inóru" toki
no | TÉ wa || TE-nó-hira no | kotó de || "TÉ ni hureru" no | TÉ wa || YUBI
no kotó desѝ. || konna BA.AI no TÉ wa || minna | NIN.ḠEN no | karada no BÚ.
BUN desu ḡa || "huraipan no TÉ" to Iu to | DOO.ḠÚ no | MÓtѝ | tokoró da
sѝ || "HATAKE no | tómato no | TÉ" to | Iéba | SYOKÚ.BUTU o sasaeru |
boo no kotó desѝ. ||

mukasi wa || KAN.ZI o "OTOKO.DE" || hiraḡána o | "ONNA.DE" to Ii-másíta
ḡa || kono BA.AI wa || MÓ.ZI no | Í.MI desѝ. || "UTAi-TE" || "OYOḡi-TE" no
"TÉ" wa || HÍTO || túmari || UTAu HÍTO || OYÓḡu HÍTO to iu | Í.MI da sѝ ||
"HѶKA-DE o Ou" no TÉ wa || keḡa no kotó de || mata || "kono TÉ no SINA.
MONO" to iu to || SYÚ.RUI to iu | Í.MI ni nari-masѝ. || "MIḠI.TE no KOO.EN"
no TÉ wa || MIḠI no HÓO || túmari || HOO.KOO o simesite i-masѝ. || "TE-
MÁWAsѝ" to iu no wa || sѝtakѝ | ZYÚN.BI to iu | Í.MI de || "TE-ḡótae" to iu
no wa || HAN.NOO to iu Í.MI desѝ. || konó hoka ni mo | iron na TѶKAi-KATA
ḡa ari-masѝ. ||

HÍTO.DE ḡa nái || HATARAkѝ HÍTO ḡa | TArinái. ||

TÉ o aḡeru || MAkeru. || koosan suru. ||

TÉ ḡa aḡaru || úmaku | náru. || ZYOO.TATѶ suru. ||

TÉ o | tѝkéru || ATARAsíi | SI.ḠOTO nádo o | HAZImeru. ||

TÉ o Utѝ || TAI.SAKU o tatéru. ||

TÉ o hѝkѝ || ZÍ.KEN || MON.DAI nádo kara | KAN.KEI o TÁtѝ. ||

TÉ ḡa akѝ || hima ni náru. ||

TÉ o yakѝ || mendóo na | MON.DAI nádo de | komáru. ||

TÉ o | kakéru || yókѝ | SE.WÁ o suru. ||

TÉ ni | kakéru || KOROsѝ. ||

TE-BANÁsṵ || Uru. || hoka no TOKORÓ e yaru. ||

TÉ ḡa | NAḠÁi || HĮTO no monó o | nusúmu | kṵsé ḡa aru. ||

TÉ o | komanékṵ || ude -ḡúmi o sįte || KANḠAe-kómu. || NANI mo sezu ni iru. ||

TÉ ḡa | hṵsaḡatte iru || isoḡasíi. || SI.ḠOTO -TYUU de || hima ḡa nái. ||

máda || takṵsan TṴKAi-KATA ḡa ari-masṵ. ||

ONAzi | "TÉ ḡa | nái" to | iú no mo || HANASÍ ya | BÚN.SYOO no | NAI.YOO ni yotte || "HOO.HOO ḡa | nái" to iu | Í.MI ni mo | náru sį || "HĮTO.DE ḡa TArinái" to iu | Í.MI ni mo nari-masṵ. || "TÉ o hįku" mo || "móo | ano ZÍ. KEN kara wa || TÉ o | hįki-másįta yo" to | iéba || "KAN.KEI o | TÁtta" to iu | Í.MI de || "kodomo no TÉ o hiite || sanpo suru" to | iéba || "Kodomo no TÉ o | tótte || mitibiki-náḡara | sanpo suru" to iu Í.MI desṵ. ||

kotobá to | iu monó wa || HṴKU.ZATU na monó desṵ.

DÁI | ZYUU-KYÚU -KA ||

sumoo || zyúuDOO || kénDOO || karaTE nádo wa || NI.HON no | DEN.TOO -TEKI na | sṵpóotu desu ḡa || sono náka de || ITI.BAN | TAI.SYUU ni | NIN. KI ḡa | áru no wa || sumoo desṵ. || kore wa || KIN.DAI - sṵpóotu no | résuringu ni NIte ite || BÚ.KI o TṴKAwazu ni | AITÉ o | taósṵ | KÓ.ZIN TAI | KÓ.ZIN no | SYÓO.BU desṵ. || "sumoo SI-ZYUU HÁT -TE" to iwareru hodo || iroiro na KATÁ ya | KĮ.SÓKU ḡa | átte || ITI-NIN-mae no RÍKĮ.SI ni | náru no ni wa || NAḠÁi SYU.ḠYOO o | sinákereba | nari-masén. || mukasi no samurai no yóo ni || "maḡe" o YUtte irú no wa || ÍMA de wa || RIKĮ.SI Í.ḠAI ni wa | ari-masén. ||

zyúuDOO || karaTE || kénDOO mo || yahári || KÓ.ZIN TAI | KÓ.ZIN no | SYÓO.BU desu ḡa || zyúuDOO wa || AI.TÉ o | seméru yori wa || músiro || ZI.BUN o | mamóri || TEKI o HṴSÉḡu tame no | monó de || zyúuDOO no | kokoróe ḡa | áreba || ONNÁ de mo || AI.TE no TIKARÁ o | RI.YOO sįte || OO.ÓTOKO o | NAḡe-taosṵ kotó ḡa | deki-masṵ.

karaTE wa || mukasį || NI.HÓN ni | BÚ.KI o TOri-Aḡerareta | ryuukyúu || (okinawa) de || kṵhuu | KEN.KYUU sare || HAT.TATṴ sįta monó desṵ. || TÉ.ASI o TṴKAtte || TEKI o | tuitári || kéttari sį | ZI.BUN o mamóru | BÚ. ZYUTU desṵ. || REN.SYUU o túmeba || NÁN-mai mo KASAneta | kawará o | kata- TE de | ITI-DÓ ni | watte simau kotó mo | dekíru yoo ni nari-masṵ. ||

kénDOO wa || BÚ.SI no HĮTU.YOO kara Umareta | ZYÚN- NI.HON -TEKI na | monó de || "MEN" || "kote" || "dóo" nado o | MI ni tuke || KATANA || (hṵtuu wa | BOKṴ.TÓO ya | TAKE no "sínai") o TṴKAtte || ÁI-utṵ || ISAmasíi | BÚ.ZYUTU desṵ. || koré -ra no | BÚ.ZYUTU wa || wazá o | miḡakṵ to DOO.ZI ni || SÍN.SIN o | kįtaéru to iu MOKṴ.TEKI de | OKOnaware-másįta. ||

KÓN.NITĮ || NI.HÓN de wa || RIKU.ZYOO - KYÓO.ḠI || SUI.ZYOO - KYÓO.ḠI o hazime || hotóndo | arayúru | KIN.DAI - sṵpóotu ḡa | OKOnaware || orinpikkṵ - TÁI.KAI ni mo | SAN.KA sįte i-masṵ.

DÁI | NÍ-ZYUK -KA ||

YÁS∅.KO   "SOTU.ḠYOO si̷tára || dónna | SYOKÚ.ḠYOO ni | túitara | íi ka
sira . ."

HÁRU.KO   "sóo ne || watasi wa || KYÓO.SI ni naru | tumori dá kedo . .|| dá
kara || íi KYOO.ZYU no | sorótte iru DAI.ḠAKU ni | NYUU.ḠAKƲ
suru kotó ḡa || SEN.KETU - MÓN.DAI da wa."

YÁS∅.KO   "watasi wa ne || BEN.KYOO wa NIḠA.TE dá kara || KAI.SYA ka |
GIN.KOO e || súḡu | o-TƲTOme si̷-tái wa. || ZIMÚ -IN de mo ||
hi̷syó de mo | íi kara . ."

HÁRU.KO   "KEI.EI no | si̷kkári si̷te iru | tokó dattara || MATI no KO-URI
-TEN no hóo ḡa || SYUU.NYUU ḡa íi n zya | nái ka sira . ."

YÁS∅.KO   "dé mo || NIKƲ.YA -san ya | SUMÍ.YA -san nan ka de || héi ||
irassyái nan te | Iú no | iyá da wa."

HÁRU.KO   "sonna SI.ḠOTO zya náku̷te || OOkíi o- MISE no | ZÍ.MU ya | KAI.
KEI nán ka yo. || sore yóri || anáta | GEI.ZYUTƲ -TEKI na sénsu
ḡa | áru kara || YOO.HƲKU no ZAI.RYÓO ne || KÍ.ZI ya | bótan nan
ka | Urú no || dóo ka sira . ."

YÁS∅.KO   "soryaa || omosiro-sóo da wa ne."

SYUU.ITI̷   "KIMÍ -tati̷ || NÁNI | HANÁsi̷te 'ru no?"

HÁRU.KO   "SYOKÚ.ḠYOO yo. || dónna | SYOKÚ.ḠYOO ḡa | íi ka tte . ."

YÁS∅.KO   "SYUU.ITI̷ -san || NÁN ni | náru | tumori ná no?"

SYUU.ITI̷   "sóo da | náa. || GUN.ZIN ḡa NAku nattyattá kara | náa || máa || KOO.
MÚ -IN da ne. || bóku wa || SÉI.HU no SI.ḠOTO ḡa | si̷-tái n da yo. ||
móto wa || saibán -KAN ya | BENḠÓ -SI ni | nari-tái to | OMÓtta
kotó mo | áru n da kedo || NAN-MÁN to iu HOO.RITU o | NOKÓrazu |
oboéru nan te | KANḠÁeta | daké de mo || KI ḡa | TOOku náttyai-soo
da."

HÁRU.KO   "watasi wa || ne || NÁNI ka | SEN.MON no GÍ.ZYUTU o | MI ni
tu̷kéta hoo ḡa | íi to | OMÓu no yo. || tatóeba || ne || GÍ.Si̷ to ka ||
I.SYA tó ka . .||HÁ - I.SYA mo | íi to | OMÓu kedo."

SYUU.ITI̷   "dá kedo || sore ní wa || DAI.ḠAKƲ ka | SEN.MON no GAK.KOO e |
Ikanákya | nánnai si̷ || KEI.ZAI -TEKI ni | RAKÚ zya | nái kara ||
dáre de mo tte | iu wáke ni wa | ikanái yo. || bóku wa || TIIsái |
TOKÍ ni wa ne || KI̷.SYA no UN.TÉN -SYU ni | nari-tákatta n da yo."

YÁS∅.KO   "OTOKÓ-no-KO wa || taiteî sóo ne. || watasi wa || GEI.ZYUTƲ -KA
ni | akoḡarete itá no yo. || SI.ZIN ya | GA.KA ya | KEN.TI̷KƲ -KA
nán ka ni . ."

SYUU.ITI̷   "sore wa sóo to || bóku wa ne || minná ḡa | mótto || hyaku̷syóo ya |
RYÓO.SI no SI.ḠOTO no | ZYUU.YOO -sa o mitomenákya | ikenái to
OMÓu yo. || SƲKUnái SYUU.NYUU ni amanzite || TA.NIN no tamé ni ||
SYOKU.RYOO no SEI.SAN ni | haḡénde | irú n da kara . ."

HÁRU.KO   "motíron yo. ‖ DÁI.KŲ -san ya │ SA.KAN -YA -san ḡa │ inákattara ‖
IÉ ḡa │ TAtánai sỉ ‖ KÁN.NUSỈ -san ya │ boo-san dá tte │ inákattara ‖
komáru desyo? ‖ ÍMA wa ‖ BUN.ḠYOO no ZI.DAI désu mono ‖ soré
−zore ‖ ZI.BUN ni TEKỈsỉta │ SYOKÚ.ḠYOO ni │ túite ‖ o- taḡai ni ‖
tasỉke-átte │ SEI.KATŲ sinákyaa . ."

DÁI │ NÍ-ZYUU │ ÍK -KA ‖

NI.HON no NOO.ḠYOO - ZÍN.KOO wa ‖ ZEN- ZÍN.KOO no │ YON-ZYUP
-paasento Í.ZYOO de │ áru no ni ‖ KOKU.MIN - SYÓ.TOKU ya │ SEI.SÁN -ḠAKU
no │ MÉN kara │ MÍta │ NÓO.KA no │ TÍ.I wa ‖ kiwámete │ HỈKÚi no desỉ. ‖

KÓO.TI no │ semái │ NI.HÓN de wa ‖ íkura │ SYUU.YAKU - NÓO.ḠYOO ‖
(semái │ TÁ ya │ HATAKÉ ni ‖ RÓO.RYOKU ya │ HÍ.RYOO o │ takỉsan ataete ‖
dekiru dake ÓOku no │ SAKÚ.MOTU o │ tóru HOO.HOO) o │ OKOnatté mo ‖
KÓO.TI ni │ TÁIsỉte ‖ NOO.MIN ḡa │ OO-suḡirú no desỉ. ‖ sỉtaḡatte ‖ NOO.
ḠYOO - TÍN.ḠIN mo │ YASÚi wake desỉ. ‖

NÓO.KA ni wa ‖ ZI.SAKÚ -NOO to │ KO.SAKÚ -NOO ḡa ari-masỉ. ‖ ZI.SAKÚ
-NOO to │ iú no wa ‖ ZI.BUN no KÓO.TI de │ NÓO.ḠYOO o │ ITONÁmu │ NÓO.
KA de ‖ KO.SAKÚ -NOO wa ‖ ZI.NUSỈ kara │ TO.TI o KArite │ NÓO.ḠYOO o │
ITONÁmu │ monó desỉ. ‖

SEN.ZEN wa ‖ KO.SAKŲ -TI ḡa │ ZEN- KÓO.TI no HAN.BUN TỈKÁku o │
símete │ i-másỉta. ‖ KO.SAKÚ -NOO wa ‖ KO.SAKÚ -RYOO to sỉte ‖ tóreta │
KOMÉ no │ HAN.BÚN o │ ZI.NUSI ni │ harawánakereba │ nari-masén desỉta
kara ‖ KOMÉ o │ TỤKŲtte mo │ KOMÉ ḡa │ TAberarénai │ MAZUsíi │ "MIZU
-NOmi -byákỉsyoo" ḡa │ ÓOkatta no desỉ. ‖ SEN.ḠO ‖ REN.ḠOO -GUN - SI.
RÉI- -BU no KAN.KỤKU de ‖ NÓO.Tỉ - KAI.KAKU ḡa │ DAN.KOO sare-másỉta. ‖
HU.ZAI - ZÍ.NUSỈ ‖ (KÓO.TI o │ MÓtte ite mo ‖ NÓO.ḠYOO mo │ sézu ‖ soko
ní mo │ SÚmazu ‖ taitei │ TO.KAI ni SÚnde ‖ KO.SAKÚ -NOO ni ‖ SYO.YÚU
-TI o │ KAsỉte ita ZI.NUSI) ya ‖ OO- ZÍ.NUSỈ ‖ (KOO.DAI na TO.TI no │ SYO.
YÚU -SYA) no │ KO.SAKŲ -TI o │ SÉI.HU ḡa │ KYOO.SEI -TEKI ni │ KAi-áḡete ‖
sore o ‖ KÓO.TI no │ hosíi │ KO.SAKÚ -NOO ni │ YÁSỤkỉ │ KAwasetári │ KO.
SAKÚ -RYOO o │ KEI.ḠEN sase │ KIN.NOO ni sasetári │ sỉtá no desỉ. ‖ túmari ‖
semái │ NI.HON no KÓO.TI o ‖ YOWÁi │ TATI-BÁ ni │ átta │ KO.SAKÚ -NOO ni │
KAI.HOO sỉtá no desỉ. ‖

kono KAI.KAKU ḡa ‖ KO.SAKU - NÓO.KA o │ KYUU.SAI sỉ ‖ sono KEI.EI to │
SEI.KATU no KAI.ZEN o TASỤke ‖ NOO.SON - MIN.SYU -KA no │ MOTÓI o │
TỤKÚru no ni │ SEI.KOO sỉtá to │ Itté mo ‖ KA.ḠON dé wa │ nái to OMOi-masỉ.

DÁI │ NÍ-ZYUU │ NÍ -KA ‖

"Ókita? ‖ yuube no zisin de."

"Ókite 'ta n da yo ‖ ano TÓKI wa │ máda . . SỈ.KYUU ‖ kono KÁ.SI ni │ SAK.
KYOKŲ sỉte kuré tte │ tanomáreta mon de ‖ SI.ḠOTO sỉté 'ta n da kedo ne ‖
SÁI.ḠO no │ SYOO.SETU no tokó ḡa ‖ dóo mo │ úmaku │ ikanákỉte ne ‖ MAN-
NÉN -HỈTU │ MÓtta manma ‖ boṅyári │ KANḠÁete ita │ tokoró e ‖ KYUU ni │
gata-gatá tto │ Kítá n de ‖ OMÓwazu │ NIWA e TObi-dásỉtyatta yo."

"nyúusŭ KIita? || hidói | TOKORÓ de mo || HASIRA -DÓ.KEI ḡa | TOmatta
TÉI.DO datta n da tte."

"ún. || sóo da tte ne. || go-ZÓN.zi no | tóori || bóku wa || zisin to | kaminári
ḡa | DÁI- kirai da kara | née. || OO- zísin ka to | OMÓttyatta n da yo."

"KIMI wa || kaminári de | KAO.IRO o KAerú n da kara | née. || bóku wa ||
KÁ.ZI no hoo ḡa | iyá da na."

"KÁ.ZI tte | Iéba || HI-no-MI no kane ḡa | zyán-zyan | NAri-dásŭ to || ÍKĬ
-sekĬ-kĬtte || NÁN-TYOO mo SAKI no | KA.ZI -BÁ made | HASĬtte Itte || HÍ-
no-KO mo | kamáwazu || KEN.BUTŬ suru yátu ḡa | irú kedo || MATTAkŭ |
KI ḡa SIrenái ne."

"bóku wa || SYOO.BÓO -SYA no | sáiren ḡa | DÁI- kirai sa."

"KAZE mo iyá da ne."

"sóyo-soyo hŭku | HARÚ.-KAZE nan ka | íi zya nai ka."

"pyúu-pyuu | hŭkaréru no wa | gomen dá yo. || sore ni || mádo ya | TO ḡa |
gáta-gata suru to | KI ḡa TĬtte || NÁNI o | YÓnda tte || ATAMÁ ni | háiryaa |
sinái yo."

"KAZE ni KURAberéba || ÁME no hoo ḡa | íi ne. || sĬto-sĬto huru | HARU . SAME
ya || zaat to kúru | NATU no YUU.DATI nán ka || WÁRUku | nái | née."

"At! || génkan no | béru ḡa || rín-rin | NAtte 'rú kara || sĬkkéi."

DÁI | NÍ-ZYUU | SÁN -KA ||

SYOO.YOO || KAN.KOO || KEN.KYUU || sonó TA no | MOKŬ.TEKI de | RAI.
NITĬ suru | ameriká -ZIN no | DAI- BÚ.BUN wa || TOO.KYOO - KOKŬ.SAI -
KÚU.KOO || matá wa || yokohamá (YOKO.HAMÁ) -KOO ni | TŬkŭ. ||

iwaba || NI.HON no génkan ni ataru | yokohama mo || ZYUU-KYUU - SÉI.KI
no | NAKÁ-ḡoro made wa || TĬIsa na | GYO.SON de átta. || GAI.KOKŬ tó no |
OO.RAI ḡa HAZImatta | MEI.ZI - ZÍ.DAI kara || BOO.EKĬ -KOO to sĬte |
KYUU.SOKU ni | HAT.TEN sĬta. || ÍMA de wa || MINATO no SÉTU.BI mo |
yókŭ | TOTONÓi || SÉ.KAI | YUU.SUU no | RYOO.KOO ni nátte iru. || KYAKŬ
-SEN nomi nárazu || KA.MOTŬ -SEN || YU.SOO -SEN no HAT.TYAKU mo |
ÓOi. ||

yokohama ní wa || GAI.KOKU no SYÓO.SYA ya | RYOO.ZÍ -KAN o hazime ||
hóteru || miyáḡe - MONO -YA || résŭtoran nado ḡa | ÓOi. || koko ni SÚmu |
GAI.KOKÚ -ZIN no | KÁ.ZOKU mo | kánari | ÓOkŭ || íka ni mo | KOKŬ.SAI -
TO.SI rasíi. || mata || koko ní wa || SYUTU.NYÚU.KOKU no | HĬTÓ – BITOˋ
ya || YU.SYUTU.NYUU -HIN o SIRAbéru | ZEI.KAN ḡa áru. || ZEI.KAN dé wa ||
NI -aḡe sĬta | NÍ.MOTU no | SÓO.KO ya || NYUU.KOO sĬta HÚNE no | KÁN.RI
mo | sĬte iru. ||

yokohama wa || MINATO to sĬte || SI.ZEN -TEKI ZYOO.KÉN ḡa | YÓkŭ ||
HUYÚ de mo | kooranái. || mata || SUI.SIN mo ÓOkĬkŭ || KAI.TEI ḡa | ikari
o orósu no ni | TEKĬsĬ || SIN.SEN no SA ḡa | SŬKUnái. ||

sono ue || NI.HON no SYÚ.HU de ari || DAI- SYOO.HĮ -TI de mo aru | TOO.
KYOO ni TĮKÁkų || RIKU.ZYOO - KÓO.TUU no | BÉN mo | îi no de || TOO.
KYOO no GAI.KOO to sįte | HAT.TEN sĮ || ROKU- DAI- TÓ.SI no | hĮtó-tu ni |
nátte iru. ||

TOO.KYOO - yokohamá -KAN wa || DAI- KOO.ḠYOO - TĮ.TAI de || KÓO.ḠYOO
no | SYÚ.RUI mo | ÓOkų || KEI- KÓO.ḠYOO to | ZYUU- KÓO.ḠYOO || KA.
ḠAKŲ - KÓO.ḠYOO nado ḡa | sorótte | HAT.TATŲ sįte iru.

DÁI | NÍ-ZYUU | YÓN -KA ||

KOKU.MIN no SYUKŲ- SÁI.ZITŲ to sįte | SADAmeráreta HĮ. ||

GAN.ZITŲ || ITI-ḠATŲ | ITI.ZITŲ ||

TOSI no HAZIme o | IWÁu. ||

SEI.ZIN no HĮ || ITI-ḠATŲ | ZYÚU-GO -NITĮ ||

otona ni nátta | kotó o | ZI.KAKŲ sįta SEI.NEN o | IWÁi | haḡemasų. ||

SYUN.BUN no HĮ || SÁN-ḠATŲ | NÍ-ZYUU ITI -NITĮ ||

Ikí- MONO o | tatáe || SI.ZEN o AIsúru. ||

TEN.NOO tanzyóo -BI || SI-ḠATŲ | NÍ-ZYUU | KÚ -NITĮ ||

TEN.NOO - HÉI.KA no | o-Umare ni nátta HI o | IWÁu. ||

KEN.POO - KI.NÉN -BI || GÓ-ḠATŲ | MIK-KA ||

NI.HON -KOKŲ - KÉN.POO ḡa | ÁRAta ni | OKOnawareta HÍ o | KI.NEN sĮ ||
KUNI no SEI.TYOO o | KĮsúru. ||

kodomo no HĮ || GÓ-GATŲ | ITŲ-KA ||

kodomo no ZIN.KAKU o OMOnzi || sono KOO.HŲKU o HAKÁri || ZÍ.DOO o |
MAMÓru to | tómo ni || HÁHA ni |KÁN.SYA suru. ||

SYUU.BUN no HĮ || KÚ-ḠATŲ | NÍ-ZYUU | SÁN -NITI ||

SÓ.SEN o | UYAMÁi || naku natta HĮTÓ—BITO o | sinóbu. ||

BÚN.KA no HĮ || ZYUU-ITI -ḠATŲ | MIK-KA ||

ZI.YÚU to HEI.WA o| ÁIsĮ | BÚN.KA o TAKAméru. ||

KIN.ROO - KÁN.SYA no HĮ || ZYUU-ITI -ḠATŲ | NÍ-ZYUU | SÁN -NITĮ ||

KIN.ROO o TATTÓbi || KOKU.MIN taḡai ni | KÁN.SYA | si-áu.

DÁI | NÍ-ZYUU | GÓ -KA ||

"mósi mosĮ."

"mósi mosĮ. || ORÍ.HARA -san desų ka."

"hái || sóo desų."

"IWA.TA désu yo. || ano ne || GETU.MATU ni | KURUMA o KAttá n desu yo. ||

sore de ne ‖ KYUU désu ḡa ne ‖ ANE ḡa │ asƗta │ doráibu ni │ TUrete Iké tte │ Iú n desu ḡa ‖ issyo ni dóo desƗ ka."

"tóotoo │ KAi-másƗta ka. ‖ NÁN desu?"

"KURÓi │ dattósan desu yo. ‖ asƗtá wa ne ‖ ÁNI o │ HIPPÁri-dasƗte ‖ UN.TEN sƗte morai-másƗ kedo ne ‖ GO-NÉN -KAN │ MU- ZÍ.KO tte iu │ SEI.SEKI désƗ kara ‖ go- SIN.PAI nákƗ. ‖ yókattara │ dóozo."

"sore wa sore wa. ‖ YOROKÓnde │ o-TÓMO │ simásu yo. ‖ dótti no │ HÓO e. │ Ikú n desƗ ka."

"TÍBA no KAI.ḠAN ‖ KU-ZYUU KÚ -RI (kuzyuukúri) no │ HÓO e │ Ikóo tte │ Itte 'rú n desu ḡa ‖ yókattara ‖ IMOOTO -san ya │ OTOOTO -san mo ‖ dóozo."

"ITÍ-DAI ni │ sonna ni NOre-másƗ ka."

"o- takƗ kara │ SAN-NÍN ‖ uti no │ ÁNI to │ ANE to │ bóku de │ ROKÚ-NIN desu ne. ‖ NOre-másƗ tomo. ‖ TÍ.ZU de │ MƗru to ‖ SAN-ZI.KAN ḡúrai no │ TOKORÓ desƗ kara ‖ ÁSA ‖ HATI-ZI ḡóro ‖ sotira ni YOtte ‖ mukoo de │ HIRU.MESI ni sƗte ‖ KURAku náru │ máde ni wa │ KÁEtte KUru │ kotó ni │ sƗtára ‖ dóo desyoo."

"íi desu ne. ‖ KÓN.YA wa │ HOSI ḡa takƗsan DÉte iru kara ‖ asƗtá wa ‖ ZYOO- TÉN.KI │ UTAḠAi nási desu yo."

"TÉN.KI wa │ SIN.PAI na-sasóo desu ne. ‖ zya ‖ asƗta no ÁSA │ HATÍ-ZI ni. ‖ a̲! ‖ sore kara ‖ MÓO.HƗ to │ KE.ITO no séetaa wa │ YÓO.I sƗta │ hóo ḡa │ íi desu yo."

"wakari-másƗta. ‖ dóo mo │ aríḡatoo. ‖ TANOsími ni sƗte i-másƗ."

"zya ‖ sayonára."

"sayonára. ‖ o-yasumi-nasái."

DÁI │ NÍ-ZYUU │ RÓK -KA ‖

Í.RYOO wa ‖ SYOKÚ.RYOO ni TUide │ ZYUU.YOO na │ SEI.KATƗ - HƗTU.ZYU -HIN de áru. ‖ sono │ DAI.HYOO -TEKI na monó wa ‖ MEN- ÓRI.MONO ‖ KE - ORI.MONO ‖ KINU - ÓRI.MONO │ óyobi │ ZIN.KOO - sén'i de aru. ‖

NI.HÓN de wa ‖ GO-HYAKU -NEN bákari │ MÁE made wa ‖ KÍ no │ KAWÁ ya ‖ asá kara │ TÓtta │ TƗYÓi │ sén'i de │ Ótta NUNO ḡa ‖ NITI.YOO ni │ TƗKAwarete itá ḡa ‖ GÉN.ZAI de wa ‖ SI.YÓO -RYOO no │ MOTTÓmo │ Óoi no wa ‖ momen de áru. ‖ momen wa ‖ Í.RYOO no │ ÓO to │ SYOOsáre ‖ MIZU ni TUYÓi no de ‖ tabi-tabi aratte ‖ SEI.KETU ni si-yásƗkƗ ‖ zyoobu de ‖ hada -záwari mo │ yói │ ué ni ‖ ÁN.KA de aru. ‖ momen wa ‖ WATÁ kara │ TÓtta │ ÍTO de │ Ótta │ Í.RYOO de aru ḡa ‖ NI.HÓN de wa ‖ WATA no SEI.SAN wa ‖ hotóndo │ NÁi ḡa ‖ MÉN.KA o YU.NYUU sƗ │ KƗ.KAI -Ori no │ GÍ.ZYUTƗ to ‖ YASÚi │ ROO.DÓO -RYOKU ni yori ‖ ITI-RYUU no │ MEN- ÓRI.MONO │ SEI. SÁN -KOKƗ to │ nátte iru. ‖

KE - ORI.MONO wa ‖ MUSI ḡa tƗkƗ │ KET.TÉN wa │ áru ḡa ‖ HO.ON ḡa yókƗ ‖ HUYU no Í.RYOO to sƗte ‖ NÁkƗte wa │ naránai │ monó de aru. ‖ wázuka no │ REI.ḠAi wa │ BETƗ to sƗte ‖ hƗtuzi no KE o │ ÍTO ni sƗte │ Ótta │ NUNO de áru. ‖ YÚTAka na │ BOKƗ.SÓO -TI mo │ NÁkƗ ‖ KƗ.KOO mo ‖ hƗtuzi o káu no ni │

TEKɪsánai | NI.HÓN de wa ‖ GEN.MOO o YU.NYUU sɪ ‖ KE - ORI.MONO o TʊKʊtte iru. ‖

KÍNU wa ‖ KÁIKO no | máyu kara | TÓtta | KÍ.ITO de | Ótta NUNO de ‖ UTʊKʊsíi | zeitáku na | ORÍ.MONO de aru. ‖ NI.HÓN de wa ‖ NÓO.KA no | HʊKU.ḠYOO to sɪte ‖ YOO.SAN ḡa | OKOnawarete iru. ‖

WATÁ ya | KÁIKO ya | hɪtuzi no | SEI.SÁN -DAKA ni wa | KAḠIrí ḡa aru. ‖ sono Hʊ.SOKU o OḠINÁu | tamé ni | párupu o | GEN.RYÓO to sɪta | réeyon nado no | ZIN.KOO - sén'i ḡa | TʊKUraréru yoo ni | nátta. ‖ KÍNU no | NAN- BAI mo TUYÓi | náiron wa ‖ SEKɪ.TAN -SAN kara Umareta | KA.ḠAKʊ -TEKI - GOO.SEI -HIN de áru. ‖ KÓN.NITI de wa ‖ KÁ.ḠAKU no | SÍN.PO to tomo ni ‖ KÁK.KOKʊ KYOO.SOO de ‖ ZIN.KOO - sén'i no | KEN.KYUU KAI.RYOO ni | DÓ.RYOKʊ sɪ ‖ TUḠÍ-TUḠI ni ‖ SIN- SÉI.HIN ḡa ‖ Sɪ.SAKʊ | HATU.BAI sarete iru.

DÁI | NÍ-ZYUU | SɪTÍ -KA ‖

KYUU- KEN.POO - ZÍ.DAI ni wa ‖ KA.TYOO ‖ (ÍK.KA no | SYÚ.ZIN) no | ZET.TAI -TEKI na | KÉN.RI ḡa ‖ HOO.RITU ni yotte | MAMOrárete ite ‖ KA.TYOO wa ‖ IÉ to | KÁ.ZOKU no | Sɪ.HÁI -SYA de atta. ‖ KA.TYOO no TÍ.I o | SÓO.ZOKʊ suru | MONÓ wa ‖ daitai | TYOO.NÁN de ‖ KO.DOMO no utɪ kara ‖ TÓKU ni | DAI.ZÍ ni | YÓO.IKʊ sare ‖ TɪTÍ no | SÍ.ḠO ‖ matá wa ‖ IN.TAI -ḠÓ wa ‖ sono ZEN- ZÁI.SAN o | Úke ‖ ÍK.KA no | SEKI.NÍN -SYA ni | nátta. ‖ KÁ.ZOKU no | ZYÓ.RETU mo | GEN.KAKU de ‖ SYOKU. ZI no SÉKI ya | NYUU.YOKU no ZYUN sáe mo | KImerarete ita. ‖ HU.ZIN no TÍ.I wa ‖ HɪKʊku ‖ TÚMA wa ‖ OTTO ya | TɪTÍ ni | HʊKU.ZYUU surú no ḡa | DOO.TOKU de átta. ‖

kekkon mo ‖ KA.KEI tó ka ‖ IE no KAKʊ.SɪKɪ ‖ ZÁI.SAN no | ZYOO.TAI nádo o | ZYUU.YÓO -Sɪ sɪte ‖ TÓO.NIN no | Í.SI o | MÚ.Sɪ sɪta | monó mo | kánari | átta. ‖ kekkon -ḠÓ mo | OYÁ to | DOO.KYO sɪta | monó ḡa | ÓOkʊ ‖ kóto ni | Tɪ.HÓO de wa ‖ DAI- KÁ.ZOKʊ to sɪte ‖ KO mo MAḠÓ mo | ONAzi YÁNE no SɪTA de ‖ NITI.ZYOO - SÉI.KATU o | tómo ni sɪta. ‖

kono yóo na | HURÚi | KA.ZOKʊ - SÉI.DO ni mo ‖ TYÓO.SYO ḡa | NÁi | kotó wa | nái ḡa ‖ syuuto to yome ‖ ROO.ZÍN to | wakái | MONÓ to no AIDA ni ‖ KAN. ZYOO ya | Sɪ.SOO no masatu ḡa | Okóri ‖ KÁ.ZOKU no AIDA no | HʊKU.ZATU na MON.DAI ni | nátta koto mo | síba-siba | átta. ‖

SIN- KEN.PÓO -KA no | GÉN.ZAI de wa ‖ OTOKÓ mo | ONNÁ mo | HOO.RITʊ -TEKI ni | BYOO.DOO de átte ‖ IÉ to wa ‖ KÁ.ZOKU ḡa | taḡai ni | KYOO. RYOKʊ si-Átte | SEI.KATʊ suru | BA.SYO de áru to | KANḠAéru yoo ni | nátta. ‖ TO.KAI no SEI.NEN - DÁN.ZYO wa ‖ sono KANḠAe-KÁTA mo | KOO. DOO mo | HI.ZYOO ni | KAI.KATU de | ZI.YÚU ni | nátta to iwareru. ‖ tádasi ‖ HO.SYU -TEKI na | ROO.ZÍN no | AIDA ní wa ‖ máda ‖ HURÚi | KA.ZOKʊ - SÉI.DO ya | syuukan ḡa | NE-ZUYÓku | MAMOrárete iru | yóo de aru.

DÁI | NÍ-ZYUU | HÁK -KA ‖

bóku wa ‖ áru KAI.SYA ni | TʊTÓmete iru | sararíiman desɪ. ‖ KYÓ.NEN ‖ DAI.ḠAKʊ SOTU.ḠYOO to DÓO.ZI ni | NYUU.SYA - Sɪ.KÉN o | Úkete ‖ SYÁ.IN

ni | nari-másįta. || máda || GEK.KYUU g̃a | YASÚi no de || GE.SYUKĮ - SÉI.
KAKU desį. ||

MÁI.ASA || SYOKU.ZI g̃a SÚmu to || ÉKI e | kake-tįkéte || ÍP-PUN | ITÍ-BYOO
o | ARASÓu | HĮTO no MUré de | MAN.IN no | DÉN.SYA ni | osi-ái | hesi-ái |
NOri-komi-masį. || ZI.KA -YÓO -SYA de | TUU.KIN surú no g̃a | boku no yumé
desu g̃a . . ||

KAI.SYA dé wa || GO.ZEN -TYUU wa || DEN.WA to SYO.RUI ni Oware || ZYUU-
NÍ -ZI ni | náru to || SYA.NAI - SYÓKU.DOO de | EI.YÓO -SI g̃a | károrii o |
KEI.SAN sįte | tįkįtta TYUU.SYOKU o | tori-masį. || SYOKU.G̃O wa || ITÍ-ZI
made | HIRU - YÁSUmi de || SAN.PO suru MONO || YA.KYUU ya | ténisu o suru
MONO | ZYO.SĮ - SYÁ.IN to | GAS.SYÓO -DAN o | tįkįtte | REN.SYUU suru
MONO || soré – zore TANÓsįkį sug̃osi-masį. ||

GÓ.G̃O wa || KAI.G̃Í ya SOO.DAN || RAI.KYAKU no OO.SETU nádo de || isog̃asíi |
HÍ ni wa || o- TYA o NÓmi ni Iku hima mo | ari-masén. ||

kono KAI.SYA wa || KOO.SEI - SÉTU.BI mo | naka-naka yókį || ÍMA || SYA.IN -
SYUKĮ.SYA o KEN.TĮKĮ -TYUU de || KÍN.KEN ni wa | "YAMA no IÉ" mo |
"ÚMI no IE" mo ari-masį. ||

KEN.KOO - KÁN.RI mo | yóku | OKOnawarete ite || EI.SEI ya | BYOO.KI no YO.
BOO ni túite wa || I.MU -KA g̃a | NÉS.SIN ni SI.DOO sįte i-masį. ||

motíron || ROO.DOO - KÚMI.AI mo | ári || KUMI.ÁI -IN no | NÁKA kara |
erabáreta | Í.IN g̃a || KAI.SYA no KÁN.BU to | TÓO.G̃I sįte || RÓO.SI KYOO.
RYOKĮ sįte || KAI.SYA no HAT.TEN to | SYÁ.IN no KOO.HĮKU ni | DÓ.RYOKĮ
sįte i-masį.

DÁI | NÍ-ZYUU | KYÚU -KA ||

SYOO.WA | NÍ-ZYUU | NÍ -NEN || (SÉN | KYÚU-HYAKU | YÓN-ZYUU | SĮTÍ
-NEN) || GÓ-G̃ATU MIK-KA ni | HAK.KOO sįta | ATARAsíi | NI.HON -KOKĮ
- KÉN.POO wa || ZEN.BUN to | HYAKĮ SAN -káZYOO kara | NÁtte iru. ||

sono KĮ.TYOO o násį | SÉI.SIN wa || mázu || SYU.KEN - ZAI.MIN || (SYU.KEN
wa | KOKU.MIN g̃a MÓtį) to iu | KANG̃Áe de || TEN.NÓO g̃a | MÓtte ita | ZET.
TAI -TEKI na | KÉN.RYOKU wa || KAN.ZEN ni | HĮ.TEI sare || TEN.NÓO wa ||
KOKĮ.SEI ni KANsúru SYOKU.NOO o | MOtánai | kotó g̃a | SADAmerárete iru. ||
KYUU- KÉN.POO ni | óite wa || SIN.SEI na KÁMI to sareta ita | TEN.NÓO wa ||
KOO.G̃ÓO to | tómo ni || NIN.G̃EN to sįte || KOKU.MIN ni | SĮTAsimaréru yoo
ni nátta. ||

TUide || SIN- KÉN.POO ni | óite wa || KOKĮ.SAI - HÉI.WA o | SEI.ZITU ni KĮ.
KYUU sį || EI.KYUU ni | SEN.SOO o sinai kotó o | SADÁme || GÚN.TAI no | HÓ.
ZI mo || KUNI no KOO.SÉN -KEN mo | MITOmete inái. || kono kotó wa || HĮ.
KOKĮ - KYOO.HEI o | MOKĮ.TEKĮ to sįta | KYUU- KÉN.POO ni KURAbete ||
SIN- KÉNPOO g̃a || MATTAkį HAN.TAI no | HEI.WA o MOKĮ.TEKI to sįte iru
kotó o | SIMÉsįte iru. ||

mata || KYUU- KÉN.POO ni | óite wa || TYÚU·KOO || ZIN·G̃I || HAKU.AI nádo ||
KOKU.MIN to sįte | MAMOránakereba | naránai | DOO.TOKU ya | G̃Í.MU g̃a
KYOO.TYOO sarete itá g̃a || SIN- KÉN.POO de wa || KOKU.MIN no RĮ.EKI o |
TYUU.SIN ni || sono KÉN.RI ya || G̃ÍMU o | KOMÁkaku | NÓbete iru. ||

sára ni ‖ KÓ.ZIN no │ ZI.YÚU to ‖ KĮ.HON -TEKI - ZIN.KEN no SON.TYOO o │ TÓKU ni │ KYOO.TYOO sįte iru. ‖ ZIN.KAKU no BYOO.DOO to iu │ KÉN.TĮ kara ‖ KI.ZOKῼ - SÉI.DO o yame ‖ DÁN.ZYO BYOO.DOO no │ KÉN.RI o │ MITOmete iru. ‖ sįtagatte ‖ NI.HON - KOKU.MÍN de aru │ SEI.ZIN - DÁN.ZYO wa ‖ BYOO.DOO ni ‖ SÉN.KYO ni yori ‖ KOK.KAI o TUUzite ‖ SEI.ZI ni SAN. KA dekíru koto ni │ nátte iru.

DÁI │ SAN-ZYÚK -KA ‖

wá ḡa KUNI wa ‖ KÓO.BUTU no │ HYOO.HÓN -SĮTῼ to iwareru hodo ‖ KOO-SÁN.BUTU no │ SYÚ.RUI ḡa │ ÓOi. ‖ KÍN ‖ GÍN ‖ DÓO ‖ TETῼ ‖ SEKĮ. TÁN ‖ SEKI.YU nádo │ taitei no monó wa │ SAN.SYUTῼ surú ḡa ‖ izure mo ‖ sono RYÓO ḡa │ SῼKUnákų ‖ ZI.KYUU si-ḠATÁi. ‖

EKĮ.TAI - NÉN.RYOO de aru │ SEKI.YU wa ‖ hotóndo │ SAN.SYUTῼ sézu ‖ GEN.YU wa ‖ DAI- BÚ.BUN │ arabiya kara ‖ SEI.HIN wa │ amerika kara │ YU. NYUU sįte iru. ‖ móto wa │ TOO.KA -YOO ni SI.YOO sareta SEKI.YU mo ‖ NAI. NEN - KĮ.KÁN no HATU.MEI to │ tómo ni ‖ DOO.RYOKU -YOO to sįte │ ZYUU. YOO ni nátta. ‖ mata ‖ KA.ḠAKῼ - KÓO.ḠYOO no │ GEN.RYÓO to sįte ‖ GOO. SEI - gómu no SEI.ZOO o hazime ‖ TA- HÓO.MEN ni │ RI.YOO sarerú no de ‖ KÁK.KOKῼ tomo │ YU.DEN no KAI.HATU ní wa ‖ TI.MANAKO ni nátte iru. ‖

SEKĮ.TÁN wa ‖ KĮTA- KYÚU.SYUU to │ HOK.KÁI.DOO no │ TAN.DEN kara ‖ wá ḡa KUNI de │ SAN.SYUTῼ sareru SEKĮ.TAN - SOO.ḠAKU no │ HATI-ZYÚP -paasénto made │ TÓtte iru ḡa ‖ wá ḡa KUNI no TAN.DEN wa ‖ TĮ.SĮTῼ to TĮ. SEI ḡa │ GEN.IN de ‖ TAN.MYAKU ḡa MIZIKÁkų ‖ haba mo semái no de ‖ OO-ḡákari na ‖ KĮ.KAI -KA sįta HOO.HOO de │ SAI.TAN suru kotó wa ‖ hotóndo │ Hῼ- KÁ.NOO de aru. ‖ sono tame ‖ DAI- BÚ.BUN ḡa ‖ NOO.RITU no aḡaranai │·GEN.SĮ -TEKI na HOO.HOO de │ SAI.TAN sįte irú no de ‖ sono · SYUT.TÁN -RYOO wa ‖ ÓOku │ nái. ‖ WARE.WARE no TĮ.SĮKĮ to │ GĮ.ZYUTU no │ SÍNPO ni yori ‖ SEKĮ.TÁN mo │ NEN.RYÓO to sįte │ SI.YOO sareru Į.ḠAI ni ‖ GEN.RYÓO to sįte ‖ KÁKῼ.SYU no YAKῼ.HIN ya │ GOO.SEI - zyúsį ‖ ZINKOO - sén'i no SEI.ZOO ni │ SI.YOO sare ‖ sono TῼKAi- miti wa ‖ TA- HÓO.MEN ni │ KAKU.DAI sare-tątu aru.

DÁI │ SÁN-ZYUU │ ÍK- KA ‖

TĮ.KYUU ḡa │ ZI.TEN sį-tątu ‖ TÁI.YOO no MAWAri o │ KOO.TEN surú ni │ sįtaḡatte ‖ SĮ-KĮ ḡa meḡuru. ‖ NI.HÓN wa ‖ SĮ-KĮ no │ HÉN.KA mo ‖ TÉN.KI no │ HÉN.KA mo │ HῼKU.ZATU de ‖ HUU.SÚI.ḠAI ni yoru │ SON.ḠAI mo │ SῼKUnáku nái. ‖ TÓKU ni ‖ MAI.NEN no yóo ni ‖ HÓN.DO ni ZYOO.RIKῼ suru │ TAI.HÚU ni │ yoru SON.ḠAI wa ‖ HI.ZYOO ni ÓOkų ‖ KEN.TĮKÚ -BUTU ya │ HASI no RYUU.SĮTU wa │ motíron ‖ SĮ-SYA no │ déru │ kotó sae │ mare dé wa │ nái. ‖ sįtaḡatte ‖ KĮ.SYOO ya │ TEN.TAI no KEN.KYUU ḡa ‖ TÓKU ni │ ZYUU.YOO da. ‖

KAḠAMI no yóo ni │ SÍZUka na │ MIZUÚMI ni ‖ yawarakákų │ TÉtte ita │ TÁI. YOO ḡa │ KYUU ni │ KURÓi │ KÚMO ni │ oowárete ‖ BOO.HÚU.U ḡa │ yatte kúru. ‖ HĮTÓ—BITO wa ‖ É no yoo ni │ UTῼKῼsíi │ HÚU.KEI o │ TANOsímu │ dókoro de wa │ nákų ‖ tatimatį ‖ TEI.DEN ya │ TETU.DOO - SÉN.RO ‖ DEN. SIN ‖ DEN.WA no Hῼ.TUU ni náru no o │ SIN.PAI sinákereba │ naránai. ‖

TÉN.KI no | HÉN.KA ḡa | YO.TI dekíreba || MU.YOO no SIN.PAI mo irazu ||
mata || SAI.ḠAI mo | MI.ZEN ni | BOO.SI dekíru WAKE da. || kono HʮTU.YOO
kara || rázio ya | terebízyon de wa || MÁI.NITI | IT.TEI no ZI.KAN ni || TEN.
KI - YÓ.HOO ḡa | HOO.SOO sare || SIN.BUN ní mo | MÁI.NITI | TEN.KÍ -ZU
ya | TEN.KI - YÓ.HOO ḡa | déte iru. ||

KI.ON || sitúDO || KI.ATʮ || KAZE || KÚMO || Ú.RYOO nado no | HÉN.KA o |
yóku KAN.SATʮ sʮte iru to || TÉN.KI no | HÉN.KA ḡa | wakáru. || GÉN.ZAI ||
Kʮ.SYOO -DAI ya | SOK.KOO -ZYO kara | DAsárete iru | TEN.KI - YÓ.HOO wa ||
TEN.KÍ -ZU o | motó ni sʮte iru. || TEN.KÍ -ZU wa || KÁKʮ.TI no | kimatta ZI.
KAN no | SÉI.U || KAZA-MUkʮ || HUU.SOKʮ || KI.ATU o hazime || TOO.ATʮ
-SEN || KOO- KÍ.ATU ya | TEI- KÍ.ATU no | TYUU.SIN - Í.TI nado o | KI.ROKʮ
sʮ || sono TÓKI no | HIRÓi | hán'i no | TÉN.KI ḡa || HʮTÓ.ME de | wakáru yoo
ni | sʮta monó da. ||

TYUU.OO - KʮSYOO -DAI dé wa || KÁKʮ.TI no | SOK.KOO -ZYO ya || KOO.KAI
-TYUU no HÚNE kara | ATÚmeta | KAN.SOKʮ - KÉK.KA ni | motozúite || TEN.
KÍ -ZU o SEI.SAKʮ si || IT.TEI - ZI.KAN ḡóto ni | TEN.KÍ -ZU o | TʮKÚru koto
ni yotte || KOO- KÍ.ATU ya | TEI- KÍ.ATU no I.DOO ya | KʮSYOO no HÉN.KA o
SIri || mata || DÉN.PA o TʮKAtte || ZYOO.KUU no ZYOO.TAI o | KAN.SOKʮ
si || soré -ra no | SÍ.RYOO kara | TEN.KI - YÓ.HOO o | HAP.PYOO sʮte iru.

DÁI | SÁN-ZYUU | NÍ-KA ||

WATAKʮSʮ -tati wa || MAI.NITI no yóo ni || SYO.ZYOO || haḡakʮ || KO.ZÚTUMI
o hazime || SIN.BUN || zassi nádo no | TEI.Kʮ - KAN.KÓO -BUTU o | OKʮttári ||
Uke-TOttári sʮte i-masʮ. || yuubín -KYOKU no SI.ḠOTO ḡa || NI.TI.ZYOO - SÉI.
KATU ni || ZÉ.Hʮ | HʮTU.YOO da to iu kotó ni wa || dare mo | I.ZON wa | nái
desyoo. ||

NI.HON no yuubin - ZÍ.ḠYOO no REKʮ.SI o | Mʮru to || mázu || MÉI.ZI | YO-
NEN || (SÉN | HAP-PYAKʮ | SʮTI-ZYUU | ITʮ) ni || KOKU.EI - ZÍ.ḠYOO ni |
nári || SAI.SYO no KIT.TE ḡa | HAK.KOO sare-másʮta. || sore máde wa ||
"hʮkyaku" nádo ḡa | RI.YOO sarete itá no desʮ. || DÓO | HATÍ-NEN ni wa ||
amerika tó no AIDA ni || HAZÍmete | GAI.KOKU - yúubin ḡa | atʮkaware-
másʮta. || BÁN.KOKU|yuubin - REN.GÕO - ZYÓO.YAKU ni | KA.MEI sʮtá no
wa || MÉI.ZI | ZYÚU-NEN desʮ. ||ZYUU-ROKÚ -NEN ni wa||RYÓO.KIN o|ZÉN.
KOKʮ|KIN.ITU ni si-másʮta. ||KO.ZUTUMI - yúubin wa||NÍ.ZYUU.GO - NEN
ni||KOO.KUU - yúubin wa||TAI.SYOO|ZYUU-SÁN -NEN ni||HAZImatte i-masʮ. ||

yuubín -KYOKU no SI.ḠOTO no | ómo na | monó wa || SYUU.HAI désʮ. || MATʮ -
kado no pósʮto kara | ATÚmeta | yuubín -BUTU o || mázu || yuubín -KYOKU
de | KÉN.SA sʮ || KESI.IN o osi-masʮ. || sore kara || Ikʮ- SAKI ni yotte || KÚ.
BETʮ sʮte || UN.SOO sʮ || Uke-TOtta KYÓKU de wa || HʮTATAbi | HAI.TATʮ -
KÚ.BUN o sʮte || MITI - ZYUN o KUmi-TÁte || KO.BETU ni HAI.TATʮ si-
masʮ. || NEN.ḠÁ -ZYOO de | KÓN.ZATʮ suru | NEN.MATU ní wa || KYOKÚ-
IN | daké de wa || TÉ ḡa TArazu || RIN.ZI ni | arubaito - GÁKʮ.SEI nado o |
DOO.IN suru sóo desʮ. ||

SYUU.HAI no hoka || yuubín -KYOKU de wa || kawase || TYO.KIN || hurikae -
TYÓ.KIN || NEN.KIN || ON.KYUU || kan'i - HÓ.KEN nado mo | TOri-'atʮkatte
i-masʮ. ||

yuubín -BUTU o | SᴷKÓsi de mo | HÁYAkᴷ | SEN.POO ni | TODÓkete | morai-
tai TOKÍ ni wa ‖ SOKᴷ.TATU o RI.YOO sᴵ ‖ GAI.KOKU é wa ‖ KOO.KUU -BIN
o RI.YOO suru kotó ḡa | deki-masᴺ. ‖ mata ‖ yuubín -BUTU ḡa | naku nattári |
HA.SON sᴵtári sᴵta BA.AI no | SON.ḠAI - báisyoo no | tamé ni ‖ HAI.TATU
máde no | KI.ROKU o sᴵte okᴷ | KAKᴵ.TOME mo | ari-masᴺ. ‖ konó hoka ‖
NAI.YOO - SYÓO.MEI ‖ HAI.TATᴷ - SYÓO.MEI nado mo | ari-masᴺ. ‖

RYÓO.KIN wa ‖ NAI.KOKᴷ - TUU.ZYOO - yúubin no SYO.ZYOO wa ‖ NI-ZYUU
-guramu ḡóto ni | ZYUU-EN ‖ TUU.ZYOO - háḡaki |GÓ-EN ‖ HEN.SIN -YOO -
haḡaki -Tᴷki | OO.HᴷKU - háḡaki wa | ZYUU-EN desᴺ.

DÁI | SÁN-ZYUU | SÁN -KA ‖

NI.HON - ZÉN.KOKU de ‖ MAI.NEN | kimatta ZÍ.KI ni ‖ kimatta GYÓO.ZI ḡa |
kuri-KÁEsi | OKOnawarete i-masᴺ. ‖ tatóeba ‖ SYOO.GATᴷ ‖ hina - MÁTUri ‖
o- bón ‖ ZÍN.ZYA no | SAI.REI nádo desᴺ. ‖ motíron ‖ TOKORO ni yotte ‖ TA.
SYOO | SYUU.KAN ya | MÍN.ZOKU no tiḡai wa | ari-másu ḡa ‖ konna GYÓO.ZI o|
NEN.ZYUU - GYÓO.ZI to ii-masᴺ. ‖

SYOO.ḠATÚ ni wa ‖ KADÓ - matu o | TÁte ‖ o- sonae o kazari ‖ HATᴷ.HÍ-no-
DE o | OḠÁndari ‖ UZI-ḠAMI no o- MIYA ni | HATU-móode o | sᴵtári si-masᴺ. ‖
mata ‖ KÍN.PEN no | TI.ZIN ní wa ‖ NEN.SI -MÁWAri ‖ EN.POO no Tᴵ.KÍ ni
wa ‖ NEN.ḠÁ -ZYOO de ‖ SÍN.NEN no | áisatu o si-masᴺ. ‖ GAN.ZITᴷ kara |
ZYÚU-GO -NITI made ‖ iro-iro na GYÓO.ZI ḡa | TUZUki-masᴺ. ‖

NI-ḠATÚ ni | náru to ‖ SETÚ.BUN ḡa ari-masᴺ. ‖ RIS.SYUN no ZEN.ZITU no
YUU.ḠATA ‖ OO.ḠÓE de ‖ "HᴷKÚ wa UTᴵ ‖ oní wa SOTO" to | kuri-KAEsi-
náḡara ‖ uti -zyuu ni | mamé o | máku no desᴺ. ‖

SÁN-ḠATU ni wa ‖ hina - MÁTUri ḡa ari-masᴺ. ‖ ÍMA de wa ‖ UTᴷKᴷsíi |
hina - NÍN.ḠYOO o kazaru | ONNÁ-no-KO no | MATUrí ni | nátte | i-másu ga ‖
mukasi wa ‖ HᴵTÓ-BITO ḡa ‖ ÚMI ya | KAWÁ e Itte ‖ karada o KIYÓme ‖
NIN.ḠEN no keḡaré o | NIN.ḠYOO ni UTᴷsᴵte ‖ kore o | MIZU ni NAḠÁsᴵta no
ḡa ‖ móto no KATATI desᴺ. ‖ SÍN.TOO ‖ túmari ‖ NI.HÓN KO.YUU no | SYÚU.
KYOO no | GYÓO.ZI desᴵta. ‖ mata ‖ SYUN.BUN ‖ SYUU.BUN no kóro o |
"hiḡán" to itte ‖ HAKA -MÁIri o | surú no wa ‖ BUK.KYÓO no MATUri desᴺ. ‖

GÓ-ḠATU ni wa ‖ OTOKÓ-no-KO no | SEK.KÚ ḡa ari | yoroi ya | kábuto o
kazari ‖ AO.ZORA TÁKAkᴷ | koi - nóbori o | TÁte ‖ syoobú -YU ni hairi-
masᴺ. ‖

NOO.SON de ‖ ITI.BAN TANOsími na | monó wa ‖ o- bón to | UZI-ḠAMI no |
SAI.REI desyóo. ‖ o- bón wa ‖ SᴵTI-ḠATU | ZYUU-GO -NITI o TYUU.SIN ni |
OKOnawareru | BUK.KYOO no GYÓO.ZI de ‖ SInda SÓ.SEN o | MATUrú no
desᴺ. ‖ kono kóro ‖ "TYUU.ḠEN" to itte ‖ Tᴵ.ZIN ni | okuri- mono o suru
SYUU.KAN ḡa ári ‖ mata ‖ ZYO.TYUU ya | SI.YOO -NIN ní wa | KOzukái -SEN
o yatte ‖ uti e KÁEsᴵtari ‖ ASObi ni yattári simasᴺ. ‖ mata ‖ YÓRU wa ‖ ZEN.
KOKᴷ -TEKI ni | bon - ódori ḡa | OKOnaware-masᴺ. ‖ ZÍN.ZYA no | KÉI.DAI
ya | HÍRO.BA nado ni | TAKÁi yaḡura o | TÁte ‖ ÁKA ‖ KI ‖ MÍDORI nado no |
DEN.TOO ya ‖ KO.BATA ‖ tyootín mo | UTᴷKᴷsikᴷ ‖ taiko ni Awásete ‖
OTOKÓ mo | ONNÁ mo | KO.DOMO mo | issyo ni | WÁ ni natte ‖ odori-
MAWAri-masᴺ. ‖

ZÍN.ZYA no SAI.REI wa || MURA no MAMOrí-ĞAMI de aru | UZI-ĞÁMi ni ||
HÁRU ni wa || HOO.SAKƱ to | HEI.WA o NEĞÁi || ÁKI ni wa || tóreta | KOKÚ.
MOTU o | SONÁete || KÁN.SYA suru to | tómo ni || MURA -zyuu no | HƗTÓ
-BITO ğa || sorótte | TANOsímu | rikuriéesyon mo | KÁnete i-masƗ. ||

NEN.ZYUU - GYÓO.ZI no | KƗ.KÁN || TAbéru koto o | KINziráreta mono ||
mata || KANARAzu | TAbéru koto ni | nátte iru | monó nado || TOKU.BETU
na | SYOKƱ- SYÚU.KAN mo ari-masƗ. ||

koré -ra o | táda | MEI.SÍN to ka || ZÉN.DAI no | I.HÚU to sƗte || waratte
simau MÁE ni || sono MÍN.ZOKƱ | SYUU.KAN o | KEN.KYUU suru kotó ğa ||
NI.HON -ZÍN no | SEI.KATƱ - KÁN.ZYOO ya | KANĞAe-KÁTA o | SIru ué ni |
TAI.SETU na kotó desyoo.

DÁI | SÁN-ZYUU | YÓN -KA ||

1. NI.HÓN de wa || SEI.ZI no UN.EI ni túite || SÁN-KEN - BUN.RITƱ | SÉI.DO
   o | TÓri || RIP.PÓO -KEN wa | KOK.KAI ni || GYOO.SÉI -KEN wa | NÁIkaku
   ni || SI.HÓO -KEN wa | saiBAN -SYO ni | SYO.ZOKƱ sƗte iru. ||

1. NI.HON no KOK.KAI wa || KOK.KEN no | SAI.KOO - KƗ.KÁN de ari || SYUU.
   ĞÍ.IN to | SAN.ĞÍ.IN kara | NÁru. ||

1. KOK.KAI no || RIP.POO ni KANsúru | ómo na | KEN.ĞÉN wa || KÉN.POO
   KAI.SEI no | HÁTU.ĞI || HOO.RITU no SEI.TEI || ZYOO.YAKU no SYOO.NIN
   de áru. ||
   ZAI.SEI ni KANsúru | KEN.ĞÉN no | ómo na | monó wa || YO.SAN no GI.
   KETƱ || KÉS.SAN no SYOO.NIN || KÓKƱ.HƗ SƗ.SƗTU no | KET.TEI de áru. ||
   KÓKU.MU ni | KANsúru | KEN.ĞÉN no | ómo na | monó wa || SOO.RI - DÁI.
   ZIN no | SI.MEI || KOKƱ.SEI ni KANsúru | TYÓO.SA || saiBÁN -KAN no |
   danğái -KEN de aru. ||

1. KOK.KAI - GÍ.IN wa || ZÉN- KOKU.MIN o | DAI.HYOO suru MONÓ de ||
   KOKU.MIN no TOO.HYOO ni yori | SÉN.KYO sareru. ||
   MÁN | NI-ZYUS -SAI Í.ZYOO no KOKU.MIN wa || TOKU.BETU na BA.AI o
   NOZOkƗ || SEI.BETƱ || KAI.KYUU no | SÁ.BETU | nákƗ || SEN.KYÓ -KEN
   ğa | áru. ||

1. SYUU.ĞÍ.IN - GÍ.IN wa || TEI.IN | YÓN-HYAKU | ROKU-ZYUU | SƗTƗ -MEI ||
   NIN.KI | YO-NEN || SAN.ĞI.IN - GÍ.IN wa || TEI.IN | NI-HYAKU | GO-ZYÚU
   -MEI || NIN.KI | ROKÚ-NEN de aru. ||

1. RYOO.IN no GI.KETU ğa | KOTOnáru | BA.AI ní wa || IT.TEI no TE- TÚZUki
   o | HÉte || SYUU.ĞÍ.IN no GI.KETU ğa || KOK.KAI no GI.KETƱ to sareru. ||

1. KOK.KAI wa || SOO.RI - DÁI.ZIN o | SI.MEI surú ğa || TÓO.HA o | KOTÓ ni
   suru SEI.TOO no utƗ || TA.SUU -TOO no TÓO.SYU ğa | SI.MEI sareru. ||

1. SOO.RI - DÁI.ZIN wa || GAI.MÚ -SYOO || OO.KURÁ -SYOO nado || KÁKƱ.
   SYOO no | DÁI.ZIN o | KIme || NÁIkaku o | SÓ.SƗKƗ suru. ||

1. NÁIkaku wa || GYOO.SEI no | SAI.KOO no TƗ.I ni ari || KÁKƱ.SYOO ni | sono
   SI.ĞOTO o MAKÁsete || kore o kantokƗ suru. ||

1. NÁIkaku no KEN.ĞÉN no | ómo na | monó wa || HOO.RITU no KÓO.SƗ to |
   KÓKU.MU no | SÓO.RI || GAI.KOO - MÓN.DAI no | SYÓ.RI || ZYOO.YAKU

o MUSUbu koto ‖ YO.SÁN -AN no SAKÝ.SEI to │ KOK.KAI TEI.SYUTU nádo de aru. ‖

1. GÍ.KAI ni oite ‖ NÁIkaku no │ HYOO.BAN ḡa Ótí ‖ SYUU.GÍ.IN ḡa │ HÝ-SÍN.NIN o │ KÉTU.ḠI síta │ toki wa ‖ SYUU.GÍ.IN ḡa ‖ TOO-KA Í.NAI ni │ KAI.SAN sarenai KÁḠIri ‖ NÁIkaku wa ‖ SOO- ZÍ.SYOKÝ suru. ‖

1. TÍ.HOO - GYÓO.SEI wa ‖ SEN.ḠO ‖ TÍ.HOO - ZÍ.TI ḡa │ SUI.SIN sare ‖ GEN.SOKÝ to síte ‖ súbete ‖ TÍ.HOO - KOO.KYOO - DÁN.TAI ni │ MAKÁsete aru. ‖

1. HOK.KÁI.DOO ‖ HÓN.SYUU ‖ SÍ.KÓKÝ ‖ KYÚU.SYUU wa ‖ ITÍ-DOO ‖ ÍT-TO ‖ NÍ-HÝ ‖ SI-ZYUU NÍ -KEN ni │ WAkeráre ‖ soré-zore ‖ DOO- GÍ. KAI ‖ TO-KAI ‖ HÝ-KAI ‖ KEN-KAI ḡa │ ári ‖ sára ni │ KÁKU │ SÍ │ TYÓO │ SÓN ni wa ‖ SI-KAI │ TYOO-KAI │ SON-KAI ḡa ári ‖ KÁKU- GI.IN │ óyobi ‖ TO │ DÓO ‖ HÝ │ KÉN no │ TÍ.ZI SÍ ‖ TYÓO ‖ SÓN-TYOO wa ‖ ZYUU.MIN ni yori ‖ TYOKÝ.SETÝ │ KOO.SEN sareru. ‖ (GÉN.ZAI de wa ‖ GÚN wa ‖ TÍ.HOO - GYÓO.SEI no │ TÁN.I ni │ nátte inai.) ‖

1. SÍ.HÓO -KEN wa ‖ saiBAN -SYO ‖ (SAI.KOO - saiBAN -SYO ‖ KA.KYUU - saiBAN -SYO) ḡa │ DOKU.RITÝ síte │ tíkasadóru. ‖

1. KÓ.ZIN no │ ZI.YÚU │ óyobi │ KÉN.RI o │ MAMÓri ‖ HAN.ZAI ya │ KOO.TUU no │ TOri-simari o OKOnau tamé ni wa ‖ keisatu ḡa áru. ‖

Í.ZYOO ‖ SÓOzite ‖ SEN.ḠO no SEI.ZI wa ‖ MIN.SYU -KA ‖ TI.HOO - BUN. KEN -KA sare ‖ KOKU.MIN no SÓO.I ‖ SE.RON ḡa │ ZYUU.YÓO -SÍ sareru │ yóo ni │ nátta. ‖ SE.RON wa ‖ MIN.SYU - SÉI.ZI no │ ZYUU.YOO na YÓO.SO de │ áru ḡa ‖ <u>masý-komyunikéesyon</u> no │ HAT.TATÝ síta ZI.DAI ní wa ‖ SEN.DEN ni │ SÁ.YUU sareru │ osoré mo │ áru no de ‖ TYÚU.I ḡa │ HÍTU.YOO de áru.

DÁI │ SÁN -ZYUU │ GÓ -KA ‖

KÁ.ZITÝ ‖ TOO.KYOO ZAI.ZYUU no │ SEI.NEN - DÁN.ZYO o │ TAI.SYOO ni síte ‖ "síkí na goraku" ni │ túite │ TYÓO.SA síta │ KYOO.MI -BUKÁi HOO. KOKU o Yómu │ KÍ.KÁI ḡa │ átta. ‖

DAN.SEI no KOTÁe de wa ‖ ITÍ-I ḡa │ éiḠA ‖ NÍ-I ḡa │ sýpóotý ‖ ZYO.SEI no KOTÁe de wa ‖ ITÍ-I ḡa │ RYO.KOO ‖ NÍ-I ḡa │ éiḠA to │ nátte iru. ‖

sýpóotu ni │ túite wa ‖ ZYÚU.RAI no ‖ YA.KYUU ya │ sumoo o ‖ "Míru" koto │ yóri mo ‖ ZI.BUN de ‖ "suru" kotó ḡa │ síkí da to │ KOTÁe ‖ <u>góruhý</u> │ ténisu o hazime ‖ TO.ZAN ‖ <u>síkíi</u> ‖ <u>síkéeto</u> ‖ yótto ‖ <u>síkúutaa</u> ‖ ZI.DOO -SYA - ÚN.TEN nado o │ aḡete iru. ‖ kono kotó wa ‖ RYO.KOO ḡa │ ITÍ-I ni │ nátta koto to │ tómo ni ‖ KEI.ZAI - SÉI.KATU │ AN.TEI no KEK.KA to │ KÁI. SYAKÝ │ síté mo │ yokaróo. ‖

konó hoka ‖ KEI.BA ‖ KEI.RIN ‖ <u>máazyan</u> ‖ <u>patinko</u> no NIN.KI mo │ otoróezu ‖ ÓN.ḠAKU de wa ‖ <u>zyázu</u> ḡa │ ITÍ-I o │ síme ‖ "SÍ.KÓO -RYOKU o │ ubáu DOKU. YAKÝ" to │ iwaraté mo ‖ ZYÚU-DAI no │ KOO.KÓO -SEI no │ zyázu ni │ TAIsúru │ I.ZYOO na KOO.HUN wa │ samenai rasíi. ‖ KAwatte irú no wa ‖ "KABU no BÁI.BAI" to iu │ KOTÁe de ‖ "BA.KEN o KAú yori ‖ <u>súriru</u> ḡa │ áru to ka. ‖

éiḠA no | "KA.SÓO - TEKÍ" | térebi wa || AN.ḠAI TÉI-I de || ROKÚ-I ni | nátte
iru. || sík̇ás̟í || NOO.SON no SEI.NEN - DÁN.ZYO o | TAI.SYOO ni suréba ||
NOO.SON -ḠAWA dé wa || osórakú || térebi ḡa | rázio to | tómo ni | ITI-, NÍ-I
o | siméru no de wa | aru mái ka. || terebí -KYOKU SOO.SETU ni | tomonái ||
SAK.KON no | terebi - ZYU.ZÓO -KI no | NOO.SON SIN.Sí̇TU wa || makoto ni
ITIZIRÚsík̇ú || YUKI no YÓRU || KOME.DÁWARA o | Ami-náḡara || térebi o |
TANOsímu | NÓO.KA wa || móhaya || mezurásíku wa | nái. || éiḠA ya | sibai
ḡa || SYOO.ḠÁK.KOO no | KOO.DOO nádo de || NÉN ni | NÁN-DO ka | ZYOO.
EN sarerú ni | suḡ̇ínai | goraku no SÚ̇KUnái || SEI.KATU no TAN.TYOO na NOO.
SON de || térebi ḡa | KANḡei sarerú no wa·|| TOO.ZEN de aróo. ||

konó hoka || MAI.TÚ̇KÍ | SYUP.PAN sareru | goraku - zássí || TAN.KOO -BON
no KÁZU mo | obitadásík̇ú || TÓKU ni || SYUU.KAN - zássi no | SYOO.KIN
-TÚ̇kí - kuízu wa || TO.KAI | NOO.SON no | BETU nákú || ÓOku no | DÓKÚ̇.
SYA ni | TANOsimárete | iru yóo de aru.

Part III

VOCABULARY AND GRAMMAR NOTES

INTRODUCTORY NOTE

These notes are intended to help the students understand the structure of the sentences. We attempt to show how complex sentences are built up by systematic changes in simple sentences. The sentence derivations are based on the analysis in the forthcoming book "The Sentences of Japanese," but practical considerations have led us to simplify many points; the intention is to be helpful rather than definitive, and we have relied on illustrative examples to bring home the structure. For some of the lessons, the sentences are each analyzed in considerable detail; for other lessons, the treatment is more cursory; for some lessons, there are only brief notes on puzzling points. In the examples, A B C usually refer to people, X Y Z to things, and P Q R to places; but we have not tried to be strictly consistent. The symbol → means 'changes into' and the opposite symbol ← means 'changes from.' The symbol + means 'combined with.'

The lessons in this Manual contain materials in both spoken and written styles as used today; they do not attempt to cover the older literary style, called Bungo, but a few elements from that style are found in the modern written style.

Here are some general peculiarities of modern written Japanese to watch for:

1. Use of de áru for the COPULA dá.

2. Use of the INFINITIVE, -(i) for VERBS and -ku for ADJECTIVES, in place of the GERUND, -te/-de for VERBS and -kute for ADJECTIVES, to mean 'does/is and (so).'

3. Use of the TENTATIVE to mean 'probably.' In the colloquial -masyoo means 'let's do it' or 'I think I'll do it,' so that the form arimasyóo is usually not said; to say 'there probably exists' you use áru daroo/desyoo. The dialect form -karoo (abbreviation of -ku aroo) is also used, corresponding to standard ADJECTIVE -i daróo, so that nakaróo = nái daroo. From the usages of written Japanese, of course, a number of idioms have entered into the spoken language.

4. Use of the TENTATIVE to modify NOUNS, especially koto, hazu, mono, hito, etcetera. Examples: siyóo koto = (1) suru koto, (2) suru hazu no koto, (3) siyoo to omóu koto; X de aróo hito = (1) X no hito, (2) X no hazu no hito, (3) X da to omowaréru hito, etcetera. In the colloquial, only present or past sentences can be embedded in another sentence as a NOUN modifier: Míru./ Míta. Ookíi./ Ookíkatta. Hón da. [Hon no . . .]/Hón datta. Génki da. [Génki na . . .]/ Génki datta.

5. NOUN no NOUN is often replaced by a compound NOUN-NOUN. natu no yasumi 'a vacation in the summer' natu-yásumi 'a summer vacation.'

6. NOUN to/ya NOUN is often replaced by NOUN . NOUN or NOUN - NOUN. rázio to/ya térebi 'radio and TV' razio•térebi 'radio-TV' gen'in to kekka 'cause and result' gen'in - kekka 'cause and effect'

7. Subject and object PARTICLES (ḡa and o) freely drop, especially when next to the VERB.

8. Clichés are frequently borrowed from Bungo and inserted in the midst of otherwise colloquial sentences.

44

Lesson 1

ka	a lesson
Dái Ík-ka	Lesson 1
áto no . . .	the rest [of the . . .], the remaining . . .
aói	is blue, is green
tomo	both, all; [+NEGATIVE] neither, none
ni-satu tomo	both books, [+NEGATIVE] neither book
san-nin tomo	all three people [+NEGATIVE] none of the three
tetyoo	a memo book
(A ni X o) situmon suru	asks (A about X), questions (= <u>kiku</u>)

1. Hón ḡa arimasu
     + Sán-satu arimasu
     → Hón ḡa | sán-satu arimasu

   There is a book (or There are books)
   There are three [bound objects]
   There are three books

2. Teeburu no ué ni arimasu

     + Hón ga | sán-satu arimasu
     → Teeburu no ué ni ‖ hón ḡa | sán-satu arimasu

   There are some on the table (or It is on the table)
   There are three books
   There are three books on the table

3. Is-satú wa | ookíi desu
     + Áto no | ní-satu wa ‖ tiisái | hón desu
     → Is-satú wa | óokikute ‖ áto no | ní-satu wa | tiisái | hón desu

   One [of the books] is big
   The remaining two [books] are small books
   One [of the books] is big, and the remaining two are small books

4. Ookíi hon $\begin{Bmatrix} \text{ḡa} \\ \text{wa} \end{Bmatrix}$ | aói desu

     + Tiisái no $\begin{Bmatrix} \text{ḡa} \\ \text{wa} \end{Bmatrix}$ | áoku | arimasén

     → Ookíi hon wa | $\begin{Bmatrix} \text{áokute} \\ \text{aói desu ḡa} \end{Bmatrix}$ ‖ tiisái no wa | áoku | arimasén

   The big book is green (or blue)

   The small ones aren't green

   The big book is green, and/but the small ones aren't green

5. Aói | hón no | sita ni arimásu

     + Siról | kamí ḡa | si-, ḡo-mai arimásu
     → Aói | hón no sita ni ‖ siról | kamí ḡa | si-, ḡo-mai arimásu or
   Aói | hón no | sita ní wa ‖ siról | kamí ḡa | si-, ḡo-mai arimásu

   There are [some] under the green book (or It is under the green book)
   There are 4 or 5 sheets of white paper
   There are 4 or 5 sheets of white paper under the green book
   Under the green book [as opposed to other places] there are 4 or 5 sheets of white paper

6. (Sóba ni) | tiisái tetyoo ḡa arimasu
     + Pén ḡa | íp-pon arimasu
     → (Sóba ni) | tiisái tetyoo to | pén ḡa | íp-pon arimasu

   (Nearby) there is a small notebook

   There is one pen
   (Nearby) there is a small notebook and one pen

7. muzukasii tokoro   difficult parts (<u>or</u> places)
  + wakaránai tokoro   parts which I do not understand
  → muzukásikute wakaránai tokoro   difficult parts which I do not understand

8. Muzukásikute│wakaránai tokoro   I'll write down on that paper [to have
      o│sono kamí ni│káite okimasu   ready for later] the difficult parts
                                      which I do not understand

    + Áto de‖senséi ni│situmon simasu   Afterwards I'll ask the teacher
    → Muzukásikute│wakaránai tokoro   I'll write down on that paper the dif-
      o│sono kamí ni│káite oite‖   ficult parts which I do not under-
      áto de‖senséi ni│situmon   stand
      simasu

9. Senséi ni│situmon simasu   I'll ask the teacher
  + . . . tumori désu   It is my intention to . . .
  → Senséi ni│situmon suru tumori   I intend to ask the teacher
    désu

    Muzukásikute│wakaránai tokoro   I intend to write down on that paper
    o│sono kamí ni│káite oite‖   the difficult parts which I do not
    áto de‖senséi ni│situmon suru   understand and afterwards ask the
    tumori désu   teacher [about them]

Lesson 2

móto wa	originally, formerly
móto	the beginning, the origin
móto no	former . . . , ex- . . .
gaikokugo	a foreign language
gaikoku	a foreign country
gairaigo	a word of foreign origin, a loanword
tatóeba	for example
tatoé	an example, an allegory, a proverb
mánto	a cape, a manteau
sukíi	ski, skiing, a pair of skis
porutogarugo	Portuguese language
mázu	first of all
térebi	TV
ópera	an opera
báree	ballet
rekóodo	a phonograph record
zyúusu	juice
sandoítti	a sandwich
kéeki	a cake
X o hazime	including of course X, not to speak of X
sókkusu	socks
súrippa	slippers
reinkóoto	a raincoat
ténisu	tennis
ténisu o suru	plays tennis
góruhu	golf
doráibu	a drive
doráibu suru	takes a ride
doráibu ni iku	goes for a drive
cf. unten suru	drives = operates a vehicle
háikingu	hiking
píkunikku	picnicking
seikatu	life, living, existence
X ga Y ni tokekómu	X melts into Y, X merges into Y
wakái	is young
. . . bákari de náku	not only . . . (but also)
tosiyóri	an aged person, old people

1. (Íma wa) ‖ (móo) | Nihon-go ni
   narimásita

   (Now) it has (already) become a Japanese word

✓ 2. Íma wa ‖ móo | Nihon-go ni nátte |
   simaimásita

   Now it has already become a completely Japanese word

   + Nihon-zín ga | máiniti tukaimasu

   The Japanese use it every day

   ⇢ Íma wa ‖ móo | Nihon-zín ga |
   máiniti tukau | Nihon-go ni nátte |
   simaimásita

   Now it has already become a completely Japanese word which the
   Japanese use every day

3. (Móto wa) | gaikoku-go désita

   (Formerly) it was a foreign word

   + Íma wa ‖ móo | Nihon-zín ga |
   máiniti tukau | Nihon-go ni
   nátte | simaimásita

   Now it has already become a completely Japanese word which the
   Japanese use every day

Móto wa ‖ gaikoku-ḡo dátta keredomo ‖ íma wa ‖móo . . .

Formerly it was a foreign word, but now it has already . . .

4. Móto wa ‖ gaikoku-ḡo dátta keredomo ‖ íma wa ‖ móo| Nihon-zín ḡa|máiniti tukau| Nihon-ḡo ni nátte simatta kotoba

Words which formerly were foreign words but now have already become completely Japanese words which the Japanese use every day

+ Gairai-ḡo to iimásu

We call them "gairai-go"

→ Móto wa ‖ . . . simatta kotobá o|gairai-ḡo to iimásu

Words which formerly . . . every day we call "gairai-go"

5. (Tatóeba)‖X, Y, Z nado

(for example), X, Y, Z, and the like

+ Ei-ḡo ‖ porutogaru-ḡo ‖ huransu-ḡo ‖ doitu-go kara kita|gairai-ḡo désu

They are loanwords which came from English, Portuguese, French, and German

→ Tatóeba‖X, Y, Z nado wa ‖ ei-ḡo ‖ porutogaru-ḡo ‖ huransu-ḡo ‖ doitu-go kara kita|gairai-ḡo désu

For example, X, Y, Z and the like are loanwords which came from English, Portuguese, French, and German

6. Konna kotobá o kakimasu

We write words of this kind . . .

+ katakána de

in/with katakana

→ Konna kotobá {o / wa}|katakána de kakimasu

We write words of this kind in katakana

7. Mé de|mítari simasu

We do things like looking [at it/them] with our eyes

+ Mimí de|kiitári simasu

We do things like listening [to it/them] with our ears

→ Mé de|mítari ‖mimí de|kiitári simasu

We do things like looking with our eyes and/or listening with our ears

8. Mé de|mítari ‖mimí de|kiitári| suru monó ni wa

Among the things which we look at with our eyes and/or listen to with our ears . . .

+ X, Y, Z nádo ḡa arimasu

There are X, Y, Z and the like

→ Mé de|mítari‖ mimí de|kiitári| suru monó ni wa ‖ X, Y, Z, nádo ḡa arimasu

Among the things which we look at with our eyes and/or listen to with our ears are X, Y, Z, and the like

9. Kuti ni ireru monó ni mo

Also among the things which [people] put in their mouths . . .

10. X, Y, Z o hazime ‖ arimasu

There are some, beginning with X, Y, and Z [as outstanding examples]

+ Takusán no gairai-ḡo ḡa arimasu

There are many loanwords

→ X, Y, Z o hazime ‖ takusán no gairai-ḡo ḡa arimasu

There are many loanwords, from X, Y, Z on down [to less prominent examples]

11. X, Y, Z {o / wa}|té de tukaimasu

We use X, Y, Z with our hands

+ Así ni wa ‖ P ya Q o hakimasu

On our feet, we wear P and Q [among other things]

    X, Y, Z wa‖té de│tukaú si‖así   We use X, Y, Z with our hands; and
    ni wa‖P ya Q o hakimasu   on our feet we wear P and Q

12. áme ḡa│húru to   when it rains (, then . . .)
    Reinkóoto o kimasu   We wear a raincoat
    Áme ḡa│húru to‖reinkóoto o   When it rains, we wear a raincoat
    kimasu

13. samúi hi ni   on cold days
  + Óobaa o kimasu   We wear an overcoat
  → Samúi hi ni wa ‖ óobaa o kimasu On cold days [as opposed to other
                           times] we wear an overcoat

14. Áme ḡa│húru to ‖ reinkóoto o   When it rains, we wear a raincoat
    kimasu
  + Samúi hi ni wa ‖ óobaa o kimasu On cold days we wear an overcoat
  → Áme ḡa│húru to ‖ reinkóoto o│ When it rains, we wear a raincoat;
    kirú si ‖ samúi hi ni wa ‖ óobaa   and on cold days we wear an over-
    o kimasu   coat

15. Háikingu ya│píkunikku ni ikimasu We go hiking or for a picnic
  + . . . kotó mo arimasu   It sometimes also happens that . . .
  → Háikingu ya│píkunikku ni│iku kotó It sometimes also happens that we
    mo arimasu   go hiking or for a picnic

16. Kono yóo na gairai-ḡo wa ‖ toke-   Loanwords of this type are com-
    konde simatte imasu   pletely merged . . .
  + Nihon-zín no│seikatu no náka   inside the life of the Japanese
  → Kono yóo na gairai-ḡo wa ‖ Nihon- Loanwords of this type are com-
    zín no│seikatu no náka ni│toke-   pletely merged into the life of the
    konde simatte imasu   Japanese

17. Wakái hitobito│bákari de (wa)│   It is not only young people
    arimasén
  + Roku-, siti-zyúu no│tosiyóri mo│   Old people of 60 or 70 also use them
    yóku tukaimasu   regularly
  → Wakái hitobito│bákari de│náku(te)‖ Not only young people but also old
    roku-, siti-zyúu no│tosiyóri mo│   people of 60 or 70 use them regu-
    yóku tukaimasu   larly

18. X o/wa│tosiyóri mo│yóku tukai-   Old people also use X regularly
    masu
  → X ḡa/wa│tosiyóri ni mo ‖ yóku   X gets used regularly by old people
    tukawaremasu   also

19. X ḡa/wa (A ni) tukawarete imasu   (1) X is used (by A) regularly (all
                                the time, repeatedly)
                                (2) X is [in the midst of] getting used
                                (by A)
                                (3) X [has come into use and now] is
                                in use (by A)

Lesson 3

X ni naréru	gets accustomed to X
tosyókan	a library
osyooḡatú	the New Year, January
ikébana	flower arrangement, the art of floral arrangement
zituḡyooka	a businessman, an industrialist
benḡósi	a lawyer
sínsetu (na)	is kind
syuukan	a custom, a habit
sáhoo	(good) manners, etiquette

1. Hak-káḡetu ni narimasu — It becomes 8 months
   + móo — already
   → Móo│hak-káḡetu ni narimasu — It is already 8 months

2. Nihón e│kimásita — We came to Japan
   + X kara — since/after X
   → Nihón e│kité kara — since coming to Japan

3. Nihón e│kité kara — since coming to Japan
   + Móo│hak-káḡetu ni narimasu — It is already 8 months
   → Nihón e│kité kara ‖ móo│hak-káḡetu ni narimasu — It is already 8 months since we came to Japan

4. Kánai wa│naremásita — My wife has gotten accustomed [to] . . .
   + Musumé wa│naremásita — My daughter has gotten accustomed [to] . . .
   → Kánai mo│musumé mo│naremásita — Both my wife and my daughter have gotten accustomed [to] . . .

5. X mo Y mo (daibu) naremásita — Both X and Y have gotten (for the most part) accustomed [to] . . .
   + Nihon no seikatu — Japanese life
   → X mo Y mo│daibu│Nihon no seikatu ni naremásita — Both X and Y have pretty much gotten accustomed to Japanese life

6. Isikawa to iimásu — His name is Ishikawa, They call him Ishikawa
   + Tomodati désu — It's a friend
   → Isikawa to iu tomodati désu — It's a friend named Ishikawa

7. Watakusi wa│Nihon-ḡo o naraimásu — I learn Japanese language
   + Isikawa to iu tomodati — a friend named Ishikawa
   → Watakusi wa ‖ Isikawa to iu tomodati ni│Nihon-ḡo o naraimásu — I learn Japanese from a friend named Ishikawa

8. Watakusi {ḡa / wa}│tosyókan e ikimasu — I go to the library
   + Watakusi {ḡa / wa}│benkyoo simásu — I study
   → Watakusi {ḡa / wa}│tosyókan e itte│benkyoo simásu — I go to the library and/to study

9. Get-, |sui-, |kin-yóo ni wa‖
    Nihon-g̱o o naraimásu

On Mondays, Wednesdays, and Fridays [as opposed to other days] I learn Japanese

  + Ka-yóo to|moku-yóo ni wa ‖
    tosyókan e itte|benkyoo simásu

On Tuesdays and Thursdays [as opposed to other days] I go to the library to study

  → Get-, |sui-, |kin-yóo ni wa ‖
    Nihon-g̱o o narái ‖ ka-yóo to|
    moku-yóo ni wa ‖ tosyókan e
    itte|benkyoo simásu
    (<u>narái</u> - <u>narátte</u>: see Introduction, Point 2)

On Mondays, Wednesdays, and Fridays I learn Japanese; and on Tuesdays and Thursdays I go to the library to study

10. Onná-no-ko desu
  + Nihon-zín desu

It's a little girl
It's a Japanese

  → a. Onná-no-ko $\begin{Bmatrix} \text{g̱a} \\ \text{wa} \end{Bmatrix}$ |Nihon-zín
      desu

The little girl is Japanese

    b. Nihon-zín no|onná-no-ko desu

It's a little Japanese girl

11. Musumé wa asobimasu
  + tikáku no|Nihon-zín no|onná-no-ko

My daughter plays . . .
The little Japanese girl in the neighborhood

  → Musumé wa|tikáku no|Nihon-zín
    no|onná-no-ko to|asobimásu

My daughter plays with the little Japanese girl in the neighborhood

12. (máiniti) . . . asonde imásu

. . . regularly plays (every day)

13. Ikébana o|narátte imasu
  + o-syoog̱atú kara

She is learning flower arrangement since January

  → O-syoog̱atú kara ‖ ikébana o|
    narátte imasu

She has been [and still is] regularly studying flower arrangement since January

    <u>cf</u>. Kyónen kara byooki desu

He has been sick since last year

14. A to iu B
    <u>cf</u>. No. 6

a B called/named A

  a. Yamanaka-san to iimásu
  + Zitug̱yoo-ka désu

His name is Yamanaka
He's a businessman

  → Yamanaka-san to iu zitug̱yoo-ka
    désu

He's a businessman named Yamanaka

  b. Mórita-san to iimasu
  + Beng̱ó-si g̱a|súnde imasu

His name is Morita
A lawyer lives . . .

  → Mórita-san to iu|beng̱ó-si g̱a|
    súnde imasu

A lawyer named Morita lives . . .

15. Mig̱i-dónari $\begin{Bmatrix} \text{g̱a} \\ \text{wa} \end{Bmatrix}$ |X desu

The right-hand side [= neighbor] is X

  + Hidari-dónari ni (wa)|Y g̱a súnde
    imasu

On the left-hand side [comparatively speaking] lives Y

  → Mig̱i-dónari wa X de ‖ hidari-
    dónari ni wa ‖ Y g̱a súnde imasu

The right-hand neighbor is X, and on the left-hand side lives Y

16. . . . osiete kumemásu

They [do us the favor of teaching us =] teach us

17. <u>Giving favors</u>
    a. A ḡa B ni site yaru/aḡeru   A does it for B

    b. A ḡa B ni site kureru/kuda-   A does it for B
       sáru

18. <u>Getting favors</u>
    a. B ḡa A ni site morau/itadaku   B has A kindly do it

    b. B ḡa A ni site morau/omorai   B has A do it
       ni náru

Lesson 4

urayamasíi	is enviable
ryokoo suru	makes a trip, travels
Toohoku-tíhoo	The Tōhoku Region = Northeastern Japan
arúite miru	tries walking
X ni yoru	depends on X
X ni yotte	depending on X
Kánsai	The Kansai Region = Western Japan
Simoda	Shimoda (place name)
kí no me	a leaf bud

1. Kinóo kara | haru-yásumi desu — It has been spring vacation since yesterday

+ $\left\{\begin{array}{l}\text{no}\\\text{n}\end{array}\right\}$ — fact/act

→ Kinóo kara | haru-yásumi na $\left\{\begin{array}{l}\text{no}\\\text{n}\end{array}\right\}$ desu — [It is a fact that] it has been spring vacation since yesterday

(désu occurs as na before no 'fact' or its abbreviation n)

2. Génki desu — He's healthy
+ Hito désu — It's a man
→ Génki na hito desu — He's a healthy man

(désu occurs as na after COP-ULAR NOUNS such as génki before any other NOUN.)

3. Note the following pairs:

Simásu → Surú $\left\{\begin{array}{l}\text{no}\\\text{n}\end{array}\right\}$ desu — He does it

Ookíi desu → Ookíi $\left\{\begin{array}{l}\text{no}\\\text{n}\end{array}\right\}$ desu — It's big

Kore désu → Kore ná $\left\{\begin{array}{l}\text{no}\\\text{n}\end{array}\right\}$ desu — It's this

Simásita → Sitá $\left\{\begin{array}{l}\text{no}\\\text{n}\end{array}\right\}$ desu — He did it

Ookíkatta desu → Ookíkatta $\left\{\begin{array}{l}\text{no}\\\text{n}\end{array}\right\}$ desu — It was big

Kore désita → Kore dátta $\left\{\begin{array}{l}\text{no}\\\text{n}\end{array}\right\}$ desu — It was this

4. Note: There are 3 words no with several meanings:

a. NOUN:
  1. ikú no wa — the one who goes [etc.]
  2. ikú no wa — the fact that one goes; a case of go-ing [etc.]

  3. benkyoo-surú no wa — [the act of] studying [etc.]

b. PARTICLE:
   1. Tanaka-san no hón   Mr. Tanaka's book
   2. Watakusi $\left\{\begin{array}{c} \text{no} \\ (\bar{\text{g}}\text{a}) \end{array}\right\}$ yónda hon   the book which I read . . .

(no optionally replaces ḡa as
subject of a modifier clause)

c. COPULA FORM (replaces
   désu between nouns whenever na is inappropriate):
   1. tomodati no Tanaka-san   Mr. Tanaka who is my friend = My
                                       friend Mr. Tanaka

5. Note the following:
   Haru-yásumi ḡa│urayamasíi   Your spring vacation is enviable/ex-
      desu ne   cites my envy, you know
   Haru-yásumi o urayámu   I envy your spring vacation

   Note: the polite form urayami-
   másu is seldom heard.

6. Bóku-tati wa ‖ natu-yasumi   We have summer vacation only
      daké desu
   + Háru ya│áki ni wa ‖ yasumí   In the spring and fall [comparatively
      ḡa│nái n desu   speaking] there is no vacation
   → Bóku-tati wa ‖ natu-yasumi   We have summer vacation only, and/
      daké de ‖ háru . . .   but in the spring . . .

7. ryokoo dé mo   even being a trip, a trip or the like,
                                       maybe a trip
   + Surú n desu ka   Are you going to do it?
   → Ryokoo dé mo│surú n desu ka   Are you perhaps going to take a trip?

8. Inaka no hóo e│ikimásita   I went to the country
   + (sita) kotó ḡa│arimasén   have never (done)
   → (Máda)│inaka no hóo e│itta   I have never (as yet) gone to the
      kotó ḡa│arimasén   country

9. inaka no hóo e│itta kotó ḡa│nái Since I have never gone to the
      no de . . .   country, . . .

10. Murá o arukimasu   I walk about the villages
    + (site) mimásu   try (doing)/(do) and see
    → Murá o│arúite mimasu   I'll try walking about the village

11. Murá o│arúite mimasyoo   Let's try walking about the villages
                                     I guess I'll try walking about the
                                        villages
    + . . . to omótte│irú n desu   I'm thinking of . . .
    → Muráo│arúite miyoo to│omótte│ I guess I'll try walking about the
       irú n desu   villages
    → Murá o│arúite│miyóo ka to│   I'm wondering if I should/might try
       omótte│irú n desu   walking about the villages

12. Máda│yukí ya│koori ḡa arimásu   There is still snow and ice [and such
                                        things]
    + . . . ká mo│siremasén   maybe/perhaps [—who can tell] ·

→ Máda|yukí ya koori ḡa|áru ka
   mo|siremasén

Maybe/perhaps there is still snow
  and ice [and such things]

Compare:
Ookíi ka mo|siremasén
Akákatta ka mo|siremasén
Kore ká mo|siremasén
Sono hón datta ka mo|siremasén

Maybe it is big
Maybe it was red
Maybe it is this
Maybe it was that book

13. (dé mo)|yukí ḡa|áru $\left\{\begin{array}{l}\text{no de wa}\\\text{n zya}\end{array}\right\}$

(but) if we have snow [lit. as for its
  being a case of having snow]

14. Kánsai ni wa ‖mitái tokoro ḡa
   arimasu
 + yamá hodo

→ Kánsai ni wa ‖ mitái tokoro ḡa|
   yamá hodo arimasu

In the Kansai there are places which
  I want to see
[to the extent of mountains, enough to
  make a mountain =] lots
In the Kansai there are loads/heaps
  of places I want to see

15. sí-, ḡo-niti no|ryokoo $\left\{\begin{array}{l}\text{dé wa}\\\text{zya}\end{array}\right\}$ . . .
  (cf. No. 13)

If it is a 4- or 5-day trip . . .

16. Simoda no hóo e|itte mimasu
 + Dóo desu ka
→ Simoda no hóo e|itte mítara|dóo
   desu ka

  cf. Simoda o mí ni|ittára|dóo ka

I'll go and see Shimoda
How is it? How would it be?
How about going to see Shimoda?
How would it be if you try visiting
  Shimoda?
Why don't you go see Shimoda?

17. Atarasíi sakana mo|
   $\left\{\begin{array}{l}\text{taberaremasu}\\\text{tabéru koto ḡa dekimasu}\end{array}\right.$

One can eat fresh fish too

18. Sore ḡa íi desu
   Sore ḡa yo-sasóo desu

THAT [emphatic] is good
THAT seems best, THAT sounds
  good

Compare:
Ooki-sóo desu
Ookíi soo desu
Na-sasóo desu
Nái soo desu
Genki-sóo desu
Génki da soo desu
Áme ḡa|huri-sóo desu
Áme ḡa|húru soo desu

It looks [as if it were] big
I hear that it is big
It looks as if there aren't any
I understand that there aren't any
He looks healthy
I hear that he is well
It looks as if it would rain
They say that it will rain

Note: The formation of yo-sasóo
and na-sasóo is irregular.

Lesson 5

roomázi	the roman alphabet, roman letters, romanization
hutuu no	is usual, normal
hutuu wa	in ordinary circumstances
Y ni X o mazéru	mixes X with Y
Tyúuḡoku	China
X o wataru	crosses over X (water, bridge)
P kara wataru	gets imported from P
mózi	a letter, a character
ziten	a Chinese character dictionary
Ueda daizíten	Ueda (Kazutoshi)'s Japanese dictionary of Chinese characters
zyuubún (na)	is sufficient, enough
X o oboéru	memorizes X, learns X by heart, masters X
to iú no wa	what I mean to say is, the reason we can say this is . . . because
katati	form, shape
yomikáta	a pronunciation (of written symbols), a way of reading
ími	meaning
tutawaru	gets handed down (transmitted)
X o tutaeru	hands X down, transmits X
Nihonka suru	Japanizes
X o Y ni áteru	makes X correspond to Y
náma	is uncooked, raw
ikíru	lives, exists
kí no	is pure, genuine
X to Y o kumiawaseru	combines X and Y, joins X and Y together
betu no (betu na)	is additional, separate, different, another
zyukuḡo	a compound word, a phrase
séimei	life
ínoti	life
kazoéru	counts it
X to tiḡau	differs from X, is different from X
issyoo	one's whole life
kakáru	it takes/requires (time or money)
X ḡa oboekiréru	is able to learn all of X, gets X learned all the way through
tooyoo-kánzi	the Chinese characters for general use
syooḡákusei	a primary school pupil
syooḡákkoo	an elementary school
tyuuḡákusei	a junior high school pupil
tyuuḡákkoo	a middle school, a junior high school

1. Nihon-ḡo $\begin{Bmatrix} \bar{g}a \\ wa \end{Bmatrix}$ kana de

    $\begin{Bmatrix} kakemásu \\ káku\ koto\ ḡa\ dekimasu \end{Bmatrix}$ Japanese can be written in kana

2. Kana daké de kakemasu   It can be written only in kana

+ Roomázi de kakemasu

→ Kana daké de mo ‖roomázi de
  mo kakemasu

It can be written in romanization
It can be written both in kana alone
  and in romanization

3. { Katakána | hiragána
    Katakána to/ya | hiragána } o
  mazemasu

They mix <u>katakana</u> and <u>hiragana</u>

+ Kanzi { to
        ni } mazemasu

They mix [it] in with kanzi

→ Kanzi { to
       ni } | { katakána |
              katakána to/ya |
  hiragána
  hiragána } o mazemasu

They mix <u>katakana</u> and <u>hiragana</u> with
kanzi

4. Kanzi to | katakána | hiragána o
  mazemasu

+ kakimasu

→ Kanzi to | katakána | hiragána o |
  mázete kakimasu

They mix <u>katakana</u> and <u>hiragana</u> with
kanzi
They write [it]
They write it by mixing <u>katakana</u> and
<u>hiragana</u> with kanzi

5. sén | suu-hyakú-nen mo

PATTERN: NUMBER + <u>mo</u> +
AFFIRMATIVE
NUMBER + <u>mo</u> + NEGATIVE
Ni-zíkan mo | kakarimasén
  desita

all of a thousand and several hundred
  years
all of, as much as, as many as

not even, not as much as
It didn't even take two hours

6. Sono kázu { ḡa
          wa } | taihen óoi desu

+ Tyúuḡoku no | hurúi ziten nì wa ‖
  yon-mán | go-hyaku-zi-ízyoo |
  áru soo desu

→ Sono kázu wa | taihen óoku ‖
  Tyúuḡoku . . . (<u>óoku</u> = <u>óokute</u>;
  see Introduction Point 2)

Their number is very large

They say there are more than 40,500
  characters in the old Chinese dictionary
Their number is very large, <u>and</u> . . .

7. (Sono kázu wa) | zyuubún desu
+ hutuu no hito
→ Hutuu no hitó ni wa ‖ zyuubún
  desu

(That number) is enough/sufficient
the average person
It is enough for the average person

8. X <u>de mo</u>
  san-zen-zi dé mo

even [being] X
even 3,000 characters

9. oboéru no wa
  (<u>cf.</u> Lesson 4, Note 4-a-3.)

the act of remembering

10. to iú no wa . . .

what I mean to say is, the reason why
  we [can] say this is . . . [because]

11. Kanzi ní wa ‖ X to Y to Z ḡa
  arimasu

+ . . . kara desu

→ Kanzi ní wa ‖ X to Y to Z ḡa
  áru kara desu

Kanzi consists of X, Y, and Z

it is because . . .

It is because kanzi consists of X, Y,
  and Z

12. Compare:
     Yomi-káta ni wa, ‖X to Y ḡa   The readings consist of X and Y
     arimasu
     Yomi-káta ni mo ‖X to Y ḡa   The readings, in turn, consist of X
     arimasu   and Y

13. X to iú no wa   what we mean by X, the thing that is
                                                    called X

14. Tyúuḡoku no|yomi-káta ḡa| Chinese readings got handed down
     tutawarimásita
   + X o Nihon-ka simásita   They Japanized X
     cf. X ḡa Nihon-ka simasita   X is Japanized
   → Tyúuḡoku no|yomi-káta ḡa tuta-   Chinese readings got handed down
     watte ‖Nihon-ka simásita   and were Japanized
     (In the text, this sentence modi-
     fies monó "thing")

     Note PATTERN: VERB-(i/e)-kata,   manner of . . .-ing, way of . . .-ing
     as in:
       yomikáta   manner of reading
       arukikáta   manner of walking
       iikata   manner of saying
       tabekáta   manner of eating

     Note SUFFIX: -ka suru, as in: . . .-izes it, it . . .izes
       Nihon-ka suru   Japanizes
       kikai-ka suru   mechanizes

15. Kanzi o kokuḡo ni atemasu   We apply/adjust/correlate kanzi to
                                                    the native words
   + Yomimásu   We read [them]
   → Kanzi o kokuḡo ni atete yomi-   We read them by applying kanzi to the
     másu   native words
     (In the text, this sentence modi-
     fies yomi-káta "readings")

     Note these PATTERNS:
     A ḡa X o Y ni ateru   A adjusts X to Y or A makes X cor-
                                                    respond with Y
     X wa Y ni ataru   X corresponds with Y

16. Iti-on|ik-kun no monó mo ari-   There are also/even some [Chinese
     masu   characters] having one on and one
                                                    kun

17. Ití-zi ni|takusán no|on ya kun   There are also/even some which have
     {ḡa}   many on and kun for one single
     {no} áru mono mo arimasu   character

18. Kanzi o hutatu-ízyoo|kumi-awa-   It is a thing [=something] in which
     seta monó desu   more than two Chinese characters
                                                    have been joined together
   + Betu no ími o motimasu   It carries a special meaning
   → Kanzi o hutatu-ízyoo|kumi-awa-   It is something in which more than
     seta monó de ‖betu no ími o   two Chinese characters have been

motimasu
(in the text, this sentence modi-
fies zyuku-ḡo "compound word")

joined together and it carries a
special meaning

19. Compare:
X wa│Y to iu ími desu
X to iú no wa│Y to iu ími desu

X means Y
By X we mean Y

20. Tiḡaimásita

tiḡatta yomi-káta

They have diverged, They were
different
different readings

21. oboekiréru

oboekirénai

Note PATTERN: VERB-(i)-
kiréru
Tabekiréru
Matikirenai

I can learn them all, I can learn it
thoroughly
It is impossible to learn them all

It is possible to do exhaustively

It is possible to eat them all
I can hardly wait

22. sore de

that being the case, in consequence

23. X o Y to simasu
Sén│hap-pyaku│go-zyúu-zi o│
tooyoo-kánzi to simasu

We fix/designate X as Y
We fix/designate 1,850 characters
as Tooyoo-kanzi

24. Tyuuḡáku-sei ḡa benkyoo simasu
+ hón
→ Tyuuḡáku-sei {ḡa/no}│benkyoo
suru hón

Middle-school pupils study [them]
books
Books which middle-school pupils
study

25. Compare:
Tyuuḡáku-sei ḡa│benkyoo suru
hón ni tukau
Tyuuḡáku-sei ḡa│benkyoo suru
hón nado ni tukau

They use [it] in the books which
middle-school pupils study
They use [it] in the books which
middle-school pupils study and
elsewhere [= and in other similar
publications]

26. Compare:
X o kimeru
X ḡa kimaru
X ḡa kimete áru (= kimatte iru)

fixes/designates/decides upon X
X is fixed/designated/decided upon
X has been, is fixed/designated/
decided upon

27. Sono on, kun ḡa│kimete arimásu

+ hón nado ni tukau kanzi
→ Hón nado ni tukau kanzi to ‖sono
on │kun ḡa│kimete arimásu

Their on and kun have been decided
upon
kanzi used in books, etc.
Their on and kun have been decided
upon as the kanzi [to be] used in
books, etc.

28. yómu koto ḡa│dekíru yoo ni suru
kanzi
+ káku koto ḡa│dekíru yoo ni suru
kanzi
→ yómu koto mo ‖káku koto mo│
dekíru yoo ni suru kanzi

characters to be learned [lit. done]
so as to be able to read them
characters to be learned so as to be
able to write them
characters to be learned for both
reading and writing ability

29. Benkyoo suru kóto ni│simasyóo   Let's decide to study

     <u>Compare:</u>
     Yameru kotó ni│simasyóo   Let's give it up, Let's not do it,
     Yamenai kotó ni│simasyóo   Let's not give it up

Lesson 6

X o tatéru	builds/constructs X
syóotai suru	invites
mut to suru	becomes angry, is offended
zitú wa	the fact is, in reality
zitu no	is real, actual
zitú ni	truly, surely, very, indeed
gomí	dust, rubbish, trash, garbage
goma	sesame, sesame seed
tyóoon	a long vowel/sound
tán'on	a short vowel/sound
X nante = { X nado to / X nado wa	such a thing as X
moosiwake	an apology, an excuse
ákusento	accent
(X ni) tyúui suru	pays attention (to X), is careful (about X)
hana	a nose
sitá	a tongue
ryakuḡo	an abbreviation, an abbreviated word
tóire	a toilet
X o hósu	airs X, dries out X
basyo	a place, a spot, a section
gyaku (na, no)	is contrary, reverse, opposite

1. Tomodati ḡa|Súmisu-san o|syóo-
   tai simasita

   A friend invited Mr. Smith

   Súmisu-san ḡa|tomodati ni|syóo-
   tai saremasita

   Mr. Smith got invited by a friend

2. iwareta tomodati
   (iwareru is the PASSIVE of iu)

   the friend spoken to [in this unfavorable way]

3. Mut to simásita

   He took offense [i.e., reacted by ex-
   claiming mu!]

   Compare:
   Tanaka-san wa|hat to simásita

   Mr. Tanaka was startled

4. Súmisu-san ḡa|iitái desita
   + . . . no
   → Súmisu-san { ḡa / no }|iitákatta no
   (wa) . . .

   Mr. Smith wanted to say [it]
   thing (which) . . .
   the thing Mr. Smith wanted to say . . .

5. Compare:
   A ḡa B o X ni yobu
   B ḡa A ni X ni yobareru
   (PASSIVE; cf. Note 1)

   A invites B to X
   B gets invited by A to X

6. A ḡa|oba-san o|obáa-san
   { nante / nado to }|yobimásita

   A called "oba-san" such a thing as
     "obaa-san"

7. hana mo

   one and the same hana

8. haná "flower" and hana "nose"
   are identical in isolation or
   before the PARTICLE no "of":

   hana no   of the flower or of the nose

   But with other PARTICLES and
   with désu the accentual difference is clear. Compare:
   haná desu   It's a flower
   hana désu   It's a nose

   Note:
   Haná ni narimasu   It becomes haná ("flower")
 + Hana ni narimásu   It becomes hana ("nose")
 → Haná ni mo│hana ní mo nari-   It becomes both haná ("flower") and
   masu   hana ("nose")

9. Compare also:
   Sitá ni oku   He puts it on his tongue
   Sita ni oku   He puts it underneath [something]

10. . . . no ka . . . no ka ‖hakkíri│   Please speak so that one can under-
    wakáru yoo ni│hanásite kudasai   stand clearly whether . . . or . . .
    X ná no ka ‖ Y ná no ka ‖hakkíri│   Please speak so that one can under-
    wakáru yoo ni│hanásite kudasai   stand whether it is X or Y

11. Hósite aru│monó ni narimasu   It becomes [i.e., comes to mean]
                                                things which have been dried/which
                                                are hung up to dry

  + Hósu koto ni narimasu   It becomes [i.e., comes to mean] the
                                                act of drying

  → Hósite aru│monó to ka ‖hósu   It comes to mean [either] things
    koto ni narimasu   which are hung up to dry or the act
                                                of drying

Lesson 7

sina	a thing, an article, goods
hanasikótoba	spoken language
hooḡén	a dialect
zénkoku	the whole country
kyootuu no	is common
hyoozyun no	is standard
áisatu	greeting
X o hirou	picks up X, finds X
yukiwatáru = ikiwatáru	it extends/pervades/reaches
zenzen	wholly, completely
zenzen + NEG.	not at all
tuuziru	gets understood, makes itself clear
P-ben	P dialect (preceded by place-name)
taḡai no	is mutual, is reciprocal
gokai suru	misunderstands
seikatuḡo	language/words of daily life
túuyoo suru	circulates, passes (for)
hán'i	scope, sphere, extents, limits
kenkyuu suru	studies, researches
seisitu	nature, character, qualities
búnka	culture
rikai suru	understands

1. Tokoró (ḡa)│kawaréba‖sina (ḡa)
   kawaru
   (Note the omission of PARTICLES
   frequent in written Japanese,
   and especially in proverbs;
   cf. Introduction Point 7)

   "Each country/place has its own
   customs"

2. $\left\{ \begin{array}{l} \text{. . . to iu tóori} \\ \text{. . . to iu yóo ni} \end{array} \right\}$

   as they say, as the saying goes . . .

3. X ni táisite . . .

   in contrast with X, as opposed to X

4. Nihon-zénkoku de tukaimasu
   + Kyootuu ni tukaimasu
   → Nihon-zénkoku (de)│kyootuu ni
     tukaimasu
     (Note omission of PARTICLE de)

   They use [it] all through Japan
   They use [it] commonly
   They use it commonly all through
     Japan

5. tokoro ni yori hito ni yotte . . .
   (Note use of yori for yotte within the larger phrase ending
   with yotte)

   depending on the person and on the
     place . . .

6. Kotobá ḡa│tuuzimasén

   The languages are not understood,
     The languages are incomprehensible
     [to each other]

   + . . . to iu kotó wa│arimasén

   It never happens that . . .

   → Kotobá $\left\{ \begin{array}{l} \text{no} \\ \text{ḡa} \end{array} \right\}$│tuuzinai to iu kotó
     wa│arimasén

   It never happens that the languages
     are not understood

7. A-dóosi de
   Nihon-zin-dóosi de
   gakusei-dóosi de
   roodoosya-dóosi de
   kaiin-dóosi de

among fellow-A's
among fellow-Japanese
among fellow-students
among fellow-workers
among fellow-members

8. VERB-(i)+-áu
   X to hanasi-áu

does mutually
talks/converses with X

9. Náni ḡa | nán da ka | wakarimasén

They do not understand what is what
   (which word is which)

10. Komáru koto ḡa | óoi

It often happens that they are embar-
   rassed/inconvenienced

11. -teki (na)
    tihoo-teki (na)
    kaḡaku-teki (na)

is . . .-ic/-ical/-istical/-al
is regional
is scientific

12. káku-
    káku-ti
    káku-si
    kák-koku

each
each area/land
each city
each country

13. Nihon-ḡo no seisitu ḡa | yóku |
    wakáru yoo ni narimasu

We will get to the point of being able
   to understand the essence/nature
   of the Japanese language

  + Nihon-zín no | kanḡae-káta mo |
    yóku | rikai dekíru yoo ni nari-
    masu

We will get to the point of being able
   to understand the Japanese ways of
   thinking also

  → Nihon-ḡo no seisitu ḡa | yóku |
    wakaru bákari de | náku(te) ‖
    Nihon-zín no | kanḡae-káta mo |
    yóku | rikai dekíru yoo ni nari-
    masu

We will get to the point of being able
   to understand not only the nature
   of the Japanese language but also
   the Japanese ways of thinking also

14. Compare:
    Rikai simasu
    Rikai (suru kotó ḡa) dekimasu
    Rikai suru yóo ni narimasu
    Rikai (suru kotó ḡa) dekíru yoo
      ni narimasu

We understand
We can understand
We get to the point of understanding
We get to the point of being able to
   understand

Lesson 8

Ikeda	Ikeda (family name)
Usiyama	Ushiyama (family name)
sitúrei suru	acts rudely
bangóo	a number
Mítiko	Michiko (female name)
zimúsyo	an office, one's place of business
Akásaka	Akasaka (place-name)
noti hodo = áto de	later on, after a while
denwa suru	makes a telephone call
kotozuke	a message
kotozukéru	gives a message
Kyóoto	Kyoto (place-name)
tátu	leaves for a trip
Itábasi	Itabashi (place-name)
kenkyuusyo, kenkyuuzyo	a research laboratory

The sentences in Notes 1–5 illustrate various VERBS used in HONORIFIC and HUMBLE senses.

1. Tanaka-san wa│denwa o kake-
   másita
   (NEUTRAL)   Mr. Tanaka telephoned

   Nán-ban e│o-kake ni narimásita
   ka
   (HONORIFIC)   What number did you (or someone
                                              esteemed) call?

   Odénwa o│o-kake ⎰simasu⎱
   (HUMBLE)   ⎱itasimasu⎰   I will phone you (or someone es-
                                              teemed)

2. Súmisu-san wa│dóko ni│imásu
   ka
   (NEUTRAL)   Where is Mr. Smith?

   Wada-senséi ḡa/wa⎰irassyai-
                    ⎱oide ni
   másu ⎱ ka
   narimásu⎰   Is Dr. Wada in?
   (HONORIFIC)

   Musuko-san ḡa/wa│ ⎰irassyai-
                    ⎱oide ni
   másu ⎱ ka
   narimásu⎰   Is your son in?
   (HONORIFIC)

   Háa, orimasu   Yes, he's in (or I'm in)
   (HUMBLE)

3. Tanaka-san désu   He is Mr. Tanaka
   (NEUTRAL)

   Itoo-san de irassyaimásu ka   Are you (or Is he) Mr. Ito?
   (HONORIFIC)

   Tanaka-san de gozaimásu   It is (or He is) Mr. Tanaka
   (POLITE)

   Tanaka de gozaimásu   I am Mr. Tanaka (or I am of the
   (POLITE)   Tanaka household)

$\begin{Bmatrix} \text{Dótira-sama} \\ \text{Dónata-sama} \end{Bmatrix}$ de|irassyaimásu   Who is it?
ka
(HONORIFIC)

4. Ítu|kaerimásu ka   When are you (<u>or</u> is he) returning?
   (NEUTRAL)
   Tanaka-san wa ‖ítu|o-kaeri   When is Mr. Tanaka returning?
   $\begin{Bmatrix} \text{désu} \\ \text{ni narimásu} \end{Bmatrix}$ ka
   (HONORIFIC)
   Gó-zi made ni|káette mairimasu   I'll return by 5 o'clock
   (HUMBLE)

5. Dáre ḡa|simásita ka   Who did it?
   (NEUTRAL)
   Dónata ḡa|odénwa|nasaimásita   Who (= what esteemed person) tele-
   ka   phoned?
   (HONORIFIC)
   Kotira kara o-dénwa|itasimasyóo   Shall I phone (someone esteemed)?
   ka
   (HUMBLE)

6. A-san wa Kyóoto e|tatimásita   Mr. A left [town] for Kyoto
7. . . . (suru) yóo ni $\begin{Bmatrix} \text{iu} \\ \text{tutaeru} \end{Bmatrix}$ Tell someone to (do)

   Kité kudasaru|yóo ni‖$\begin{Bmatrix} \text{ossyátte} \\ \text{o-tutae} \end{Bmatrix}$ Would you please tell him to come
   kudasaimasén ka   [as a favor to me]?
   (HONORIFIC)

Note:	NEUTRAL	HUMBLE	HONORIFIC
imásu		orimásu	irassyaimásu
arimásu	gozaimásu		
ikimasu/kimasu		mairimásu	irassyaimásu
désu	de gozaimásu		de irassyaimásu
simásu		itasimásu	nasaimásu

8. Note: SUFFIXES:
   -sama (Tanaka-sama) }
   -san (Tanaka-san)   }   'Mr., Mrs., Miss.'
   -syo (zimú-syo)   }
   -zyo (kenkyuu-zyo)   }   'place'
   -hasi (óo-hasi)   }
   -basi (isí-basi)   }   'bridge'
   -saka (Aká-saka)   }
   -zaka (nobori-zaka) }   'hill'
   -ban (100-ban)   '(telephone) number'
   -ḡoo (3-ḡoo)   'number'
   -goositu (5-ḡoositu)   '(room) number'
   -ḡoosya (1-ḡoosya)   '(train) car number'

Lesson 9

daihyooteki (na)	is typical, is representative
daihyoo suru	represents
senséesyonaru (na)	is sensational
midasi	a headline
dókusya	a reader, a person who reads
(X ni) odoróku	is surprised, gets startled (at X)
kízi	news, an article, a statement
seikaku (na)	is correct, authentic
insatu	printing
ayamári	an error, a mistake
ayamáru	makes a mistake, mistakes it
sin'yoo	trust, confidence, faith
seizi	politics
kéizai	economy, economics, finance
syákai	society, the community
gakuḡei	art and science
supóotu	sports
X o wakéru	divides/splits X
X o kúmu	composes/constructs/assembles X
sinbúnsya	a newspaper (office/company)
íken	an opinion, an idea
X o nobéru	states/expresses X
syasetu	an editorial
syoosetu	a novel, fiction
manḡa	a cartoon, a caricature
toosyo	a letter from a reader to the editor
ninki	popularity
ninki ḡa áru	is popular
ninki ḡa nái	is unpopular
kesyoohin	toilet articles
kesyóo	makeup
kámera	a camera
kookoku	an advertisement
syuunyuu	an income

1. The following nouns are followed
   by <u>na</u> when modifying another
   NOUN:

   a. Native words with SUFFIXES
      -<u>ka</u>, -<u>yaka</u>, -<u>raka</u>:

sízuka (na)	is quiet
niḡíyaka (na)	is gay
hoḡáraka (na)	is cheerful

   b. Other native (<u>or</u> obscure)
      words:

árata		new
ainiku	(na) is	unfortunate
damé		no good
báka		foolish, crazy

c. Chinese words with attributive meaning:

génki	⎫			⎧ healthy
téinei	⎬ (na)	is		⎨ polite
taihen				terrible
seikaku	⎭			⎩ precise

génki)   (healthy
téinei } (na)   is { polite
taihen }   { terrible
seikaku)   (precise

d. Words with the SUFFIX -teki
(See Note 11, Lesson 7)

e. English (and other European) ADJECTIVES borrowed into Japanese:

senséesyonaru)   (sensational
síkku } (na)   is { chic
sumáato)   (smart, stylish

f. . . . yóo   seeming to be . . ., of the kind that . . .

as in:
dókusya o│odorokaséru yoo na sinbun   a newspaper of the kind that shocks the readers

Tanaka-san no musuko-san no yóo na gakusei wa│ sukunái desu   Students like Mr. Tanaka's son are rare

g. . . . -sóo   appearing to be . . .

as in:
Genki-sóo na│ákatyan desita ḡa . . .   It was a baby which appeared to be healthy, but . . .

2. YOMI-URI lacks "send-off" kana because it is a name; compare YOmí-MONO 'reading or reading material,' Uri-MONO 'things to sell.'

3. Note the following PSEUDO-PARTICLES which are suffixed to nouns:

-íḡai	outside of, besides
-ínai	inside of, within
-írai	since/from [that time]
-ízyoo	above
-íka	below
-ínan	south of
-íhoku	north of
-ítoo	east of
-ísei	west of
-íḡo	after
-ízen	before

4. ⎰ X ya Y-íḡai ni ⎱   aside from X and Y, in addition to X
   ⎱ X ya Y no hoka ni ⎰   and Y

5. Compare:
Dókusya ḡa│odorokimásita   The readers were surprised/startled

Sono kízi ḡa|dókusya o|odoroka-semásita

That article shocked the readers [lit. made the readers be surprised]

6. Sinbun o yásuku|kau kotó ḡa| dekíru $\begin{Bmatrix} \text{no} \\ \text{wake} \end{Bmatrix}$ wa, . . . kara desu

The reason why we can buy newspapers cheaply is that . . .

Lesson 10

dái nízi taisen	the Second World War, World War II
kyooiku	education
séido	a system
iwáyuru X	what is called X, what is known as X, the so-called X
-séi	-system
kootoo-gákkoo	a senior high school
séito	a pupil, school children
zyog̅ákkoo	a girl's middle school
kyoog̅aku	coeducation
sin̅gaku suru	enters into a school of higher grade
susumu	it proceeds, goes forward, makes progress
senmon-gákkoo	a professional school
nyuug̅aku	entrance into a school
X o yurúsu	permits/admits X
sig̅ánsya	an applicant
síg̅an suru	applies
kanarazu	certainly, without fail, by all means
gimu-kyóoiku	compulsory education
gímu	a duty, an obligation
nobíru	it extends/stretches/expands
nobásu	extends/expands it
kooritu	a public institution, public
siritu, watakusíritu	a private establishment, private
sotug̅yoo suru	graduates
sára ni	anew, again, furthermore, still more
daig̅akúin	a graduate school

1. iwáyuru roku·san·san·sei

what is called/what is known as the 6-3-3 system

2. X ‖sunáwati│Y

X, i.e. Y/X, namely Y

3. Syoog̅ákkoo (wa)│rokú-nen to│nátte│imásita

The syoogakkoo [was fixed at =] consisted of 6 years

4. A mo sukunákatta si ‖B mo sukunákatta no de, . . .

Since both A were few and, in addition, B were few, . . .

5. Zyog̅ákusei wa│kazoéru (koto g̅a dekíru) hodo sika│imasén desita

There were female students only to the extent of being able to count them [on one's fingers] (= the number of female students could be counted on one's fingers)

6. Syoog̅ákkoo wa│rokú-nen desu
+ Onazi desu
→ Syoog̅ákkoo wa│rokú-nen de│onazi désu

The syoogakkoo is 6 years
It's the same
The syoogakkoo is the same, [remaining] at 6 years

7. Tyúug̅aku made no│kyúu-nen ni│nobimásita

It extended to the 9th year, [which is] up until the tyuugaku

8. A no tamé ni   for the benefit of A

9. PREFIXES:

    zyo- (zyo-ḡákusei)   'girl, woman'
    dan- (dan-sei)   'boy, man'
    kyuu- (kyuu-sei)   'old'
    sin- (sin-sei)   'new'

10. SUFFIXES:

    -ḡo (taisen-ḡo)   'after, post-'.
    -zen (sen-zen)   'before, pre-'
    -sei (6, 3, 3-sei)   'system'
    -ḡaku (daiḡaku) 1)   'school'
        (keizái-ḡaku) 2)   'study, -ology'

    -in (daigakúin)   'institution'
    -sei (daiḡáku-sei)   'student (of)'
    -ritu (koku-ritu)   'established (by)'

Note: Since siritu is the pronunciation of both 'private-established' and 'city-established' municipal,' they are sometimes distinguished as watakusí-ritu 'private' and iti-ritu 'municipal.'

Lesson 11

sizen	nature, natural phenomena
bí	beauty, grace, charm
X o meḡumu	blesses with X
X ni meḡumareru	is blessed with (abundant) X
míḡoto (na)	is beautiful, fine, superb, splendid, brilliant
zinkoo no	is man-created, artificial
X ni yoru	is based upon X, is due to X
X ni yotte	on the ground of X
X o osímu	spares/grudges X
neuti	value, worth
wareware = watakusí-tati	we [LITERARY]
yosó no	is other, alien
yosó	other place(s), elsewhere
dokutoku no	is peculiar, unique
yakimono	ceramic ware, crockery, pottery, porcelain
mumei no	is nameless, obscure
tesíḡoto	hand work
kikái	a machine, machinery, mechanism
seihin	manufactured goods, a product, finished goods
tasúu no	is many, is a (large) number of
sómatu (na)	is coarse, crude
yorokóbi	joy, delight, pleasure
yorokóbu	is delighted, glad
kanzyoo	feelings, emotion, sentiment, passion
kanasimi	sorrow, sadness, grief, woe
kanasii	is sad, sorrowful
kanasímu	feels sorrow, grieves
kurusimi	pains, agony, anguish, torture
kurusíi	is painful, tormenting
kurusímu	feels pain
X ḡa komóru	is full of X, is filled with X
issyookénmei ni	with all one's might, as hard as one can, (as if) for one's very life

1. Note carefully the PARTICLES associated with <u>meḡumu</u> and <u>meḡumareru</u>:

    a. Kámi-sama ḡa│Nihón <u>ni</u>│sizen   God blessed Japan with the beauty of
        no bí <u>o</u>│meḡumimásita   nature

    → Nihón ḡa│(kámi-sama <u>ni</u>)│   Japan has been blessed (by God) with
        sizen no bí o│meḡumare-   the beauty of nature
        másita (PASSIVE)

    → Nihón ḡa/wa│sizen no bí ni│   Japan has been blessed with beauty
        meḡumaremásita   of nature

    b. Sizen no bí ni│meḡumareta   Japan which has been blessed with
        Nihón   the beauty of nature

2. A wa B $\begin{Bmatrix} \text{desu} \\ \text{de aru} \end{Bmatrix}$ A is B
    (see Introduction Point 1)

→ 3. X $\begin{Bmatrix} \text{ni yotte} \\ \text{no tamé ni} \end{Bmatrix}$ | sékai ni | yuumei   They are world-famous for/because
     désu   of X

4. sono tatémono ya | niwa no bí   the beauty of their buildings and
                                              gardens
   + mígoto na bí   splendid beauty
   + zinkoo no bí   man-made beauty
   → Sono tatémono ya | niwa no mí-   The splendid man-made beauty of
     goto na | zinkoo no bí   their buildings and gardens

5. kane o $\begin{Bmatrix} \text{osímazu (ni)} \\ \text{osimánai de} \end{Bmatrix}$ without begrudging money
   + tukurimásita   He produced/made [it]
   → Kane o $\begin{Bmatrix} \text{osímazu (ni)} \\ \text{osimánai de} \end{Bmatrix}$ | tukuri-   He produced it without begrudging
     másita   money [i.e., with no regard/concern
                                              for expense]

6. Rippa $\begin{Bmatrix} \text{de} \\ \text{de ári} \end{Bmatrix}$ ‖ neúti ga arimásu   They are splendid and have value
   de áru = désu; de ári = de átte
   (see Introduction Point 2)

→ 7. . . . hitó mo | nái koto wa | nái ga   It isn't the case that even people who
                                              . . . are totally lacking, but . . .
                                              [i.e., there ARE some people who
                                              . . .]

8. Yosó no kuni $\begin{Bmatrix} \text{ni} \\ \text{de} \end{Bmatrix}$ | míru koto ga | It cannot be seen in another country
     dekimasén

   dokutoku no utukúsisa   unique beauty
   → Yosó no kuni ni | míru koto $\begin{Bmatrix} \text{ga} \\ \text{no} \end{Bmatrix}$ | A unique beauty which cannot be seen
     dekínai | dokutoku no utukúsisa   in other countries

→ 9. . . . kotó mo | wasureté wa | $\begin{Bmatrix} \text{naru} \\ \text{nará-} \end{Bmatrix}$ Surely we mustn't forget the fact
     mái $\Big\}$ that . . .
     nai desyoo
   VERB-u mai is a semi-literary
   form for the NEGATIVE TENTATIVE
   -(a)nái desyoo

10. Koré-ra no | yakimono ní wa, . . .   Among these ceramic pieces there
     monó ga | sukunáku | arimasén   are quite a few which . . .

→ 11. te-sígoto $\begin{Bmatrix} \text{de} \\ \text{ni yotte} \end{Bmatrix}$ | tukuráreta | It's a thing made by/with hand(-work)
      monó desu

→ 12. . . . kotó wa | iu máde mo | nái   It goes without saying that . . . [lit.
                                               It is not necessary to go to the ex-
                                               tent of mentioning it]

→ 13. Dekiru dake tasúu no | monó o | They manufacture inexpensively as
      yásuku tukurimasu   great a number of things as possible

+ Mizikái zikan ni│tukurimásu

They manufacture [them] in a short time

→ Mizikái zikan ni ‖dekiru dake tasúu no│monó o│yásuku tuku-rimasu

They manufacture inexpensively in a short time as great a number of things as possible

14. X o tukúru tame ni

for the purpose of manufacturing X

+ Kikái ḡa tukawaremasu

Machines are used

→ Kikái wa ‖X o tukúru tame ni│tukawaremásu

Machines are used for the purpose of manufacturing X

15. Note the following:

Sómatu ni tukurimasu

They make [them] without devotion

Sómatu ni tukuraremasu

They are made without devotion

Sómatu ni│tukurare-yasúi desu

They are easily [= are apt to be] made without devotion

16. Dóre mo│onazi yóo desu

Every one of them looks the same

+ (mata)‖sómatu ni│tukurare-yasúi desu

(and what's more) they are easily made without devotion

→ Dóre mo│onazi yóo de ‖mata ‖ sómatu ni│tukurare-yasúi desu

Every one of them looks the same, and what's more, they are easily made without devotion

17. Kikái ḡa│ninḡen o tukaimásu

Machines use human beings

Ninḡen ḡa│kikái ni tukawaremasu

People get used by machines

(PASSIVE)

18. (A kara) hataraku yorokóbi o│tótte simaimasu

It completely takes away (from A) the joy of working

19. A ni (wa)‖X ḡa komótte imasu

A is filled with X

20. Kane o kakénakute mo, . . .

cf. kane o tukau "spends (=uses) money"

Even if [people] don't spend money on it . . .

21. Issyookénmei ni│tukurimásita

He made it with all his heart

22. The following COPULAR NOUNS in this lesson are followed by na:

yuumei ⎫   famous
míḡoto │   splendid
rippa ⎬ (na)   is splendid
sómatu │   crude, poor, coarse
issyookénmei⎭   eager, earnest

Lesson 12

Túnoda	Tsunoda (family name)
Sanpei	Sampei (male name)
gobusata suru	neglects to write/call
tanosíi	is merry, pleasant, happy, enjoyable
sugósu	passes/spends (time)
kyuu (na)	is sudden
musiburo	a steam bath
musiatúi	is muggy, sweltering, sultry
kisetuhuu	a seasonal wind
suizyóoki	(aqueous) vapor
X o hakobu	carries/conveys/transports X
kion	(atmospheric) temperature
nóogyoo	agriculture, farming, agricultural industry
hituyoo (na)	is necessary, needed
gáman suru	shows patience; is patient
kusáru	it rots/decomposes/decays
i-tyoo	the stomach and intestines
huéru	it increases/multiplies/accrues
sinrui	a relative, a relation
naminóri	surf-riding
nihyakutooka	"the 210th Day": the storm day expected every year in September
Nihonbare	a clear sky, beautiful weather
táyori	news, tidings
Kóozi	Kōji (male name)

1. Gobusata itasimásita
   cf. sata "notes, communica-
   tion"; busata, "neglect, failure
   to write or call"

   I have neglected you/I have failed to
   write

2. Háwai no│miná-san

   all you people in Hawaii

3. Kaimono ni ikimásu

   I go shopping

   + Kenbutu ni ikimásu

   I go sightseeing

   → Kaimono ya│kenbutu ni ikimásu

   I go shopping and sightseeing [and
   the like]

4. Tomodati ni aimásu

   I see friends

   + Kaimono ya│kenbutu ni ikimásu

   I go shopping and sightseeing [and
   the like]

   → Tomodati ni áttari ‖kaimono
   ya│kenbutu ni ittári simasu

   I see my friends and [at other times]
   go shopping and sightseeing

5. Tanósiku│sugósite imasu

   I am living pleasantly

6. Musiburo no yóo desu

   It's like a steam bath

   + . . . to iu tóori $\begin{Bmatrix} ni \\ de \end{Bmatrix}$

   as they say, . . .

   → Musiburo no yóo da to│iu tóori
   $\begin{Bmatrix} ni \\ de \end{Bmatrix}$

   As they say, it's like a steam bath,
   and . . .

7. Compare the following pairs:

a. Iku kotó ḡa arimasu   It sometimes happens that we go
   Iku kotó mo arimasu   It sometimes even happens that we go

b. Itta kotó ḡa arimasu   We have gone [at least once]

   Itta kotó $\begin{Bmatrix} \bar{g}a \\ wa \end{Bmatrix}$ | arimasén   We have never gone

c. Iku kotó ḡa | arimásita   It sometimes happened that we went,
                                              we would sometimes go

   Iku kotó mo | arimásita   It sometimes even happened that we
                                              went

d. Itta kotó ḡa | arimásita   We had gone [at least once]

   Itta kotó $\begin{Bmatrix} \bar{g}a \\ wa \end{Bmatrix}$ | arimasén   We had never gone
        desita

8. Yóru | $\begin{Bmatrix} \text{neraremasén} \\ \text{neru kotó } \bar{g}a \text{ | dekimasén} \end{Bmatrix}$ At night I can't sleep

   + . . . kotó mo arimasu   It sometimes even happens that . . .

   Yóru | neraTenai   It sometimes even happens that I
                                              can't sleep at night
        neru kotó $\begin{Bmatrix} no \\ \bar{g}a \end{Bmatrix}$ | dekínai |
   + kotó mo arimasu

9. Suizyóoki o hakobimasu   It bears vapor
   Suizyóoki o | hakonde kimásu   It comes bearing vapor

10. Úmi no | suizyóoki o | hakonde   It comes bearing the ocean's vapor
    kimásu
   + Musi-atúi no da | sóo desu   They say it is [a fact that it is] muggy
   → Úmi no | suizyóoki o | hakonde   They say it is muggy because it comes
     kúru no de ‖ musi-atúi no da | bearing the ocean's vapor
     sóo desu

11. Nóoḡyoo ni | hituyoo désu   It is necessary for agriculture
   + Komé o | tukúru no ni | hituyoo   It is necessary for the growing of
     désu   rice
   → Nóoḡyoo ‖ (tóku ni) ‖ komé o | It is necessary for agriculture and
     tukúru no ni | hituyoo désu   (especially) for the growing of rice

12. Hituyoo désu   It is necessary
   + no   fact that . . .
   → Hituyoo ná no desu   It's a fact that it is necessary

13. Compare:
    Tabemóno ḡa | kusarimásu   Foodstuffs spoil
    Tabemóno ḡa | kusari-yasúi desu   Foodstuffs spoil easily

14. Tabemóno ḡa | kusari-yasúi desu   Foodstuffs spoil easily
   + Ityoo no byooki mo huemásu   Intestinal disorders also spread
   → Tabemóno ḡa | kusari-yasúi si ‖   Foodstuffs spoil easily and intestinal
     ityoo no byooki mo huéru (no   disorders spread, (so) . . .
     de) ‖ . . .

15. Suzúsiku narimasu   It gets cool, It will get cool
    Suzúsiku/náreba | íi desu ḡa . .   I hope it gets cool

16. atúi aida (wa),   [during the time] while it is hot,

17. Compare the following pairs:
   a. Yamá ni noborimasu   We climb the mountain
       yamanóbori   mountain-climbing

   b. Namí ni norimasu   We ride the waves
       naminóri   surf-riding

18. Yamanóbori o simasu   We do mountain-climbing
   + Naminóri o simasu   · We do surf-riding
   → Yamanóbori o│sitári ‖naminóri   We do [things like] mountain-climb-
       o│sitári simasu   ing and surf-riding [at different
                                              times]

19. Nihyakutooka ḡa súḡitara   When the 210th day will pass . . .
   + Nihonbare ḡa tuzuku yóo ni│   When the Nihon-bare weather will
       náttara   become firmly established . . .
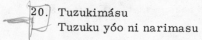→ Nihyakutooka ḡa súḡite ‖Nihon-   When the 210th day passes and the
       bare ḡa tuzuku yóo ni│náttara   Nihon-bare weather becomes firm-
                                              ly established . . .

20. Tuzukimásu   It continues
     Tuzuku yóo ni narimasu   It gets to the point of continuing [i.e.,
                                              becomes firmly established]

Lesson 13

hatten	expansion, extension, enlargement, develop- ment, growth
zyuuyoo (na)	is important, is of importance, is essential
booeki	trade, commerce between nations
syóogyoo	commerce, trade, business
toríhiki	transactions, dealings, business (deal)
yusyutu	exportation, export
yunyuu	importation, import
syoohin	a commodity, an article of commerce, merchandise
yusyutuhin	export goods (commodities)
P muke	(bound or headed) for P
menséihin	cotton goods
orimóno	a (textile) fabric, woven goods
ánka (na)	is cheap, inexpensive, lowpriced
zakka	miscellaneous goods, sundries, notions
ómo (na)	is a great part of, is the majority of
kínnen	recent years, in recent years, of late years
sidai ni	gradually
toranzisutaa-rázio	a transistor radio
zooka suru	increases, gains
ménka	raw cotton
kóogyoo	industry, the manufacturing industry
genryóo	raw material
kakoo	processing, industrial processes
X o simesu	shows/indicates X
tariru	suffices; is sufficient, enough
múgi	barley, wheat
aite	partner, the other party, an opponent
saikóoi	the highest position, the highest place
X o siméru	occupies/holds/takes (up) X
Tyuukyoo (= Tyúugoku - Zinmín - Kyoowá-koku)	Communist China
músiro	rather (than), preferably
Ázia	Asia
syókoku	various countries
yuubóo-si suru	hopefully looks upon
yuuboo (na)	is hopeful, promising

1. Kéizai no | hatten no $\begin{Bmatrix} ué \\ tamé \end{Bmatrix}$ ni |
   zyuuyoo désu

   It is important in/for the development
   of the economy

2. Kéizai no | hatten no $\begin{Bmatrix} ué \\ tamé \end{Bmatrix}$ ni |
   zyuuyoo na mono no hitótu ni ‖
   X ga arimasu

   As one of the things important for
   the development of the economy,
   there is X

3. Syoogyoo-tórihiki wa ‖ gaikoku
   tó desu

   The commercial transactions are
   with foreign countries

Gaikoku tó no│syoogyoo-tórihiki
desu

They are commercial transactions
with foreign countries

4. Kore ní wa│A to B ḡa arimasu

As an example of this we have A and
B, In this are included A and B

5. A wa, . . . uru kotó de ‖B wa,
. . . kau kotó desu

A is a matter of selling . . . and B
is a matter of buying . . .

Compare the following:
Nán no│kotó desu ka
Tanaka-san no kotó o itte imasu
Amerika no kotó o│káite kudasai

What is it about
They are talking about Mr. Tanaka
Please write about America

6. Yusyutuhin ní wa ‖orimóno ḡa│
óoku(te), . . .

Imports consist largely of textiles,
and . . .

7. Compare:
Nihón wa ‖menséihin o│Amerika
$\begin{Bmatrix} e \\ ni \end{Bmatrix}$ mukemásu

Japan sends cotton goods to America

Amerika-muke no menséihin desu

They are cotton goods bound for
America

8. (yusyutuhin ní wa) ‖móto wa ‖X, Y,
Z nádo ḡa│sono ómo na│monó
desita

(Among exports) the important things
were formerly X, Y, Z, and the
like

9. P, Q, R nádo mo│zooka site imásu

P, Q, R, and the like are also increasing

10. Nihon no booeki ni ‖kakoo-bóoeki
ḡa│óoi desu
+ Kore wa ‖. . . kotó o│simesite
imásu

In Japanese commerce the processing
trade is large
This reveals the fact that . . .

→ Kore wa, ‖Nihon no booeki ni ‖
kakoo-bóoeki $\begin{Bmatrix} no \\ ḡa \end{Bmatrix}$│óoi koto o│
simesite imásu

This reveals the fact that in Japanese
commerce the processing trade is
large

11. genryóo o yunyuu suru booeki

trade in which raw materials are imported

+ seihin o yusyutu suru booeki

trade in which finished products are
exported

→ genryóo o yunyuu site ‖seihin o
yusyutu suru booeki

trade in which raw materials are imported and finished products exported

12. Compare:
Zinkoo ḡa óoi desu
Zinkoo ḡa óoi no ni ‖. . .

The population is large
Although the population is large = Considering the large [size of the] population, . . .

13. X to sité wa

as X [comparatively]

14. X yori mo ‖músiro‖Y no hoo
ḡa│yuubóo-si sarete imasu

Rather than X, [the alternative of] Y
is being looked upon [more] hopefully

15. X tó no booeki o│yuubóo-si site
    imasu

They are hopefully looking upon the
trade with X

→ X tó no booeki (no hóo) ḡa│
    yuubóo-si sarete imasu
    (PASSIVE)

The trade with X is being looked upon
[more] hopefully

Lesson 14

syuusyoku suru	finds employment, gets a job
meḡúsuri	eye drops, eye lotion
tyokusetu no	is direct, immediate
X o omoikíru	gives up X, abandons X
omóikitte	boldly, daringly
zyookyoo suru	comes/goes up to the capital
sabisíi	is lonesome, cheerless, solitary
tanima	a ravine, a gorge, a chasm
miyako	a capital, metropolis
wakaréru	it branches off, parts (from), separates
gokuraku	paradise (of Buddhism), Elysium
ziḡoku	hell, the inferno
kotowáza	a proverb, a (common) saying, a maxim
ikiuma (ikinma)	a living horse
X o nuku	extracts/pulls X, takes/plucks X out
daitókai	a large city
kentóo ḡa tukánai	has no idea (of), has not the slightest idea (of)
kentóo	aim, estimate, guess
boo	a stick, a rod, a pole
X ni ataru	hits (on/against) X, strikes (on) X, crashes into X, comes across X
X ḡa ataru	X hits
katappasi kara	taking them up one by one, one after another
arukimawáru	walks around
mizikási = mizikái	is short
náḡasi = naḡái	is long [LITERARY sentence –final]
tekitoo (na)	is suitable, is proper, is adequate, is appropriate
zenzáisan	entire (total) fortune (property)
saihu	a billfold, a coin-purse, a wallet
nakittura	a crying face, a tearful face
nasakenái	is pitiful, wretched, miserable
yakuba	a public office, a city hall
íken	an opinion, a view, an idea, a suggestion
A/X ni sitaḡáu	obeys A/X (a person/an order), complies with (a request), agrees to (a proposal)
sassoku	at once, immediately, right away

1. Kookoo o sotuḡyoo simásita   I graduated from high school
+ Tookyoo de syuusyoku sitái to omoimásita   I thought I would like to get a position in Tokyo
+ Tookyoo no tomodati ni kakimásita   I wrote to my friend in Tokyo

Kookoo o sotuḡyoo sitá no de ‖ Tookyoo de syuusyoku sitái to omótte ‖ Tookyoo no tomodati ni kakimásita   I graduated from high school, and (so) thinking I would like to get a position in Tokyo, I wrote to my Tokyo friends

2. nán-do mo   ever so many times

3. Inaka ni imásu   I am in the country
 + Tomodati ni│siḡoto o saḡasite   I get a friend to hunt work for me
    moraimásu

 → Inaka ni ite ‖tomodati ni│siḡoto   While [myself] staying in the country,
    o saḡasite moraimásu   I get a friend to hunt work for me

4. . . . saḡasite moraú no de wa,   If it's the case where one has a
    . . .   friend hunt . . .

5. "Nikai kara│meḡúsuri [o‖mé ni│   [It is like] eye lotion [dropped into
    sásu yoo desu]"   the eyes] from upstairs [i.e., it is
                                                    obviously ineffectual]

6. X ni kosita kotó wa│arimasén   There is nothing better than X
    (kosu "surpasses, is better
    than")

7. Tyokusetu│zibun de saḡasimásita   He looked for it himself [= in person]

8. Omoikirimásita   I made up my mind
 + Zyookyoo suru kotó ni│kime-   I decided to go up to Tokyo
    másita

 → Omóikitte ‖zyookyoo suru kotó   I made up my mind and decided to go
    ni│kimemásita   up to Tokyo

9. sabisíi│tanima no murá de mo,   Even if it's a lonely valley town . . .
    . . .

10. Tookyoo ni tukimásita   I arrived in Tokyo
 + (site) mimásu   try (doing), (do) and see
 → Tookyoo ni túite│mimásita   I arrived in Tokyo [to see what it was
                                                    like]

    Tookyoo ni túite│míru to, . . .   Upon arriving in Tokyo I found . . .

11. "Kiité [wa] gokuraku [de]‖míte   When you hear about it, it is a para-
    [wa] zigokú [desu]"   dise; and when you see it, it is hell.

    In this sentence, kiité (wa) is
    equivalent to kiku to, and míte
    (wa) is equivalent to míru to.

12. ". . ." no kotowaza no tóori   like the proverb which goes ". . ."
    de . . .

13. "Ikiuma no mé o nuku"│yóo na│   It was a metropolis of the kind that
    daitókai desita   "plucks the eyes right out of a live
                                                    horse"

14. ittai + INTERROGATIVE   just (what, who, etc.), (what, who, why
                                                    etc.) in the world
    Ittai dóo site│Nyuuyóoku e│ittá   I don't understand why in the world
    ka│wakarimasén   he went to New York

15. Note the following:
    Siḡoto o saḡasitára, . . .   If/when one hunts work
    Siḡoto o saḡasitára│íi   It would be good/better to hunt work
    Dóo site│siḡoto o saḡasitára│íi   I didn't have the slightest idea, I
    ka ‖kentóo mo│tukimasén   couldn't even guess how I should
    desita   hunt for work

16. "Inú mo|arúkeba‖boo ni ataru"

    A ḡa X ni ataru

"Even a dog will come across a stick if he just walks"
A hits upon X

17. $\begin{Bmatrix} \text{Katahasi} \\ \text{Katappasi} \end{Bmatrix}$ kara|tazúnete| mimásita

I looked [for them] (= visited them) one after another

18. dóre mo kore mo

each and every one

19. "Óbi ni mizikási ‖tasukí ni| náḡasi" = óbi ni wa|mizikái, tasukí ni wa|naḡái

"It is good neither for one thing nor the other" [lit. It's too short for an obi 'wide belt' and too long for a tasuki 'sash for sleeves']

20. Íi siḡoto o|mitukemásita
Tekitoo na siḡoto ḡa mitukari-masén desita

    Tekitoo na siḡoto wa|arimasén

I found a good job
I was not able to find a suitable job,
There was not any suitable work [to be found]
There isn't any suitable work

21. Watakusi $\begin{Bmatrix} \text{no} \\ \text{ga} \end{Bmatrix}$ zenzáisan o ireta|saihu désu

It is the purse into which I put all my money

22. Mattaku ‖"nakitura ni hati" $\begin{Bmatrix} \text{tó wa} \\ \text{to iú no wa} \end{Bmatrix}$ ‖kono kotó desu

This is just what is meant by "a crying face stung by a bee"

+ . . . to (omótte) ‖nasakenáku narimásita

→ Mattaku ‖"nakitura ni hati" tó wa‖kono kotó da to ‖nasake-náku narimásita

Thinking that/with the feeling that . . . , I got depressed
Thinking that this is just what is meant by "a crying face stung by a bee," I got depressed

23. (tití kara) . . . to itte kimásita

There came word (from father) [say-ing] that . . .

24. Siḡoto ḡa arimásu
+ Náni ka arimasu
→ Náni ka|siḡoto ḡa arimásu

There is a job
There is something
There is some work

25. Inaka ni imásu
Inaka ni í wa simasu

Inaka ni í mo simasu
Inaka ni í sae simasu
Inaka ni í sae|suréba, . . .

I am in the country
I AM in the country, I DO stay in the country
I even/also STAY in the country
I even/just stay in the country
Provided I just stay in the country . . .
As long as I stay in the country . . .

26. A ḡa X ni komáru
Watakusi ḡa tabéru no ni| komarimásu

A is troubled by X
I have trouble eating

27. Káette|kitára|dóo desu ka
+ . . . to itte kimásita
→ Káette|kitára|dóo ka to|itte kimásita

How would it be if you came back?
word came [saying] that . . .
Word came asking how it would be if I came back

Lesson 15

wá ḡa kuni	our country, my country
wá ḡa = watakusi no	my, our [LITERARY]
tairiku	a continent
simáḡuni	an island country
simá	an island
kókudo	a country, a realm, a domain, a territory
hukín	neighborhood, vicinity
sanzén-yo	over three thousand
X kara náru	consists of X, is composed of X
zen-ménseki	entire area, square measure, total size (of land)
heihoo	the square (of a number)
Tyoosén	Korea
Kánkoku	the Republic of (South) Korea
Minami-Kárahuto	Southern Saghalien (Sakhalin)
ryóodo	a territory, a possession
haisen	a lost battle, a defeat
kekka	result, consequence, outcome
X o usinau	loses X, is deprived of X
hikiaḡéru	withdraws (from), evacuates (a place)
X óyobi Y	X and Y, X as well as Y
kikokúhei	a soldier who has returned to his own country
kikoku suru	returns to one's country
kuwawáru	it joins (in), enters for
hizyoo ni	exceedingly, excessively, extremely
syussyóo-ritu	birthrate
ití-oku	one hundred million
tisei	geographical features, topography
(. . . no) daibúbun	a greater part, a great portion, a large percentage (of . . .)
santi	a mountainous district
kóoti	arable land, cultivated field, farmland
X ni taisúru	towards X, as against X
mítudo	density
génzai	at present time
sitaḡatte	accordingly, consequently, therefore
suizyun	level, standard
seikatu-súizyun	living standard
takaméru	raises, elevates, exalts, improves, enhances
yasinau	feeds, rears, supports, provides for, cares for
ten	a point, a respect
zyuuyoo (na)	is important
mondai	a problem, a question

1. X wa ‖Y to Z (to) no│aida ni arimásu — X is [found] between Y and Z

2. Kókudo wa ‖X to Y (to) kara nátte imasu — [Its] territory consists of X and Y, [Its] territory is made of X and Y

3. haisen no kekka, . . .

as a result of losing the war, . . .

4. Koré-ra no|ryóodo o|usinaimásita
+sono ué ni . . .
→Koré-ra no|ryóodo o|usinatta ué
ni . . .

We lost these colonies
on top of that . . .
In addition to losing these colonies
. . .

5. A|óyobi|B nado ḡa|kuwawari-
másita (óyobi "and, as well as"
is LITERARY usage)

A and B and the like were added [to
the total]

6. Heitai ḡa|kikoku simásita

The'soldier returned home/got repatriated

→kikoku sita heitai
→kikokú-hei

a soldier who got repatriated
repatriated soldier

7. Tookú wa|$\begin{cases}\text{aru mái} \\ \text{nái desyoo}\end{cases}$
(cf. Note 9, Lesson 11)

It probably isn't distant

8. X ni taisúru Y

kooti-ménseki ni|taisúru|zinkoo-
mítudo

Y as $\begin{cases}\text{contrasted with} \\ \text{seen in light of}\end{cases}$ X

the population density as contrasted
with the arable-land area

9. Seikatu-súizyun o|takamemásu
+ Óoku no zinkoo o|yasinaimásu
→ Seikatu-súizyun o|takamenáḡara ‖
óoku no zinkoo o|yasinaimásu

They raise the standard of living
They feed a large population
They support a large population while
[at the same time] raising the living standard

10. . . . zinkoo o yasinau tamé ni (wa)

For the purpose of feeding the population . . .

+ Dóo sitara|$\begin{cases}\text{íi} \\ \text{yói}\end{cases}$$\begin{cases}\text{desu} \\ \text{desyoo}\end{cases}$ ka

How should we/one do it?

+ . . . to iu ten
→ . . . zinkoo o yasinau tamé ni
wa ‖dóo sitara|yói ka to iu
ten . . .

the point/question of . . .
The point/question of what one/we
should do in order to feed/support
the population . . .

Lesson 16

símen	the four sides, all sides
X o kakomu	surrounds/encircles/encloses X
sanmyaku	a mountain range
táiga	a big river
tyooryuu	a long stream
daihéiya	a big plain, a big open field
heiya	a plain, a field
kyuuryuu	a rapid stream, a swift current
suiryoku-hátuden	waterpower generation
súiryoku	waterpower, hydraulic power
hatuden	generation of electric power
suigai	a flood damage, a water calamity
husoku	shortage, insufficiency, deficiency, deficit
imi-súru	means
kootuu	traffic
kázan	a volcano
(sore ni) sitagatte	in accordance (with that), accordingly
onsen	a hot spring
hoyoo	health seeking, preservation of health
X ni tekisúru	fits/suits X, is fit for X
sono hanmén	on the other hand
zisin	an earthquake
katudoo	activity, action, operation
itáru tokoro	everywhere, wherever one goes, all over
syokúbutu	a plant, vegetation, flora
syúrui	a kind, a sort, a species, a denomination, a type
húukoo	scenery, natural (scenic) beauty
ontai	the temperate zone, the warm latitudes
kikoo	climate
onwa (na)	is mild, is gentle, is clement, is temperate
sikí	the four seasons
kúbetu	difference, distinction
hanaréru	it separates/parts from
búnka	culture, civilization
kooryuu	interchange, an alternating current
kookúuki	a flying machine, aircraft
kikán	a medium, an organ, an instrument
hattatu	development, growth, progress, advancement
kaiketu suru	settles (a problem), solves (a question)

1. Úmi ga│Nihón o│kakomimásu   The ocean surrounds Japan
   Nihón ga│úmi ni│kakomaremásu   Japan gets surrounded by the ocean
      (PASSIVE)
   Nihón ga│úmi ni│kakomarete   Japan is surrounded by the ocean
      imásu

2. símen   [on] four sides, [on] all sides

3. sono tamé (ni), . . .   for that reason, . . .

4. X $\begin{Bmatrix} \text{wa} \\ \text{ḡa} \end{Bmatrix}$ ‖ Y ni | bénri desu

X is convenient for Y

Kyuuryuu $\begin{Bmatrix} \text{no} \\ \text{ḡa} \end{Bmatrix}$ óoi koto wa ‖
suiryoku-hátuden ni | bénri
desu

The fact that there are many rapid
streams is convenient for the generation of hydroelectric power

5. Suiḡai o ukéru koto ḡa | óoi desu

It often happens that they suffer
flood damage

→ Suiḡai o ukéru koto mo | óoi desu

It also/even often happens that they
suffer flood damage

6. Zinkoo ḡa óoi no ni, . . .

Despite the fact that the population
is large, . . .

7. . . . kotó wa, . . . o | imi-
simásu

The fact that . . . means that . . .

8. X $\begin{Bmatrix} \text{wa} \\ \text{ḡa} \end{Bmatrix}$ ‖ Y ni | húben desu
(cf. Note 4)

X is inconvenient for Y

9. Compare:
Toti ḡa | hoyoo ni tekísite imasu

The land/place is suitable for health
recuperation

Hoyoo ni tekísita toti desu

It is a place suitable for health recuperation

Note: Many sentences with -te
iru "is in the state resulting from
[VERB]" become modifiers with
the simple PAST -ta:
Hito ḡa | tukárete imasu
Tukáreta hito desu

The man is tired
It's the man who is tired

10. sono hanmén (ni)

on the other hand

11. itáru tokoro $\begin{Bmatrix} \text{de} \\ \text{ni} \end{Bmatrix}$

everywhere

12. Hayasí o mimasu
Hayasí ḡa miraremasu
(PASSIVE)

I see the woods
The woods are/get seen [by me/some-
one]

13. ontai ni áru $\begin{Bmatrix} \text{‖ tamé ni} \\ \text{kara} \end{Bmatrix}$, . . .

Because it is in the temperate zone,
. . .

14. Hakkíri simasu
Kúbetu ḡa | hakkíri site imasu
→ Hakkíri sita | kúbetu desu
(Cf. Note 9)

It makes itself clear/distinct
The divisions are clear-cut/distinct
They are distinct divisions

15. A ḡa | B kara | hanárete imasu

A is separated from B

16. X no hattatu ni $\begin{Bmatrix} \text{yotte} \\ \text{yori} \end{Bmatrix}$, . . .

Depending on (or Because of) the
development of X, . . .

17. a. Sarete iru $\begin{Bmatrix} \text{tokoró desu} \\ \text{totyuu désu} \end{Bmatrix}$ It is getting done

Sare-tútu aru [LITERARY]   It is getting done

b. Site iru tokoró desu   They are doing it, They are in the
                                   process of doing it

Si-tútu aru [LITERARY]   They are doing it, They are in the
                                   process of doing it

Lesson 17

ún-waruku	unfortunately, unluckily
ún	destiny, fate, one's lot, luck
ún-yoku	fortunately, luckily
uoítiba	a fish market
síromi	white meat
sioyáki	(fish) broiled with salt
mitukurou	selects (thing) according to one's own judgment, choose (thing) at one's own discretion
syokuyoku	an appetite
zoosin	increase, promotion, improvement, advance
sansei	agreement, approval, assent
kái	a shellfish
su-nó-mono	a vinegared dish, Japanese sweet and sour salad
sú	vinegar
syooti suru	consents to, agrees to
umái (nmái)	is delicious (used more often by men)
omówazu	without intention on one's part, unintentionally, unconsciously, before one knew it
kaikei	a bill, account
arígatoo zonzimasu	Thank you very much.

1. Tyótto│mátte (kudasai)

   Wait a moment (please)

2. Hayasi-kun
   (= Hayasi-san)
   (-kun is used among male colleagues, fellow students, etc.)

   (Mr.) Hayashi

3. Moo kúru daroo
   (moo = "shortly now")

   I think he'll be here soon

4. Tori ni siyóo ka

   Shall we make it chicken?/Shall we decide on chicken?

5. Dóo da i?
   (Less POLITE than dóo desu ka)

   How about it?/How would it be?

   Compare:
   Dáre da i?
   Sóo ka i?
   (Less POLITE than sóo desu ka)
   Kore ka i?
   Íi ka i?
   Note that da i follows question words while ka i used mostly in yes-or-no questions.

   Who is it?
   Is that so? Oh?

   Is it this one?
   Is it good/OK?

6. Tenpura ni sité mo│íi ka i?
   Íi ka i?║Tempura ni sité mo . . .
      [AFTERTHOUGHT]

   Is it all right if we have tempura?
   Is it all right? [I mean . . .] if we have tempura . . .

7. Íi tomo   Of course it's all right

   Compare:
   Kúru tomo   }
   Kimásu tomo }   Of course I'm coming
   Sóo da tomo   Of course it's that way
   Sóo datta tomo   Of course it was that way

8. Compare:
   Ún g̃a | warúi desita   He had bad luck
   Ún g̃a|íi desita   He had good luck
   Ún waruku | byooki ni narimásita   Unfortunately he got sick
   Ún yoku|íi isya g̃a | imásita   Fortunately there was a good doctor

9. Kaig̃í g̃a | átta {kara   Because there was a meeting
                     {mon(o)

   Kaig̃í g̃a | átta {kara   }
                     {mon(o) de } . . .   It is because there was a meeting
                                                      that . . .

   This use of mon(o) is colloquial.

10. Kita ba(k)kári/bákari desu   We've just arrived

11. Tenpura dé mo|tyuumon siyóo   We were talking about whether we
       ka tte| {itté 'ta   should order perhaps tempura
               {itte ita

   + . . . {tokó   } desu   [at the] point [of] . . .
           {tokoró}

   + no   fact that . . .
   → Tenpura dé mo|tyuumon siyóo   [It's a fact that] we were just discuss-
       ka tte|itté 'ta toko|ná n(o) desu   ing whether we should order temp-
                                                      ura

12. O-bíiru g̃a|o-sumi ni nátte kara, . . .   When you have finished your beer, . . .
    (= bíiru g̃a | súnde kara)
    (o-bíiru is an affected form
    mostly used by waitresses)

13. Soo site (kudasái)   (Please) do that

14. Tabe-sug̃imásita   I ate too much
    Tabe-sug̃ite simaimásita }
    Tabe-sug̃ityaimásita   }   I ended up overeating

15. Note accent:
    Íppai désu   I'm full
    Íppai desu   It's one cupful

16. O-azukari {simásu   }   I take charge of [something pertain-
              {itasimásu }   ing to you]
    (HUMBLE)

Lesson 18

kakaeru	holds (a thing, a person) under one's arm
káta	the shoulder
yubisáki	the tip of a finger, a fingertip
tékubi	a wrist
inóru	prays, says a prayer
te-nó-hira	the palm (flat) of the hand
hureru	touches, feels (see Note 2)
huraipan	a frying pan
tómato	a tomato
sasaéru	supports, sustains, holds, keeps, props, bolsters
utaite	a singer
oyoḡite	a swimmer
hukade	a severe wound, a serious wound
X o ou	receives/sustains X
keḡá	an injury, a wound
hookoo	a direction, a course
temáwasi	preparation, arrangement
zyúnbi	preparation, arrangement
teḡótae	response, result, resistance
hannoo	reaction, response, effect
A ḡa B ni koosan suru	A surrenders to B
zyootatu suru	makes progress, improves
taisaku	a countermove, counterplan
taisaku o tatéru	devises a countermove, takes steps (measures) to meet the situation, studies how to cope with the situation
zíken	an event, an occurrence, an incident
X o tátu	cuts X (off), breaks/chops X off
mendóo (na)	is troublesome
A o korosu	kills/murders/slays A
X o nusúmu	steals X
kusé	a habit, a characteristic, a trait
komanéku	folds (one's arms)
udeḡúmi suru	folds one's arms
kanḡaekómu	is absorbed in thought, is in deep thought
husaḡaru	gets occupied, engaged, filled
búnsyoo	a composition, a writing, a style, a sentence
naiyoo	content(s), substance, import
hoohoo	a method, a way, a device, a mean
A o mitibíku	guides/leads A

1. Káta kara|yubisaki máde no|
   kotó desu

   It is a matter of (it refers to)[the area] from the shoulder to the fingertips

2. X o|té ni|tóru
   X ḡa|té ni hureru
   X ni|té ḡa hureru
   A ḡa|X ni|té de hureru
   A ḡa|X ni|té o hureru

   Take [up] X in[to] one's hand
   X touches the hand
   The hand touches X
   A touches X with the hand
   A touches X

3. A to iu to | B desu
    + C to iéba | D no kotó desu
    → A to iu to | B dá si ‖ C to iéba |
      D no kotó desu

When we say A, it is B
If we say C, it refers to D
When we say A, it is B; and if we say
  C, it refers to D [so, . . .]

4. Utaite no té wa ‖ hito ‖ túmari ‖
    utau hitó to iu | ími desu

The "te" of "utai-te" means a person
  —to be specific, a person who sings

5. X to iu ími desu
    X to iu ími ni narimasu

It means X
It comes to mean X

6. Iroiro ⎱ na tukaikata ḡa arimásu
    Iron ⎰

There are various uses

7. Mendóo na mondai de | komari-
      másita

I was bothered by an annoying problem

8. A wa | hito no monó o | nusumi-
      másu
    + A wa . . . kusé ḡa arimasu
    → A wa | hito no monó o | nusúmu |
      kusé ḡa arimasu

A steals [other] people's belongings/
  things
A has the unpleasant habit of . . .
A has the habit of stealing people's
  belongings

9. A wa | nani mo simasén
    + A wa imásu

    → A wa | ⎰ nani mo sinái de imasu
          ⎱ nani mo sezu ni imásu

A doesn't do anything
A is/exists/stays

A stays/sits around doing nothing

10. Siḡoto-tyuu désu
    + Hima ḡa arimasén

    → Siḡoto-tyuu de ‖ hima ḡa ari-
        masén

He's in the midst of work
There is no free time, He has no free
  time
He is in the midst of work and [for
  that reason] has no free time

Lesson 19

sumoo	Japanese wrestling
kéndoo	Japanese fencing, the art of defense with a sword
dentooteki (na)	is traditional, conventional
dentoo	tradition
taisyuu	the masses, the general public
kíndai	modern ages, modern times
búki	a weapon, arms
taósu	throws/blows/knocks down, throws (a person/ thing) to the ground
kózin	an individual, a person in his private capacity
syóobu	victory or defeat, a match, a contest
katá	a style, a type, a pattern
kisóku	a rule, regulations
itininmae no	is full-fledged, respectable
ríkisi	a wrestler of Japanese wrestling
syuḡyoo suru	trains oneself in, practices, studies
maḡe	a topknot, a chignon
yuu	dresses (the hair)
yahári	likewise, as well, like the rest, too, also
X o seméru	launches an attack upon X
X o mamóru	protects/defends/guards X
teki	an enemy, a foe
X o huséḡu	resists X, keeps/wards/fends X off
kokoróe	knowledge, information
tikará	(physical) strength, might, energy
X o riyoo suru	utilizes X, makes good use of X
naḡetaosu	throws (a person) to the ground
toriaḡeru	takes away (something from a person), deprives (a person of something), dispossesses (a person of his property)
kuhuu suru	devises, designs, invents
kenkyuu suru	studies, does research into, investigates
X o tuku	pushes/thrusts/pokes/strikes X
X o kéru	kicks X
búzyutu	military arts
X o tumu	piles/heaps/stores X up, accumulates X
X o kasaneru	lays X('s) one on top of another
kawara	a (roof) tile
X o waru	splits/cleaves/rips/chips/breaks/smashes X
katate	one hand
búsi	a samurai, a warrior
zyún-Nihonteki (na)	is purely Japanese (style), is orthodox Japanese (fashion)
men	a mask, a face guard
kote	fencing gloves, a gauntlet, a bracer
dóo	the trunk, the torso, the plastron, the body armor
mi	one's body, one's person
X o tukéru	attaches, joins, fastens, sews on, glues

mi ni tukéru	puts on, wears, has on (one's person), acquires skill in an art
kataná	a sword, a blade
bokutoo	a wooden sword
take	bamboo
sínai	a bamboo sword, a fencing stick
aiútu	hit each other, strike each other
isamasíi	is brave, is courageous, is valiant, is gallant
wazá	a performance, art, a trick, work, an act, skill
sínsin	body and mind
A o kitaéru	drills/trains/hardens in A
mokuteki	a purpose, an aim, an object
rikuzyoo-kyóoḡi	field and track events
suizyoo-kyóoḡi	aquatic sports
Orinpikku-táikai	the Olympic games
X ni sanka suru	participates in X

1. Taisyuu ni│ninki ḡa arimásu   It has popularity for the masses
  + . . . no   the one (or the ones) which . . .

  → Taisyuu ni ninki $\begin{Bmatrix} ga \\ no \end{Bmatrix}$ áru no wa   The one/ones which has/have
    . . .   popularity for the masses . . .

2. A wa│B ni│nite imásu   A resembles B

3. búki o $\begin{cases} \text{tukawanái de} \\ \text{tukawázu ni} \end{cases}$ without using weapons

4. A│tai│B desu   It is A versus/against B

   A│tai│B no│syóobu desu   It is a contest of A against B

5. X to iwareru hodo . . .   To the extent that they say it is X . . .

6. Ríkisi ni│náru no ni (wa)‖   In order to become a champion
    . . . sinákereba│narimasén   wrestler, one must . . .

7. X-íḡai ni wa│arimasén   There are none outside of X

8. Zibun o mamóru│tamé desu   It is for the purpose of protecting oneself

  + teki o huseḡu tamé desu   It is for the purpose of warding off the enemy

  + . . . monó   thing which . . .

  → Zibun o mamóri ‖teki o huseḡu   It is a thing which is for the purpose
    tamé no│monó desu   of protecting oneself and warding off the enemy

9. Nihón ḡa│Ryuukyúu kara│búki o│   Japan took weapons away from the
   toriaḡemásita   Ryukyus

   a. Búki ḡa│Nihón ni│Ryuukyúu   The weapons got taken away from the
      kara│toriaḡeraremásita   Ryukyus by Japan
   b. Ryuukyúu ḡa│Nihón ni│búki o │   The Ryukyus suffered [by] Japan's
      toriaḡeraremásita   taking away of their weapons
      (PASSIVE)

10. Kuhuu saremásu
    + Kenkyuu saremásu
    ⇥ Kuhuu ‖kenkyuu saremásu

It is devised
It is studied, Research is done on it
It is devised and studied

11. Teki o tukimásu
    + Teki o kerimásu
    ⇥ Teki o tuitári ‖kéttari simasu

They strike [at] the enemy
They kick the enemy
They hit and kick the enemy [in alter-
nation]

12. Teki o tuitári ‖kéttari si ‖
    zibun o mamóru│búzyutu desu
    (si = site)

It is a military art in which one hits
and kicks the enemy and protects
oneself

13. Rensyuu o túmeba . . .

If one accumulates/continues practice . . .

14. Katate de warimásu
    + Iti-dó ni warimasu

    ⇥ Katate de│iti-dó ni warimasu

He splits it with one hand
He splits it at one time (= with one
stroke)
He splits it with one [single] blow of
the hand

15. Búsi no hituyoo kara│umare-
    másita

It was born out of (= it developed from)
the needs of the warrior

16. Búsi ḡa│ái-utimasu

The warriors hit each other

17. X to doozi ni

at the same time as (= together with)
X

18. A ḡa│Q to iu mokuteki de‖X o
    okonaimásu
    (A ni)│Q to iu mokuteki de‖
    (X ḡa) okonawaremásu
    (PASSIVE)

A performs X for the purpose of Q

It (X) is performed (by A) for the
purpose of Q

19. arayúru X

all sorts of X

20. X ni│sanka simásu

    X ni│sanka site imásu

They participate [habitually] in X/
they will participate [once] in X
They are participating [repeatedly/
regularly] in X
They are [continuing] participants in
X

Lesson 20

Yásuko	(a female name)
syokúḡyoo	an occupation, a profession, a vocation, a trade, a line of business
syokúḡyoo ni túku	takes up an occupation, enters (upon) a profession
Háruko	(a female name)
kyóosi	a teacher, an instructor
kyoozyu	a professor; (school) teaching
soróu	it becomes complete, is all present
senketu no	is of previous decision, is preconsidered
senketu-móndai	a previous question, a preconsideration
niḡate	a weak point; a person (a subject) hard to deal with
keiei	management, administration, operation, running, enterprise, business
sikkári site iru = (sikkári sita)	is strong, is firm, is solid, is steady
kouriten	a retail store
syuunyuu	an income, earnings, revenue, proceeds
sumíya	a charcoal dealer
sumí	charcoal
geizyututeki (na)	is artistic
geizyutu	art, the arts
geizyutuka	an artist
sénsu	a sense
Syuuiti	Shuichi (a male name)
gunzin	a soldier, a military man
koomúin	a civil servant, public service personnel
séihu	the government, the Federal Government, the administration
saibánkan	a judge
sáiban suru	judges, tries (a case)
saibansyo	a court of justice, a courthouse
hooritu	a law, the law
ki ḡa tooku náru	blacks out, loses consciousness
gízyutu	technique, skill, technical know-how
gísi	an engineer, a technician, a technical expert
rakú (na)	is comfortable, easy
sizin	a poet
gaka	a painter
kentikuka	an architect
X o mitomeru	recognizes/observes/notices X
X ni amanzúru = (amanzíru)	contents oneself with, is contented with X
tanin	other person, others, an unrelated person, strangers
sakan'ya	a plasterer
kánnusi	a Shinto priest, the guardian of a shrine
boosan	a Buddhist priest, a monk
bunḡyóo	division of labor
zidai	an era, a period, an age

This lesson illustrates the kinds of sentences used among young people. Note the frequent dropping of <u>dá</u> and PARTICLES in PLAIN STYLE sentences.

1. Náni o|sitára|íi ka sira   I wonder what it would be good to do

   Compare:
   Tanaka-san wa|ikú ka sira   I wonder if Mr. Tanaka is going
   Sátoo-san no|hón ka sira   I wonder if it's Mr. Sato's book
   (The above sentences are used
   more by girls and women)

   Náni o|sitára|íi ka na   I wonder what it would be good to do
   (used more by boys and men)

2. Daigaku ni|kyoozyu ga|sorótte   The university is full of good profes-
   imasu   sors [i.e., has a full staff]

3. Compare:
   Mondai dá wa
   (used by girls and women as
   PLAIN STYLE)
   Mondai désu wa   It's a problem
   (used by girls and women as
   POLITE STYLE and by middle-
   aged men when pontificating)

4. watasi wa ne   as for me, . . .
   (= watasi wa)
   Insertion of <u>ne</u>, especially after
   topic, is frequent in Tokyo speech,
   especially that of women; compare its use in telephone conver-
   sations.

5. A (ni) wa|X $\begin{Bmatrix} ga \\ wa \end{Bmatrix}$|nigate désu   X is A's weak point, A has no apti-
                                                      tude for X

6. Ginkoo ni o-tutome sitái   I want to get employed (= work) in
   (HUMBLE form, often used   a bank
   by girls)

7. Keiei ga sikkári site imasu   Business is steady/good

8. X ya Y nánka desu   It is X and Y and the like
   (in this sentence, <u>nánka</u> is
   somewhat deprecatory: "the likes
   of X and Y")

9. Héi = hái   yes
   (used by lower-class people or
   shopkeepers in downtown
   Tokyo)

10. X nánte|iú no (wa)
    X nádo to|iú no wa   saying such things as X

11. X zya arimasén   It isn't X

+ Y desu   It's Y

→ X zya nákute ‖ Y desu   It's not X, it's Y; It's not X, <u>but</u> Y

12. soryaa = sore wa   that
     [COLLOQUIAL]

13. Náni o│site irú no desu ka ⎫
     Náni│site (i)rú no? [less ⎬   What is it you're doing,
     FORMAL]   ⎭

14. Dónna│syokúgyoo ga│íi ka   (We were discussing) what occupa-
     {tte}│(itte imásita)   tion would be good
     {to }

15. Sóo da│náa = sóo desu│née   Let me see, now . . .
     (used mostly in men's and boys'
     INFORMAL speech; <u>naa</u> is some-
     what more vigorous than <u>nee</u>)

16. nan-mán to iu hooritu   laws amounting to many thousands
                                            = many thousands of laws

17. X o│nokórazu│oboénakereba│   You must learn [all of] X with no ex-
     narimasén   ception
                                            You must memorize X without leav-
                                            ing anything out

18.   oboéru nante   ⎫
      oboéru nado to│iu kotó wa ⎭   learning [them], etc.

19. Kangáeta│daké desu   I just [only] thought [about it]
     → Kangáeta│daké de mo . . .   Even just thinking [about it] . . .

20. Ki ga tooku {nátte simau}   (a) One grows completely faint
                 {náttyau   }   (b) One ends up growing faint

     Ki ga tooku {nátte simai} -soo   It looks as though one grows com-
                 {náttyai   }   pletely faint
     desu

21. Náni ka│mi ni tukemásu   She acquires something ["attaches
                                            something to herself"]

     + Senmon no gízyutu o│mi ni   She acquires professional skills
     tukemásu
     → Náni ka│senmon no gízyutu o│   She acquires some kind of profes-
     mi ni tukemásu   sional skill(s)

22. X tó ka│Y tó ka . . .   for example, X or Y

23. Ikanákya│nánnai   ⎫
     Ikanákya│naránai   ⎬
     Ikanákereba│naránai ⎬   You have to go
     Ikanákereba│ikenái ⎭

24. Dáre de mo {tte}│iu wáke   [the case of] anybody at all
                {to }
     + . . . wáke ni wa ikanai   It doesn't stand to reason that . . .
     → Dáre de mo tte│iu wáke ni   It doesn't stand to reason [to say]
     wa│ikanái   that anybody at all [can do it]

25. A ḡa│B ni│akoḡareru

A is $\left\{\begin{array}{l}\text{drawn toward}\\ \text{attracted to}\end{array}\right\}$ B = A adores B

26. A ḡa│X ni│amanzíru

A contents himself with X

27. A ḡa│X ni│haḡému

A strives/works diligently for X

28. Ié ḡa │ tatimásu

A house goes up, A house is (or will be)built

Ié o │ tatemásu

We build a house

Ié ḡa │ tateraremásu
   (PASSIVE-POTENTIAL)

We can build a house

29. A ya B dá tte
    = A ya B dé mo

even [being] A or B

30. Komáru desyo?
    = Komáru desyoo?

We will be in trouble, won't we?

31. X desu mono
    = X desu kara

Because it's X

32. O-taḡai ni│tasuke-aimásita

They helped each other [mutually]

33. Sinákyaa . . . nánnai
    = sinákereba naránai

You have to [do it]

Lesson 21

syótoku	income, earnings
kokumin-syótoku	the national income
seisángaku	production, output, yield
seisan suru	produces
nóoka	a farmhouse, a farm family
tíi	a position, a status, a station in life, social standing
kiwámete	very, exceedingly, extremely, to a high degree
syuuyaku-teki (na)	is intensive
nóogyoo	agriculture, farming
róoryoku	labors, toil, effort
híryoo	fertilizer, manure
(A ni) X o ataeru	gives X (to A)
sakúmotu	crops, farm products
X o okonau	does/acts/carries out X, puts X into practice
tíngin	wages, pay
zisakúnoo	an owner farmer
kosakúnoo	tenant farming, tenancy
kosakúti	tenant farmland
kosakúryoo	farm rent, rent for tenancy
X o itonámu	performs/conducts/runs/operates X
zinusi	a landlord, a landowner, a landholder
mazusíi	is poor, needy, destitute, meager
rengóogun	the allied forces, the Allies
siréibu	the headquarters, the command
kankoku	advice, counsel, expostulation
kaikaku	reform, reformation
dankoo suru	acts decisively, enforces, executes
huzai no X	absent X
huzai-zínusi	an absentee landlord
syoyuu suru	owns, possesses
syoyúuti	land owned by (a person)
koodai (na)	is vast, extensive, huge
kyooseiteki (na)	is compulsory, coercive, forceful
kyoosei suru	forces, compels, coerces
keigen suru	reduces, alleviates
kinnoo	cash payment, payment in money
tatibá	a standpoint, a ground, a position, a footing
kaihoo suru	opens, throws open
kyuusai suru	relieves, helps, delivers, gives relief to, saves
kaizen	improvement, betterment, reform, change for the better
minsyuka	democratization
motói	the basis, the foundation, the root
seikoo suru	succeeds, proves successful
kagon	saying too much, exaggeration

1. A wa |X $\begin{Bmatrix} \text{de áru} \\ \text{ná} \end{Bmatrix}$ no ni ‖B wa
   hikúi no desu

   (In contrast with the fact that =)
   Though A is X, B is low

2. (Watakusí-tati ḡa) |tíi o|seisán-
   ḡaku no|mén kara|mimásita
   Seisán-ḡaku no|mén kara mita|
   tíi wa ‖hikúi desu

   (We) observed the position from the
   standpoint of amount-of-production
   Their position, seen from the standpoint of amount-of-production, is
   low

3. Ikura X o okonatté mo, . . .

   No matter how much X we engage
   in, . . .

4. . . . wáke desu

   It means that . . .

5. A ḡa |B kara|X o kariru
   B ḡa |A ni|X o kasu

   A borrows/rents X from B
   B lends/rents X to B

6. Nóoḡyoo o|itonámu|monó desu

   It is a matter of engaging in farming

7. Hanbun tikáku desu

   It is nearly half [but not over half]

8. Komé ḡa|tóreta

   They were able to get (= They produced) rice

   → Tóreta|komé da

   It is the rice they produced

9. Komé ḡa|taberaremasén
   + Mazusíi|hyakusyóo desu

   [People] cannot eat rice
   They are poor farmers

   → Komé $\begin{Bmatrix} \text{ḡa} \\ \text{no} \end{Bmatrix}$|taberarénai ‖mazu-
   síi|hyakusyóo desu

   They are poor farmers who cannot
   eat rice

10. mizu-nomi-byákusyoo

    water-drinking farmers [i.e., poor
    farmers who can't even eat rice]

11. Kóoti o|mótte ite mo . . .
    + Nóoḡyoo o|simasén desita
    + Soko ní (wa)|sumimasén desita
    + (Taitei) tokai ni sumimásita
    + Kosakúnoo ni ‖syoyúuti o|
    kasite imásita
    → Kóoti o|mótte ite mo ‖nóoḡyoo
    mo|sézu ‖soko ní mo|súmazu ‖
    taitei tokai ni súnde ‖kosakúnoo
    ni|syoyúu-ti o|kasite imásita

    Even though he owns arable land . . .
    He did not farm
    He did not live there
    (Usually) he lived in a large city
    He was renting his property to ten-
    ants
    Even though he owned arable land,
    he neither farmed nor lived there
    [on the farm], but usually lived in
    a large city and was renting his
    property to tenants

12. Sore o|kosakúnoo ḡa kaimasu
    → Séihu ḡa|sore o|kosakúnoo ni|
    kawasemásu (CAUSATIVE)

    The tenants buy that
    The government lets the tenants buy
    that

13. a. Zinusi ḡa|kosakúryoo o|
    keiḡen simásita
    Séihu ḡa|zinusi ni|kosakúryoo
    o|keiḡen sasemásita

    The landlord eased the tenant rent

    The government made the landlords
    ease the tenant rent

    b. Zinusi ḡa|kosakúryoo o|
    kinnoo ni simásita

    The landlords made the tenant rent
    [so that it would be] cash payment

Séihu ḡa│zinusi ni│kosakúryoo
o│kinnoo ni sasemásita

The government made the landlords
make the tenant rent [so that it
would be] cash payment

14. A ḡa│X o│B ni kaihoo suru

A opens X for [the benefit of] B = A
turns X over to B

15. . . . no ni│seikoo simásita

It succeeded in . . .(ing) . . .

16. . . . to itté mo│kaḡon dé wa│
arimasén

It is no exaggeration to say that . . .

Lesson 22

sikyuu (no)	is urgent, pressing, immediate
kási	the libretto, the text, lyric, words (of a song)
sakkyoku suru	composes (music)
sáigo no . . .	the last . . ., the very end of . . .
syoosetu	a bar of music
bonyári (to)	blankly, vacantly, absent-mindedly
tobidásu	it flies/runs/rushes out
nyúusu	news
hasiradókei	a wall clock
hasira	a pillar, a column, a post, a pole
téido	degree, extent, measure
kaminári	thunder, a thunderbolt
kaoiro	complexion
kaoiro o kaeru	changes color/countenance
kázi	a fire
kaziba	the scene of a fire
hi-no-mi no kane	bell of the fire lookout
zyán-zyan (to)	(with a) clangor, dingdong, clang-clang
íkiseki kíru	pants for breath, gasps
hí no ko	sparks
yátu	a so-and-so, a damn fellow, a creep, a guy, a (damn) thing
ki ḡa sirenái	is incomprehensible, is hard to understand
syoobóosya	a fire engine
sáiren	a siren
sóyo-soyo (to)	(wind blows) softly, gently
pyúu-pyuu (to)	(the wind) whistles/hisses
ki ḡa tiru	has one's attention distracted
síto-sito (to)	(it rains) gently, softly
harusame	spring rain
zaat (to)	(with the sound) ZAA! = gushing
zaat to|mizu o kakéru	showers water over
zaat to|áme ḡa|huridásu	rain comes pouring down
yuudati	an evening shower, a (sudden) shower
rín-rin (to)	(with a) ting-a-ling, tinkling
sikkéi (= sitúrei)	rudeness, impertinence, incivility, discourtesy
Aa! Sikkéi	Excuse me. (used by men)

This lesson contains sentences in men's PLAIN STYLE; note the dropping of PARTICLES and forms of dá.

1. yuube no zisin de   at last night's earthquake
   (de = a mild "because of")

2. Ókite $\begin{Bmatrix} \text{'ta} \\ \text{ita} \end{Bmatrix}$ n da yo   I was up, you know

3. Sakkyoku site kure   Compose music [for me/us]
   (kuré is the PLAIN IMPERATIVE
   of kureru)

4. (Watakusi ni│hito ḡa│) sakkyoku   They ask me to compose music
    site kuré tte│tanomimásu
    (Watakusi ḡa│hito ni│) sakkyoku   I am asked/requested to compose
    site kuré tte│tanomaremásu   music
    (PASSIVE)

5. Dóo mo│úmaku│$\begin{Bmatrix} \text{ikanákutte} \\ \text{ikanákute} \end{Bmatrix}$ . . .   Somehow just wouldn't come out
    Note double tt for emphasis and   right and . . .
    liveliness.

6. X (o) mótta $\begin{Bmatrix} \text{manma} \\ \text{mama} \end{Bmatrix}$ . . .   Just as I was holding X = with X in
    Note insertion of n for emphasis   hand . . .
    and liveliness.

7. kanḡáete ita│tokoró   [just] when I was thinking
  + Gata-gatát to│kimásita   There came a sound of rattling

  → Kanḡáete ita│tokoró $\begin{Bmatrix} \text{ni} \\ \text{e} \end{Bmatrix}$ ‖   [Just] when I was thinking . . . ,
    gata-gatát to│kimásita   there came a sound of rattling
    (final clottal catch is for em-
    phasis)

8. Nyúusu kiita?   Did you hear the newε [broadcast]?
    = Nyúusu o│kiitá ka

9. . . . téido│dátta $\begin{Bmatrix} \text{n(o) da tte} \\ \text{(no da)│sóo da} \end{Bmatrix}$ They say it was [only] to the extent
                                                 that . . .

10. Oo-zísin ka to│$\begin{Bmatrix} \text{omóttyatta n da yo} \\ \text{omótte simatta yo} \end{Bmatrix}$ I really wondered if it was a big
                                                 earthquake, you know

11. kaminári de   because of/at thunder
    (cf. Note 1)

12. kaoiro o kaeru   change countenance
    kaoiro ḡa kawaru   turn pale
    kaoiro o kaenai (hito)   (a man who) does not show any emo-
                                                 tion

13. Íki-seki│kítte│hasirimásita   He ran [there] all out of breath

14. Nán-tyoo mo│saki désu   It is a good many blocks ahead

15. X mo kamáwazu   regardless of [the] X

16. Ki ḡa sirenai   Their minds can't get understood =
                                                 I can't understand their minds

17. Dái-kirai sa   I really hate 'em!
    The emphatic PARTICLE sa is
    very popular in assertive Tokyo
    speech.

18. Hito ḡa│kaze ni hukaremásita   People were blown by the wind [i.e.,
                                                 adversely affected by being blown
                                                 upon]

19. Náni o $\left|\begin{matrix} \text{yónda tte} \\ \text{yónde mo} \end{matrix}\right|$ ··· .   Whatever I read . . .

20. Atamá ni $\left|\begin{matrix} \text{háirya sinai} \\ \text{hairí wa} \end{matrix}\right|$ sinái   It doesn't enter/sink into my head

Lesson 23

syooyoo	commercial business, business
kankoo	sightseeing
kankoo-ryókoo	a sightseeing tour
kankóokyaku	a tourist
sonó-ta = sonó-hoka	other than that, others
rainiti suru	comes to Japan
kokusai-kúukoo	an international airport
kokusai-tósi	cosmopolitan city
kokusai-teki (na)	is international
iwaba	so to speak, in a sense, in a way, sort of
séiki	a century
zyuukyuu-séiki	the 19th century
gyoson	a fishing village
oorai	comings and goings, traffic
kyuusoku (na)	is rapid, swift, hasty
totonóu	is arranged, is in good order, is regulated
yuusuu no . . .	prominent, eminent, foremost, leading, distinguished . . .
ryookoo	a good harbor
kyakusen	a passenger boat
. . . nomi-nárazu = daké de náku(te)	not only . . . but [LITERARY]
kamotusen	a freighter, a cargo boat
yusoosen	an oil tanker
hattyaku	departure and arrival
syutunyúukoku	entry into and departure from the country
zeikan	a custom(s) house
niage suru	unloads
sóoko	a warehouse, a storehouse
nyuukoo suru	enters port, docks
kánri	administration, management, supervision, superintendence, control
zyooken	condition
suisin	the depth of water
kaitei	the bottom of the sea
ikari	an anchor
ikari o orósu	drops anchor
sa	difference, variance, disparity, inequality
syúhu	a capital (city)
syoohi	consumption, spending
syoohíti	a consumption area
gaikoo	an outer port
roku-daitósi	the Six Big Cities
koogyoo-títai	an industrial area, a manufacturing district
keikóogyoo	the light industry
zyuukóogyoo	the heavy industry
kagaku-kóogyoo	the chemical industry

1. Kankoo ‖kenkyuu ‖sonó-ta no│   It is for the purpose of sight-seeing,
   mokuteki désu   research, and other things

+ Rainiti simásita

→ Kankoo ‖kenkyuu ‖sonó-ta no mokuteki de‖rainiti simásita

They came to Japan

They came to Japan with (=for the purpose of) sight-seeing, research, and other things

2. Iwaba|Nihon no génkan ni ataru Yokohama
Iwaba is a LITERARY equivalent of ittára, used as a cliché in the modern written language.

Yokohama—equivalent, so to speak, to Japan's entrance-hall

3. A $\begin{Bmatrix} \bar{g}a \\ wa \end{Bmatrix}$‖B ni ataru

A corresponds to (=functions as) B

4. (. . .) Yokohama mo

even Yokohama (=the very Yokohama) (which . . .)

5. Sétubi $\bar{g}$a|(yóku|) totonóu

Hito $\bar{g}$a|sétubi o|totonoéru

The facilities are (well)arranged/prepared

People prepare/arrange the facilities

6. X ni nátte iru

It has become X and it is [now] X

7. X $\begin{Bmatrix} \text{nomi-nárazu} \\ \text{daké zya|nákute} \end{Bmatrix}$ ‖Y |Z mo| óoi

Not only X, but also Y and Z are numerous

8. $\begin{Bmatrix} \text{Íka ni mo} \\ \text{Hontoo ni} \end{Bmatrix}$|X rasíi

It is really like X

9. X ni tekisúru
Ikari o orósu no ni|tekisúru

It is suitable for X
It is suitable for lowering anchor

10. A dé ari ‖B dé mo áru X

X which is A and also is B

11. Rikuzyoo-kóotuu no|bén $\bar{g}$a|íi

Land-transportation facilities are good

12. Tokyoo-Yokohamá-kan
= Tokyoo to Yokohama no aida

between Tokyo and Yokohama

Lesson 24

syukusáizitu	a public holiday
X o sadaméru	decides/determines/appoints X
ganzitu	New Year's Day
X o iwáu/ióo	celebrates/commemorates/congratulates X
seizin = otona	an adult, a grown-up person
X o zikaku suru	becomes X, is aware of X
A o haḡemásu	encourages/urges A, gives encouragement to A
syunbun	the vernal equinox
ikímono	a living thing, a (living) creature
X o tataéru	praises/extols/admires X
X o aisúru	loves X, is fond of X
tennóo	the Emperor
kénpoo	a constitution, constitutional law, organic law
kinénbi	a memorial day, commemoration day
árata (na) = atarasíi	is new, fresh, novel [LITERARY]
árata ni = atarásiku	newly
seityoo	growth, increment
X o kisúru	expects/anticipates/hopes for X
zinkaku	character, personality, individuality
X o omonzíru/omonzúru	attaches importance to X
koohuku (na)	is happy, felicitous, is fortunate
X o hakáru	plans/devises/design X
zídoo	a child, a juvenile, boys and girls, children
X to tómo ni	(together) with X
X ni kánsya suru	thanks/appreciates X
syuubun	the autumnal equinox
sósen	an ancestor, a forefather, one's forbears
X o uyamáu	respects/reveres/honors X
X o sinóbu	recalls/recollects X
ziyúu (na)	is free, liberal, unrestricted
heiwa (na)	is peaceful, pacific
X o takaméru	promotes/advances/elevates X
kinroo	labor, exertion
X o tattóbu/tootóbu	values X, sets a (high) value on X

1. Hi o sadaméru   They fix/set/designate the day

    Hi ḡa | sadameraréru   The day gets fixed/designated/set-
                                         tled

    Hi ḡa | sadamerárete iru   The day is fixed

2. Note that Haḡemásu 'He encourages [them]' is the PLAIN form; the PO-
LITE form is Haḡemasimásu. Compare Haḡemásu the polite form of
Haḡéru 'He gets bald.'

3. X ḡa | $\begin{Bmatrix} \text{árata ni} \\ \text{atarásiku} \end{Bmatrix}$ | okonaware-   X was newly put into effect
    másita

4. Háha ni | kánsya simasu   They thank (= show gratitude to)
                                         mothers

    (Taḡai ni |) kánsya | si-aimásu   They give thanks to each other (mutu-
                                          ally)
                                          = They show mutual gratitude

5. A o ái-su [LITERARY] = ai-súru   loves A
     X o kí-su [LITERARY] = ki-súru   expects X
     X o omonzúru [LITERARY]   attaches importance to X
        = omonzíru

Lesson 25

getumatu	the end of the month
dattósan	a "Datsun" (a Japanese compact car)
X o hipparidásu = X o	takes/gets X out, drags out X
hikidásu	
muzíko no	is without an accident, trouble-free
zíko	an accident
seiseki	record, showing, result, score
o-tómo	<u>tomo</u>: an attendant, a companion; a retinue
otómo suru	goes along with, accompanies
Tíba = Tibá-ken	Chiba prefecture (east of Tokyo)
kaiḡan	the seashore, the coast, the seaside
Kuzyuukúri	Kuzyuukuri ("99 League") Beach
-ri	Japanese league (= 2.44 miles)
zyooténki	fine weather, splendid weather
utaḡai	doubt, uncertainty, a question
X o utaḡáu	doubts/questions X, has a doubt about X
móohu	a blanket
keito	woolen yarn, knitting wool
X o yóoi suru	prepares/arranges X

1. sore de ne . . .   And so, then, you see

2. Issyo ni ({ sitára / ittára })|dóo desu ka   How about ({ doing it / going }) together?

3. Turete iké { tte / to } iu   [She] says "take [me] along" = [She]
                                                           asks me to take [her] along

4. Áni o|hippari-dasimásita   I dragged my brother out

5. muzíko { tte / to } iu seiseki   a [driving-]record without accidents

6. sore wa sore wa   Well, well . . .
   [showing one is overwhelmed by
   an honor or favor]

7. { Ikóo tte|itte 'rú n desu / Ikóo to|itte irú (no desu) }   [We] are talking of going

8. Hito ḡa|zidóosya ni noru   People get [ride] in the car
   (Hito ḡa)|hatí-nin|(zidóosya ni)   Eight people can get in (the car)
     noreru

9. tízu de|míru to . . .   when one looks at it with a map . . .

10. sotira = anáta (no tokoro)   there, where you are, your place
    kotira = watakusi (no tokoro)   here, where I am, my place
    atira = anó hito (no tokoro)   there, where he/she is, his/her place

11. kuraku náru made ni (wa)   by the time it gets dark

12. Hosi ḡa|takusan demásita   Lots of stars came out
    Hosi ḡa|takusan déte imasu   Lots of stars are out

13. Nási [LITERARY] = Nái   There are none
     Utaǧai nási desu   There are no doubts

14. X o yóoi suru   prepare/equip oneself with X

15. X o tanosími ni suru   looks forward to X

Lesson 26

íryoo	clothing
X ni tuide	next to X, second only to X, after X
hituzyuhin	a necessity, a requisite, an essential, a necessary article
sén'i	a fiber, textiles
kawá	the skin, the integument; leather, bark, rind, peel
asá	flax, hemp
nuno	cloth
nitiyoo no . . .	of daily use, used everyday
siyóoryoo	the amount used, the quantity consumed
siyoo suru	uses, consumes
mottómo	most, -est
óo	a king
A o X to syoosúru	calls/names A 'X'
seiketu (na)	is clean, neat
hadazáwari	the touch, the feel (to the skin)
háda	the skin
sawaru	touches, feels
ánka (na)	is inexpensive, cheap, low-priced, low-cost
íto	thread, yarn, filament, gut
ménka	raw cotton, cotton wool
itiryuu no . . .	first-class, top-ranking . . .
kettén	a fault, a defect, a flaw, a weak point
hoon	keeping warm, heat insulation
wázuka (na)	is few, little, scanty, trifling
reigai	an exception
hituzi	a sheep
yútaka (na)	is abundant, plentiful, ample, rich
bokusóoti	a pasture (land)
X o káu	raises/rears X, keeps (an animal)
genmoo	raw wool
káiko	a silkworm
máyu	a cocoon
kíito	raw silk
zeitáku (na)	is luxurious, extravagant, lavish
hukugyoo	a side job
yoosan	sericulture
husoku	insufficiency, shortage, deficiency, deficit
X o ogináu	compensates (makes up) for X
párupu	pulp
réeyon	rayon
sekitansan	carbolic acid
gooseihin	a synthetic product, a compound/composite product
goosei suru	synthesizes, compounds
sínpo	evolution
kyoosoo	competition, contest, race
kairyoo	improvement, betterment, reform

dóryoku suru   does one's best, endeavors
sisaku   trial manufacture
hatubai suru   sales

1. Íryoo $\begin{Bmatrix} \bar{g}a \\ wa \end{Bmatrix}$ | syokuryoo ni tuḡi-   Clothing ranks next after/to food
   másu

   + Íryoo wa | zyuuyoo désu   Clothing is important

   → Íryoo $\begin{Bmatrix} \bar{g}a \\ wa \end{Bmatrix}$ | syokuryoo ni tuide ‖   Clothing ranks next in importance
   zyuuyoo désu   after food

2. Sono daihyooteki na monó wa ‖   Their representative items are A,
   A ‖ B ‖ C ‖ óyobi ‖ D de aru   B, C, and D

3. Asá kara | tótta | sén'i desu   They are fibers taken from flax
   + Sén'i de | ótta | nuno désu   It is cloth woven from fibers
   → Asá kara | tótta | sén'i de | ótta | It is cloth woven from fibers taken
   nuno désu   from flax

4. Siyóoryoo $\begin{Bmatrix} \bar{g}a \\ no \end{Bmatrix}$ | mottómo | óoi no   The one whose amount of use is
   wa ‖ momen de áru   greatest is cotton

5. (Hito ḡa) | momen o | íryoo no | óo   People call cotton the king of cloth
   to | syoosimásu

   Momen ḡa | íryoo no | óo to | syoo-   Cotton is/gets called the king of cloth
   saremásu (PASSIVE)

6. Tabi-tabi | araimásu   They wash it frequently
   + Seiketu ni si-yasúi desu   It is easy to clean
   + Zyoobu désu   It is durable

   + Hadazáwari mo | $\begin{Bmatrix} íi \\ yói \end{Bmatrix}$ desu   The feel to the skin is also good

   + . . . ué ni   in addition to (being/doing) . . .
   + Ánka desu   It is inexpensive
   → Tabi-tabi aratte | seiketu ni si-   In addition to the fact that it is easy
   yásuku ‖ zyoobu de ‖ hadazáwari   to clean by frequent washing, that
   mo | yói ue ni ‖ ánka desu   it is durable, and that the feel to the
                                    skin is also good, it is inexpensive

7. Ménka o yunyuu simásu   They import raw cotton
   X to Y ni yorimásu   They rely/depend on X and Y
   Z to nátte imasu   They have come to be [considered] Z
   Ménka o yunyuu si ‖ X to Y ni   They import raw cotton; and relying
   yori ‖ Z to nátte imasu   on X and Y, they have come to be
                                    [considered] Z

8. X to site ‖ nákute wa | naránai | It is indispensable as X
   monó de aru

9. Wázuka no reiḡai wa | betu désu   A few [trifling] exceptions are sepa-
                                    rate

   → Wázuka no reiḡai wa | betu to   Excluding a few [trifling] exceptions,
   site, ...

10. Hituzi no ke o | íto ni suru   They make wool into thread
    Hituzi no ke o | íto ni site | ótta | It is cloth woven with the thread made
    nuno désu   from wool

11. tekísu [LITERARY] = tekisúru   is suitable
    Kikoo ḡa | hituzi o káu no ni | The climate is suitable for the rais-
    tekísu   ing of sheep

    Kikoo $\begin{Bmatrix} no \\ \bar{g}a \end{Bmatrix}$ | hituzi o káu no ni | (It is) Japan, whose climate is not
    tekisánai | Nihón (desu)   suitable for the raising of sheep

12. X ni (wa) | kaḡirí ḡa arimasu   There is a limit to X

13. Réeyon $\begin{Bmatrix} \bar{g}a \\ wa \end{Bmatrix}$ | párupu o | genryóo   Rayon had pulp for its raw material

    $\begin{Bmatrix} to \\ ni \end{Bmatrix}$ sita

    → Párupu o | genryóo $\begin{Bmatrix} to \\ ni \end{Bmatrix}$ sita | (It is) rayon, which took pulp for its
    réeyon (desu)   raw material

14. Sén'i ḡa | tukuraremásita   Fibers got made
    Sén'i ḡa | tukuraréru yoo ni | Fibers came to be made
    narimásita

15. nan-bai mo   ever so many times
    kínu no nan-bai mo | tuyói desu   It is every so many times stronger
         than silk

16. Kákkoku | kyoosoo désu   It is worldwide competition
    + X ni dóryoku simasu   They strive for X
    + (Tuḡí-tuḡi ni) | Y ḡa | hatubai   Y are put on sale (one after another)
    sarete imásu

    → Kákkoku | kyoosoo de ‖ X ni dóryoku   They strive for X in worldwide com-
    si ‖ (tuḡí-tuḡi ni) | Y ḡa | hatubai   petition, and Y are put on sale (one
    sarete imásu   after another

Lesson 27

katyoo	the head of a family, a patriarch, a matriarch
kénri	a right, a claim
siháisya	a ruler, a master, an administrator
sîhai suru	rules, dominates, manages, controls
sóozoku suru	succeeds, inherits
tyoonán	the eldest (oldest) son
yooiku suru	brings (a child) up
sekinin	responsibility, accountability, liability
intai	retirement (from active/public life)
zyóretu	rank, grade, order
nyuuyoku	taking a bath, bathing
huzin	a lady, a woman
túma	a wife
otto	a husband
hukuzyuu suru	obeys
dootoku	morality, morals
kakei	a family line, a family tree, lineage
kakusiki	status, social standing
zyootai	a condition, the state (of things), a situation, an aspect
tóonin	the person in question, the person concerned, the man himself
ísi	will, volition
X o musi suru	takes no account of X, ignores X
dookyo suru	lives together, lives in the same house
nitizyoo no . . .	daily, every-day, ordinary . . .
tyóosyo	a strong point, a good point, a merit
syuuto	a father-in-law, a mother-in-law
yome	a (young) wife, a daughter-in-law
roozín	an old (aged) person
sisoo	thought, an idea
masatu	chafing, rubbing, friction
sîba-siba = tabi-tabi	often
byoodoo no . . .	equal, even, impartial . . .
kyooryoku suru	cooperates
koodoo suru	acts, conducts
tádasi	but, however
nezuyóku	firmly, steadfastly, inveterately
nezuyói	is strong, firm, deep-seated, deep-rooted

1. -ḡo = . . . no áto, . . . sita áto   after . . .
   titi no sí-ḡo   after the father's death
   kekkon-ḡo   after marriage
   (sono) intai-ḡo   after (his) retirement
   syuusen-ḡo   after the end of the war
   ANTONYM: -zen = . . . no máe,   before . . .
     . . . suru máe

2. A ‖matá wa│B wa   As for A or B

3. kodomo no uti kara   from the time of childhood

Note: uti here is equivalent to tokí or aida (compare wakái uti ni 'while young'). Uti ni can also mean 'within (a certain time)': mikka no uti = mikka-ínai 'within three days.' You are familiar with the other meaning of uti 'among, in the midst of' (= náka): Kodomó-tati no uti de‖dáre ḡa itiban│ookii ka 'Who is the biggest of the children?' With the PARTI-CLE kara, uti can also have this meaning, provided the following VERB is one that calls for kara: Kodomo(-tati) no uti kara‖hitóri│eránde kudasai 'Choose one of (from among) the children.'

4. íkka no . . .   . . . of the whole family

5. kaikatu (na)   is lively
    genkaku (na)   is strict
    hukuzatu (na)   is complicated
    zettai-teki (na)   is absolute
    hooritu-teki (na)   is legal
    hosyu-teki (na)   is conservative

6. . . . surú no ḡa│dootoku de átta   It was the virtuous thing to do to . . .

Note: The word dootoku takes no as a modifier: Dootoku no hazu da 'It ought to be virtuous,' but its opposite takes na: Hu-dóotoku na hazu da 'It ought to be unvirtuous.'

7. . . . monó mo│kánari│átta   There were a fair number of regular
                                                     happenings such that . . .
                                                     There used to be quite a bit of (doing)

Note: monó here means 'usual situation, frequent happening, habitual doing.'

8. . . . sita monó ḡa│óokatta   There were many cases where they
                                                     did . . . , there were many people
                                                     who did . . .

9. X ḡa│nái koto wa│nái ḡa, . . .   Is not completely lacking in X; DOES
                                                     have SOME X, to be sure, but . . .

10. . . . sita kotó mo│síba-siba│   The experience of having it happen was
        átta   frequent; It often happened that . . .

11. Masatu ḡa okóru   A friction arises
  + Hukuzatu na mondai ni náru   It becomes a difficult problem
  → Masatu ḡa okóri,‖hukuzatu na   A friction arises, and becomes a dif-
      mondai ni náru   ficult problem . . .

12. . . . ≤ka   under (the system, power, era, etc.)
                                                     of . . .

13. uti tó wa = uti to iú no wa   what is meant by "home"

14. Kaikatu da   It is happy
  + Ziyúu da   It is free
  → Kaikatu de‖ziyúu da   It is happy and free
  → Kaikatu de‖ziyúu ni│náru   It becomes happy and free
    . . . nátta   It has become . . .
  → . . . natta to iwareru   It is said (reported) that it has be-
                                                     come . . .

    cf. . . . to ieru   It can be said that . . .

Lesson 28

sararíiman	a salaried man, a white collar worker
nyuusya	entering (=joining) a company
gekkyúu	a monthly salary
P ni kaketukeru	rushes/runs/hastens to P
muré	a group, a crowd, a throng
man'in no . . .	. . . with no vacancy, full (house, car, etc.)
osiái hesiái	hustling and jostling
zikayóosya	an automobile for one's personal/private use
	a private automobile
zikayoo no . . .	private . . . ; . . . for the use of one's own family
tuukin suru	commutes (to work)
yumé	a dream, a reverie
syorui	a document, a paper
X o ou	chases/pursues X, runs after X
eiyóosi	a dietitian, a nutritionist
eiyoo	nutrition
károrii	a calory, a calorie
X o keisan suru	calculates/counts X
sanpo suru	takes a walk
gassyóodan	a choir, a chorus, a singing group
gassyoo suru	sing in chorus
soodan	consultation, conference, discussion
raikyaku	a caller, a visitor, a guest
koosei	the welfare of the people, public welfare
syukúsya	quarters, lodgings, residence, billet, dormitory
kínken	neighboring prefectures
kenkoo (na)	is healthy.
eisei	hygiene, sanitation
yoboo	prevention, protection (against), precaution
imu-ka	the medical affairs division
ímu	medical affairs
néssin (na)	is enthusiastic, assiduous, eager, ardent
A o sidoo suru	guides/leads A
íin	a member of a committee, a delegate
kánbu	the management, the governing body, the managing staff, the executive
tóogi suru	discusses, debates
róosi	capital and labor, labor and management

1. X to doozi ni	at the same time with/as X; together with X
2. Gesyuku-séikatu desu	It is boardinghouse life
3. kakéru	runs
kake-tukeru	runs (to the spot or scene)
4. X o arasóu	struggles for X
5. osu	pushes

osi-áu   jostles, pushes each other

osi-ái   a jostle

osi-ái|hesi-ái [SLANG, hesi-au   pushing and shoving each other
and hesu do not exist]

6. kómu   gets crowded/packed

→ kónde iru   is crowded

   VERB-(i)-kómu   (does) in

   nori-kómu   boards and enters (also 'rides/
                              drives in')

   nomi-kómu   swallows down, drinks in

7. X no muré de|man'in dá   It is full with a crowd of X (= 'It is
                          a crowd of X and so it is full.')

8. zíka   a private home, one's own home

→ zíka no . . .   private . . . (for family only)

+ (-)yoo . . .   (for the) use (of . . .)

→ zika-yoo   for private (family) use

+ -sya   car

→ zikayóo-sya   private automobile

9. . . . surú no ḡa|bóku no|yumé   It is my dream to do . . .
   da

10. A ḡa B o ou   A pursues B

   B ḡa A ni owareru   B gets pursued by A

   denwa to syorui ni oware(te) is pursued by phone calls and docu-
                           ments, and . . .

11. . . . suru mono, . . . suru mono, some doing . . . , some doing . . . ,
   . . . suru mono, sorézore . . . some doing . . . (we all) various-
                         ly . . .

Note the use of a comma instead of a PARTICLE (to or ya) to show the
series, the omission of any PARTICLE at the end of the series (we might
expect to or wa), and the lack of specific topic or subject (we would expect watakusí-tati or the like).

12. Tokí o|suḡósu   [We] pass (time)

   X o suḡósu   overdoes X

   nesuḡósu   oversleeps

13. A ya|B ‖C nado de   There is A and B, and C and so on,
                         and . . .

Note the use of a comma to show a wider break in the series than a PARTI-
CLE would show.

14. a. Syukúsya o|kentiku site iru They are building dormitories

  → Syukúsya o|kentiku-tyuu dá They are (in the midst of) building
                             dormitories

This is possible for any suru-NOUN.

   b. -tyuu   during (a time)

     gozen-tyuu   during the morning

     sensoo-tyuu   during the war

cf. -zyuu 'all through (a place or time)' as in <u>Tookyoo-zyuu</u> 'all over Tokyo,' <u>itiniti-zyuu</u> 'all through the whole day, all day long.' A minimal contrast is shown by <u>Yasumi-tyuu</u> '(in) the midst of resting' and <u>Yasumi-zyuu</u>
'all through the holiday.'

15. X ni túite│sidoo site iru | They guide [them] with respect to X

16. -in | member
    kumiái-in | union member
    (kai)syá-in | staff member, employee
    kaiin | member (of a society)
    ten'in | clerk (in a shop)
    zimú-in | clerk (in an office)
    íin | committee member(s)
    sen'in | sailor, crew(man)

17. róo-si = roodoo to sihon | labor and capital (management)
    roosi-kánkei | labor-management relations
    roosi-kyóoryoku | labor-management cooperation
    róosi kyooryoku suru | engages in labor-management cooper-
    ation

18. koohuku (no tamé) ni ‖ doryoku | strives (works) for happiness
    suru

Lesson 29

Syóowa	the Showa Era (1926 --)
hakkoo suru	comes into effect
zenbun	a preamble
kazyoo	an article, a clause, an item
kityoo	the keynote, the underlying tone, the basis
séisin	mind, spirit, sentiment
kénryoku	power, authority, influence
kanzen (na)	is perfect, complete, consummate
hitei suru	denies
kokusei	(national) administration, government
syokunoo	function
sinsei (na)	is sacred, holy, divine
koogóo	an empress
ningen	a human (being), a mortal
B ni sitasímu	grows intimate with B, makes friends with B
seizitu (na)	is sincere, faithful, honest
X o kikyuu suru	seeks/hunts X, quests for X
eikyuu no . . .	eternal, permanent, perpetual . . .
gúntai	the troops, armed forces
hózi	maintenance, preservation, retention
koosénken	the right to join a war, the right of belligeren-cy
X o mitomeru	recognizes X, approves of X
hukoku kyoohei	national prosperity and military strength, wealth and military power (of a state)
tyúu koo	loyalty and filial piety
zín gi	humanity and justice, benevolence and righteousness
hakuai	philanthropy, charity, benevolence, humanity
kyootyoo suru	emphasizes, stresses
ríeki	profit, gain(s), return(s)
X o nobéru = X o hanásu/iu	states/explains X, expresses (one's opinion)
kihonteki (na)	is fundamental, basic
zinken	human rights, the rights of man
sontyoo	respect, esteem, deference
kénti	a standpoint, a viewpoint, an angle
kízoku	the nobility, the peerage, the aristocracy
sénkyo	election, voting
kokkai = gikai	the Diet

1. X kara nátte iru   is composed (made up) of X

    X $\left\{\begin{matrix} \text{ga} \\ \text{wa} \end{matrix}\right\}$ | Y kara | náru   X comes from (originates in) Y

    X ga | Y o násu   X forms (creates, makes, makes up) Y

2. syuken zaimin   "the ruling power rests with the peo-
    [a typical COMPOUND NOUN   ple"="popular sovereignty"
    made up from a classical Chinese
    sentence]

3. X ni kansúru Y

   X ni kánsite

Y which has to do with (= concerns)
  X
concerning X

4. X ni óite wa
   (1) X ni/de wa
   (2) X wa
   (3) X ni kánsite (wa)
  X ni okéru Y
   (1) X no Y
   (2) X ni áru Y

   (3) X no baai no Y

at/in X
as for X
concerning X

Y which is X
Y which is in X; Y which is a
  part/member of X
Y which is (on) the occasion of X

These are SEMI-LITERARY clichés; óite is from oite, the GERUND
of oku 'puts'; okéru . . . is a LITERARY PERFECT MODIFIER equivalent
to COLLOQUIAL oita . . . '. . . which has been put.'

5. A o|X to suru

  A ḡa|X to sarete iru

  Tennóo wa|kámi to sarete ita

treats A as X; considers A to be X;
  thinks of A as X
A is thought of (considered, treated
  as) X
The emperor was thought of as a god

6. Tennóo ${\text{ḡa} \atop \text{wa}}$|zettaiteki na
  kénryoku o|mótte ita
  Tennóo ḡa|mótte ita|zettaiteki
  na kénryoku ${\text{wa} \atop \text{ḡa}}$|hitei sarete
  iru
  X ni kansúru Y (see No. 3)
  Tennóo ḡa|mótte ita X wa|hitei
  sare‖tennóo wa|Y o motánai
  koto ḡa|sadamerárete iru

The emperor had absolute power

The absolute power which the emper-
  or possessed is denied

Y concerning X
It's decided that X which the emper-
  or formerly possessed is denied
  and it is decided that the emperor is
  not to possess Y

7. sitasimaréru yoo ni|nátta

has come to be loved

8. X mo mitomete 'nái
  Sin-kénpoo ni|óite wa‖A o
  kikyuu si‖B o sadáme‖C mo
  D mo|mitomete nái

They do not recognize X either
Under the new consitution it aspires
  for A, decides B, and recognizes
  neither C nor D

9. X o mokuteki to suru
  X o mokuteki to sita Y
  cf. Y wa X to iu mokuteki de . . .

makes/considers X one's aim
Y which has made X its aim
Y is for the purpose of X and . . .

10. X o Y to/ni kuraberu

compares X with/to Y

11. mattaku hantai da
  mattaku hantai no heiwa

is completely opposite
peace which is the complete opposite
  (of it)

12. Kyuu-kénpoo ni|óite wa‖A‖B‖
  C nado‖X ya Y ḡa|kyootyoo
  sarete ita

In the old constitution X and Y which
  were represented by A, B, C and others were stressed

13. X o tyuusin ni = X o tyuusin ni   Taking X for its heart/center = with
    site   X for its center, centering on/
                                                  around X

14. X de aru Y [FORMAL STYLE] =   Y which is X
    X no/na Y
    Nihon-kókumin de aru│seizin-   Adult men and women who are Jap-
    dánzyo   anese citizens

15. Sénkyo ni yori = Sénkyo ni yotte   with (= by means of) elections
    = sénkyo de

16. Kokkai o tuuzite   going through the [instrumentality
                                                  of the] Diet

17. Dekíru koto ni│nátte iru   It is arranged that they can,
                                              it is arranged that they get to be
                                                  able to (do)

Lesson 30

kóobutu	the mineral
hyoohónsitu	a speciment room/gallery
hyoohon	a specimen
koosánbutu	a mineral product
dóo	copper
tetu	iron, steel
sekitán	coal
sekiyu	petroleum, kerosene
sansyutu suru	produces
zikyuu	self-support/-supply
ekitai	a liquid, fluid
nenryóo	fuel
gen'yu	crude petroleum
Arabia	Arabia
tooka-yoo	use for lamplight
nainen-kíkan	an internal combustion engine
hatumei	invention, contrivance
dooryoku-yoo	use for (motive) power
gómu	gum, rubber
seizoo	manufacture, production, making
tahóomen	many quarters, many directions, various fields
yuden	an oil field; a petroleum well
kaihatu	development, exploitation
timanako no . . .	bloodshot-eyed, frantic, frenzied, wild . . .
timanako ni náru	becomes frantic, gets wild
tanden	a coal field
soogaku	the total amount
tisitu	geology, geological features, (the nature of) the soil
gen'in	a cause, a factor; the origin, the source
tanmyaku	a coal seam
oogákari (na)	is large-scale, elaborate
saitan suru	mines coal
hukánoo (na)	is impossible, unattainable
kanoo (na)	is possible
nooritu	efficiency
gensi-teki (na)	is primitive, primeval, archaic
syuttánryoo	the output of coal
tîsiki	knowledge, knowhow, learning attainments
kákusyu no . . .	every kind of, all sorts of, various . . .
yakuhin	medicines, drugs, medical supplies
zyúsi	resin, rosin
tukaimiti	a use, a way to use
X o kakudai suru	spreads/expands/enlarges X

1. wá ga kuni (see Voc. L. 15)   our country

2. . . . to iwareru hodo   to the extent that it is said to be . . .

3. taitei no (monó)   the usual (things); most (things)

4. X o sansyutu suru   They produce X
   X wa sansyutu suru   X they produce

5. izure [LITERARY] = dóre, dótti   which one
   izure mo   both/all of them

6. si-ḡatái = si-nikúi   it is difficult to do
   ariḡatái   'is grateful/obliged' from 'it is hard
                          to have (= bear)'

7. A wa | P kara yunyuu suru   A imports it from P; He imports A from P
   B wa | Q kara yunyuu suru   B imports it from Q; He imports B from Q
   A wa | P kara yunyuu site ‖ B wa | A imports it from P and B imports it from
      Q kara yunyuu suru   Q; He imports A from P and he im-
                          ports B from Q

   A wa | P kara ‖ B wa | Q kara yunyuu   A imports it from P, and B from Q; He
      suru   imports A from P, and B from Q

8. Ooḡákari na hoohoo   a large scale method
 + kikaika sita hoohoo   a mechanized method
 → ooḡákari na | kikaika sita hoohoo   a large scale mechanized method
   cf. ooḡákari ni kikaika sita   a method which has been mechanized
      hoohoo   on a large scale

9. X ni | timanako ni náru   gets red-eyed in pursuit of X, makes
                          desperate efforts for X

10. X ḡa gen'in de   with X as the cause; owing to X

11. Hoohoo { wa / ḡa } | nooritu ḡa   The way (of doing) is inefficient
     agaranai

[→ Nooritu no aḡaranai hoohoo da   It is an inefficient way

   Hoohoo { ḡa / wa } | gensi-teki da   The way (of doing) is primitive

+ [→ Gensi-teki na hoohoo da   It is a primitive way
 [Nooritu no aḡaranai | gensi-teki   It is an inefficient and primitive way
     na hoohoo da

   → Nooritu no aḡaranai | gensi-teki   By inefficient and primitive means,
     na hoohoo de, ...

[Dai-búbun ḡa | saitan site iru   The majority is mined or Almost all
                          of them are mined

+ [Nooritu no aḡaranai | gensi-teki   It is mined by inefficient and primi-
     na hoohoo de | saitan site iru   tive means

→   Dai-búbun ḡa | nooritu no aḡara-
     nai | gensi-teki na hoohoo de ‖
     saitan site iru =
   (1) Dai-búbun (no | tanden no hitó-   Almost all of them (the coalmine
      bito) ḡa . . . saitan site iru   people) mine by . . .
   (2) Dai-búbun (no | sekitán) ḡa . . .   The majority (of the coal) is mined
      saitan sarete iru   by . . .

Note: In long sentences when the VERB is well removed from the subject,
an intended PASSIVE is sometimes forgotten; strictly speaking, the sentence is "ungrammatical" in Meaning 2 (which was the meaning intended

by the writer) unless we change the PARTICLE g̱a to o̱ or produce the proper
PASSIVE.

12. sínpo ni yori = sínpo ni yotte   with (by means of) progress
       = sínpo de

13. suru íḡai ni = suru hoka ni   in addition to doing

14. si-tútu aru [LITERARY] = site   is doing, is in process of doing
       iru (totyuu/tokoró da) [COL-
       LOQUAL]
       VERB-i-tutu = VERB-i-naḡara   while doing; though doing
       nomi-tútu kataru [LITERARY]   talks over a drink
         = nomi-náḡara|hanásu
       (cf. Note 17, Lesson 16)

Lesson 31

táiyoo	the sun
kooten suru	moves around the sun
X ḡa meḡuru	X comes around, returns
Y o meḡuru	has to do with Y, (surrounds Y)
	is connected/involved with Y
hóndo	the mainland, the country proper
taihúu	a typhoon
sísya	a dead person, the deceased, the dead
boohúuu	a rainstorm, a storm
yatte kúru	comes along/around, it/one turns/shows up,
	makes its/one's appearance
tatimati no . . .	instant, immediate, instantaneous . . .
teiden	interruption of electric current, power failure
mizen ni	before (anything) happens
sítudo	humidity
kiatu	atmospheric (barometric) pressure
kookíatu	high atmospheric pressure
teikíatu	low atmospheric pressure
úryoo	rainfall
kisyoodai	a meteorological observatory, a weather sta-tion
sokkoozyo	a meteorological station, a local weather bureau
séiu	fair or rainy weather, rain or shine, weather conditions
kazamuki	the direction of the wind
huusoku	the velocity of the wind
tooatusen	an isobar, an isobaric line
íti	a situation, a position, a location, a place
X o kiroku suru	records X
tyuuóo no . . .	central, middle . . .
X o seisaku suru	manufactures/produces/makes X
idoo	movement, transfer, locomotion

1. Tikyuu ḡa | ziten suru   The earth rotates around its axis
→ Tikyuu no ziten da   It is the rotation of the earth

2. $\left\{\begin{matrix}A\\x\end{matrix}\right\}$ ḡa | $\left\{\begin{matrix}B\\Y\end{matrix}\right\}$ ni | sitaḡau   A/X obeys B/Y; A/X complies with (accedes/agrees to) B/Y; A/X follows (accompanies) B/Y

    X ni sitaḡatte   in accordance with X, in conformity to X

    Compare:
    sitaḡatte   consequently, accordingly

3. X ḡa | hénka suru   X changes
→ X no hénka da   It is the change(s) of/in X

4. huuḡai   storm damage
+ suiḡai   flood damage
→ huu, súi-ḡai   storm and flood damage

5. Songai $\left\{\begin{matrix} \bar{g}a \\ wa \end{matrix}\right\}$ | huu-súigai ni yoru   The loss is due to storm and flood damage

   → Huu-súigai ni yoru songai da   It is loss due to storm and flood damage

6. Mainen da   It is every year
   → Mainen no yóo da   It seems to be every year
   → mainen no yóo ni   like every year; almost every year; yearly(-like)

7. Taihúu $\left\{\begin{matrix} \bar{g}a \\ wa \end{matrix}\right\}$ | hóndo ni zyooriku suru   The typhoons hit Japan proper

   → Hóndo ni | zyooriku suru | taihúu da   They are typhoons hitting Japan proper

8. Kentikúbutu $\left\{\begin{matrix} \bar{g}a \\ wa \end{matrix}\right\}$ | ryuusitu suru   The buildings are washed away

   + Hasí $\left\{\begin{matrix} \bar{g}a \\ wa \end{matrix}\right\}$ | ryuusitu suru   The bridges are washed away

   → Kentikúbutu ya | hasí $\left\{\begin{matrix} \bar{g}a \\ wa \end{matrix}\right\}$ | ryuusitu suru   The buildings and bridges [among other things] are washed away

   → Kentikúbutu ya | hasí no | ryuusitu da   It is the buildings and bridges being washed away

9. X wa | motíron da   X is obvious (goes without saying)
    X wa ‖ motíron | mare da   X of course (it goes without saying) is rare

   + Y sáe mare da   Even Y is rare

   → X wa | motíron ‖ Y sáe mare da   Even Y is rare, to say nothing of (not to mention) X

10. Kisyoo o kenkyuu suru   They study weather
   + Tentai o kenkyuu suru   They study heavenly bodies
   → Kisyoo ya | tentai o | kenkyuu suru   They study [such things as] weather and heavenly bodies

   → Kisyoo ya tentai no kenkyuu da   It is the study of weather and heavenly bodies; it is meteorological and astronomical study

11. Kagami no yóo da   It is like a mirror
   + Sízuka da   It is quiet
   → Kagami no yóo ni | sízuka da   It is quiet like a mirror

    Mizuúmi $\left\{\begin{matrix} \bar{g}a \\ wa \end{matrix}\right\}$ | kagami no yóo ni | sízuka da   The lake is calm as a mirror

    Kagami no yóo ni | sízuka na | mizuúmi da   It is a lake that is calm as a mirror

12. Táiyoo ga | téru   The sun shines
   → Táiyoo ga | tétte iru   The sun is shining
   → Táiyoo ga | tétte ita   The sun was shining
   → Tétte ita | táiyoo da   It is the sun that has (or had) been shining

13. Kúmo ḡa│táiyoo o│oóu   The clouds cover up the sun

   Taiyoo {ḡa / wa}│kúmo ni│oowaréru   The sun gets covered up by the clouds
   (PASSIVE)

14. É no yoo da   It is like a picture
   + Utukusíi   It is beautiful
   → É no yoo ni│utukusíi   It is pretty as a picture

   Huukei {ḡa / wa}│é no yoo ni│utukusíi   The scenery is pretty as a picture

   → É no yoo ni│utukusíi│húukei da   It is scenery that is pretty as a
                                           picture

15. Sanpo (suru) dókoro de wa│nái   Taking a walk is out of the question

16. Tanosimu (koto) dókoro de wa│   Enjoying it is out of the question
   nái

   → . . . náku(te)   Enjoying it is out of the question and
                                           . . .

   Compare:
   Tanosimu dókoro ka, . . .   Far from enjoying it, (on the contrary)
                                           . . .

   X dókoro ka│Y mo nái   Far from (having) X, he doesn't even
                                           have Y, He hasn't even got Y, much
                                           less X

17. X o sinpai suru   We worry about X
   X o sinpai sinákereba│naránai   We have to worry about X

18. Tetudoo-sénro ḡa│hutuu ni náru   Rail lines get disrupted
   + Densin ḡa│hutuu ni náru   The telegraph gets cut off
   + Denwa ḡa│hutuu ni náru   The telephone gets interrupted
   → Tetudoo-sénro, ‖densin, ‖denwa   The rail lines, telegraph, and tele-
     ḡa│hutuu ni náru   phone get disrupted
   Tetudoo-sénro ‖densin ‖denwa   It is a matter of . . . getting disrupted
     ḡa│hutuu ni náru no da
   Tetudoo-sénro ‖densin ‖denwa   We worry about the [matter of] the
     no hutuu ni náru no o│sinpai   rail lines, telegraph, and telephone
     suru   getting disrupted

19. X (suru kotó ḡa)│dekíreba ‖Y   If you can do X, it means that Y can
   dekíru wake da   be done

20. Ténki ḡa│hénka suru   The weather changes
   Ténki no│hénka da   It is the changes in weather
   Ténki no│hénka o│yoti suru   We foresee (forecast) the changes in
                                           weather

   Ténki no│hénka ḡa│yoti dekíru   The changes in weather can be fore-
                                           cast
   Ténki no│hénka ḡa│yoti dekíreba‖   If we can foresee the changes in
   . . . wáke da   weather, it means that . . .

21. Sinpai {ḡa / wa}│muyoo da   The worry is needless
   → Muyoo no sinpai da   It is needless worry
   Sinpai {ḡa / wa} iranai   Worry is not necessary

22. Saiḡai o boosi suru
    Saiḡai o boosi (suru kotó ḡa|)
    dekíru

We prevent disaster damage
We can prevent disaster damage

23. Sinpai ḡa iranai
  + Saiḡai ḡa|boosi dekíru
  → Sinpai mo írazu‖saiḡai mo boosi
    dekíru

Worry is not necessary
We can prevent disaster damage
We both avoid anxiety and are able
    to prevent disaster damage

24. kono hituyoo kara

(springing) from this necessity

25. Zikan ḡa ittei da
  → Ittei no zikan da
    Ittei no zikan ni|(hoosoo suru)

The time is fixed
It is a fixed (set regular) time
(They broadcast) at a regular time.

26. Tenki-yóhoo o hoosoo suru
    Tenki-yóhoo ḡa hoosoo sareru
    (PASSIVE)

They broadcast weather forecasts
Weather forecasts are broadcast

27. Tenkízu ḡa|déru
    . . . déte iru

A weather map appears
. . . keeps appearing, appears [reg-
    ularly]

Note. that déte iru can have two meanings: (1) Déru → Déte iru 'They keep appearing (regularly).' (2) Déta → Déte iru 'They are out (visible—as a result of having appeared).'
The same is true for most INTRANSITIVE VERBS as well as a number of TRANSITIVE VERBS:

    (1) Ikú—Gakkoo e itte iru   'He goes to school [regularly].'
    (2) Itta—Gakkoo e itte iru   'He is at school, He's gone off to school.'

28. X o kansatu suru
    X o kansatu site iru

We observe (study) X
We keep observing X, observe X
    regularly

    X o kansatu site iru to‖Y ḡa
    wakáru

When we observe X regularly, we
    understand Y

29. (Hito ḡa)|X to Y kara|tenki-
    yóhoo o|dásu

They (People) issue weather fore-
    casts from X and Y

  → Tenki-yóhoo ḡa|(hito ni)|X to
    Y kara|dasaréru
    . . . dasárete iru   (PASSIVE)
    X ya Y kara|dasárete iru|tenki-
    yóhoo da

Weather forecasts get issued (by
    people) from X and Y
    . . . get regularly issued
They are weather forecasts which
    get regularly issued by X and Y

30. A $\left\{ {ḡa \atop wa} \right\}$|X o motó ni site iru

A has taken X for its basis, A is
    based on X, A regularly bases it-
    self on X

31. (Kiatu $\left\{ {ḡa \atop wa} \right\}$|kákuti no da)

(The atmospheric pressure is of each
    place)

  → Kákuti no kiatu da

It is the atmospheric pressure of each
    place

+ Kimatta zikan no kiatu da

    It is the atmospheric pressure of a set time

→ Kákuti no│kimatta zikan no kiatu da

    It is the atmospheric pressure, at a set time, of each place

32. Ténki $\left\{ \begin{matrix} \bar{g}a \\ wa \end{matrix} \right\}$│sono tóki no da

    The weather is of that particular time

+ Ténki $\left\{ \begin{matrix} \bar{g}a \\ wa \end{matrix} \right\}$│hirói han'i no da

    The weather is of a wide area

→ Sono tóki no│hirói│hán'i no│ ténki da

    It is the weather, at that particular time, of a wide area

33. . . . (wakáru) yoo ni suru

   . . . yóo ni site iru

   . . . yóo ni│sita monó da

    arranges it so that you understand . . .

    . . . have arranged so that . . .

    It is the thing which they have arranged so that . . .

34. Húne $\bar{g}a$│kóokai site iru

   Húne $\bar{g}a$│kookai-tyuu da

→ Kookai-tyuu no húne da

    Ships are navigating/sailing

    Ships are under sail (at sea)

    It is the ship(s) at sea

35. Kisyoodai de│(hito $\bar{g}a$)│X ya Y kara│kansoku-kékka o│atuméru

    At the weather station they (people) gather the observation results from X and Y

   Kisyoodai de│(hito $\bar{g}a$)│X ya Y kara│atúmeta│kansoku-kékka da

    It is the observation results gathered (by people) from X and Y at the weather station

Note: A better translation treats <u>kisyoodai</u> as the subject; <u>de</u> often substitutes for $\bar{g}a$ when the subject is an organization or an impersonal body.

36. X $\left\{ \begin{matrix} wa \\ \bar{g}a \end{matrix} \right\}$│Y ni motozúku $\left(= X \left\{ \begin{matrix} \bar{g}a \\ wa \end{matrix} \right\}\right|$ Y o motó ni site iru)

   Y ni motozúite Z o suru

    X is based on Y

    They do Z on the basis of Y

37. . . . $\bar{g}$óto ni

   Zikan $\bar{g}$óto ni

   ittei-zikan $\bar{g}$óto ni

    every . . .

    every hour

    every designated hour (or time)

38. X o tukúru koto ni yoru

   X o tukúru koto ni yotte│Y o siru

    It is due to the construction of X

    You learn (find out) Y by creating X

39. Dénpa o tukau

  + Zyookuu no zyootai o│kansoku suru

  → Dénpa o tukatte‖zyookuu no zyootai o│kansoku suru

    They use radio waves (= radar)

    They investigate the conditions of the sky (= the upper air)

    They use radar to investigate the condition of the sky

40. Síryoo kara│yohoo o happyoo site iru

    They regularly publish forecasts from their data.

Lesson 32

syozyoo	a letter
haḡaki	a postcard
eháḡaki	a picture postcard
kozútumi	a parcel, a package
zíḡyoo	an undertaking, an enterprise, an activity
kokuei	government management/operation; government-run
saisyo no . . .	the first, initial . . .
kitte	a postage stamp
hakkoo suru	issues, publishes, puts into circulation
hikyaku	a postman of bygone days (an express messenger)
bánkoku yuubin renḡoo- zyóoyaku	Universal Postal Union Treaty
bánkoku	world nations, all nations, all countries on earth
zyooyaku	treaty, an agreement, a pact
kookuu	aviation, flying, aerial navigation
kookuu-(yúu)bin	an air mail
syuuhai	collection and delivery
hutatabi	again, twice, a second time, once more/again
haitatu	delivery, distribution
kúbun	division, section, subdivision
mitizyun	a route, an itinerary, the way
X o kumitatéru	constructs/frames/assembles X
kobetu no . . .	. . . of each house
kobetu ni	from house to house, from door to door
rinzi no . . .	temporal, provisional . . .
kawase	a money order, money exchange
tyokin	savings, a deposit
hurikae	change, transfer
nenkin	an annuity, a pension
onkyuu	a pension
kan'i-hóken	postal life insurance
kan'i (na)	is simple, easy, plain
senpoo	the other party/side
sokutatu	express delivery
naiyoo	contents, substance
syoomei	proof, evidence, testimony, attestation
tuuzyoo no . . .	normal, common, general

1. Monó o│kankoo suru   They publish things

    Kankóobutu da   It is a publication

    Kankóobutu $\begin{Bmatrix} \bar{g}a \\ wa \end{Bmatrix}$│téiki no da   The publication is periodic(al)

→ Téiki no│kankóobutu da   It is a periodical publication

→ Teiki-kankóobutu da   It is periodical

    Teiki-kankóobutu $\begin{Bmatrix} \bar{g}a \\ wa \end{Bmatrix}$‖ sinbun ‖   Periodicals are newspapers, maga-

    zassi nádo da   zines, and so on

Sinbun │zassi nádo no│teiki-
kankóobutu da

They are the periodicals that are
newspapers, magazines, and so on

2. X, Y, Z o hazime ‖kankóobutu
o okuru

They send X, Y, Z, in particular,
and also publications

3. Monó o okuru

They send things

+ Monó o uke-toru

They accept/receive things

→ Monó o│okuttári│uke-tottári
suru

They send and receive things [in al-
ternation, off and on, or typically]

→ Monó o│okuttári│uke-tottári site
iru

They send and receive things [reg-
ularly, all the time]

4. Hituyoo da

It is necessary

Zéhi hituyoo da

It is by all means necessary

Seikatu ni│zéhi hituyoo da

It is by all means necessary for life

Nitizyoo (no) seikatu da

It is everyday life

Sigoto $\left\{\begin{matrix} wa \\ ga \end{matrix}\right\}$ │nitizyoo-séikatu ni
hituyoo da

Work is necessary for everyday life

5. Hituyoo dá

It is necessary

Hituyoo dá to iu

We say it is necessary

Hituyoo dá to│iu kotó da

It is a matter of our saying it is necessary = It is a matter of it's being
necessary

Hituyoo dá to│iu kotó ni│izon
ga áru

There is an objection to the statement
(or fact) that it is necessary

6. X (to iu kotó) ni│izon ga áru

There is an objection to X

X ní (wa)│hito (ni)│izon ga áru

People have an objection to X

X ní wa│dáre ni│izon ga áru ka?

Who has an objection to X?

X ní wa│dare (ni) mo│izon ga nái

Nobody has an objection to X

. . . nái daroo

Surely (nobody has an objection to X)

7. X o riyoo suru

They use X

X ga riyoo sareru

X gets used

X ga riyoo sarete iru

X is used [regularly, all the time]

X ga riyoo sarete ita

X was [regularly] used

X ga riyoo sarete itá no da

[It is a fact that] X was [regularly]
used

8. Méizi│yo-nen ‖. . . dóo│hatí-nen

In the 4th year of Meiji, . . . in the
8th year of the same [Meizi]

9. Yuubin o atukau

They handle mail

Yuubin ga atukawareru

Mail gets handled

10. A ga│zyúu-nen ni│X ni kamei
sita

A joined X in the year 10

Zyúu-nen ni│X ni kamei sita A da

It's the A that joined X in the year 10

A ga│zyúu-nen ni kamei sita X da

It's the X that A joined in the year 10

A ga│X ni kamei sita zyúu-nen da

It's the [particular] year 10 that A
joined X

A ga X ni kamei sitá no wa│
zyúu-nen da

The one (=year) that A joined X was
the year 10 or A's joining X was
(in) the year 10

Compare:

A ḡa|zyúu-nen ni|kamei sitá no   The one that A joined in the year 10
wa|X da   was X

Zyuu-nén ni|X ni kamei sitá no   The one that joined X in the year 10
wa|A da   was A

Note: This pattern could be extended, of course, by including the place
where (tokoró de) the joining took place.

11. Ryóokin ḡa|(zénkoku) kin'itu da   The fee is uniform (for the whole
    country)

(Séihu ḡa)|ryóokin o|zénkoku-   (The government) makes the fee uni-
kin'itu ni suru   form for the whole country

12. . . . tokí ni hazimatte iru   . . . was begun at the time [and con-
    tinues to this day], is under way
    [since a certain time]

13. a. Yuubínkyoku ḡa siḡoto o suru   The post office does work

→ Siḡoto $\begin{Bmatrix} ḡa \\ wa \end{Bmatrix}$|yuubínkyoku no da   The work is the post office's

→ Yuubínkyoku no siḡoto da   It's the post office's work

b. Yuubínkyoku de|(hito ḡa)| At the post office they (people) do
→   siḡoto o suru   work

→ Siḡoto $\begin{Bmatrix} ḡa \\ wa \end{Bmatrix}$|yuubínkyoku (de)   The work is of at the post office
   no da

→ Yuubínkyoku (de) no siḡoto da   It's the work at the post office; It's
    post office work

14. Yuubínbutu o|pósuto kara| They collected the mail from the
   atúmeta   mailboxes

→ Pósuto kara|atúmeta|yuubínbutu   It's the mail collected from the mail-
da   boxes

15. Yuubínbutu o|kénsa suru   They examine the mail
+ Sore ni|kesiin o osu   They apply postmarks (cancellation
    stamps) to it

→ Yuubínbutu o|kénsa si ‖(sore ni)| They examine the mail and postmark
kesiin o osu   it

Note: The ADVERB mázu applies to both kénsa suru and kesiin o osu.

16. Yukisaki ni yoru   It depends on the destination
+ Kúbetu suru   They divide them
→ Yukisaki ni yotte|kúbetu suru   They divide them according to desti-
    nation

+ Unsoo suru   They transport them
→ Yukisaki ni yotte kúbetu site| They divide them according to desti-
unsoo suru   nation and transport them

17. Kyóku wa|(yuubínbutu o)|uke-   The (post) office received it (the mail)
totta

→ Uke-totta kyóku da   It's the office that received it

Uke-totta kyóku de (wa) . . .   At the office that has received it, they
   kobetu ni haitatu suru   . . . and deliver it house-to-house

18. Nenmatu ni│(yuubin ḡa)│kónzatu   At the year-end it (the mail) is con-
    suru   gested
  → (Yuubin ḡa) kónzatu suru nen-   It is the year-end, when it (the mail)
    matu da   is congested

19. Nenḡázyoo da   It's a New Year's card
    Nenḡázyoo de│kónzatu suru   It is congested with New Year's cards

20. Kyokúin│daké da   It's only the (post) office staff
    kyokúin│daké de (wa)│té ḡa│   With it's being (= if it is) only the of-
    tarinai   fice staff, there are insufficient
                             hands

    Arubaito-gákusei o│dooin suru   They mobilize working students
    Kyokúin│daké de (wa)│té ḡa   With only the office staff, they are
    tarazu (=│tarinái de) ║arubaito-   shorthanded and they mobilize work-
    gákusei o dooin suru   ing students

Note: LITERARY   COLLOQUIAL
    taru   tariru   'suffices'
                ⎧ tarizu (ni) ⎫
    tarazu   ⎨ tarinái de ⎬   'not sufficing'
                ⎩ tarináku(te) ⎭

21. Sukósi da   It's a little bit
    sukósi de   being a little bit, with [its being] a
                          little bit

    sukósi de mo   even [being] a little bit
  + hayái   it is early/fast
  → Sukósi de mo│hayái   It's even a little bit early/earlier
                          (or fast/faster)

  + Todokéru   They deliver it
  → Sukósi de mo│háyaku│todokéru   They deliver it [so that it is] even a
                          little bit earlier; They deliver it as
                          soon as possible

22. A ḡa│B ni│X o todokéru   A delivers X to B
    C ḡa│A ni│B ni│X o todókete   C gets A to deliver X to B
    morau
    (C ḡa)│A ni│B ni│X o todókete│ The time when C wants to get A to
    moraitái tóki   deliver X to B

23. Gaikoku da   It's abroad
    gaikoku e   to abroad
    gaikoku é wa   if it's to abroad, to abroad [as com-
                         pared with, say, to <u>Kyushu</u>]

24. Yuubínbutu ḡa│naku-naru   Mail gets lost
  + Yuubínbutu ḡa│hason suru   Mail gets damaged
  → Yuubínbutu ḡa│naku-nattári│ Mail gets lost or damaged [or the
    hason sitári suru   like]
    . . . sita baai da   It's a situation where (mail has been
                         lost or damaged)

... sita baai no|(soṇ̄gai no)
  baisyoo da

It's the indemnity (of the loss) in the situation where . . .

... baisyoo no tamé da

It is for the sake/purpose of indemnity . . .

... tamé ni|X mo áru

For the purpose of . . . there is also/even X

25. Yuubínbutu o|haitatu suru

They deliver mail

→ (Yuubínbutu no) haitatu da

It is the (mail) delivery

Haitatu máde da

It is up to the (point of) the delivery

Haitatu máde no|kiroku da

It is the record up to the delivery

26. Kiroku o suru

They make a record

Kiroku o site oku

They make a record [and keep it for later use], They keep a record

27. (Hito ḡa|sore o)|kiroku site oku

People record it

(Hito ḡa|sore o)|kiroku site oku
  kakitome ḡa áru

There is registered mail of which they keep a record [of it]

Haitatu máde|kiroku site oku

They record it up to the delivery

→ Haitatu máde no kiroku da

It is the record up to the delivery

+ Kiroku site oku kakitome da

It is registered mail that is recorded

→ Haitatu máde no kiroku o site
  oku|kakitome da

It is registered mail that they record up to the delivery

28. X $\left\{\begin{array}{c}\text{ḡa}\\\text{wa}\end{array}\right\}$|zyuu-en da

X is 10-yen

+ Y $\left\{\begin{array}{c}\text{ḡa}\\\text{wa}\end{array}\right\}$|gó-en

Y is 5-yen

+ Z $\left\{\begin{array}{c}\text{ḡa}\\\text{wa}\end{array}\right\}$|zyuu-en da

Z is 10-yen

→ X wa|zyuu-en (de) ‖ Y (wa)|gó-en
  (de) ‖ Z wa|zyuu-en da

X is 10-yen and Y is 5-yen and Z is 10-yen

29. hensin

reply (mail)

+ -yoo

use

→ hensin-yoo

for reply

+ haḡaki

postcard

→ hensin-yoo - haḡaki

reply postcard

+ -tuki

attached

→ hensin-yoo - haḡaki-tuki

(with) reply postcard attached

oohuku

round trip

+ haḡaki

postcard

→ oohuku-háḡaki

round-trip postcard

hensin-yoo -haḡaki-tuki oohuku
  - háḡaki

a (round-trip) postcard with reply postcard attached

Note the arbitrary lack of send-off kana in the following words (where we would have expected the consonant-base INFINITIVE to have send-off kana):

kesi-in (from kesu 'cancels, erases' + ín 'stamp'), kaki-tome (from káku 'write' + tomeru 'leaves, keeps').

Lesson 33

zíki	the time, the time of the year, season
hinamáturi	the Doll Festival, the Girls' Festival (March 3rd)
obón	the Bon Festival, the Lantern Festival,.the Festival of the Dead
bon-ódori	A Bon Festival Dance
sairei	a ritual, a festival, a feast
tasyoo no . . .	somewhat (of a . . .), to some degree, more or less
kadómatu	gate pinetree, New Year decoration pines
osonae	an offering, a rice-cake offering
X o sonaéru	offers X (to a god)
X o kazaru	decorates/ornaments/dresses X
hatuhí-no-de	the sunrise on New Year's Day
X o oḡámu	worships/adores/prays to X
uzíḡami	a tutelary deity, a patron deity, a guardian god
hatumóode	the visit to a temple or a shrine on New Year's Day
kínpen	the neighborhood, the vicinity, the region about
tízin	an acquaintance
enpoo	a great distance, a long way, a distant place
tíki	an acquaintance, a friend
setubun	the day before (the eve of) the beginning of spring
ríssyun	the first day of spring, the opening of spring
hukú	(good) fortune, blessing, (good) luck
oní	demon, evil, an ogre, a fiend
"Hukú wa uti, oní wa soto"	"In with fortune! Out with the demon(s)!"
hiḡán	the equinoctial week
sekku	March 3rd (the Girls' Festival) and May 5th (the Boys' Festival)
yoroi	a suit of armor
kábuto	a helmet, a headpiece
syoobúyu	a sweet-flag bath
syóobu	a sweet-flag, an iris
tyuuḡen	July 15th; a midsummer gift (traditional to this time of year)
kozukáisen	pocket money, spending money
kéidai	the precincts (compound) of a shrine or a temple, (within) shrine/temple grounds
híroba	a plaza, an open space, a (public) square
yaḡura	a tower, a turret, a scaffold
tyootín	a paper lantern
hoosaku	an abundant harvest
kokúmotu	grains

1. Gyóozi o|kurikáesu	They repeat the functions (events)
+ Gyóozi o okonau	They perform the functions
➜ Gyóozi o|kurikáesi(te) okonau	They perform the functions repeatedly

Gyóozi ḡa|kurikáesi(te) okona-
wareru (PASSIVE)

. . . okonawarete iru

The functions are repeatedly performed

. . . are repeatedly performed [all
the time, as a regular thing]

2. Syuukan ḡa tiḡau
+ Mínzoku ḡa tiḡau
→ Syuukan ya|mínzoku ḡa|tiḡau

→ Tiḡai wa‖syuukan ya|mínzoku da

→ Syuukan ya|mínzoku no|tiḡai da

The customs are different
The folkways are different
The customs and the folkways are
different
The difference is in the customs and
folkways
It is the difference in customs and
folkways

3. Tiḡai ḡa áru
Tiḡai wa áru ḡa

There is a difference
There IS a difference [to be sure], but

4. A ni (wa)|áisatu o suru
A ni (wa)|nensi-máwari de|áisatu
o suru
+ B ni (wa)|nenḡázyoo de|áisatu
o suru
→ A ni wa|nensi-máwari (de) ‖B
ni wa|nenḡázyoo de|áisatu o
suru

They greet A
They greet A with the New Year's
round of visits
They greet B with the New Year's
cards
They greet A with the New Year's
round of visits, B with cards

5. Sínnen ni|áisatu o suru

→ Áisatu {ḡa / wa}|sínnen no da

→ Sínnen no|áisatu da

They greet them at New Year's

The greetings are [of] New Year's

They are New Year's greetings

6. "X" to kurikáesu
+ Mamé o maku
→ "X" to|kurikaesi-náḡara|mamé
o maku

They repeat "X"
They scatter beans
They scatter beans while repeating
"X"

7. Uti da
Uti-zyuu da

It's the house
It's all over the house; It's all through
the house

8. Maturi ni náru
Maturi ni nátte iru

It becomes a festival
It has become (= is now) a festival

9. Karada o kiyómeta
+ Keḡaré o|ninḡyoo ni utúsita

They cleansed their bodies
They transferred their contamination to dolls

+⌈ → Karada o kiyóme(te) ‖keḡaré o|
 ⌊ ninḡyoo ni utúsita
   Kore o|mizu ni naḡásita

They cleansed their bodies and transferred their contamination to dolls
They floated these (the dolls) down
the river

→⌈ Karada . . . utúsi(te)‖kore o|
 ⌊ mizu ni naḡásita

They cleansed their bodies and transferred their contamination to dolls,
and then floated the dolls on the
water

+ Kawá e itta

They went to the river

→ Kawá e itte ‖karada . . .   They went to the river to cleanse
   naḡásita   their bodies and transfer their
                                         contamination to dolls, and then
                                         float the dolls on the water

10. . . . naḡásita no ḡa│moto no   The original form [of the ceremony]
    katati da   was that they went . . .

11. Kore wa│gyóozi da   This is a function
    Kore wa│gyóozi datta   This was a function
    Kore wa│Síntoo no│gyóozi desita   This was a Shinto function
    Síntoo wa│syúukyoo da   Shinto is a religion

    Síntoo $\begin{Bmatrix} \text{ḡa} \\ \text{wa} \end{Bmatrix}$│Nihón koyuu da   Shinto is peculiar to Japan

┌─┌ A ‖túmari│B = A ‖sunáwati│B   A, equivalent to B = A, that is B; A,
│ │   in other words B; A, which is to
│ │   say B
│ │
│ │ Kore wa Síntoo no│gyóozi desita   This was a function of Shinto
+ │ + Síntoo wa│Nihón│koyuu no syúu-   Shinto is a/the religion peculiar to
│ │   kyoo da   Japan
│ ┌─→ Kore wa│Nihón koyuu no│syúu-   This was a function of Shinto, [which
└─┘   kyoo no (= de aru)│Síntoo no│   is] the religion peculiar to Japan
       gyóozi desita
  ┌─ Kore wa│Síntoo ‖túmari│Nihón   This was a function of Shinto, that is
→ │   koyuu no│syúukyoo no│gyóozi   to say of the religion peculiar to
  └   desita   Japan

12. Haká e/ni│máiru   They humbly visit the graves
  → Haka-máiri da   It is a grave visit
    Haka-máiri o suru   They visit the graves

13. X no kóro o│Y to itte ‖haka-   Calling the time around X "Y" and
    máiri o│surú no wa ‖Bukkyóo   visiting the graves is a Buddhist
    no│maturi da   festival

14. Sóra ḡa│aói   The sky is blue
    Aói│sóra da   It's a blue sky
    Aozóra da   It's a blue sky
    Aozóra ni│takái   It is high in the blue sky
    Aozóra│tákaku│X o tatéru   They raise X [so that it is] high in
                                         the blue sky

15. Kói ḡa noboru   The carp goes up
    koi-nóbori   a carp streamer

16. Tanosíi   It is pleasant
    Tanosímu   They enjoy it
    tanosími   enjoyment
    Tanosími da   It is a pleasure = It is pleasant
    Tanosími na│monó da   It is a pleasant thing

17. X o tyuusin ni suru   They make X the center (heart) of it,
                                         They center it on/around X

    X o tyuusin ni (site)│gyóozi o   They perform the function centering
    okonau   it around X

➤ X o tyuusin ni│gyóozi ḡa okona-
　wareru

The function gets performed center-
　ing around X

➤ X o tyuusin ni│okonawareru
　gyóozi da

It is a function that gets performed
　centering around X

18. (Kore o) "Tyuuḡén" to iu

They call it "Chūgen"

+　Syuukan da

It is a custom

　Syuukan de│okurimono o suru

By custom they give presents

　Tyuuḡén to itte ‖syuukan de│
　okurimono o suru

By custom they give presents, calling
　it "Chūgen"

　"Tyuuḡén" to itte ‖okurimono o
　suru syuukan da

It is a custom by which they give
　presents, calling it "Chūgen"

19. Zenkoku-teki da

It is nationwide

　Zenkoku-teki ni okonau

They perform it nationwide

20. Dentoo $\begin{Bmatrix} \text{ḡa} \\ \text{wa} \end{Bmatrix}$│áka da

The light is red

➤ Áka no dentoo da

It is a red light

+　Dentoo $\begin{Bmatrix} \text{ḡa} \\ \text{wa} \end{Bmatrix}$│kiiro da

It is a yellow light

➤ Kiiro no dentoo da

+　Dentoo $\begin{Bmatrix} \text{ḡa} \\ \text{wa} \end{Bmatrix}$│mídori da

It is a green light

➤ Mídori no dentoo da

➤ Áka ‖ki(iro)‖mídori (nado) no
　dentoo da

They are lights that are red, yellow,
　green, and so on

In written Japanese, kiiro 'yellow' can be shortened to ki in citing groups of
colors (with or without linking PARTICLES such as to and ya).

21. X $\begin{Bmatrix} \text{ḡa} \\ \text{wa} \end{Bmatrix}$│utukúsiku(te)

X are beautiful and

22. (Odori o)│taiko ni awaséru

They adjust it (the dance) to the
　drums = They do it (the dance) to the
　accompaniment of drums

　Taiko ni awásete odoru

They dance (adjusting their dance
　rhythm) to the drums

23. Wá ni naru

They become/form a circle

+　Odori-mawáru

They dance around

➤ Wá ni natte‖odori-mawáru

They form a circle and dance around
　= They dance around in a circle

24. Kámi $\begin{Bmatrix} \text{ḡa} \\ \text{wa} \end{Bmatrix}$│murá o│mamóru

The god protects the village

➤ Mura no mamorí-ḡami da

It is the village protection-deity

　mura no mamoríḡami $\begin{Bmatrix} \text{de aru} \\ \text{no} \end{Bmatrix}$
　uzíḡami da

It is the tutelar deity that is the
　guardian deity of the village

25. Kánsya suru

They give thanks

+　Rikuriéesyon o│kanéru

They combine it with recreation

➤ Kánsya suru to│tómo ni ‖
　rikuriéesyon mo kanéru

At the same time with giving thanks,
　they combine it with recreation too

26. Hitóbito ḡa│soróu · · · · · · · · · · · · · · · · The people are all present

+ Hitóbito $\begin{Bmatrix} \text{ḡa} \\ \text{wa} \end{Bmatrix}$│rikuriéesyon o│ · · · · · · The people enjoy recreation
   tanosímu

→ Hitóbito $\begin{Bmatrix} \text{ḡa} \\ \text{wa} \end{Bmatrix}$│sorótte│rikuriée- · · · · · The people all enjoy recreation
   syon o│tanosímu

→ Hitóbito ḡa sorótte│tanosímu│ · · · · · · · · It is recreation that the people all
   rikuriéesyon da · enjoy

27. A ḡa│B ni│X (suru kotó) o│ · · · · · · · · · A forbids B to do X
   kinzíru

   ┌ a. B ḡa│A ni│X o kinziraréru · · · · · · · B gets forbidden (to do) X by A
   │   B ḡa│A ni│X o kinzirárete iru · · · · B is forbidden X by A
   →│ b. (A ni│yotte)│B ni│X ḡa · · · · · · · · · X was forbidden for B (by A)
   └   kinziráreta (PASSIVE)

→ (A ni yotte)│B ni kinziraréru X · · · · · · X which gets forbidden for B (by A)
   A ḡa│B ni│monó o│tabéru koto o│ · · · · A forbids B to eat the things
   kinzíru

   B ḡa│A ni│monó o│tabéru koto o│ · · · · B was forbidden by A to eat the
   kinziráreta (PASSIVE) · · · · · · · · · · · · · · · things

→ (B ḡa│A ni│) tabéru koto o · · · · · · · · · · The things that have been forbidden
   kinziráreta mono · (by A for B) to eat

28. Monó o│kanarazu tabéru · · · · · · · · · · · They eat the things unfailingly
   Monó o│kanarazu tabéru koto ni│ · · · · · It has come about that they eat the
   nátte iru · things unfailingly
→ Kanarazu tabéru koto ni│nátte · · · · · · It is the things that they have come
   iru│monó da · to eat unfailingly

29. Koré-ra o│meisín to suru · · · · · · · · · · · We consider these [to be] supersti-
                                                            tions

+ Koré-ra o│(zéndai no)│ihúu to · · · · · · We consider these [to be] customs
   suru · (of earlier ages)

→ Koré-ra o meisín to ka ‖(zéndai · · · · · We regard (consider) these as super-
   no)│ihúu to suru · · · · · · · · · · · · · · · · · · stitions or [as] customs of earlier
                                                            ages

30. Warau · We laugh
   Waratte simau · We end up laughing <u>or</u> We laugh them
                                                            off <u>or</u> We laugh in an undesirable
                                                            way

   . . . to site‖waratte simau · · · · · · · · · We laugh them off [considering them]
                                                            as . . .

31. Siru ué ni│taisetu da = Siru tamé · · · · It is important in order to find out
   ni│taisetu da
   (<u>cf</u>. Note 1, Lesson 13)

Lesson 34

un'ei	operation, management, administration
sánken bunritu	division of powers, separation of the three powers (executive, legislative, and judiciary)
rippóoken	legislative power, lawmaking power
rippoo	legislation, lawmaking
gyooséiken	administrative power
gyoosei	administration
náikaku	a cabinet, a ministry, the Council of Ministers
sihóoken	judicial (judiciary) power
sihoo	judicature
saibansyo	a court of justice, a courthouse
saikoo-saibansyo	the Supreme Court
kakyuu-saibansyo	a lower court
X ni syozoku suru	belongs to X
kokken	national rights, sovereign rights, state power
syuugíin	the House of Representatives, the Lower House,
sangíin	the House of Councilors, the Upper House
giketu	a resolution, a decision, passing a vote of, voting on (a bill)
késsan	settlement of accounts, closing accounts
kókuhi	national expenditure
kókumu	the affairs of State
gíin	a member of an assembly, a member of the Diet, a Congressman
senkyóken	the franchise, suffrage, the right to vote
sénkyo	election
ninki	one's term of office, one's tenure
X o héru	passes/goes by, passes through X
tasuutoo	the majority party
tóosyu	the leader of a party
ookurásyoo	the Ministry of Finance
X o sósiki suru	organizes/forms X
kantoku suru	supervises, charges
kóosi	use, exercise, employment (of one's privilege)
syori	disposition, management, disposal
X o musubu	ties/allies with X
teisyutu	presentation, filing, submission
hu-sínnin	non-confidence
kétugi suru	resolves, decides
soo-zísyoku suru	resigns in a body
zisyoku suru	resigns (from a post)
súbete	all, everything, the whole
kookyoo	the public, society, the community
dantai	a group, a corps, a company, an organization, an association
dóo	(in old Japan) a district; Hokkáidoo
hu	an urban prefecture, a metropolitan prefecture

tízi	a governor (of a prefecture)
gún	a sub-prefecture, a county, a district
tán'i	a unit, a denomination
hanzai	a crime, an offense, a delict
torisimari	control, discipline, supervision
X o torisimaru	keeps control over X
keisatu	the police
soozite	generally, as a rule, generally speaking
tihoo bunken	decentralization of power
sóoi	consensus (of opinion)
kokumin no sóoi	the collective will of the people
seron (or yoron)	public opinion
yóoso	an (essential) element, an important factor, the essence
masukomyunikéesyon	mass communication

The itemizing format in which this lesson is written is called "kazyoo-ḡaki" or "hitotu-ḡaki."

1. Nihón de wa | X ni túite | Y o tótta — In Japan they took/adopted/choose Y with respect to X

2. X $\begin{Bmatrix} \bar{g}a \\ wa \end{Bmatrix}$ | A ni zokúsite iru — X belongs to A

+ Y ḡa | B ni | zokúsite iru — Y belongs to B
+ Z ḡa | C ni | zokúsite iru — Z belongs to C
→ X wa | A ni (zokúsite) ‖ Y wa | B ni (zokúsite) ‖ Z wa | C ni zokúsite iru — X belongs to A, Y to B, and Z to C

3. Kenḡén $\begin{Bmatrix} \bar{g}a \\ wa \end{Bmatrix}$ | kokkai nó da — The powers are of the Diet

→ Kokkai no kenḡén da — They are the powers of the Diet
Ómo na kenḡén da — They are the principal powers

Kenḡén $\begin{Bmatrix} \bar{g}a \\ wa \end{Bmatrix}$ | rippoo ni kansúru — The powers affect/concern legislation

→ Rippoo ni kansúru | kenḡén da — They are the powers that concern legislature

Rippoo ni kansúru | ómo na | kenḡén da — They are the principal powers that concern legislature

Kokkai no ‖ rippoo ni kansúru | ómo na | kenḡén da — They are the principal legislative powers of the Diet

4. A de aru — It is A
+ B de aru — It is B
+ C de aru — It is C
→ A ‖ B ‖ C de aru — They are A, B and C

5. Kaisei o | hátuḡi suru — They initiate amendments
→ Kaisei no hátuḡi da — It is the initiation of amendments
Hooritu o | seitei suru — They enact laws
→ Hooritu no seitei da — It is the enactment of laws
Zyooyaku o | syoonin suru — They approve treaties
→ Zyooyaku no syoonin da — It is the approval of treaties

6. Ómo na│monó $\begin{Bmatrix} \bar{g}a \\ wa \end{Bmatrix}$│kengén da The principal ones are (of) the powers

⌐[→ Kengén no│ómo na│monó da They are the principal ones of the powers

+   Kengén $\begin{Bmatrix} \bar{g}a \\ wa \end{Bmatrix}$│zaisei ni kansúru The power affects/concerns finance

└[→ Zaisei ni kansúru│kengén da They are the powers that concern finance

→[Zaisei ni kansúru│kengén no│ They are the principal ones of the
     ómo na│monó da powers that concern finance

7. Yosan o│giketu suru They decide the budget
   → Yosan no giketu da It is the decision of the budget
     Sisyutu o│kettei suru They fix expenditures
   → Sisyutu no kettei da It is the fixing of expenditures

8. Soori-dáizin o│simei suru They name the Prime Minister
   → Soori-dáizin no simei da It is the naming of the Prime Minister

   Tyoosa $\begin{Bmatrix} \bar{g}a \\ wa \end{Bmatrix}$│kokusei ni kansúru The investigation affects/concerns the government

   → Kokusei ni kansúru│tyóosa da It is an investigation concerning the government

9. Saibánkan o│dangai suru They impeach the judges
   → Saibánkan no dangai da It is the impeachment of judges
   → Saibánkan no│dangáiken da It is the power of impeaching judges

10. Monó $\begin{Bmatrix} \bar{g}a \\ wa \end{Bmatrix}$│zen-kókumin o│ The person represents the whole
      daihyoo suru country

+   Monó $\begin{Bmatrix} \bar{g}a \\ wa \end{Bmatrix}$│kokusei o okonau The person conducts the government

→   Monó $\begin{Bmatrix} \bar{g}a \\ wa \end{Bmatrix}$│zen-kókumin o The person represents the whole
      daihyoo site ‖ kokusei o okonau country and conducts the government

→   Zen-kókumin o daihyoo site ‖ They are the persons who conduct the
      kokusei o okonau monó da government, representing the entire nation, or . . . who represent the entire nation in conducting the government

11. Kokumin $\bar{g}$a toohyoo suru The citizens vote
   → Kokumin no toohyoo da It is the voting of/by the citizens
     Toohyoo ni yoru They rely on voting; It is due to voting; It depends on voting

     Toohyoo ni yori sénkyo suru They elect him by voting

12. Nízis-sai da He is 20 years of age
     Mán│nízis-sai da He is fully 20 years of age; He is 20 years of age according to the Occidental count

   cf. Kazoé-dosi de│nízis-sai da He is 20 years old according to the Oriental count [i.e. Since his birth he has lived in 20 calendar years]

Mán|nízis-sai|ízyoo da — He is over 20 years of age (by Occidental count)

13. Baai $\left\{\begin{matrix} \bar{g}a \\ wa \end{matrix}\right\}$|tokubetu da — The situation is special

→ Tokubetu na baai da — It is a special situation

Tokubetu na baai o nozoku — We except special situations

tokubetu na baai o nozoki/ nozoite/nozokéba — except for special situations

14. Sábetu (ḡa)|nái — There is no discrimination

sábetu|náku — without discrimination

Seibetu no sábetu da — It is discrimination of/by sex

+ Kaikyuu no sábetu da — It is discrimination of/by class

→ Seibetu (ya) ‖kaikyuu no| sábetu da — It is discrimination by sex and/or class

15. Teiin ($\left\{\begin{matrix} \bar{g}a \\ wa \end{matrix}\right\}$)|yón-hyaku| rokuzyuu naná-mei da — The full complement is 467 persons

+ Ninki ($\left\{\begin{matrix} \bar{g}a \\ wa \end{matrix}\right\}$)|yo-nen da — The term [of office] is 4 years

→ Teiin yón hyaku|rokuzyuu naná-mei (de) ‖ninki yo-nen da — The full complement is 467 persons, (and) the term (is) 4 years

16. Ryooin ḡa giketu suru — The two Houses make decisions

→ Ryooin no giketu da — It is the decisions of the two Houses

17. Sono baai ní (wa)‖giketu ḡa kotonáru — The decisions differ in that situation

→ Giketu ḡa kotonáru baai da — It is a situation where the decisions differ

18. Tetúzuki ḡa ittei da — The procedure is fixed

→ Ittei no tetúzuki da — It is a fixed procedure

19. (Hito ḡa) X o A to suru — (People) consider X to be (as) A

X $\left\{\begin{matrix} \bar{g}a \\ wa \end{matrix}\right\}$|(hito ni)|A to sareru — X is considered (by people) as A

20. X o kotó ni suru — It differs with respect to X, It varies in X

X ḡa kotonáru — X is different

Seitoo $\left\{\begin{matrix} \bar{g}a \\ wa \end{matrix}\right\}$|tóoha o|kotó ni suru — The political parties differ (with respect to faction)

→ Tooha o kotó ni suru seitoo da — They are differing/different political parties

21. Gyoosei no tíi da — It is the position of the administration

+ Saikoo no tíi da — It is the highest position

→ Gyoosei no|saikoo no tíi da — It is the highest position of administration

22. A ḡa|B ni|X o makaséru — A entrusts B with X, A assigns X to B

A ḡa|B ni|X o makásete ‖kore
o kantoku suru

A entrusts B with X and oversees it

23. A {ḡa / wa}|hyooban ḡa warúi

As for A his reputation is bad, A has
a bad reputation

Náikaku {ḡa / wa}|gíkai de|hyooban
ḡa otíru (= hyooban ḡa wáruku|
náru)

The cabinet gets a bad reputation
with the Diet

24. Syuuḡíin o kaisan suru
→ Syuuḡíin ḡa kaisan sareru
Syuuḡíin ḡa kaisan sarenai
Syuuḡíin ḡa|kaisan sarenai
kaḡiri da
. . . kaḡiri, . . .

They dissolve the House
The House is dissolved
The House is not dissolved
It is as long as the House is not dis-
solved
as long as (the House is not dis-
solved) . . .

25. Tihoo-zíti o suisin suru

They push (forward) local govern-
ment

Tihoo-zíti ḡa suisin sareru

Local government gets pushed/pro-
moted

26. A ḡa|X o|gensoku to suru
X o gensoku to site
gensoku to site

A makes X its principle
with X as its principle
as a principle

27. A ḡa|X o|B ni|makaséru
X ḡa|B ni|makásete aru

A entrusts B with X
X is (has been) entrusted to B

28. A ḡa|B o|X|Y|Z ni|wakéru
B ḡa|(A ni yotte)‖X|Y|Z ni|
wakeraréru

A divides B into X Y Z
B gets divided (by A) into X Y and Z

29. Zyuumín ḡa|A o|koosen suru
A {ḡa / wa}|zyuumín ni (yori)‖
koosen sareru

The residents publicly elect A
A gets publicly elected by the res-
idents

30. A {ḡa / wa}|X ni nátte iru

A is (has become) X

A {ḡa / wa}|X ni nátte inai

A is not X (any more)

31. Saibansyo {ḡa / wa}|dokuritu suru

The court becomes/is independent

Saibansyo {ḡa / wa}|dokuritu site‖
sihóoken o|tukasadóru
Sihóoken wa|saiban-syo ḡa|
dokuritu site tukasadóru

The court independently controls
law enforcement
Law enforcement is independently
controlled by the courts

32. Y o mamóri‖Z o okonau tamé
ni wa ‖X ḡa aru

For the purpose of protecting Y and
of performing Z there is X

33. X ḡa hattatu sita

X has developed

X {ḡa / wa}|hattatu sita zidai da

It is an era when X has developed

34. Senden ḡa│hito o sáyuu suru   Propaganda controls men
   ⇀ Hito ḡa│senden ni│sáyuu sareru   Men get controlled by propaganda
     (Hito ḡa)│senden ni│sáyuu   There is a fear/danger that we (men)
       sareru│osoré ḡa│áru   get controlled by propaganda

Lesson 35

kázitu	the other day, some days ago, recently
goraku	amusement, recreation, entertainment
zyúurai	hitherto, up to now, in the past
tozan	mountain climbing, mountaineering
yótto	a yacht, yachting, a sailboat
aḡeru	mentions (a fact), adduces (proof), cites (an instance)
keiba	horse racing, a horse race
keirin	a bicycle race
maazyan	mahjong
patinko	a pinball game
otoróéru	becomes weak, loses vigor
zyázu	jazz
sikóoryoku	thinking faculty
X o ubau	takes X (by force), robs/deprives of X
dokuyaku	a poisonous drug
dokú	poison, poisonous substance
kabu	stocks, shares
báibai	buying and selling
baken	a ticket on a horse race, a pari-mutuel ticket
suríru	a thrill
kasóo-teki	a hypothetical enemy
anḡai (na)	is unexpected, surprising
soosetu	establishment, creation, founding, inauguration
X ni tomonáu	goes (hand in hand) with X
sakkon no . . .	recent . . . , . . . of these days
itizirusíi	is remarkable, marked, distinguished, striking
komedáwara	a straw rice-sack
tawara	a straw bag
X o ámu	knits/crochets X
koodoo	a lecture hall, an auditorium
tantyoo (na)	is monotonous, flat, drab, dull
tankoobon	an independent volume, a book
obitadasíi	is immense, vast, enormous, tremendous
syuukan-zássi	a weekly magazine
syookin	a prize, an award
kuízu	a quiz

1. Hito $\begin{Bmatrix} \text{ḡa} \\ \text{wa} \end{Bmatrix}$ | Tookyoo ni zaizyuu suru   People reside in Tokyo

→ Tookyoo ni zaizyuu suru hitó da   They are the people who reside in Tokyo

→ Hito $\begin{Bmatrix} \text{ḡa} \\ \text{wa} \end{Bmatrix}$ | Tookyoo-zaizyuu da   People are resident in Tokyo

→ Tookyoo-zaizyuu no hitó da   It is the people resident in Tokyo

2. X $\begin{Bmatrix} \text{ḡa} \\ \text{wa} \end{Bmatrix}$ | tyóosa no | taisyoo da   X is the object of the investigation

Tyoosa $\begin{Bmatrix} \text{ḡa} \\ \text{wa} \end{Bmatrix}$ | X o taisyoo ni suru　　　The investigation makes X its object

X o taisyoo ni site ‖ tyóosa suru　　　They investigate with X as its object

+ Y ni túite ‖ tyóosa suru　　　They investigate with respect to Y

→ X o taisyoo ni site ‖ Y ni túite |　　　They investigate Y, with X as the
　tyóosa suru　　　　　　　　　　object

3. Kyoomí ḡa | hukái　　　The interest is deep; It is deeply
　　　　　　　　　　　　interesting; I have a deep interest
　　　　　　　　　　　　[in it]

→ Kyoomi-bukái　　　It is deeply interesting

Hookoku $\begin{Bmatrix} \text{ḡa} \\ \text{wa} \end{Bmatrix}$ | kyoomi-bukái　　　The report is deeply interesting

⌐[→ Kyoomi-bukái hookoku da　　　It is a deeply interesting report

　　Hookoku $\begin{Bmatrix} \text{ḡa} \\ \text{wa} \end{Bmatrix}$ | Y ni túite | tyóosa　　　The report investigated Y
+
└　　sita

└[→ Y ni túite | tyóosa sita | hookoku da　　　It is the report which investigated Y

⌐　Y ni túite | tyóosa sita | kyoomi-　　　It is a deeply interesting report which
→└　　bukái hookoku da　　　　investigated Y

4. Sono kikái ni | yómu　　　I will read it on that occasion (op-
　　　　　　　　　　　　portunity)

　Yómu | kikái da　　　It is an opportunity (change, occasion)
　　　　　　　　　　to read it

　Yómu | kikái ḡa | áru　　　There is an opportunity = I have an op-
　　　　　　　　　　　　portunity to read it

5. Dansei no kotáe da　　　It's the men's answers
　Dansei no kotáe de (wa) ‖ X ḡa |　　　In the men's replies, X is considered
　　Y to nátte iru　　　　　　(treated as) Y
　A ḡa | X o | Y to suru　　　A treats (considers) X as Y
　X ḡa | Y to náru　　　X gets treated (considered) as Y

Note: A no kotáe de wa ‖ití-i ḡa | éiḡa (de) ‖ ní-i ḡa | supóotu (de) ‖ B no kotáe
de wa ‖ití-i ḡa ryokoo (de) ‖ ní-i ḡa | éiḡa to | nátte iru: The entire sentence
is to be derived from . . . da . . . to nátte iru; the underlying sentence is
a compound of two double COPULAR sentences (éiḡa da, supóotu da; ryokoo da,
éiḡa da), with the COPULAR GERUNDS suppressed and topics derived from
COPULAR sentences (kotáe da) inserted for each half of the underlying sentence.

6. X yori (mo) | Y ḡa | sukí da　　　We like Y better/rather than X

7. Yokaróo [Abbreviation of yóku +　　　It probably is good
　　aróo] = Íi daroo

The -karóo [←-ku aróo] form is dialect or written, equivalent to standard
spoken ADJECTIVE-i daróo.

8. Sono kekka da　　　It is the result of that
　Sono kekka to káisyaku suru　　　They understand it as the result of
　　　　　　　　　　　　that

　. . . káisyaku | sité mo | íi　　　You may accept it as . . .

9. Seikatu $\begin{Bmatrix} \text{ḡa} \\ \text{wa} \end{Bmatrix}$ | antei suru　　　Life gets stabilized

→ Seikatu no antei da

It is the stabilization of life

→ Seikatu-antei da

It is life stabilization

Keizai-séikatu antei da

It is the stabilization of economic life

10. Ninki $\left\{\begin{array}{l}\bar{g}a\\wa\end{array}\right\}$ |X|Y|Z no da

The popularity is of X Y Z

X|Y|Z no ninki da

It is the popularity of X Y Z

X|Y|Z no ninki ḡa (→ mo) otoroénai

The popularity (also) of X Y Z has not diminished

11. Koohun $\left\{\begin{array}{l}\bar{g}a\\wa\end{array}\right\}$ |izyoo da

The excitement is unusual (abnormal)

→ Izyoo na koohun da

It is unusual excitement

+ Zyázu ni|taisúru koohun da

It is excitement directed toward jazz

→ Zyázu ni taisúru|izyoo na koohun da

It is unusual excitement about jazz

Koohun wa|zyúu-dai no|kookóo-sei no da

The excitement is of teen-age high-school students

+ Kookóo-sei no koohun da

It is the excitement of the high-school students

→ Zyúu-dai no|kookóo-sei no| zyázu ni|tai-súru|izyoo na koohun da

It is the unusual excitement of teen-age high-school students about jazz

12. Koohun $\left\{\begin{array}{l}\bar{g}a\\wa\end{array}\right\}$ |saméru

The excitement dies down (cools off)

13. Saménai

It doesn't cool

Samenai rasíi

It seems that it does not cool

14. Kawaru

It changes

Kawatta = Kawatte iru

It changed, It is different/peculiar

Kawatta monó da

It is an odd (different, peculiar) thing

Monó $\left\{\begin{array}{l}\bar{g}a\\wa\end{array}\right\}$ |kawatte iru

The thing is odd (different, peculiar)

Kawatte irú no $\left\{\begin{array}{l}\bar{g}a\\wa\end{array}\right\}$ ||". . ." to iu kotáe da

The odd thing (one) is the answer ". . ."

15. . . . tó ka = . . . sóo da, . . . to iu kotó da

I hear that . . .

16.Ití-i o|siméru

It occupies first place

Compare:

Ití-i ka|ní-i o|siméru

It occupies first or second place

→ Iti-|ní-i o|siméru

They occupy 1st and 2nd place

17. Osóraku . . . no dé wa|aru mái ka = Tábun . . . no zya| nái daroo ka

Wouldn't it probably be the fact that . . .

18. Zyuzóoki ḡa|nooson ni sinsyutu suru

[Television] sets advance (spread) in the farm villages

Zyuzóoki no|nooson-sinsyutu da

It is the spread of television sets in the farm villages

19. Móhaya (= móo) | mezurásiku
wa | nái

It is no longer rare, It isn't rare anymore [but common]

20. A wa | X ni suḡínai

A is nothing but X, A is no more than
X

A wa | . . . surú ni | suḡínai =
A wa | . . . suru daké da

A does nothing more than [to do] . . .

21. nén ni = ití-nen ni

per year

22. (Hito ḡa) | éiḡa ya sibai o |
zyooen suru

(People) put on films and plays

→ Éiḡa ya sibai $\left\{ {ḡa \atop wa} \right\}$ | (hito ni)
zyooen sareru

Films and plays get put on (by people)

23. (Hito ḡa) | térebi o | kanḡei suru

(People) welcome television

→ Térebi $\left\{ {ḡa \atop wa} \right\}$ | (hito ni) kanḡei
sareru

Television gets welcomed (by people)

Térebi ḡa | kanḡei sarerú no wa |
toozen de aróo (= toozen daróo)

The fact that television gets welcomed is surely to be expected, It is
surely natural for television to get
welcomed

24. (Hito ḡa) | zassi o syuppan suru

(People) publish magazines

→ Zassi $\left\{ {ḡa \atop wa} \right\}$ | syuppan sareru

Magazines get published (by people)

Maituki syuppan sareru zassi da

It is magazines published every
month

25. A | B | C | D no betu da

It is the differences of/among A B C
D

A | B | C | D no betu ($\left\{ {ḡa \atop wa} \right\}$) nái

There are no differences among A B
C D

→ . . . náku

With no differences (among A B C D),
Regardless (of A B C and D)

26. Dókusya ḡa | sore o tanosímu

The readers enjoy it

→ Sore ḡa | dókusya ni | tanosimaréru
. . . tanosimárete iru
. . . tanosimárete iru | yóo da

It gets enjoyed by the readers
It is (regularly) enjoyed . . .
It seems to be (regularly) enjoyed . . .

Part IV

ENGLISH TRANSLATIONS OF THE TEXT LESSONS

INTRODUCTORY NOTE

1. In order to give some idea of the way Japanese think and at the same time to give a clear understanding of the structure of the sentences, we have stuck to the original text as closely as possible. The result is not the sort of fine "free" translation you would want to make for publication in English. Instead, it is a guide that will help you reconstruct the Japanese text.

2. In free translation, it is a good idea to break up long Japanese sentences into several short English sentences. When the Japanese sentences are long, we have broken them up with semicolons (;) or colons (:) whenever it helps make the structure clear.

3. When Japanese placenames, personal names, and the like appear in the midst of the English sentences, we have written them in the Hepburn romanization, as is usual for such purposes. Students should compare these versions with the versions in the romanized texts, where we use a system similar to the official (Kunrei-shiki) system of the Japanese government.

4. Translations of Japanese words not required by the English sentence will be found in parentheses (like these); unexpected English words and phrases that do not correspond directly to anything in the Japanese text, but are required to make a smooth English sentence, are enclosed in brackets [like these]. A word quoted inside parentheses is a translation into any other language of the immediately preceding word: pan ("pão"), distasteful ("kirai na"). In this section Japanese words appearing in the midst of the English text are underlined; but in the romanized text, only those words originally written in katakana are underlined.

5. The purpose of the translation is (1) to help you understand both the meaning and the structure of the Japanese sentences, (2) to help you reconstruct from memory the Japanese sentences verbatim. The purpose of the romanized text, on the other hand, is (1) to help you pronounce the words correctly, (2) to help you reconstruct the exact spelling in hiragana, katakana, and kanji of the original sentences.

LESSON 1

There are three books on (top of) the table.

One is large and the other two are small (books). The large book is blue but the small ones are not blue. Both [of them] are red books.

There are four or five sheets of white paper under the blue book. Nearby, there is a small notebook and [there is also] one pen.

I'm planning to write (in advance) on this paper the parts ("places") which are difficult and I don't understand, and later on question the teacher [about them].

LESSON 2

Those words which were formerly foreign words but are today used daily by the Japanese people and have become Japanese words are called gairaigo ("words of recent foreign origin"). For example, matchi ("match"), pan ("pāo"), manto ("manteau"), sukī ("ski") etc. are words which have come from English, Portuguese, French, and German [respectively]. Usually, this kind of word is written in katakana.

First of all, among the things one sees with one's eyes and hears with one's ears, there are [words like] terebi ("TV"), opera ("opera"), barē ("ballet"), rajio ("radio"), rekōdo ("records") and so on. Among the things one eats or drinks ("puts into one's mouth") there are many gairaigo including [words like] kōhī ("coffee"), jūsu ("juice"), bīru ("beer"), sandoitchi ("sandwich") and kēki ("cake"). Naifu ("knife"), fōku ("fork"), and supūn ("spoon") are used with one's hands; and one wears sokkusu ("socks") and surippa ("slippers") on the feet. When it rains, one wears a reinkōto ("raincoat"); and on cold days, one wears an ōbā ("overcoat"). On Saturdays, Sundays and holidays, one plays tenisu ("tennis") or gorufu ("golf"), and goes for a doraivu ("drive") and so forth. Occasionally one also goes haikingu ("hiking") and goes on a pikunikku ("picnic").

These kinds of loanwords have ultimately been absorbed into ("have fused into") the daily life of the Japanese, and they are often used not only by young people but also by old people of sixty and seventy as well.

LESSON 3

We came last year in September, so it has already been eight months since we came to Japan.

(Both) my wife and daughter have pretty well accustomed themselves to life in Japan. Every week, on Monday, Wednesday, and Friday, I learn the Japanese language from a friend called Ishikawa, and on Tuesday and Thursday, I go to the library and study. Every day my daughter plays with the little Japanese girl in our neighborhood. My wife has been studying flower arranging since January.

My next-door neighbor on the right is a businessman called Yamanaka; and a lawyer named Morita is living on the left. [Our neighbors] are all kind and always teach us Japanese customs and manners.

LESSON 4

Yamada: "Is today a school holiday?"

Smith : "Yes. It's been spring vacation since yesterday."

Y: "That's nice, isn't it? How long does it last?"

S: "Since it's one week, it's until next Thursday."

Y: "I envy you. We only have summer vacations, and in spring and fall, there aren't any vacations at all. Are you going on a trip (or something like that)?"

S : "Yes. I've never yet been to the country(side), so I have been wondering if I might try hiking around ("walking in") [some] villages of
Tōhoku (the Northeastern Area), but . . . [I haven't decided yet]."

Y : "Tōhoku? There may be snow and ice there, depending on the place.
Since the winters up there are long, you know. Are you going by
train?"

S : "Yes. But, if there is snow . . . I guess a trip to Tōhoku would be
better in the summer, wouldn't it?"

Y : "Yes. It's still cold there [now]. How about Kansai (the Western
Area)?"

S : "There are loads of places I'd like to see in Kansai; so [if it is] a trip
of four or five days . . . [it wouldn't do]."

Y : "Well, why don't you try visiting Shimoda? Since it's pretty far south,
I should think the leaf buds are already pretty. Besides, you can get
fresh ("new") fish there (to eat)."

S : "THAT sounds good, doesn't it?"

LESSON 5

The Japanese language can be written either in kana alone or in roman letters;
but it is usually written by mixing katakana and hiragana (in) with Chinese characters.

Chinese characters are letters which were introduced from China (all of) a
thousand and some ("five or six") hundred years ago. There are a great number of Chinese characters and those in a [certain] old Chinese dictionary are
said to number over 40,500. There are about 15,000 Chinese characters in the
Ueda Dictionary of Japan. For most people, however, it is sufficient if they
know 3,000 of them.

It is not easy to learn even 3,000 Chinese characters. That is because a Chinese
character has form(s), reading(s), and meaning(s). The readings [of a charac-
ter] in turn consist of the on and the kun. The on is the Japanized form of the
pronunciation which has been brought from the Chinese reading. The kun is a
manner of reading the character [so that] its meaning corresponds to Japanese
("the native word"). For example, the on of the Chinese character 山 is san,
and its kun is yama. Some Chinese characters have only one on and one kun,
while there are others which have many on and kun. The character 生 has, in
addition to the (two) on, sei and shō, several kun: e.g. u(mareru), nama, i(kiru),
and ki, etc.

There are also compounds, consisting of two or more Chinese characters
bound together, which carry a separate meaning. The compound 学生 which
is composed of 学 and 生 , means a person studying at a college or the like.
The compound 生命 , (which is today pronounced) seimei, used to be pronounced inochi as well. If all the kun in the compounds using 生 were counted,
it is said that 生 would have 165 different pronunciations. It might be that
there are so many on and kun, and in addition (so many) pronunciations and
meanings of compounds, that it perhaps would be impossible to master all of

them even if one spent one's whole life(time). Consequently, in Japan today, 1,850 characters have been declared as Tōyō Kanji (Chinese characters of current use); these characters and their on and kun are designated for use in ordinary newspapers, magazines, and text books that primary and secondary school children learn.

Furthermore, 881 from among those characters have been set aside as the ones which [students] are to be enabled to read and write during primary and secondary school.

To begin with, let us study those 881 characters.

LESSON 6

Said Mr. Smith, who had been invited to visit a friend who had just built a new house:

"Such a distasteful ("kirai na") house I have never seen." The friend (who was told so) was offended at these words; yet what Mr. Smith had really wanted to say was "beautiful ("kirei na") house."

Said Mr. Jones, who had invited a friend to tea:

"This cake has dust ("gomi") in it, so it's delicious. Just try some." If you eat something with dust in it, you'll get sick, won't you? Actually, [what he meant] was "sesame ("goma")."

Please pay attention to the long and short vowels, too. For there is no excuse if you [ever] call a middle-aged lady ("obasan") an old lady ("obāsan")!

Let's also take note of the accent. Depending on the accent, hana turns out to be either "flower" or "nose." Again, for shita ni oku, speak so that you will be clearly understood: either "puts it below" or "puts it on the tongue."

Among loanwords, odd abbreviations are not infrequent; remember such words. Terebi is the abbreviation of terebijon ("television"), and toire of toiretto ("toilet").

Kanemochi is someone who has a lot of money, and mochigane is money you have with you. Monohoshi is the place where one dries clothes, and conversely, when you say hoshimono, you mean things which are hung up to dry or the action of hanging up to dry.

Also, a stonemason ("ishiya") and a doctor ("isha") are quite different, are they not?

LESSON 7

As they say, "Things differ from place to place;" both the spoken language and its accent are quite different depending on the location. Ordinarily, we call languages which differ according to geographical region dialects. In contrast to dialects, the language commonly used throughout Japan is called the common language or the standard language.

If we pick out some of the words from around the country that correspond to the common language's "Ohayō gozaimasu," an expression of greeting, we find:

Ohayo gansu

Hayai no moshi

Hayo me ga sameyashita

Kesa mada jai moshita

Kyō wa mekkari mōsan

Ohi n nari

and so on: there are quite a few unusual ways of saying [it].

According to the place, or according to the people (=speakers), there are various expressions; but it does not happen that the Japanese cannot at all communicate with one another, since television and radio are fairly popularized nowadays and the common language is taught at school. However, if two people talk to each other, one in the Kyūshū dialect and the other in the Tōhoku dialect, they may often be embarrassed by not knowing what the other is saying ("neither would know what's what"), or by misunderstanding each other.

Dialects are languages of local daily life, and their boundaries of circulation are narrow; but they are by no means inferior languages.

If one first studies the common language well and then makes a study of the dialects of various places, one will not only understand better the nature of the Japanese language but also come to appreciate ("be able to understand") the way Japanese think and their culture, too.

LESSON 8

Ikeda: "Hello?"

  X: "Hello."

  I : "Is this the Ushiyama residence?"

  X: "No, it isn't. What number were you calling?"

  I : "Number? 281-4305."

  X: "This is 4304."

  I : "Oh, I'm terribly sorry. Excuse me."

  X: "That's OK."

*   *   *

  I : "Hello?"

Maid: "Hello."

  I : "Is this the Ushiyama residence?"

  M: "Yes, it is."

  I : "Is Michiko there?"

M: "Miss [Michiko] hasn't come back from the office yet; who's calling, please?"

I : "Ikeda from Akasaka; when do you expect her back?"

M: "Today's Saturday, so I think she'll get back around 1:30. Would you like her to call you back in a little while?"

I : "Let's see . . . If you wouldn't mind, I'd like to send a message."

M: "Certainly."

I : "I'm leaving for Kyōto the day after tomorrow early in the morning, so if she has the time ("is free") tomorrow afternoon, please ask her to come visit me at my lab in Itabashi."

M: "Yes, certainly. I'll give her the message."

I : "Thank you ("Please do"). Goodbye."

M: "Goodbye."

LESSON 9

The three [newspapers], the Asahi, the Mainichi and the Yomiuri, are representative Japanese newspapers.

Among newspapers, a sizable number startle their readers by sensational headlines; however, the Asahi, through accurate articles and a minimum of mistakes, enjoys an excellent reputation.

In most of the newspapers, the articles are organized (by dividing) into sections such as political events, finance, community affairs, art and culture, sports, and radio and TV.

In addition, they also run editorials which reflect the newspaper(-company)'s views, [serialized] fiction, cartoons, and other such items.

Letters to the editor are also quite popular.

Besides articles and photographs, these newspapers have many advertisements for books, magazines, department stores, movies, medicines, cosmetics, cameras and so forth.

The reason why you can buy a newspaper cheap is due to the fact that the newspaper company's income from advertising is large.

LESSON 10

After the Second World War, the Japanese educational system was changed into what is called the "6-3-3" system.

In the old system, kyūsei, ("the old system"), the Shōgakkō ("elementary school") had consisted of six years, the Chūgakko ("junior high school") of five years, the Kōtōgakkō ("high school") of three years, and the Daigaku ("university or college") of three years. The Chūgaku were schools for boys, and the girls went to the Jogakkō ("girls' schools"). There was almost no ("hardly any") coeducation.

The K̄otogakk̄o were schools for male students preparing for college, while the students who did not continue on to college entered professional schools from the Chūgaku or Jogakk̄o. In the prewar era there were few universities which permitted the entrance of girl students and, besides, there were few [girl] applicants, so there were barely enough women college students to count [on your fingers]. Education which the citizens must receive perforce is called compulsory education, and the prewar compulsory education had only been the six-year period of the Sh̄ogakk̄o. Since the war, the Sh̄ogakk̄o has remained the same, six years; but both the Chūgaku and K̄ok̄o ("high school") have become three years each and college four. Also, the distinction between the sexes has disappeared, and compulsory education has been extended to nine years, up to the Chūgaku.

Among schools, there are both public and private ones.

There are graduate schools for those people who want to do more research after graduation from college.

LESSON 11

Japan is a country blessed with natural beauty. Furthermore, the shrines and temples (and other such things) at Nikk̄o, Kȳoto (and other such places) are known all over the world for the magnificent man-made beauty of their buildings and gardens.

There are a few people who think that only those things for which money has been freely spent are splendid and have value; but we should not forget the fact that there is a beauty all its own which cannot be found in foreign countries even in the inexpensive bowls and dishes we use daily.

In this kind of ceramic ware, there are quite a few pieces which have been made by the handicraft of anonymous people. Of course, it goes without saying that there are beautiful things among the articles made at large factories, too. But usually, since machines are used for the purpose of making the largest quantity of things as cheaply as possible in a short time, each of the manufactured products has the same appearance, and, what is more, they are likely to be poorly made. On top of this, because human beings are exploited by the machines, the enjoyment of work is taken from the working people.

Handicraft is laden with human feelings, such as joy, sorrow, and agony.

I think that there is some sort of beauty in the things which are made with one's whole heart, even if money is not spent for them.

LESSON 12

[Dear Sampei;]
I have neglected to write, but I hope everyone in Hawaii is well ("Is everyone in Hawaii well?"). I am very well, (thank you,) and I am happily spending my time every day doing such things as visiting friends and shopping or sight-seeing.

In Tokyo, the rainy season has ended and it has suddenly turned hot. It's like a steam bath, as they say; it's muggy and sometimes (even) at night you can't sleep well.

The summer seasonal wind blows the water-vapor in from the Pacific Ocean, and they say it is muggy for this reason; but since this rain and temperature are necessary for agriculture, especially for the growing of rice, we have to put up with it.   Food rots easily, and gastrointestinal disorders increase, so I hope it gets cool soon.

While it remains hot, I am planning to go to the home of my country relatives and have fun doing such things as mountain climbing and surfing on the sea.

When the typhoon [which comes annually about the two hundred and tenth day after the traditional first day of spring] has passed and the fine autumn weather has become well-established, I am going to the Kansai [region], so I will send you news from there later on.   My best to everyone.

5 July   Sincerely yours ("Goodbye"),
  (Mr. Sampei Tsunoda)
                                                 Kōji Tanaka

LESSON 13

One of the important things (= factors) in an expanding economy is [international] trade.

By "trade" we mean commercial transactions with foreign countries. It consists of exportation and importation; exportation is the selling of goods to foreign countries, and importation is the buying of goods from foreign countries.

As for export goods, there is a lot of textiles, including [in particular] cotton goods bound for America; aside from that, pottery, toys, and other inexpensive merchandise used to be the chief [export goods], but in recent years cameras, transistor radios, machinery, ships, and other such things have been gradually increasing [in amount].

Among import goods, raw cotton and raw materials for industry are numerous: and this shows the abundance, within [the whole of] Japanese trade, of the processing trade, which involves the importation of raw materials and the exportation of finished goods [in return].   Also, because there is insufficient food in Japan for the dense population, rice and wheat [and other food products] are imported.

The United States occupies top place as partner for [Japanese international] trade.   Before the war, China was the most important partner; but today, the trade with Southeast Asian countries, rather than trade with Communist China, seems to hold brighter prospects.

LESSON 14

Having graduated from high school, I thought I would certainly like to find employment in Tokyo, and I wrote letters to friends in Tokyo ever so many times. However, staying in the country and having friends look for work [for one] is [like] "eye-lotion [dropped into the eyes] from upstairs" [= obviously ineffectual], so I boldly decided to go to Tokyo, since nothing is better than looking for oneself.   Even a lonely village in a mountain valley can be "[like] the capital, if one lives there [long enough]". When it came time to leave, I grew sad.

Upon arriving in Tokyo I found it was a great metropolis (that is), as the proverb says, "a paradise when you hear about it — a hell when you see it" [a place] where they "pluck the eyes right out of a live horse" [= engage in sharp practices, "skin you alive if you give them a chance"]. I had not the slightest idea how in the world I would find a job. But they say "even a dog will come across a stick if he [just] walks" [= it takes a bit of effort to achieve anything], so I looked at the newspaper [want-]ads and inquired into them one by one.

I walked around day after day for (about) a week, but every single one of them was "too short for a belt and too long for a sash [to hold up tucked sleeves]" [= inadequate in one respect or another] and I did not find a suitable job. On top of that, last night I lost my wallet with all my money ("fortune") in it. I got depressed, with the feeling that this was really "a crying face stung by a bee" [= disaster stalking misfortune].

This morning a letter came from my father which said that there was some kind of job in the village office and as long as I would be living in my home town I would not be at a loss [for something] to eat and asked me how it would be to come home (=suggested why not come home). With that, I decided to bow to parental opinion and return home immediately.

LESSON 15

Japan ("our country") is an island country which lies between the Asian continent and the Pacific Ocean; its territory consists of the four islands of Kyūshū, Shikoku, Honshū, and Hokkaidō, and more than three thousand small islands in their vicinity.

Its total surface area is approximately 370,000 square kilometers.

In addition to this, Korea ([Communist] North Korea and the Republic of Korea), Formosa, Okinawa, Southern Sakhalin, and the Kuriles were Japanese territories until the Second World War.

As a result of the defeat in the war, these territories were lost; furthermore, as the people who returned from overseas, and repatriated soldiers and the like were added, the population rose considerably. Moreover, as the birthrate is high, the natural increase in population is not inconsiderable, so that the day when the population will number one hundred million is not too far away.

As for the geographical features of Japan ("our country"), since most of the land is mountainous, the population density as measured against the arable land is the highest in the world today.

Consequently, the question of what is best to do to support a large population while raising the standard of living is a serious problem.

LESSON 16

Japan is surrounded on four sides by the sea; its shape is long and slender, and it has many mountain ranges. For that reason, there are scarcely any large rivers, long streams, [or] vast plains.

The fact that there are many swift streams is convenient for the generation of hydroelectric power; but damage by floods is also frequent, and the scarcity of plains despite the large population means that there is an insufficiency of food production besides inconvenience in transportation.

In Japan there are many volcanoes, and for this reason, there are many hot springs and quite a few places beneficial for health purposes. On the other hand, there is quite a lot of damage attributable to earthquakes [in particular] and volcanic activity.

Peninsulas, ports, lakes, forests, and groves are to be seen everywhere, and there are many kinds of plants; [Japan] is blessed with scenic beauty.

As Japan is in the temperate zone, its climate is mild and the four seasons are clearly differentiated.

The fact that [Japan] is separated from Europe and the American continent makes for inconveniences in economic and cultural interchange; but this problem is gradually being solved through developments in aviation and other means of transportation.

LESSON 17

At a restaurant. Conversation between customers and the waitress.

Waitress: Welcome. What can we do for you?

Tamaki : There's someone else coming, so wait a while.

    W: Very well.

    T: Hayashi's late, isn't he?

Ueda   : He'll probably be along soon. What shall we have?

    T: How about chicken today (= this time)?

    U: Actually, I [just] had chicken last night.

    T: Well, how about tempura?

    U: Fine, but is it all right . . . [I mean] if we order ("decide on") tempura?

    T: Sure, it's all right.

Hayashi : Hi. Sorry to have kept you waiting. Unfortunately, I had a late conference ("a conference until the early evening").

    T: We just got here ourselves. We were just discussing whether we should order tempura; (but) what do you think?

    H: Sounds okay to me.

    U: What else? This place is close to a fish market, so they have good fish here.

    H: Well, let's order white meat of fish broiled with salt.

    T: Hey, waitress!

    W: Yes, sir. Did you call?

T: Uh . . . tempura, and white meat of fish broiled with salt for three. For vegetables, (pick out) something in season.

W: Certainly, sir. And the beverage?

T: Shall we have sake?

U: Beer would probably be better for (perking up or increasing) the appetite.

H: Agreed. (= Right.)

T: Okay, beer. Shellfish salad with vinegar would be good along with the beer.

W: All right. Shall I bring in the [cooked] rice after you finish the beer?

T: Ah, yes. Do that.

W: Very well, sir. Please wait a moment.

*   *   *

U: That was good, wasn't it?

H: I overate without realizing it.

T: How about some fruit?

H: No, thanks. How about you?

U: No, I'm full. I'd just like another cup of hot tea.

T: Hey! Hot tea.

W: Right away, sir.

T: And the bill.

W: Yes, of course.

Mr. Tamaki looked at the paper brought by the waitress on which was written "¥ 2691" and handed over ¥ 3000.

W: [That will be] out of three thousand yen. One moment, please.

T: Keep the change.

W: Thank you. Thank you very much, indeed. Come again.

LESSON 18

Te when used in ōki na nimotsu o ryōte de kakaeru ("carries a big load in both arms") means [the distance] from the shoulder to the fingertips; but te used in te ni toru ("takes in one's hand") means from the wrist to the tip [of the fingers]. Also, the te of te o awasete inoru ("clasps one's hands and prays") means the palms of the hands. Moreover, the te of te ni fureru ("touches") means finger [or fingers]. Te in all these cases refers to parts of the human body. However, when one says furaipan no te ("handle of a frying pan") one means the holding part of the utensil; and if you say hatake no tomato no te ("the prop sticks of a tomato in the field") the meaning is that of sticks holding up the plants.

A long time ago, kanji was called otokode ("gentleman's hand") and hiragana, onnade ("lady's hand"); in this case, the meaning refers to written characters. The te of utaite ("singer") and oyogite ("swimmer") means a person: in other words, a person who sings or a person who swims. Also, the te in fukade o ou ("suffers a severe wound") refers to an injury, while kono te no shinamono ("goods of this kind") has come to mean class or variety. The te of migite no kōen ("the park on the right") points out the right-hand side, in other words, (it shows) the direction. Temawashi means preparation or arrangement and tegotae has the meaning of reaction. Besides these, there are many other usages:

hitode ga nai ("lacks of manpower") — there are not enough workers

te o ageru ("raises the arms") — is defeated; gives up

te ga agaru ("the hands go up") — becomes skillful; progresses [or improves].

te o tsukeru ("puts one's hands to it") — begins new work or the like.

te o utsu ("claps the hands") — devises a counterplan.

te o hiku ("withdraws one's hands") — washes one's hands of ("severs relationships with") an affair, a problem, etc.

te ga aku ("the hands become empty") — becomes free [unbusy].

te o yaku ("burns one's hands") — is disturbed by a troublesome problem.

te o kakeru ("hangs one's hands on") — takes good care of.

te ni kakeru ("hangs something on one's hand") — kills [someone].

tebanasu ("lets something go from one's hand") — sells; sends [something or someone] to another place.

te ga nagai ("one's hands are long") — has a habit of stealing things [= "has sticky fingers"].

te o komaneku ("folds one's arms") — meditates with one's hands in one's pockets; does nothing.

te ga fusagatte iru ("the hands are engaged") — is busy; is in the middle of work and has no [free] time.

There are many more ways of using it.

The same expression, te ga nai, depending upon the content of the statement or sentence, has the meaning of "no way to do" as well as the meaning of "lack of manpower." Also, as for te o hiku, if you say mō ano jiken kara wa te o hikimashita yo ("I have withdrawn my hand from that affair"), you mean kankei o tatta ("I severed relations"); and if you say kodomo no te o hiite, sanpo-suru ("I take the child's hand and go for a walk"), you mean kodomo no te o totte, michibiki-nagara sanpo-suru ("taking the child's hand, I go for a walk while leading the way").

(What we call) "words" [or "language(s)"] are complicated things.

LESSON 19

Sumō, Jūdō, Kendō, Karate, and the like are traditional Japanese sports; but among them, the one which is most popular with the general public is Sumō. This resembles the modern sport of wrestling; it is a match between two persons ("individual vs. individual"), in which [to win] you down your opponent without using a weapon. There are various [traditional] forms and rules, so many as to be called "the 48 Techniques of Sumō," and one has to undergo a long period of training in order to become a full-fledged [Sumō] wrestler. Today, none but [Sumō] wrestlers dress the hair in a mage ("topknot") as the samurai ("warrior") did in the old days.

Jūdō, Karate, and Kendō are likewise matches between individuals; but Jūdō is rather more a matter of self-defense and warding off the enemy than of attacking. And if one has some knowledge of Jūdō techniques, even a woman can throw a large man down by utilizing her opponent's [physical] force.

Karate was worked out and improved years ago in the Ryūkyūs (Okinawa) where the people had been deprived of their weapons by Japan. It is a martial art of self-defense which uses the hands and feet [or arms and legs] for striking and kicking the enemy. If one continues to practice, eventually one will be able with a single blow of the hand to split up any number of roof-tiles piled on top of each other.

Kendō, which was born out of the warrior's need, is truly a Japanese sport. It is a heroic military art in which [two persons], wearing men ("mask"), kote ("gloves"), and dō ("body armor"), attack each other with a sword: usually a wooden sword or one of bamboo called shinai. These martial arts were practiced for improving one's skill [in the arts] and also ("at the same time") for the purpose of cultivating one's mind.

In Japan, today, practically all kinds of modern sports, including [especially] field-and-track events and aquatic sports, are pursued; and they [or we] participate in the Olympic Games, too.

LESSON 20

Yasuko: I wonder what kind of occupation I should go into when I graduate.

Haruko: Well, I plan to be a teacher, so entering a college where they have a good faculty is the first consideration.

Yasuko: Since I'm not much good at studying, I'd like to go to work in an office ("a company") or bank right away. Even an office-girl or a secretary would be okay.

Haruko: The income at a retail store in town might be better if [it were a store where] business is steady. I wonder . . .

Yasuko: Even so, it's disgusting to say "Yessir! At your service!" at the butcher's or charcoal-dealer's or the like.

Haruko: Oh, I don't mean that kind of work, but something like office work or bookkeeping in a big store. Since you have an artistic sense, I wonder how you'd like selling materials for Western clothes, like dry goods, buttons, and so on?

Yasuko: It sounds like fun, doesn't it?

Shūichi: What are you both talking about?

Haruko: Occupations. [We are talking about] what kind of occupation would be the best.

Yasuko: What do you plan to be, Shūichi?

Shūichi: Let me see . . . We don't have any military men anymore, so I guess [I will be] a public worker. I'd like to do work in the government. At one time I wanted to be a judge or a lawyer; but even just thinking about such things as having to remember unconditionally tens of thousands of laws . . . well, it's enough to make me faint.

Haruko: I think acquiring skill in any kind of profession would be good. Such as an engineer or a doctor . . . A dentist would be good too.

Shūichi: That's true, but to do that, you have to attend a university or a professional school; and besides, it is not easy financially ("economically"), so just not everyone can [afford to] do so. When I was a kid, I wanted to be a train engineer.

Yasuko: Boys usually do. I used to yearn to be an artist: a poet, a painter, an architect, or the like.

Shūichi: By the way, I believe that everyone should recognize more the importance of the work of people like fishermen and farmers. Since they work hard at the production of food for other people while contenting themselves with a small income.

Haruko: Surely! If it weren't for carpenters and plasterers houses wouldn't be built; and we'd be in quite a fix, wouldn't we, if there weren't any [Shintō] priests and [Buddhist] monks. Since today (= this) is the "division of labor" era, we have to get jobs that suit each of us individually, and live by helping each other.

LESSON 21

The agricultural population of Japan is more than 40 percent of the entire population, yet the farmers' [economic] standing considered from the aspect of national income and amount of production is extremely low.

In Japan, where the arable land is limited, however much one carries out intensive agriculture—a method of producing as many crops as possible from the small paddies and dryfields by alloting a great deal of labor and fertilizer to them—the farming population is still too large when measured against the arable land. Accordingly, this is the reason that agricultural wages are low.

Among farmers there are both landed farmers and tenant farmers. Landed farmers are those who carry out farming on their own tillable land; while tenant farmers tend lands leased from a landlord.

Before the war, tenant land accounted for ("occupied") almost half of all the land under cultivation. Because it was necessary for the tenant farmers to pay half of the rice produced to the landlord as rent for tenancy, there was a large number of poor tenant farmers, so-called "water-drinking farmers," who could not [afford to] eat rice even though they raised it. After the war, at the urging of the GHQ [= General Headquarters of the Supreme Commander for the Allied Powers: MacArthur], a farm land reform [program] was decisively carried out.

The government forcibly purchased the tenant lands of absentee landlords—landlords who, while owning tillable land, did not farm it or live on it, usually living in the large cities and renting their property to tenant farmers—and land barons—the owners of extensive property—, sold it inexpensively to tenant farmers who desired arable land of their own, and also reduced the farm rents and made them cash-payment. In other words, they turned over Japan's limited arable land to the tenant farmers who had been in a weak position.

I think it is no exaggeration to say that this reform relieved the tenant farmers, promoted the improvement of farm management and living conditions, and succeeded in providing the foundations for the democratization of the farm villages.

LESSON 22

"Did you wake up? [I mean] because of last night's earthquake?"

"I was still up at that time. I had been asked to set this song to music as soon as possible and I was working on it; but the final bar wasn't working out too well. It was just when I was idly thinking with the pen right in my hand that the rattle set in, and without thinking, I ran out into the garden."

"Have you heard the news? They say that even in the hardest [hit] areas, the greatest extent of damage was that the wall clocks stopped."

"Hmm, so I heard. As you know, I really detest earthquakes and thunder. Honestly, I thought it must be ("wondered if it was") a big earthquake."

"I know your face turns pale when it thunders. As for me, I dislike fires [more than thunder and earthquakes]."

"Speaking of fires, when the bell of the watch tower begins to clang, there are people who run off huffing and puffing to a really distant scene of a fire to look at it in spite of the sparks; but I simply can't understand such people."

"I especially hate the siren of a fire engine."

"Wind is also unpleasant, don't you think?"

"A gently blowing spring breeze is nice though, isn't it?"

"When it comes to getting blown at by a 'howler,' I want no part of it. What's more, when the windows and doors rattle, my attention is distracted, and no matter what I read, nothing enters my head."

"Compared to wind, rain is better, isn't it? Softly falling spring rains and sudden heavy showers in the summer aren't bad, are they?"

"Oh! The front doorbell is ringing so excuse me."

LESSON 23

Most Americans who visit Japan for commercial business, sightseeing, study, and other purposes arrive at Tōkyō International Airport or at the port of Yokohama.

Even Yokohama, which in a sense is ("corresponds to") the doorway of Japan, was [nothing more than] a small fishing village until the middle of the nineteenth century. Since the Meiji Period, when commerce was begun with foreign countries, it has grown rapidly as a port of trade. Today, the port has many facilities and has become one of the world's leading ports. There are frequent departures and arrivals of freighters and oil tankers as well as passenger ships.

In Yokohama, besides foreign business firms and consulates, there are a great many hotels, souvenir shops, restaurants, and the like. There are also quite a large number of foreigners' families living here, and it has quite the appearance of a cosmopolitan city.

Moreover, there is a custom house which checks exports and imports and people who are entering and leaving the country. The customs also take charge of warehouses for unloaded goods [from the ships] and of boats which have entered the harbor.

As a harbor, Yokohama has (= enjoys) excellent natural conditions; (and) even in winter it does not freeze over. Furthermore, the depth of the harbor is great, and the seabed, varying little in depth, is suitable for anchoring.

On top of this, because it is located near Tōkyō—the capital of Japan and also a large consumer area—and has convenient land transportation, Yokohama has developed as the outer port of Tōkyō and has become one of the Six Big Cities.

The area between Yokohama and Tōkyō is a great industrial zone with many kinds of industries; and light industries, heavy industries, and chemical industries have been developing side by side.

LESSON 24

Days which have been designated as national holidays.

New Year's Day   January 1
   [The day on which] we celebrate the beginning of the year.

Adults' Day   January 15
   [The day on which] we celebrate and encourage the youth who have acquired awareness that they have become adults.

Vernal Equinox   March 21
   [The day on which] we admire living things and appreciate nature.

The Emperor's Birthday   April 29
   [The day on which] we celebrate the day His Majesty the Emperor was born.

Constitution Commemoration Day   May 3
   [The day on which] we commemorate the new promulgation of the constitution of Japan and look forward to the growth of the country.

Children's Day   May 5
   [The day on which] we honor the personality of the child, plan for his happiness, and take care of ("protect") the children, at the same time expressing gratitude to mothers.

Autumnal Equinox   September 23
   [The day on which] we revere our ancestors and remember those who have passed away.

Culture Day   November 3

    [The day on which] we show our love for ("love") freedom and peace, and promote culture.

Labor Thanksgiving Day   November 23

    [The day on which] we hold labor and personal service in high esteem and mutually express gratitude to the people of the nation.

LESSON 25

"Hello."

"Hello, is this Mr. Orihara?"

"Yes, that's right."

"This is Iwata [calling]. Well, I bought a car at the end of last month, you know. I should have called you sooner ("this is short notice"), but my elder sister wants me to take her for a drive tomorrow. And I was wondering if you would like to join us."

"You finally bought it, did you? What is it?"

"A black Datsun. Tomorrow, we'll drag my elder brother along and have him drive the car. He has had a good record of safe driving ("no accidents") for five years, so please don't worry. If you like please join us."

"Well, well. I would love to go with you. Where will you go?"

"We're thinking of going to Kujūkuri seashore in Chiba. Please bring your younger sister and younger brother too if you like."

"Can so many people get in a car?"

"Three from your family, (then) my elder brother and elder sister and I make six, don't we? Sure, we can all get in. According to the map, it's a place about three hours (away), so what do you say if we come to pick you up at eight o'clock in the morning, have lunch out there, and then come back before it gets dark?"

"That'll be fine. The sky is quite starry tonight, so I'm sure ("there is no doubt") it'll be excellent weather tomorrow."

"[Yes.] It looks like we won't have to worry about the weather. Well, we'll see you at eight o'clock tomorrow morning. Oh, you had better take a blanket and wool sweater [with you]."

"I see. Thanks a lot. I'm looking forward to it."

"Bye now."

"Goodbye and good night."

LESSON 26

Clothing comes next after food as an important necessity of life. Typical ("representative") kinds of clothing are cotton, wool, silk, and synthetic fabrics.

In Japan, until around 500 years ago, fabrics woven of strong fibers gathered from the bark of trees and [from] hemp were in daily use; but at present, it is cotton which is used in largest quantities. Cotton is known as the king of clothing: since it is durable in water it can be washed frequently and is easily cleaned; it is long-wearing ("durable") and agreeable to the touch; on top of [all] that, it is inexpensive. Cotton cloth is a material woven with thread produced from the cotton plant. There is scarcely any cotton production in Japan; nevertheless, [the Japanese people] import raw cotton, and, with the techniques of machine weaving and [their] cheap labor, [Japan] has become a leading cotton textile producing country.

Woolen fabric has the disadvantage of being (easily) infested by moths, but it is good for keeping warm and is indispensable for winter clothing. With few exceptions, it is a cloth woven of fibers made from sheep's wool (= fleece). In Japan, where they have neither abundance of rich pasture lands nor a climate suitable for sheep raising, they import raw wool and manufacture woolen goods.

Silk is a material woven with the raw silk produced from cocoons of the silkworm and is a beautiful, luxurious textile. In Japan, sericulture is practiced as a subsidiary business of farmers.

There are limits to the amount of production of cotton, silkworms, and sheep. In order to compensate for this insufficiency, synthetic fibers such as rayon, made by using pulp as raw material, have come to be produced. Nylon, which is many times stronger than silk, is a chemical synthetic produced from carbolic acid. Today, along with the progress of science, countries compete in their efforts toward research and improvement of synthetic fibers; and new products, one after another, are being manufactured on a trial basis, and [then] put on the market for sale.

LESSON 27

Under ("in the era of") the old constitution, the absolute rights of the head of a household were protected by law; and [this] head of the household was ruler of the family and its members. Usually the one to inherit the position of head of a household was the eldest son, who was especially cared for from childhood on; after his father's death or retirement, the son received the father's entire fortune and became the one responsible for the family. RANK in the family was strict, and even the [order of] seats at the dinner table and the order of bath-taking were fixed. The position of women was low, and it was [the proper] virtue for a wife to be obedient to her husband and her [or his] father (and such people). In marriage also, such things as family lineage, family standing, and the condition of the [family] fortune were considered important, and it often happened that the desires of the people directly involved were ignored. There were many [married] people who [still] lived with their parents even after marriage; especially in the country, [everybody] lived together [with their] children and grandchildren as a large family under the same roof.

In this type of old family system, there were, to be sure, [some] strong points ("it was not the case that there were no strong points"). However, friction of ideas and feelings did occur between the mother-in-law and the young wife and between the old folks and young people; with the result that complicated problems frequently developed within the family.

Nowadays, under the new constitution, men and women are equal under the law; and a home has come to be thought of as a place where a family lives and works together. It is reported that the young men and women of the cities have become very lively and free both in their behavior and in their ways of thinking. Yet even so, it would seem that among the conservative older people, the [way of thinking based on the] old family system and customs are still firmly rooted and followed.

LESSON 28

I'm a white-collar worker employed at a certain company. Last year, at the time of my graduation from college, I took the entrance examination and became a member of the company staff. Since my monthly wage is still small, I'm living in a boardinghouse.

Every morning, after breakfast is over, I run to the station and push and shove to get on a (electric) car crowded with people who are struggling over every single minute and second. It is my dream to commute to work by private car [= auto] but [I don't know if I'll ever be able to] . . .

Mornings, at the office, I'm hounded by phone calls and [official] papers. At noon, I go to the company's dining hall to have a lunch prepared by a dietician on the basis of a calorie computation. After the meal, there is a noon recess till one o'clock; we pass [this recess] pleasantly, some [of us] taking walks, some playing baseball or tennis, some having rehearsals in a choral group organized jointly with the female employees.

In the afternoons, there are conferences and consultations and appointments ("meetings of visitors") and so on; on busy days, I can't even find time to go out for a cup of tea.

This company has fairly good welfare facilities: a dormitory for staff members is now under construction, and in the nearby prefectures there is a "mountain cabin" and a "beach house" [maintained by the company for the employees' recreation].

The health program is also well run and the medical service section gives [us] attentive guidance with respect to hygiene and prevention of diseases.

We have a labor union, of course; the delegates, who are chosen from among the union members, do their best to promote the company's growth as well as the employees' happiness through capital-labor cooperation [achieved] by discussions with the company executives.

LESSON 29

Japan's new constitution, which was enacted on the third of May in the twenty-second year of Shōwa (1947), consists of a preamble and 103 articles.

The spirit forming the basis [of the constitution] is, first of all, the idea of popular sovereignty: that the people possess the sovereign power; it completely denies the absolute power which had been held by the Emperor and stipulates that the Emperor has no function with respect to state affairs. The Emperor, who had been regarded as a sacred deity under the old constitution, has, together with the Empress, come to be held in affection by the people as a [fellow] human being. Secondly, under the new constitution, international peace is earnestly sought, the permanent abandonment of war is prescribed, and the maintenance of an army as well as the country's right to participate in a war are not recognized (=permitted). This fact, when compared with the old constitution, whose purpose was the enrichment of the country and the strengthening of the military, shows that the new constitution has for its purpose peace, which is an entirely opposite concept.

Furthermore, in the old constitution, emphasis was laid upon morals and obligations, such as loyalty, filial piety, humanity, and benevolence, which the Japanese as a people were to uphold, while the new constitution states in detail the rights and duties of the people, with the focus on their benefits.

Also, individual freedom and respect for fundamental human rights are given particular emphasis. From the standpoint of the equality of persons [=When we look at the situation with respect to equality of person], the peerage system has been abolished and the right of equality between the sexes ("of men and women") is recognized. Consequently, adult men and women who have Japanese nationality are enabled by means of elections to participate equally in the government through the National Diet.

LESSON 30

In Japan ("our country"), there are so many kinds of mineral products that it is called a gallery of mineral specimens. Most of the usual ones such as gold, silver, copper, iron, coal, and oil, are produced; but the quantity of each is small, hardly enough [for the nation] to be self-sufficient.

There is almost no production of that liquid fuel, petroleum; for the most part, crude oil is imported from Arabia and the refined products from America. With the invention of the internal combustion engine, petroleum, once used [only] in lamps, has become important as a source of power. Moreover, since it is used extensively as a raw material in the chemical industries, particularly in the production of synthetic rubber, the nations [of the world] have grown frantic in their exploitation of oil fields.

Eighty percent of the total output of coal in Japan is taken from the coal fields of northern Kyūshū and of Hokkaidō. However, for geological and topographical reasons, Japan's coal fields have short and narrow veins. Consequently, mining with large-scale mechanized mining techniques is almost impossible. That is why most of coal is mined by inefficient and primitive means, with the result that the coal output is not great. Through progress in our knowledge and technology, coal, in addition to being employed as a fuel, is also employed as a raw material in the manufacture of different kinds of drugs, plastics, and synthetic fibers; its uses are being expanded in many directions.

LESSON 31

The four seasons come about [follow upon each other] as the earth revolves around the sun while itself revolving on its axis. In Japan, both seasonal and meteorological changes are complicated and there is quite a lot of damage caused by winds and floods. Especially the damage resulting from the typhoons which strike ("land on") Japan proper almost every year is great; it is not uncommon for lives to be lost, to say nothing of buildings and bridges being washed away. Consequently, the study of weather conditions and of the heavens [in general] ("celestial bodies") is quite important.

The sun which has been shining softly on a mirror-still lake is suddenly covered up by black clouds, and a rainstorm comes [blowing] in. The people, far from enjoying the picturesque and beautiful scenery, must [now] worry about an electrical blackout, or an interruption of the railway, telegraph, or telephone [service].

If we could predict the changes in weather, we could dispense with unnecessary worries and also prevent various natural disasters. For this reason ("out of this necessity"), the radio and television broadcast weather forecasts at fixed hours every day, and daily weather forecasts and maps are put [out] in the newspapers as well.

If we keep carefully observing the changes in air temperature, humidity, atmospheric pressure, wind, clouds, and rainfall, we can tell what the changes in the weather will be. Nowadays, weather forecasts put out by meteorological stations or observatories are based on weather maps. A weather map is something which is made so as to record, in particular, rainy or clear [weather], the wind direction and velocity, and the atmospheric pressure of every region at a specific time, plus isobaric lines and the central location of high and low pressure [areas], so that we can visualize at a glance the extent of the weather conditions over a wide area at a given time.

The central meteorological observatory [in Tōkyō] produces weather maps based on the results of surveys collected from weather stations in every region and from ships at sea: by drawing up a weather map at regular intervals of time, they find out the changes in the weather conditions and the shifts of high and low pressure [zones]; moreover, using radar ("radio waves"), they observe the conditions of the upper atmosphere. From all these data they announce weather forecasts.

LESSON 32

Almost every day we send and receive letters, postcards, and packages, as well as such periodicals as newspapers and magazines. No one would object to the statement that the post-office's business is downright essential to everyday life.

When we look over the history of Japan's postal business, [we find that] first of all, in the fourth year of the Meiji Era (1871) it became a government-operated enterprise and the first stamps were issued. Up to that time, hikyaku ("couriers") and the like were used. In the eighth year of the same period [the Meiji Period], foreign mail between Japan and America was handled for the first time. Affiliation with the Universal Postal Union Treaty dates from the tenth year of Meiji. In the sixteenth year [of Meiji] the rates were made uniform throughout the (entire) country. Parcel post was begun in the twenty-fifth year [of Meiji], and airmail was instituted in the thirteenth year of the Taishō Period.

The main matter of business for the post-office is collection and delivery. Postal matter which is collected from the mailboxes on the street corners is first examined at the post-office and postmarked. Then it is classified as to its address ("destination"), forwarded, and sorted again for delivery at the receiving post-office;[mail for]a route is put together, and the mail is delivered from door to door. At the end of the year, when New Year's cards pile up, they are short of hands with only the [regular] post-office staff; "arbeit" students [who are working on the side] and others are mobilized.

In addition to collection and delivery they also handle money orders, deposits, transfer savings, annuities, government pensions, postal[life] insurance ("easy insurance"), etc. When you would like to have postal matter sent to its destination even a little faster, you can make use of special delivery, and for [sending it] to foreign countries, you can make use of airmail. Furthermore, for compensation in case postal matter is lost or damaged, there is also registered mail of which a record is made and kept until delivery. Besides the above, there are also contents-certified mail, delivery-certified [mail] and so on.

The rate for letters of regular domestic mail is ¥10 for every twenty grams, ¥5 for a regular postcard, and ¥10 for a (double) postcard with reply-paid postcard attached.

LESSON 33

Every year at fixed times, regular events are celebrated repeatedly all over Japan. For example, there are New Year's Day, hinamatsuri ("the Doll Festival"), o-bon ("the Feast of Lanterns or the Buddhist All Souls' Day"), plus the religious festivals of Shintō shrines. Of course, there are variations in customs and folklore, more or less depending on the locality; but events such as these are generally called nenchū-gyōji ("the annual events").

On New Year's Day, people erect the pine gate ("kadomatsu"), offer ricecake-offerings, worship the first sunrise, and go out for their first worship [of the year]at the shrine of their ancestral god. They also pay a New Year's Day visit to acquaintances living nearby and send New Year's greetings to their friends far away. From New Year's Day until the fifteenth, various events are held one after another.

When it gets to be February, there is setsubun ("the parting of the seasons"). On the evening of the day before the beginning of spring[by the old lunar calendar], people scatter soybeans all through the house, crying out repeatedly "Fortune in, devils out!"

In March, there is the Doll Festival. Nowadays this has come to be a festival at which girls display pretty festival dolls. The original form [of this event], however, was a ceremony in which people of former times would go down to the sea or to the rivers to purify their bodies and float dolls on the water after [first] transferring [their] human impurities to the dolls. This was one of the religious events of Shintō, the religion peculiar to Japan. The days around the vernal and autumnal equinoxes are called higan; during these periods, people visit [ancestral] graves as part of the religious observances of Buddhism.

In May, the Boys' Festival occurs; they display helmets and armor [of the old samurai style], hoist a carp pennant high into the sky, and take an "iris bath" ("shobu-yu").

The most enjoyable events [celebrated] in the farm villages are the Feast of Lanterns and the festival of the tutelary [ancestral] deity. The Feast of Lanterns is a Buddhist event occurring around the fifteenth of July [as the main day on which] one worships one's dead ancestors. About this time of the year there is a custom called chūgen according to which people exchange presents with their acquaintances. They also give bonuses ("allowances") to maid-servants and employees and let them go home [or somewhere else] to enjoy themselves. In the evening, the Bon Festival Dance is performed throughout Japan. [For this] they build a tall scaffold in the compound of a shrine or on an open space and [decorate it] prettily [with] red, yellow, and green lamps, and small flags and lanterns; [then] men, women, and children all form a circle and dance around to the rhythm of drums.

Of the shrine festivals, the spring one is when the people pray to the local ("village") guardian deity for a rich harvest and peace, and in autumn they offer the [first] crops harvested and give thanks; these [religious ceremonies] are combined with recreational activities that people all over the village can enjoy.

During the various periods of the nenchū-gyōji, there are certain special dietary customs, such as foods which are to be abstained from and those which are to be eaten without fail.

Before laughing away these customs as superstitions or remnants of past generations, it would be well ("important") to study the customs and manners of the people in order to understand the everyday emotions of the Japanese people and their ways of thinking.

LESSON 34

In Japan, the operation of government is based on the system of separation of three powers: legislative power belongs to the Diet, executive power belongs to the Cabinet, and judicial power belongs to the courts.

The Diet in Japan is the highest organ of state power, and it consists of the Shūgiin (House of Representatives) and the Sangiin (House of Councillors).

The major legislative powers of the Diet are the initiation of amendments to the Constitution, the enactment of laws and the approval of treaties.

The major fiscal powers include resolutions on the budget, approval of the final accounts and decisions on national expenditures.

The major powers in affairs of state are the nomination of the Prime Minister, the investigation of the government and the impeachment of the judges.

The members of the Diet represent all the nation and are elected by popular vote. Except in special cases, those who are above twenty years of age have the right to vote regardless of sex, rank, or class.

The full complement of members of the House of Representatives is 467, the term of office [of each member] four years; the full complement of members of the House of Councillors is 250, with a term of office of six years.

When the House of Representatives and the House of Councillors [pass] different decisions, the decision of the House of Representatives becomes the decision of the Diet through a set procedure.

The Diet appoints the Prime Minister, who is [as a rule] the head of the majority party among the different political parties.

The Prime Minister appoints the heads of the various ministries, such as the Foreign Ministry and the Finance Ministry, and forms a cabinet.

The Cabinet occupies the highest position in the administration and delegates its responsibility to the various ministries, exercising supervision over them.

The major powers of the Cabinet are the enforcement of laws, the general supervision of government, the management of foreign affairs, the conclusion of treaties, and the preparation and presentation of the budget to the Diet.

When the Cabinet becomes unpopular in the Diet and the House of Representatives passes a vote of no-confidence, the Cabinet resigns en masse unless the House of Representatives dissolves within ten days.

Local government has been strengthened since the end of the war, and in principle has been put under the jurisdiction of local public bodies.

Hokkaidō, Honshū, Shikoku, and Kyūshū are divided into one dō (province), one to (metropolis), two fu (urban prefectures), and forty-two ken (prefectures); these have, respectively, a dō-assembly, a to-assembly, fu-assemblies and ken-assemblies. In addition to these, in each city, town, and village, there is a city council, town council, or village council. The members of these assemblies, as well as the governors of the to, dō, fu and ken, and the administrative heads of the cities, towns, and villages are all elected by direct popular vote. (Today, the gun is no longer a unit of local government.)

The judicial power is vested solely in the courts (the Supreme Court and the lower courts).

The police exist for the purpose of protecting the rights and freedom of individuals as well as for the supervision and control of crime and traffic.

The foregoing [shows that] in general, politics in postwar Japan has been democratized and decentralized; and the collective will of the people and public opinion have come to be considered (=respected as) important. Public opinion is the important and essential element in a democratic form of government, but because there is a danger ("fear") that it will be controlled by propaganda in [this] age that has developed mass communications, constant vigil is required.

LESSON 35

The other day, I had the opportunity to read an interesting report on a survey whose object was the investigation of the favorite pastimes of the young people living in Tōkyō.

Movies hold the first place [in popularity] according to the replies from men, and sports the second place; while the replies from women show traveling first and movies second.

Regarding sports, they answered that they liked "doing" sports by themselves more than "watching" sports like baseball and sumō as in the past, and they mentioned golf and tennis, as well as skiing, skating, sailboating, riding motor scooters, and driving. This fact [the preference for participating in sports], together with the fact that traveling has achieved first rank[in preference], can be interpreted as the result of the stabilization of economic livelihood.

Besides the above, the popularity of[going to the]horse races and bicycle races and of [playing] mah-jong or pinball machines has not diminished. In music, jazz occupies first place; although jazz is being called "a poison that robs one of his thinking power," the extraordinary excitement[felt by]("of") teen-age high school students toward jazz shows no signs of subsiding. An unusual reply was in regard to "stock speculation" ("buying and selling stocks") claiming it to be "more thrilling than buying pari-mutuel tickets."

The "potential rival" of movies, television, is in the sixth place, which is an unexpectedly low rank. However, if young people in the rural areas were the object [of the survey], television, along with radio, might occupy the first or second place. With the establishment of television stations, the way television sets are spreading into the agricultural districts is simply remarkable; and it is no longer unusual to see a farm family spending snowy nights enjoying television while they weave straw rice-bags. It is natural that television should be welcomed in the rural areas where the life is monotonous with very few means of entertainment, and where movies and plays are presented only a few times a year in the auditoriums of the elementary schools.

In addition to these [pastimes], a vast number of entertainment magazines and books are published every month; quizzes with prizes in weekly magazines seem to be especially enjoyed by many readers in both urban and rural areas ("regardless of area, urban or rural").

Part V

ROMANIZED VERSIONS OF THE DRILL SENTENCES

DÁI | ÍK-KA

1. yóku | wakáru made | yómu koto ḡa | DÁI ITI desu kara || kyóo wa | DÁI | ÍK-KA kara | DÁI | SÁN-KA made sika | yomimasén desita.

2. tabako ÍP-PON | iká ḡa desu ka.

3. "teeburu no UÉ no | TIIsái | KAMÍ o | ITÍ-mai | kudasai." "áa || ano SIRÓi | KAMÍ desu ka. dóozo || nán-mai de mo | A ḡemásu yo."

4. ano AÓi sebiro wa || ZYÓO ḠE | HITÓ-kumi || íkura desu ka.

5. yóku | irassyaimásita. dóozo || oA ḡari kudasái.

6. tabemóno no nedan ḡa | A ḡatta.

7. situmon ḡa | MI-Ttu arimásu.

8. KAMITE kara SANbanmé ni iru zyoyuu wa || dáre desu ka.

9. tu ḡí no | kisyá wa || NOBOri wa || SÁN-zi | NÍ-hun ni || KUDAri wa || tyoodo YÓ-zi ni | demásu.

10. ano misé de wa || DÁISYOO | iroiro na TETYÓO o | utte imásu.

11. denwaTYOO o mísete kudasai.

12. OOkíi no to | TIIsái no to || dótti ḡa | íi desyoo ka.

13. hanáya de || AKAi haná o | HUTÁ-taba katta.

14. boku no KÁ ni wa || GO-nin || hataraite imásu.

15. TÉ o | araitái n desu ḡa. .

16. HÓN no SITA ni || TE ḠAMI ḡa arimásita.

17. SENSÉI ni || kana no TEHÓN o | káite | itadakimásita.

18. súmisu-SENSEI no | MOTÓ de || benkyoo simásita.

19. nedan ḡa SA ḡáttara || kaimasyóo.

20. AÓi | KAMÍire ni || SI, ḠO-doru háitte imasu.

21. ása || yamá ni NOBOri || yuu ḡata | yamá o KUDAtta.

22. TIIsái | booru ḠAMI no hako ḡa | YO-Ttú ka | ITÚ-tu | hosíi.

23. teeburu no UÉ ni || enpitu ḡa SÍ-HON arimasu.

24. watakusi no heyá wa || YÓN-kai ni arimasu.

25. situmon ḡa wakaránakatta kara || HAKUSI no mama káesita.

26. ano SENSÉI wa || GO-nen máe ni | yoorÓppa e | irassyaimásita.

27. ISSYOO | amerika ni iru tumori da sóo desu.

28. ano ÁKAtyan wa || NIḡatú ni | Umaremásita.

29. NÁMA no sakana o | tábeta koto ḡa | arimásu ka.

30. kono sakana wa || Íkite imasu.

31. anó hito wa || uísukii o | KÍ no mama de nomimasu.

32. o-SAKI ni sitúrei simasu.

33. pén no SAKI ḡa | hútoku | narimásita.

34. NÍ-kiro SAKI no | matí made | ikanákereba | narimasén.

DÁI | NÍ-KA

1. kono HÓN ni wa || DÁI | ÍK-KA kara || DÁI | SÁNZYUU | GÓ-KA made
arimasu.   minná de | SÁNZYUU | GÓ-KA desu.

2. kinóo wa || ITI-NITI-zyuu ÁME ḡa | hútte ita kara || SÓTO e | Ikanái de ||
térebi o | MImásita.

3. MÁINITI || koko e irassyáru | EIKOKÚZIN no | EIḠO no SENSÉI wa ||
EIḠO no hoka ni || huransuḠO || supeinḠO || itariiḠO nádo || iroiro na
GAIKOKUḠO ḡa | odeki ni narimásu.

4. KOKUḠO o benkyoo sité kara || hoka no KUNÍḠUNI no | kotobá o | benkyoo
suru tumori désu.

5. kono NIHONḠO no HÓN wa || dáre ḡa | KÁita | monó desu ka.

6. "KATAru" to iu kotobá wa || KOOḠO dé wa | hotóndo | tukaimasén.

7. HITO ní wa || KUTI to hana ḡa | HITO-tu zútu || MÉ to | MIMÍ ḡa | HUTA-
tu zútu || TÉ to | ASÍ ḡa | NI-HON zútu | áru.

8. YASUmi no HÍ ni wa || dónna | kotó o | simásu ka.

9. "kyóo wa | nánNITI desu ka."
"MUIKA désu yo."

10. omosirói | kotó mo || turai kotó mo | áru no ḡa | ZÍNSEI da.

11. nyuuyóoku ni wa || GAIKOKÚZIN ḡa | óoi.

12. MEUE no HITÓ ni wa || téinei ni | hanásite kudasai.   MESITA no HITÓ
ni wa || amari téinei ni | hanasánakute mo | kamaimasén.

13. kono TEḠAMI no NÁKA ni wa || kusuri no MIHON ḡa | Irete arimásu.

14. késa no | nyúusu wa || HITÓBITO no | ZIMOKU o odorokáseta.

15. NIHON no ZINKOO wa || dono ḡurai désu ka.

16. IRIḠUTI wa | kotira désu.

17. kono tatémono wa || hurúi kara || TEIré o | sinákereba | naránai.

18. "SIRÓi kutu ḡa | NÍ-SOKU | hosíi n desu."
"IS-SOKÚ zya | TArinái n desu ka."

19. takusan TEḠAMI o KÁita no de || KAMÍ ḡa | TArinaku nátta.

20. KAMÍ wa ‖ UE kara NIbanMÉ no hikidasi ni │ arimásu.

21. KOSAME dá kara ‖ kása wa │ irimasén.

22. "SAMÚi ne."
     "ÍMA wa ‖ KÁN da kara ‖ ITIban SAMÚi n da yo."

23. ahurika no │ DOZIN no SEIKATU o sirabéru │ tamé ni ‖ ahurika e Ikimásita.

24. nyuuyóoku no │ SEIKATU dé wa ‖ hotóndo │ TUTÍ o │ MÍru koto wa │ nái
     soo desu.

25. NIHON no KUNI no KYUUZITU wa ‖ ITÍ-nen ni │ KOKONO-KA arimásu.

26. TYUUḠOKUḠO o │ narátte ‖ TYUUḠOKÚZIN to │ TYUUḠOKUḠO de │
     hanasitái n desu.

27. hude to sumí o tukatte ‖ GYOOSYO o narátte imasu.

28. ROKU, SITIZYÚU-NIN mo │ atumátte ‖ páatei ḡa │ OKOnawaremásita.

29. GO-péezi no │ SAN-ḠYOO-MÉ kara │ yónde kudasai.

30. ASImóto ni │ ki o túkete.

31. kono TEḠAMI o KÁita no wa ‖ SYO no zyoozú na │ HITÓ desu.

DÁI │ SÁN-KA

1. KYÓNEN no │ NIḠATÚ wa ‖ taihen SÁMUkatta.

2. taihúu ḡa │ SÁtte ‖ ÁME mo │ kaze mo yami ‖ ténki ḡa │ yóku natta.

3. MAINEN HATIḠATÚ ni wa ‖ YASUmí ḡa arimasu.

4. ano SEINEN wa ‖ yóku BENKYOO suru.

5. "o-TOSI wa o-ikutu?"
    "KOKÓNO-tu."

6. EIKOKU kara │ kotira e KItá TOSI ni ‖ tití ni │ sinaremásita.

7. MIḠI kara YO-NIN-MÉ no │ HITÓ ḡa │ YAMADA-san désu.

8. MAISYUU ‖ MUI-KA hataraite ‖ ITI-NITI YASÚmu.

9. RAISYUU no KIN'YÓO ni ‖ TOMOdati to │ sibai o MÍ ni Iku │ tumori désu.

10. SAMÚi kara ‖ híbati ni │ mótto │ HÍ o │ Irete kudasái.

11. natú ni │ náru to ‖ yóku │ HÁNABI o │ MÍ ni Ikimasu.

12. KÍ no SITA de ‖ HÓN o │ yomimasyóo.

13. ano MORI ní wa ‖ TAIBOKU ḡa óoi.

14. ano SIRÓi │ ISI no tatémono wa ‖ nán desyoo.

15. komé wa ‖ IK-KOKU ‖ NÍ-KOKU to │ kazoemásita.

16. KAWA no MIZU wa ‖ KAWAKAMI kara │ KAWASIMO e naḡaremásu.

17. ano KAWA no DOTE ní wa ‖ KÍ ḡa │ óoi.

18. RÁIḠETU │ TOOKA ni │ mata KImásu.

19. SIḠATU | HATUKA wa || KAYÓOBI desu.

20. TUKÍ ḡa | déte iru kara || SÓTO mo | akarúi.

21. NIHONZÍN wa || HANAMÍ ya | TUKIMÍ ḡa | sukí desu.

22. KYÓNEN no | ÓOMIZU de || TÁ mo uti mo | nakusita.

23. KAWÁ kara | SUIDEN ni | MIZU o hiki || TAué o suru.

24. ONNÁ no KO ḡa || AKAi HANÁ o | SIRÓi | KAMÍ ni | tutúnde iru.

25. AÓi koppu de || MIZU o nónda.

26. o-KANE ḡa nákereba || SEIKATU dekínai.

27. kono MIMIkázari wa || hontoo no KÍN desu.

28. KÓNNITI no | NI-DAI KYÓOKOKU wa || amerika to | sobiéto da.

29. konna TUYÓi | uísukii wa || nomemasén.

30. ano tíimu wa | TÚYOkute || ítu mo | katimásu.

31. KÍNZITU || ukaḡaimásu.

32. UEDA-san wa | OOMORÍeki no | TIKÁku ni | súnde iru.

33. ano ZYOTYUU wa | yóku | hatarakimásu.

34. ZYÓSI no IRIḠUTI wa || tatémono no | HIDARITE ni áru.

35. o-SYOOḠATÚ wa || NANOKA máde | YASUmimásu.

36. sono kotáe wa | TADAsíi.

37. SÁYUU o | yóku | MÍte kara || humikiri o | watatte kudasái.

38. taitei no HITÓ wa || MIḠITE de KÁku.

39. NIHÓN wa || YAMÁḠUNI de || MORI ya KÁZAN ḡa | óoi.

40. MORIYAMA-san wa || TANAKA-san no | sitasíi | TOMOdati da sóo desu.

41. YUUZIN no HONDA-san o | go-syookai simásu.

42. ÓOISI-san wa || iroiro na GAIKOKUḠO o | BENKYOO sitá kara || EIḠO
    mo huransuḠO mo | KAkéru desyoo.

DÁI | YÓN-KA

1. ano DAIḠÁKUSEI wa || KYÓNEN || TOODAI ni NYUUḠAKU site || ÍMA |
   EIḠO o BENKYOO site imásu.

2. "yóku MANAbi || yóku asobe"

3. KANTOO-TÍHOO no | TIIsái MURA no | SYOOḠÁKKOO o | KENḠAKU ni
   Ikimásita.

4. kono HÓN wa || dáre ḡa | KOOSEI simásita ka.

5. MAINEN || KOOYUU no atumári ḡa | áru.

6. ano TIHÓO wa || HÁRU wa | ÁME ḡa | óokute || NATÚ wa | musiátukute ||
   HUYÚ wa | OOYUKI ḡa húru kara || RYOKOO wa | ÁKI | sitára | dóo desu ka.

7. IS-SYÚUKAN ni wa │ NANOKA ári ‖ IK-káḠETU ni wa │ SANZYÚU-NITI
    aru.

8. ano IRIḠUTI no haba wa │ ÍK-KEN desu.   ÍK-KEN wa │ ROKU-fiito ḡúrai
    desu.

9. TÓSIKO-san to │ HÁRUKO-san no │ AIDA ni irassyáru │ KATÁ ḡa ‖
    HÁNAKO-san desu.

10. MURATA-san wa ‖ GAKKOO no sóba no │ HUTÁ-MA sika nai │ apáato ni │
    súnde iru.

11. kono KISYÁ kara ‖ MA-mó-naku │ húziSAN ḡa │ MIemásu yo.

12. NIHÓN wa ‖ SYÚNKA │ SYUUTOO ḡa │ hakkíri site iru.

13. RYOKOO ḡa DÁIsuki desu.

14. hitoríTABI desu ḡa ‖ tittó mo │ sabísiku │ arimasén.

15. TUKÍ wa │ HIḠASI kara │ déte ‖ NISI ni háiru.

16. koko wa ‖ TOOZAI-NÁNBOKU │ dótira o │ MÍte mo │ YAMA bákari de ‖
    ZINKOO no sukunái │ KANSON désu.

17. KITAmuki no ié wa ‖ HUYU │ SAMÚi.

18. ano bíru wa ‖ TIZYOO │ HATI-kai ‖ TIKA │ NI-kai áru.

19. kono kozútumi no MEKATA o │ hakátte kudasai.

20. ASÍ ḡa │ itái kara ‖ ARUkiKÁTA ḡa │ hén desu.

21. TIHÓO ni yotte ‖ HUYU no SÁMUsa ḡa │ tiḡau.

22. KOORI ḡa áru kara ‖ IPPO-ÍPPO ‖ ki o túkete │ ARUkinasái.

23. KURUMA wa │ MIḠIḡawa désu kara ‖ HITO wa │ HIDARIḡawa o │ ARÚite
    kudasai.

24. "ano KATA │ dónata?"
    "o-ME ni kakátta koto ḡa │ áru n desu ḡa ‖ o-namae wa │ OMOidasemasén."

25. TOOHOKU no │ áru │ TIHÓO de wa ‖ YON-kaḠETU ḡúrai │ YUKI no NÁKA
    de │ SEIKATU sinákereba │ naránai to OMOimasu.

26. YAMA no UÉ wa ‖ SINSETU de │ masSÍRO desu.

27. arásuka e Iku to ‖ HYÓOZAN ḡa │ MIéru.

28. kono GAKKOO no │ KOOTYOO-SENSÉI wa ‖ tabitabi │ GAIKOKU-RYÓKOO
    o │ sita sóo desu.

29. NINḠEN wa ‖ dandan NAḠAÍki ni │ náru soo desu.

30. NIHÓN de │ ITIban NAḠÁi │ KAWÁ wa ‖ nán desu ka.

31. TYÓOZYO wa │ ÍMA ‖ pári de │ huransuḠO o BENKYOO site imásu.

32. TEḠÚRUMA ni ‖ nímotu o nosete │ hakobu.

33. NAḠATA-san no ATARAsíi KURUMA wa ‖ AÓi │ síboree desu.

34. kono kippu de ‖ totyuu-ḠÉSYA site mo │ íi desyoo ka.

35. TYÚUḠAKU │ SAN-NÉNSEI no │ tokí ni ‖ SENSEI-ḠÁTA ya TOMOdati
    to │ KANSAI-RYÓKOO ni │ Ikimásita.

36. mukasi wa ‖ tokoro-dókoro ni | SÉKI ḡa | átte ‖ TABIBITO ḡa | soko de | siraberáreta.

37. KÚ-ZI no KUDAri de ‖ SAIKA sita.

38. kono heyá wa ‖ NISIBI ḡa atatte | atúi kara ‖ MINAMImuki no heyá ni | uturimasyóo.

39. buraziru wa ‖ MINAMI-ámerika ni | áru | KUNI désu.

40. HÁRU ni | náru to ‖ KÍ ya | kusá no | SINME ḡa déru.

41. SÍNNEN | omedetoo gozaimásu.

42. SENSYUU | kono | ATARAsíi | HÓN o katta.

43. ano KATÁ ḡa ‖ ÁRAta ni | erabáreta | kono MURA no | SÓNTYOO-san desu.

44. HITO o KÚu | kumá ḡa | iru sóo desu.

45. tuyu ní wa ‖ NAḠÁi AIDA ‖ MÁINITI ‖ MÁINITI ‖ ÁME bakari | hútte ‖ TAbemóno ḡa | súḡu | wáruku naru.

DÁI | GÓ-KA

1. watakusi wa MÁINITI ‖ EIZI-SÍNBUN o | YÓnde imasu.

2. KANZI to kana de KÁite mo‖ roomáZI de | KÁite mo | kamaimasén.

3. kono TIHÓO ni wa ‖ ZINKOO | NISEN ÍKA no | MURÁ ḡa | TASUU áru.

4. ÍMA ‖ kono heya no NÁKA ni | iru HITÓ no | NÍNZUU o | KAZÓete kudasai.

5. SUUḠAKU wa | KÁZU no | BENKYOO désu.

6. démo ni Itta GAKUSEI no uti ‖ HAPPYAKÚ-NIN wa | ITI-NÉNSEI ‖ SANBYÁKU-NIN wa | ZYOSI-GÁKUSEI desita.

7. kono kusuri wa ‖ SYOKUZEN ni | nónde kudasai.

8. kana wa ‖ zutto MÁE ni | naraimásita.

9. denwa no MÁE ni | TIIsái | TETYOO ḡa áru.

10. GAKKOO wa | éki no | TEMAE désu.

11. watakusí-tati wa | TAbéru | MÁE ni ‖ "itadakimásu" to iu.

12. EIBÚNḠAKU o | BENKYOO suru tamé ni ‖ róndon e | Ikimásita.

13. KÓKON | TÓOZAI no | BÚNKA no tiḡai o | sirábete iru.

14. KOTEN ḡa YOmitákereba ‖ TOOYOO-KANZI ÍḠAI no KANZI ya | HURÚi kana no | tukaiKATA mo | BENKYOO sinákereba | narimasén.

15. kono hen wa ‖ YUKÍ ḡa | ÓOi.

16. SENZITU | mezurasíi HURUHON o | TÉ ni | Iremásita.

17. asoko dé wa | SINSYA bákari de | náku ‖ TYUUBURU no KURUMA mo | atukatte iru.

18. daizyóobu da to | OMOimásu ḡa ‖ MÁN'ITI | náni ka | áttara | súḡu | oSIrase simásu.

19. nan-MAN-NEN mo MÁE no | KÍ no ha ḡa ‖ KASEKI ni nátte | nokótte iru.

20. kotobá ḡa | BÁNKOKU | onazi dáttara ‖ otaḡai ni | ÍSI ḡa | wakariÁete | íi desyoo ne.

21. orinpíkku ni wa ‖ BÁNKOKU no | tyánpion ḡa | atumarimásu.

22. anó HITO wa ‖ boku no HÚRUku kara no | TÍZIN de ‖ móo | ZYUU-NEN ÍZYOO ‖ TYÚUḠAKU de ‖ EIḠO no SENSÉI o site imasu.

23. DOYÓO | NITIYOO ÍḠAI wa | uti ni imasén.

24. TIIsái | DAIḠAKU dá kara ‖ GAKUSEI no KÁZU wa | SEN-NIN ÍKA desyoo.

25. ano KATÁ wa ‖ watakusi no SIriAi désu.

26. kono ATARAsíi NINḠYOO wa ‖ ARÚku koto mo | dekíru n desu yo.

27. kabuki de | ONNÁ ni naru yakusya o | ONNAḠATA to iimásu.

28. asoko wa ‖ NÁNBOKU ni | NAḠÁi TIKEI desu.

29. kono ZITEN wa | naku natta ozi no | KATAMI désu.

30. bóku wa | DÓKUSYO ḡa | sukí desu kara ‖ KISYA no NÁKA de mo | taitei | HÓN o YOmimasu.

31. bóku no TOMOdati wa ‖ NÁḠAku ‖ NIHON no DAIḠAKU de | BENKYOO sitá kara ‖ KÓBUN mo | KANBUN mo | YOmemásu.

32. kono KANZI no YOmiKÁTA o | wasuremásita.

33. TOKUHON de | YUKÍḠUNI no koto o | YOmimásita.

34. IḠAI na tokoró de | IḠAI na HITÓ ni | aimásita.

35. anáta no | go-ÍKEN o | okikase kudasái.

36. sore wa | dóo iu | ÍMI desu ka.

37. teki mo MIKATA mo | yóku | tatakaimásita.

38. dónna AZI ḡa | simásu ka.

39. hén na | OTÓ ḡa | simásita yo.

40. utukusíi piano no NE ḡa | KIkoemásu.

41. tóotoo | HONNE o háita.

42. kono KANZI no | ON no YOmiKÁTA wa | SItte imásu ḡa ‖ KUN wa | OMOidasemasén.

43. "akaruku ‖ TÚYOku ‖ TADÁsiku" to | iú no ḡa ‖ watasi no SYOOḠÁKKOO no | KOOKUN désita.

44. náiron ‖ dákuron nado wa ‖ KÁḠAKU ḡa unda | ATARAsíi | KÍZI desu.

45. oBÁke nante | imasén yo.

46. hutari zútu | KÚnde | dánsu o suru.

47. bóku no | KUMÍ ni wa ‖ ZYOSI-GÁKUSEI wa | hitori mo imasén.

48. ÍMA de wa || dónna | kaisya ní mo || hataraite iru HITÓBITO no | KUMIAI ḡa áru.

49. káre wa | udeḠúmi o site || zitto kanḡaekónda.

50. atira wa | KÁḠAKU no | SENSÉI de || GOOKIN no kenkyuu mo | site oide ni narimásu.

51. NISÍMURA-san no | MÉINITI wa | KÚḠATU | YOKKA désu.

52. NINḠEN wa || NÁḠAkute mo | HYAKU-NEN ḡúrai sika | SÉIMEI ḡa | nái.

53. INOTIḡake de níḡeta.

54. dóo iu | ÍMI ka || KENTÓO ḡa | tukimasén.

55. pisutoru no tamá ḡa | ASÍ ni | ATAttá no de || súḡu | TÉATE o sita.

56. tyótto | YÓO ḡa | arimásu kara || o-SAKI ni sitúrei simasu.

57. sonna kotó wa || o-yasui go-YÓO desu.

58. góhan no | YÓOI o | site kudasái.

59. KÓNNITI no | SINBUN dé wa || MÁE hodo | BUNḠO o MOTIinái.

60. tokubetu na YÓOSI ḡa | áru kara || sore ni | KAkiIrete kudasái.

61. mukasi no HITÓ wa || YUKI no akarí ya | hótaru no | hikarí o | MOTIite | BENKYOO sitá to ka | KIite imásu.

62. hoka no HITÓ ni KIkareru to | GAIBUN ḡa warúi kara || sonna ÓOki na | kóe de | kenka sinái de kudasai.

DÁI | RÓK-KA

1. IÉ o | TAtéru nara || mázu || íi BASYO o | erabánakereba | naránai.

2. ano NIkaiDATE no IE no YÁnusi-san wa || NIHON-KOTEN-BÚNḠAKU no | TÁIKA desu.

3. don·kihóote no | KÉRAI no namae wa || santyo·pánsa desu.

4. asoko no | usuTYA no ISI no TATÉMONO wa || GAKKOO desyóo ka.

5. TEMÁNEki site || KOdomo o yonda.

6. amerika no DAIḠAKU ni MANEkárete || ITÍ-NEN | atira de | GENḠÓḠAKU o | BENKYOO suru kotó ni | narimásita.

7. tanosíi | páatei ni | go-SYOOTAI itadaite || aríḡatoo | gozaimásita.

8. tyótto | MÁtte.

9. éki no | MATIÁIsitu de || oMAti site orimásu.

10. watakusi ní mo | HITÓ-KOTO || Iwasete kudasái.

11. tori ya kedámono ni mo | GÉNḠO ḡa | áru daroo ka.

12. náiron wa || kínu yori | zutto zyoobu dá kara || ZITUYOOmuki désu.

13. Iu kotó wa | yasasíi ḡa || ZIKKOO suru kotó wa | muzukasíi.

14. BYOOKI to iú no wa | KOOZITU de || ZITÚ wa | BENKYOO sitaku nákatta nó de || GAKKOO o YASÚnda no da | sóo desu.

15. íne ḡa | MINÓru no wa || nanḠATU ḡóro desu ka.

16. KÍ-no-MI o Ireta | okási ḡa | DÁIsuki desu.

17. NIHONZÍN wa | yóku | o-TYA o nómu.

18. TYAnoMA wa || kázoku ḡa | atumátte | HANAsiÁttari || góhan o | TÁbetari | suru TOKORÓ desu.

19. tori ya | kedámono ya | KÍ ya | kusá wa || minna SÉIBUTU desu.

20. IMÁNISI-SENSEI wa || SEIBUTU-ḠÁKUSYA desu.

21. SYOKÚMOTU ḡa | nákereba || NINḠEN wa | Íkite | ikarenái.

22. "genziMONOḠÁTARI" wa | NIHON no KOTEN-BÚNḠAKU desu ḡa || taihen NAḠÁi no de || nakanaka YOmikiremasén.

23. BYOONIN ḡa irú kara || sízuka ni | ARÚite kudasai.

24. "YÁMAI wa KUTI kara"

25. muné o | YÁnde iru.

26. tyótto no kaze kara || TÁIBYOO ni | nátta.

27. ano KÁḠAKU no | SENSÉI wa || GAKUSEI ni | taihen NINKI ḡa áru.

28. kono kudámono wa || MIZUKE ḡa ÓOkute | oisíi.

29. anó HITO no | TÁNSYO wa || KI ḡa MIZÍKAkute || okoriyasúi koto desu.

30. dáre ni mo || ITTYOO ITTAN wa | áru mono da.

31. TÁNKI na | HITÓ ni wa || konna siḡoto wa | dekimasén.

32. watakusi wa || YAMADA | yósiKO to MOOsimasu.

33. dekiru dake || NIHONḠO de HANÁsu to iu | MOOsiAwase o simásita.

34. TYUUMON sita HÓN ḡa | túita.

35. HÍ ni | abura o SOSOḡu to || masúmasu moeru.

36. TIIsái | IÉ da kara || TYÚUI sinai to | MIotosimásu yo.

37. "HÓN ḡa | áru" no | "ḡá" wa | BION désu.

38. zóo wa | HANA ḡa NAḠÁi.

39. HANAḠAMI ḡa | ITI-mai mo nái.

40. máyu ya | KÓBANA no atari || titioya ni nite iru.

41. tokonoMA ni | kono OKIMONO o | Oite kudasái.

42. iranai MONÓ wa || MONOOKI ni | simatte okimasyóo.

43. SITÁ o | dásite wa | ikemasén.

44. uti no KO wa || máda | SITATÁrazu desu. tóku ni | ZETÚON ḡa | niḡaTE na yóo desu.

45. edokko wa | makiZITA o tukatte HANAsimásu.

46. kore wa | hontoo ni átta | ZITUWA désu.

47. HANAsiTE no HANASÍ o | owari máde | KIkú no ḡa || íi | KIkiTE désu.

48. obáasan kara | mukasiBÁNASI o KIita.

49. "HANASI-zyóozu no | KIki-beta".

50. ZÉNRYAKU.   o-génki de | irassyaimásu ka.

51. kono KANZI wa | RYAKUZI désu.

52. <u>pensirubeniya</u>DÁIGAKU o | RYAKÚsite | <u>pen</u>DAI to Iu HITÓ mo iru.

53. SYOONEN SYÓOZYO no | tamé no | SINBUN ḡa áru.

54. anmari SUKUnái kara || moo SUKÓsi | kudasái.

55. osóreirimasu ḡa || SYÓOSYOO | otume kudasaimáse.

56. SYOZÍKIN o | otósite || komátta.

57. KANEMÓti ni | náreba | náru hodo || KANEMOti-buránai.

58. ano ONNÁ no KO wa || NINḠYOO o | TÉ ni | MÓtte iru.

59. TOMOdati no ZIBYOO wa || íkura | ISYA ni kakátte mo || naoránakute || KI no dóku desu.

60. koko wa || BASYO ḡa sémakute || karada no OkiBA mo nái hodo desu.

61. dónna BAAI ni || "surú"|to iu | kotobá o | tukawanái de || "OKOnau"|to iu kotobá o | tukaimásu ka.

62. kono KÍNZYO ni || dare de mo NYUUZYOO dekíru | <u>goruhu</u>ZYOO ḡa áru hazu da.

63. kyóo | EIKOKU kara KIta TEḠAMI wa || TOKOROḠAki wa átte iru ḡa || myóoZI to namae ḡa | SAKAsa ni nátte iru.

64. <u>abusutorákuto</u> no | é o | NAḠÁi AIDA || SAKAsa ni kákete oita | sóo da.

65. anó HITO wa | TÁNKI de || GYAKUZYOO siyasúi kara || dekiru dake | SAKAráwazu ni | oku yóo ni.

66. ano <u>pán</u>YA no | o-kási wa | umái yo.

67. GAKKOO no OKUZYOO kara | húziSAN ḡa | MIéru.

68. kono ḡoro wa || TOTI mo | KÁOKU mo | Aḡaru bákari da.

69. ano ISYA wa || BUNḠÁKUSYA to | sité mo | yuumei da.

70. ÍḠAKU ḡa | susunde irú no de || taitei no BYOOKI wa | naoséru.

71. oba wa ZYOI désu.   kono ḡoro wa || ONNÁ de | ÍḠAKU o | BENKYOO suru HITÓ ḡa || SUKUnáku | arimasén.

72. "<u>táimu</u>" ya | "<u>ráihu</u>" wa | DÓKUSYA ḡa | ÓOi.

73. GAIKOKU e RYOKOO suru MONÓ ḡa | húeta.

DÁI | SITÍ-KA

1. anó HITO wa || tyótto | HENZÍN desu ḡa || AKUNIN zya arimasén.

2. háwai wa || SYÚNKA | SYUUTOO no | HÉNKA ḡa | nái soo da.

3. "HÉN na | OTÓ ḡa | sitá kara || MÍte KIte kudasai."
   "NANI mo | KAwatta yoosu wa arimasén yo."

4. HINSITU no yói SINAMONO o | erábe.

5. ano o-zyóosan wa | HIN ḡa áru.

6. ane wa | HIN ḡa íi ḡa || imootó wa | HIN ḡa nái.

7. GAIKEN wa | ZYOOHÍN na HITO no | yóo da keredo || HANAsihazimeru to ||
   GEHÍN na koto | bákari | Iú no de || MATTAku odoróita.

8. SINA no íi MONO wa | TAKÁi no ḡa | TOOZEN da.

9. mósi || ZENZEN o-KI ni mesánai | yóo desitara || kotira no SINA to |
   otorikae itasimásu.

10. TYUUḠOKÚZIN no | TÉZINA o | MÍta koto ḡa | áru.

11. kono TYAwan wa | TUI ni nátte imasu.

12. zasikí ni | IT-TUI no kabin ḡa | Oite átta.

13. TOOHOKUBEN no TAIWA o KIitá ḡa || hotóndo | wakaránakatta.

14. géete to | ekkerúman no TAIWA wa || "fáusuto" to | tómo ni || DAIḠAKU
    de | yóku | YOmárete iru.

15. ÍTI TAI | ITÍ no | kenka dé wa || kotira ḡa makete simaimásu.

16. sonna HANASÍ wa | ZENZEN SIrimasén.

17. NIHON-ZÉNKOKU || dóko e | Itté mo || rázio to SINBUN no | nái TOKORO
    wa | nái desyoo.

18. sore wa || ZÉNKOKU | KYOOTUU no mondai désu.

19. sékai no KYOOTUUḠO o MOKUTEKI ni || esuperánto ḡa | tukuráreta.

20. ítu ni | náttara || TYUUKYOO e Ikerú ka || MITOOsi ḡa tukimasén.

21. KISYÁ de KAYOu | TUUḠÁKUSEI mo | ÓOi.

22. watakusi wa || KYOOḠAKU no TYÚUḠAKU ni | KAYOimásita.

23. kono TOOrí o | massúḡu Itte || tukiAtattára || MIḠI ni maḡarú to |
    OODÓOri ni demasu. soko de | zyúnsa ni | SAKI o OSIete morainasái.

24. NAḠÁi koto | ISYAḠÁYOi o site || yatto | UE no KO no BYOOKI ḡa naótta
    to | OMÓttara || kóndo wa | SITA no KO ḡa | WÁRUku | narimásita.

25. o-KANE o dásu no ni wa || hán to | TUUTYOO ḡa | irimásu.

26. TUUTYOO wa | KAYOiTYOO tó mo | Iimásu.

27. NIHONḠO o OSIeru BAAI ní wa || GAKUSEI ni | narubeku EIḠO o
    TUKAwasezu || EIḠO de KANḠAénai | yóo ni | sasenákereba | naránai.

28. tyótto || o-TUKAi ni Itte KImásu kara || MÁtte ite kudasai.

29. ATARAsíi | kanaZÚKAi o | OSOwatta koto no nái | HURÚi | HITÓ-tati wa ||
    ÍMA de mo | ÍZEN no | kanaZÚKAi o | SIYOO suru kotó ḡa | ÓOi.

30. kono kusuri wa | ISYA ÍḠAI || SIYOO dekimasén.

31. <u>amerika</u> no TÁISI ḡa | túita.

32. NATUYÁSUmi ni | kodomó-tati wa || <u>tonbo</u> ya | tyóo no | HYOOHON o tukúru.

33. NÁNI o MOKUHYOO ni site || <u>pisutoru</u> o útta ka.

34. "yóku asobi || yóku | MANÁbu" | to iú no ḡa || koko no GAKUSEI no HYOOḠO
    désu.

35. kono ÁKAtyan no MEKATA wa | HYOOZYUN ÍKA desu.

36. <u>amerika</u> wa SEIKATU-SÚIZYUN no | TAKÁi KUNI desu.

37. ÍKA | kore ni ZYUNzúru.

38. hidói BYOOKI o | simásita ḡa || íi o-ISYA-san no okaḡe de | INOTIBÍROi o |
    simásita.

39. umibé e Itte || kaiḡára o HIROtta.

40. NIHÓN ni aru | <u>kirisutoKYOO</u> no DAIḠAKU de | BENKYOO simásita.

41. OSOwarú no wa | taihen désu ḡa || OSIerú no wa | náo taihen desu.

42. kono sippai wa | watakusi ni tótte || yói | KYOOKUN ni narimásita.

43. <u>kariforuniyáSYUU</u> de | Umaremásita.

44. HÓNSYUU wa | motíron || KYÚUSYUU || SIKÓKU o RYOKOO sita.

45. KAWA no mannaka ni | TÍIsá na | NAKASU ḡa arimásu.

46. o-BENTOO o wasuretyatta.

47. sakura no KÁBEN wa | GO-mai áru.

48. BENKAI wa irimasén.   kore kara TYÚUI site kudasai.

49. ITÍ-NEN wa | NAN-SYÚUKAN desu ka.

50. GOKAI no nái yoo ni || kuwásiku | HANÁsita.

51. kono TEḠAMI ní wa | GOZI ḡa ÓOkute | komáru.

52. AYAMÁri ḡa | áttara || naósite kudasai.

53. KOdomo ḡa | AYAMÁtte | KAWÁ ni | ótita.

54. móo | NAN-SYÚUKAN mo | onazi KÁ o | BENKYOO sasete irú no ni ||
    atamá ḡa | WÁRUkute || tittó mo | obóete | kuremasén.   ZÍ o | KAkaséru
    to || GOZI bákari || YOmaséreba GODOKU bákari desu.

55. GAKUSYA to sité wa || KENKAI ḡa | tiḡaú ḡa || náka no | yói | TOMOdati
    désu.

56. TOOHOKU no HUYÚ wa | NAḠÁi no de || YUKIDOke no kisétu ḡa | KÚru
    no ḡa | MAtidoosíi soo da.

57. <u>nékutai</u> o | TÓita.

58. KOOKÓḠAKU KENKYUU no MOKUTEKI wa | NÁN desu ka.

59. watakusi wa || kore ni KÁNsite wa | ÍNOTI o | MATÓ ni site || arasóu | tumori désu.

60. kessite | HOKA no HITÓ no | WARÚGUTI o | Iwanai HITÓ desu.

61. ÁKUI no | nái HITO desu ga || BASYO o KANGÁezu ni | NAN de mo HANÁsu no de || GOKAI sareru kotó ga arimasu.

62. natisu-dóitu wa | ÍGAKU o AKUYOO site || HITÓBITO o korosita.

63. HITO wa ONÓONO || SEISITU ga tigau.

64. yooroppa-KÁKKOKU o RYOKOO si || KÁKUTI no DAIGAKU de | SEIBUTÚGAKU-KENKYUUZYO o | KENGAKU simásita.

65. watakusi wa | ZÉNKOKU | KÁKUTI o | ARUkinágara || HOOGÉN no KENKYUU o | site imásu.

66. ZYOSEI to sité wa || hagesíi KISYOO desu.

67. SINAMONO o SITÍ ni Irete || SITÍYA kara | KANE o kariru.

68. SITU no WARÚi SINA o | uru misé wa || súgu | tuburerú desyoo.

69. monógoto no | HONSITU o tukámu koto ga | daizí da.

70. KANGÁereba | KANGÁeru hodo || muzukasiku náru.

71. máda | kono hen no TÍRI ga | wakaránai kara || annái site kudasai.

72. áru GAKUSEI wa || RÍKAI wa | hayái ga || wasurerú no mo | hayái.

DÁI | HÁK-KA

1. kore wa || TOOKYOO no SUIDOO no tamé no | YOOSÚIIKE desu.

2. DENTI ga kíreta kara || ATARAsíi no o katta.

3. "KOIKE | MÁSAKO to MOOsimasu.   dóozo yorosiku."
   "MÓRITA | MÍTIKO desu. hazimemásite."

4. USI o NÍ-hiki | kátte iru.

5. "GYÚU no | sukiyaki dé mo | TAbeyóo ka."
   "íya, KOUSI no katuretu wa | dóo?"

6. SUIGYUU wa | MINAMI no KUNI no IkíMONO desu.

7. tugí wa | dáre no | BÁN desu ka.

8. IRIGUTI ni | BANNÍN ga | hutari iru.

9. otaku no BANTI wa | NAN-BÁNTI desu ka. tuide ni || DENWA-BÁNGOO mo | OSIete kudasái.

10. ZYUUNIGATU hazime ná no ni || HÓN'YA ni wa | móo | SINNÉNGOO no zassi ga | déte iru.

11. SINBUN ní wa || MÁINITI || sono HÍ no | térebi to | rázio no BANGUMI ga | déte iru.

12. asitá wa | TÓOBAN da kara || ÁSA | HÁYAku | ZIMÚSYO e | Ikanákereba | naránai.

13. tití wa SYOKA de || GÓO o | YÚUZAN to Iimasu.

14. DAInyúusu da kara || GOOĜAI ḡa déta.

15. "TAISYOO" to iú no wa || SÉN | KYÚUHYAKU | ZYUUNÍ-NEN kara || SÉN | KYÚUHYAKU | NÍZYUU | ROKÚ-NEN made no | NENĜÓO desu.

16. TÁNKI na | HITÓ wa || RÍSEI o | USINAiyasúi.

17. tyótto | SITÚREI.

18. zúibun | SITÚREI na | HANAsiKÁTA desu ne.

19. kore wa SITUĜEN o itasimásita.   aisumimasén.

20. SENSÉI ni | RÉI o site || heyá o | déta.

21. káre wa | MOKUREI site || SENSÉI ni | BASYO o aketa.

22. zyúnsa ni | MITI o OSIete moratta.

23. HANÁMITI wa || kabuki ní wa | nákute wa | naránai mono da.

24. mono no DOORI no wakaránai | HITÓ to wa || HANAsemasén.

25. "anó HITO wa || amerika no DAIĜAKU de | BENKYOO sita sóo desu ne." "DOORÍ de || EIĜO ḡa umái desu ne."

26. YOOZI ḡa arimásu kara || o-SAKI ni SITÚREI simasu.

27. KÁZI ḡa | ITIBAN kowái kara || mátti ya | tabako no HÍ ni | go-TYÚUI NEĜAimasu.

28. kóndo no | KÁZI wa || SIKKA ni yoru monó da | sóo desu.

29. ZIMÚSYO de wa || dónna KOTO o | site irassyaimásu ka.

30. TUTOmé o wasurete | ASObimawatté wa | ikenái.

31. ZIMU-TEKI ni HANAsiAimasyóo.

32. mukasi || KIKÁZIN ḡa | TYUUĜOKU-BÚNKA o | NIHÓN ni TUTAeta.

33. RAINEN no ÁKI ka | HUYÚ ni wa || KIKOKU suru tumori désu.

34. KAErímITI ni | AKÁSAKA no | MORIYAMA-san no IÉ ni | yotte miyóo. DÉNSYA o | órite kara || súḡu da kara.

35. TOKIDOKI || HIĜAEri de | TOOKYOO e | ASObi ni Ikimásu.

36. o-tóo-SAMA || go-BYOOKI da sóo desu ḡa || dónna | go-YOOSU désu ka.

37. íkura | TIKÁMITI de mo || konna SAKÁ o | KURUMA de | NOBOru kotó wa | yameyóo.

38. ZÍNSEI wa || KURUMA o hiite | SAKÁMITI o | NOBOru yóo na | monó da to Iu.   SUKÓsi de mo || KI o yuruméreba || KURUMA wa | sekkaku NOBOtta SAKÁ o | at to iu MA ni | modótte simau.

39. ITI-NITÍ wa || NÍZYUU | YO-ZÍKAN desu.

40. taitei || ZYUU NI-ZI-HÁN kara | ITI-ZI-HÁN made wa || SYOKUZI no tame | YASUmí desu ḡa || TOKÍ ni wa || ITÍ-ZI kara | ITI-ZÍKAN YASUmimasu.

41. uti máde || ITI-ZIKAN-HÁN | kakarimásu ḡa || MÁINITI || DÉNSYA de | KAYOtte imásu.

42. ZYUUḠATU NAKAbá kara │ SÁMUku naru.

43. SYÓDOO o │ naráu no ni wa ‖ HÁNSI to │ hude to │ suzurí to │ sumí ḡa │ irimasu.

44. ano DAIḠAKU ni │ NYUUḠAKU sitái no de ‖ GÁNSYO o │ dasimásita.

45. watakusi no NEḠÁi wa ‖ amerika no DAIḠAKU de │ BENKYOO suru kotó desu.

46. mósi mosi.   SÁNBYAKU ITÍ-BAN no │ HASIMOTO-san ni │ o-NEḠAi simásu.

47. DÉNKI o │ tukéte.

48. ÍMA ‖ NÁN-ZI desu ka.   YÓ-ZI ni │ náttara ‖ HENDENSYO e Ikanákereba │ narimasén kara ‖ OSIete kudasái.

49. ÁSAHI ḡa │ déru to ‖ súḡu ni │ ókite ‖ TEBAYÁku │ TYOOSYOKU no sitaku o simásu.

50. SOOTYOO kara ‖ NÁNI o │ sawáide │ irú n desu ka.

51. KYÓNEN ‖ KYÓOTO kara │ ZYOOKYOO site ‖ ÍMA ‖ TOOKYOO-DÁIḠAKU ni imasu.

52. TUḠOO ni yori ‖ GETUYÓOBI no │ GOZEN-TYUU no kúrasu wa │ YASUmásete itadakimasu.

53. KYÓOTO wa │ mukasi no MIYAKO désu.

54. SYÓOḠO no │ sáiren o KIita.

55. GÓZEN │ KÚ-ZI kara ‖ GÓḠO │ GÓ-ZI made no AIDA ni ‖ ZIMÚSYO e │ o-DÉNWA NEḠAimasu.

56. kono kusuri wa ‖ SYOKUZEN nó desu ka ‖ SYOKUḠO nó desu ka.

57. kono HÓN wa ‖ KOOHAN ḡa tumaránai.

58. mata NOTIhodo.

59. USIro kara ‖ torákku ḡa │ KImásita yo.

60. ZYOTYUU ya SIYOONIN ḡa │ ITAnoMA de │ SYOKUZI o site iru.

61. ITAgárasu o │ mádo ni hameru.

62. garéezi wa ‖ OOkíi HASI no │ mukoo ni arimásu.

63. NIHONBASI wa ‖ dono hen désu ka.

64. TÁMURA-san wa ‖ TOMOdati ni TUTAetai KOTÓ o ‖ éki no DENḠONBAN ni │ KÁite oita.

65. WARÚḠUTI wa │ súḡu TUTAwaru.

66. TUḠOO ḡa yókattara ‖ ASObi ni irassyái.

67. anó HITO wa ‖ MÓKKA │ GAIYUU-TYUU da.

DÁI | KYÚU-KA

1. anó HITO wa || KÁOKU ya TOTI no | BÁIBAI o site iru.

2. kurisúmasu to | o-SYOOḠATU-YÓOHIN no | UriDAsi ḡa hazimatta.

3. ZYÚUDAI no | HITÓBITO wa || zyázu ḡa | sukí da.

4. ZIDAI ḡa KAwaréba || KANḠAeKÁTA mo KAwaru.

5. kono SINAMONO ḡa | KI ni Iranákereba || DAIKIN o okaesi simásu.

6. watakusi wa || TUḠOO ḡa WÁRUkatta no de || DAIRI no MONÓ ni | Itte moraimásita.

7. tití no DAIRI de || KYÓOTO e | Iku kotó ni | narimásita.

8. otukare ni náttara || KAwarimasyóo.

9. ÍMA no YO de wa || sonna HURÚi koto o | Itté mo || RIKAI saremasén yo.

10. kore wa || TITI no   DÁI ni | nátte kara | TAtenaosita IÉ desu.

11. TOOKYOO || KYÓOTO wa || NIHON no | DAIHYOO-TEKI na TOKAI désu.

12. ZIKANHYOO oMÓti désitara || tyótto | MÍsete kudasai. tuḡí no | KISYÁ ḡa || NÁN-ZI ni | DÉru ka || SIritái no desu.

13. kírei na | HYOOSÍ desu ne.

14. ATARAsíi | KANZI no HYOO o | KÁita.

15. OMOTÉ de | MÁtte imasu.

16. kono KÍZI wa || dótti ḡa | OMOTÉ desu ka.

17. NIHONZÍN wa || GAIZIN hodo | KIMOti o OMOTÉ ni | ARAwasánai.

18. HÍROTA-san wa | GAISYUTU-TYUU désu.

19. SYUTUNYÚUKOKU ni wa || pásupooto to | bíza ḡa iru.

20. SYUKKE to iú no wa || boosan to iu ÍMI da.

21. asoko no musumé wa | IEDE sita sóo da.

22. TUKÍ ḡa DEta.

23. koko wa | IRIḠUTI désu kara || KURUMA wa | atira no DÉḠUTI kara | DÁsite kudasai.

24. GAKUSEI-ZÍDAI no | OMOiDE-BÁNASI o sita.

25. kyóo || amerikaTÁISI to SINBÚN-KISYA to no | KAIKEN ḡa átta.

26. NIKKI o | YASÚmazu | MÁINITI | KÁite imasu.

27. ahurika de | kirisutoKYOO no DENDOO o site iru | áru ISYA no DENKI o | YÓnde imasu.

28. "YOMIURISÍNBUN" no | KISYÁ desu.

29. ákusento wa || dónna KIḠOO o TUKÁtte | ARAwasimásu ka.

30. SEIKAKU ni KINYUU suru koto.

31. TEKIKAKU na SUUZI ḡa SIritái.

32. KIKOKU suru kotó wa | TÁSIka desu ğa || NÁNĞATU ni | KÁEru ka wa || máda | wakarimasén.

33. anó HITO ğa | KÚru ka | KÓnai ka || DENWA de | TASIkámete kudasai.

34. uti no USIro ni | ÓOki na | HANÁYA ğa | áru kara || sore o MEZÍRUSI ni site | KÚreba || súğu wakarimasu.

35. INSATU sita HÓN | bákari | YÓnde iru no de || TÉ de | UTÚsita | HURÚi SYAHON wa | YOmemasén.

36. HÓN no KOOSEIZUri o | naósite imasu.

37. INSATU ni mawasu MÁE ni || AYAMÁri ğa | nái ka | dóo ka || moo iti-do TASIkámete | mimasyóo.

38. KOOSEIZUri ğa dékite KImasita.   SIN'YOO no áru INSATUZYO dake | átte || nakanaka SEIKAKU ni | yatte arimásu.

39. ASAHISÍNBUN wa | MÁINITI | dono ğurai | SÚtte imasu ka.

40. watakusi wa | kirisutoKYOO o SÍNzite imasu.

41. úso o | túku to || SIN'YOO ğa naku narimásu yo.

42. SINzirarénai yoo na | HANASÍ desu ğa || ZITUWA da sóo desu.

43. SINĞOO ni TYÚUI.

44. KAKUSIN ğa nái kara || HANAṢemasén.

45. ZYUU-NÉNKAN mo | ONSIN no nákatta TOMOdati ğa || KIKOKU sitá no o | SINBUN de SItte || Ái ni Itta.

46. SEIZI ni túite no | ÍKEN o | SEIKEN to iimásu.

47. KASÉIĞAKU o | MANÁbu | GAKUSEI ní wa || ZYOSEI ğa ÓOi.

48. "MATURIĞOTO" wa | HURÚi | kotobá desu.

49. ano BYOOKI wa || ZENTI máde ni | IK-kaĞETU ğúrai | kakáru desyoo.

50. SEIZIKA ni nátte || IKKOKU o OSÁmete | mitái.

51. KUNI no TIAN no tamé ni || keisatu ğa áru.

52. amerika wa SIN'YOO-KÉIZAI no KUNI da.

53. o-KYOO o | KIita kotó ğa | arimásu ka.

54. kono KISYÁ wa || TOOKYOO o HÉte || AÓMORI made Ikimasu.

55. syukudai o SUmásete kara ASObu.

56. karita KANE wa || RÁIĞETU | tuitatí made ni | BENSAI sinákereba | naránai.

57. HÚRUTA-san wa || DAIĞÁISYA no | SYATYOO désu ğa || SYAKAI-GÁKUSYA to | sité mo | SIrarete imásu.

58. MURÁ ğa | áreba || YÁSIRO ğa | áru.

59. NITIYÓOBI ni wa || KYOOKAI e mairimásu kara || atira de oAisimasyóo.

60. EIKÁIWA o BENKYOO site iru.

61. KAIZYOO ḡa HIROsúḡite || USIro no HITÓBITO ni wa | KIkoenákatta.

62. GEISYA wa || NIHÓN ni sika | inái GEININ de || zasikí de | utá ya | odori o MIséru | ONNÁ desu.

63. NIHON no BÚNḠEI to || yooróppa no | BÚNḠEI wa || HONSITU-TEKI ni tiḡaimásu ka.

64. ÍMA || YÓ-ZI | ZYÚUGO-HUN desu.

65. "HANBÚN" to | "NIBUN no ITÍ" wa | onazi désu.

66. SYOOḠÁKKOO de | BUNSÚU o | OSIemásu ka.

67. HYAKU-EN no SÁN-BU wa | SAN-EN désu.

68. ITI-NÉNSEI o | HUTÁ-KUMI ni | WÁketa.

69. ITI-NÉNSEI wa | HUTÁ-KUMI ni | WAkárete iru.

70. SYASETU wa | SINBÚNSYA no | ÍKEN desu.

71. HURÚi | DENSETU no NÁKA ni wa || omosirói | HANASÍ ḡa | takusan áru.

72. áru | KEIZAI-ḠÁKUSYA no | ATARAsíi GAKUSETU o | YÓnda.

73. SEIZIKA wa | sénkyo no | MÁE ni naru to || taitei | YUUZEI ni ARÚku.

74. watakusi wa | kirisutoKYOO no SÉKKYOO o | KIité mo || SÍNZYA zya | nái kara || íkura | TOkárete mo | RIKAI dekimasén.

75. anó HITO no SETU ni yoru to || kono montaazyu-SYÁSIN wa | totemo yói deki da | sóo desu.

76. SINBUN ya | zassi ni | TOOSYO surú no ḡa | DÁIsuki desu.

77. íi | TÓOSYU ḡa | inái kara || ano tíimu wa | makerú desyoo.

78. mádo kara | MONÓ o | NAḡéru na.

79. watakusi wa | SYASIN o UTÚsu yori mo || zibun de | SYASEI suru hóo ḡa | sukí desu.

80. SYASIN no yóo na | SYAZITU-TEKI na é nara || wakarimásu ḡa . . .

81. kono TEḠAMI no | SEIKAKU na UTUsí o | tótte kudasai.

82. SÍNZITU wa | HITÓ-tu sika | nái.

83. MAKKÁ na | HANA no túite iru | kóoto o KAtta.

84. MAHUYU dé mo | amari SÁMUku | nái.

85. KOOKOKU ḡa úmakereba || SINAMONO no UreYUki ḡa HIROḡaru.

86. amerika no | KOODAI na TOTI o MÍte | bikkúri sita.

87. sínpu wa | KYOOKAI de | KOKUHAKU o KIitára || sore o | KOOḠAI sité wa | ikenai.

88. MAINEN || SYUUNYUU no SINKOKU o sinákereba | naránai.

89. HAYÁKUTI ni | YOOZI dake TUḡete || SÁtta.

90. ANZEN-DÁIITI desu.   dóozo | KI o tukéte kudasai.

91. MATTAku ANZEN na norimono nánka | arimasén yo.

92. YASÚi MONO wa || taitei | SINA ḡa WARÚi.

93. ITI-NEN-zyuu | YASUÚri ḡa | áru n desu ne.

94. kono SINA wa | tákakute | KAiTE ḡa tukánai.

95. GÓḠO kara | SITAMATI e | KAIMONO ni Iku tumori da.

96. IK-káḠETU no SYUUNYUU o | GESSYUU to iu.

97. KANE o OSÁmete kara || uketori o watasu.

98. HITÓBITO o BAISYUU site | DAIHYOO ni eránde moratta | yóo na SEIZIKA wa || damé desu.

DÁI | ZYÚK-KA

1. MOKUZI no TUḠÍ no peezi kara | YOmimasyóo.

2. ZÍZYO wa | KOOKÓOSEI desu.

3. róndon wa | TOOKYOO ni TUḡu DAITÓKAI desu.

4. SIDAI ni wakáru yoo ni | náru.

5. KÁI no | SÍDAI o | ÓOkiku | KÁite || yóku | MIéru | TOKORÓ ni | harimasyóo.

6. SENZYOO de || hitori-hitóri | SEN'YUU o USINAináḡara || TUḠÍ wa | zibun no BÁN da to | OMOituzukete ita.

7. orinpíkku de || KÁKKOKU DAIHYOO ḡa | haḡésiku TATAKAtta.

8. KOKUMIN wa || dare de mo | KYOOIKU o Ukéru | GÍMU ḡa | áru.

9. ÁKAtyan o | SODAtéru.

10. ÁKAtyan ḡa | SODÁtu.

11. RISEI-TEKI na HITÓ wa || KIMOti o SEIsúru | kotó ḡa | dekíru.

12. SYAKAI-SÉIDO ḡa | ONAzi dé wa | nái kara || amerika no | iroiro na SÉIDO o | sono mama toriiréru | koto wa | dekínai.

13. moo ITI-DO Itte kudasái.

14. koppu no MIZU o | ITI-DÓ ni | nómu.

15. kono TIHÓO wa || NATÚ de mo | SITIZYUU-DO ḡúrai desu.

16. IḠAI na TOKORÓ de || KYUUYUU ni Átta.

17. WATAKUSI no SOTUḠYOO sitá no wa | KYUUSEI-DÁIḠAKU desu.

18. SÍNNEN | omedetoo gozaimásu.   KYUUNEN ni KAwarazu || yorosiku oNEḠAi itasimásu.

19. súisu no | utukusíi|KÓOZAN no SYASIN o | moratta.

20. SYAKAI-TEKI ní wa | taihen erái | HITÓ desu ḡa || tittómo | TAKAburimasén.

21. róndon ni wa || ÍMA de mo | YAMATAKA o kabútta | OTOKO no HITÓ ḡa | ARÚite iru | sóo desu.

22. NIHÓN wa | HÚRUku kara | KÓODO no | BÚNKA o | mótte | itá ḡa ||
KEIZAI-TEKI ní wa || SÉN | HAPPYAKU-NÉN-DAI ni | nátte mo || máda |
KOOSÍNKOKU de | átta.

23. KISYÁ de | RYOKOO suru BAAI ní wa || taitei | NI-TOO ni noru.   IT-TOO
wa | TAKAsuḡirú kara . .

24. IT-TOO de RYOKOO si || TAKÁi | hóteru ni | bákari | tomattá no de wa ||
sono KUNI o MÍta koto ni wa | narimasén.

25. káre-ra no | MÉ ni wa || GIRÍ to | GÍMU to ḡa | HITÓsiku | MIéru no desu.

26. mótto | HINSITU no ZYOOTOO na MONÓ zya | nákereba || Uremasén.

27. ROKÚ no | HANBÚN to || KÚ no | SAN-BUN no ITÍ wa | HITOsíi.

28. OTOKÓ-no-KO ḡa | hutari átte || TYOONÁN wa | SYOOḠÁKKOO no | SENSÉI
de || ZÍNAN wa | GAKUSEI désu.

29. nakanaka DANSEI-TEKI na HITÓ desu.

30. TYÚUḠAKU no | SÉITO wa || TOKIDOKI || TOHO-RYÓKOO o suru.

31. SINPO-TEKI na KANḠÁe o | mótte imasu.

32. BUTURÍḠAKU no | SÍNPO ḡa || NINḠEN no SEIKATU o | kowásu mono ni |
nátte wa | komáru.

33. méedee ni | AKAi GAKUSEI ḡa | KOOSIN sita.

34. yóku | wakaránakattara ||SAKI e SUSUmázu ni || hukusyuu site kudasái.

35. DAIḠAKU de || SENMON wa | KÉIZAI desita.

36. ZYÓSI SEN'YOO no | púuru desu.

37. tabako wa SENBAI de || SENBAI-KÓOSYA ḡa | tukútte || Utte imásu.

38. amerika ní wa | MÓN no aru | IÉ ḡa | SUKUnái.

39. MÓNBAN ni | kaḡí o | akete moratta.

40. KADÓḠUTI no | pósuto ni | TEḠAMI o Irete morau.

41. ano SENSÉI wa || SYÓDOO no SENMONKA de || MONKÁSEI mo | ÓOi.

42. WATAKUSI wa | SYO ni KÁNsite wa | MONḠÁIKAN desu.

43. YURUsí ḡa | nákereba || KOOMU-TYUU || SIYOO no GAISYUTU wa |
dekimasén.

44. ÍSI no | TUYÓi HITO wa || turákute mo | KOKOROZASI o KAenái.

45. SIḠÁNSYA ḡa | ÓOi kara || sikén o | Úkete moraimasu.

46. ISYA o KOKOROZÁsite | BENKYOO site imásu.

47. o-KOKOROZASI wa aríḡatoo gozaimasu ḡa || o-KANE daké wa || oUke itasi-
kanemásu.

48. KOKUMIN no DAIHYOO ḡa | KOKKAI de | siḡoto o suru.

49. minná de | yóku | HANAsiÁtte || MINSYUTEKI ni kimemasyóo.

50. NIHON no MÍNḠEI no | utukúsisa o | GAIZIN ni OSIerareta.

51. "TÁMI no kamado" to | iú no wa || KOKUMIN no KÉIZAI to iu ÍMI desu.

52. ano SEIZIKA wa || KOKUMIN no Uké g̃a | íi.

53. GÓZEN | SÁN-ZI ni | ZYUSIN sita nyúusu o | ÁSA no SINBUN ni | INSATU dekiru n desu ka.

54. "ZINMÍN no || ZINMÍN ni yoru || ZINMIN no tamé no | SEIZI"

55. SÉIG̃I wa | TUYÓi hazu da.

56. mukasi SEWÁ ni natta | GIRÍ o | wasureté wa | ikenái.

57. ÍG̃I aru SEIKATU o | sinasái.

58. DAIG̃AKU SOTUG̃YOO to DÓOZI ni || koko e | NYUUSYA simásita.

59. DOOKÓOSYA no | nái | hitoríTABI desu.

60. SUU-NIN no GAKUSEI g̃a | KYOODOO site || KENKYUU sita.

61. ONAziMONÓ nara || YASÚi HOO g̃a | íi desyoo.

62. sig̃oto g̃a SUmánai no de || KIKOKU o | ITÍ-NEN | NObásita.

63. píkunikku wa | ÁME g̃a | húttara || HINObe simásu.

64. NÓbe | HYAKÚ-NIN no GAKUSYA g̃a | kono KENKYUU ni Atatta.

65. moo SUKÓsi || kotira ni itái no de || bíza o | ENTYOO site moratta.

66. hutarí no | HANASÍ o | KOOSEI ni KIita áto de || WATAKUSI no ÍKEN o | MOOsimasyóo.

67. KÓOMU de || amerika ni Iku kotó ni | nátta.

68. OOYAKE no KOTÓ to | WATAKUSI no KOTÓ wa || hakkíri | WAkete | KANG̃Áete kudasai.

69. kono NÁKA ni wa || MIZU g̃a KYUU-RIPPOO-méetoru Irerareru.

70. GYAKU no TATIBÁ kara mo | KANG̃Aeyóo.

71. súisu wa | TYUURITÚKOKU desu.

72. RÍSSYUN wa | HÁRU no | hazime no HÍ desu.

73. ONNA no HITÓ g̃a | heyá ni | háittara || DANSEI wa | TAtiAg̃arú no g̃a | REIg̃í desu.

74. NATU no KODAti no SITÁ de || SUKÓsi | yasumimásita.

75. "GÓO o niyasu" to | iú no wa || "gáman suru koto g̃a | dekínaku naru" to iu | ÍMI desu.

76. KAISYA no | GYOOMU-KÁTYOO o | site imasu.

77. DAIG̃AKU-BYÓOIN ni NYUUIN simásita.

78. amerika dé wa || ZYOOIN to | KAIN no | NIIN-SEI o tótte iru.

79. RAISYUN || DAIG̃AKU o SOTUG̃YOO sitára || DAIG̃AKÚIN e Itte || NIHON no KÉIZAI o | KENKYUU suru tumori désu.

DÁI | ZYUU ÍK-KA

1. dekíru ZISIN ḡa | NÁi kara || sonna SIḠOTO wa | sitaku arimasén.

2. WATAKUSI wa || BÚTURI ni wa | ZISIN ḡa arimásu.

3. tóotoo | ÁKUZI o | ZIHAKU sita.

4. ZIBUN no kotó wa | ZIBUN de sinasái.

5. káre wa || ZIKAYOO no KURUMA de || KAISYA ni KAYOtte imásu.

6. MÁINITI || NIHONZÍN to | NIHONḠO daké de | HANÁsite | iréba || SIZEN ni | úmaku | narimásu yo.

7. "BÍ" to "UTUKÚsisa" to wa || hotóndo | ONAzi ÍMI desu.

8. BIZIN zya nái ḡa || dóko ka ni | TI-TEKI na UTUKÚsisa ḡa | áru.

9. BISYOKU o suru to | hutóru.

10. NÍKKOO ni | Ataranai to || BYOOKI ni náru.

11. SINBÚNSYA no | TATÉMONO no | DENKOO-nyúusu o | MÍta.

12. píkapika | HIKÁru made || kutú o miḡaita.

13. HIKARÍ to | káḡe no | kóntorasuto ḡa | UTUKUsíi.

14. ano KATÁ wa | amerika no SINḠÁKKOO o | SOTUḠYOO sita.

15. HURÚi | ZÍNZYA ya | TERÁ ni wa || UTUKUsíi | TATÉMONO ḡa | ÓOi.

16. "KURUsíi TOKI no | KAMIdánomi"

17. KYÓOTO ni wa || SYÁZI ḡa | ÓOi.

18. ZYUUITIḠATU | ZYÚU GO-NITI wa || SITI-ḠÓ-SAN no HI desu.   ONNÁ-no-KO wa || NANÁ-tu to | MI-Ttú no TOKI || OTOKÓ-no-KO wa || ITÚ-tu no TOKI || hahaoya ni turerarete || kono HI | ZÍNZYA e | omairi ni Ikimásu.

19. are wa HURUDÉRA de || ÍMA wa || dare mo súnde inai.

20. kantaberii-MONOḠÁTARI wa || kantaberii-DAIZÍN ni | TERAmáiri ni | Iku MONÓ ḡa || DÓOTYUU no | naḡusáme ni || KAWAru-ḠÁWAru | HANÁsita | MONOḠÁTARI o | KAkitometá | to iu | KATATI ni nátte imasu.

21. YUUMEI na ZÍN no | NIWA ní wa || yóku | TEIré o sita | NIWAKI ya | NIWAISI ya | IKÉ ḡa aru.

22. KOOTEI de ASObu.

23. WATAKUSI wa || situke no kibisíi KATEI ni | SODAtimásita.

24. GAKKOO-KYÓOIKU | bákari de | náku || KATEI-KYÓOIKU mo | taisetu da.

25. tití wa | NIWA-SÍḠOTO o | surú no ḡa | suki de || hima sáe areba || NIWAKI ya | HANÁ no | TEIré o site imasu.

26. kono MITI wa || KOOZI-TYUU dá kara | TOOrénai.

27. KOOBA no TIKÁku wa | yakamasíi.

28. DÁIKU ni | IÉ o | TAtesaséru.

29. SÉKAI-ITI | TAKÁi | TATÉMONO wa || NÁN desu ka.

30. anó HITO wa || GIMU-KYÓOIKU sika | Ukénakatta keredomo || taihen
    SYUSSE simásita.

31. máda | wákakute | SEKEN-SÍrazu desu.

32. máda | wákakute | YO nó NAKA no koto o | SÍrimasén.

33. KINSEI-NIHON-BÚNḠAKU no | NÁKA de || NINḠYÓO-geki wa | taisetu na
    zyánru desu.

34. GEKAI ní wa || KURUsími mo | KANAsími mo aru.

35. kono TOTI wa || KOKUYÚU-TI desu.

36. NIHÓN de wa || HAS-SÉIKI no hazime || TYÚUḠOKU ni | narátte || ZÉNKOKU
    no | KÓKUDO o | KOKUYUU to sita kotó ḡa | arimásita.

37. syóorohohu wa ||SEKAI-TEKI ni | YUUMEI na SAKKA désu.

38. ÚMU o | Iwasézu || MÚRI ni saseta.

39. KÁKU-KATEI ni | túite || térebi no | ÚMU o | sirábeta.

40. áru HITO wa || KANE ḡa takusan Áru ḡa || áru HITO wa | SUKÓsi sika |
    NÁi.

41. kono SINAMONO no SYOYÚU-SYA wa || dónata desu ka.

42. KYÓOTO ni wa || MEISYÓ ḡa | ÓOi.

43. anó HITO wa || syooḡi no MEIZÍN desu.

44. dónna | MÉII de mo || naosénai | BYOOKI ḡa áru.

45. o-NAmae o KÁite kudasai.

46. DAIMYÓO no | yóo na SEIKATU o site iru.

47. NÍ-MEI o | DAIHYOO to site | eránda.

48. míttyan wa | adaNA de || HÓNMYOO wa | MÍTIKO desu.

49. itaríi no | runéssansu wa || ÓOku no MEISAKU o Unda.

50. kono TIHÓO no | MÉIBUTU wa | "sóba" desu.

51. MAISYUU || NIHONḠO no SAKUBUN o | KAkánakereba | naránai.

52. kono kusuri wa | WARÚi | SÁYOO o | okosánai.

53. TUKUriKÁTA o | OSIete kudasái.

54. kono tyookoku wa | mikeránzyero-SAKU to | TUTAerárete iru.

55. kono SYOOSETU no SÁKUSYA wa || dáre desu ka.

56. KYÓNEN wa | SAKÚ ḡa | yókatta ḡa || kotosi wa | HUSAKU de || SAKÚMOTU
    ḡa | SUKÓsi sika | toremasén desita.

57. hutari tomo | MUḠON de | suwatte imásita.

58. BUZI ni KÁEtta.

59. sonna MÚRI o | ossyátte mo || komarimásu.

60. húdan wa | MÚKUTI desu ḡa || bíiru nado o | nómu to | yóku syaberimasu.

61. aitu wa || BÚREI na | yátu da.

62. tibétto wa | DOKURITÚKOKU desu ka.

63. DOKUḠAKU de || YUUMEI na GAKUSYA ni nátta.

64. NÍTI-DOKU | KAIWA-GÁKUIN de || doituḠO o narátte imasu.

65. asoko wa | íi DAIḠAKU de || TÓKU ni | ÍGAKU ḡa | YUUMEI désu.

66. ano KIKÁI no TOKUTYOO wa || bótan o | osu daké de || HITODE ḡa iranái koto desu.

67. sasimí wa | NIHÓN TOKUYUU no | TAbeMÓNO desyoo.

68. kyóo wa || TOKUBAIZYOO ni | arubaito-GÁKUSEI to site || HATARAki ni Ikimásita.

69. kono SEIHIN wa || TÓKKYO o | TÓtte aru kara || YURUsí ḡa | NÁkereba || dare mo | ONAzi MONÓ o | TUKÚru koto wa | dekínai.

70. SIKATA ḡa arimasén.

71. ano ONNA no HITÓ wa | KÁMI ni | TUKÁete || ISSYOO | kekkon simasén desita.

72. kono rázio no | ZYUSÍNKI wa || subarasíi desu ne.   NÁKA wa || dónna SIKUmi ni | nátte | irú no desyoo ka.

73. zyettóKI nara || TOOKYOO kara | nyuuyóoku made || NAN-ZIKAN ḡúrai de | Ikimásu ka.

74. kodomótati wa | KIKÁNSYU ni | TÉ o | hurimásita.

75. KIKÁNSYA ḡa | NÁkereba || KISYÁ wa | hasiránai.

76. mukasi no ONNA no HITÓ wa || taitei | ZIBUN de | HATÁ o | ótte || ZIBUN de | kimono o nútta soo desu.

77. KIKÁI ḡa | áttara || Aitái.

78. kore wa || KÍ o MIte || ZIKKOO simásu.

79. ZYUUBÚN | YÓOI site | TAIKI site iru.

80. SINBUN wa | KIKÁI de | INSATU sareru.

81. SEKAIzyuu || dóko e | Itté mo || NIHONSEI no SINAMONO ḡa áru.

82. kono KAISYA no SEIHIN nára | SIN'YOO dekimásu.

83. TOKUSEI no SINA dá kara | TAKÁi.

84. KOOZYÓO de | HATARAite imásu.

85. HATI-ZÍKAN no | TUTOmé no uti || ZITUDOO-ZÍKAN wa | SITI-ZÍKAN desu.

86. go-SYÓOTAI | arígatoo gozaimasu.   YOROKÓnde | ukaḡawasete itadakimásu.

87. kono KOOZYÓO wa || ano KAISYA to | TOríhiki ḡa aru.

88. SINSYU-TEKI na HITÓ wa || ATARAsíi koto mo | osorézu ni | dóndon suru.

89. asita | KAkiTOri no <u>tésuto</u> g̃a | áru no de || BENKYOO sinákute wa | narimasén.

90. KAIMONO o sitára || UKETOri o moratte kudasái.

91. kono <u>rázio</u> wa | KÁNDO g̃a | íi kara || yóku KIkoeru.

92. totemo KANzi no íi KATA desu ne.

93. WARÚi TOMOdati no | KÁNKA o | Úkete || WARÚi koto o sita.

94. GOOZYOO na HITÓ wa || nakanaka "maketá" to wa | Iwanai.

95. aitu wa || ZENZEN ZISIN no NÁi || NASAkenai OTOKÓ da.

96. SENZYOO de Umareta | SENYUU-DÓOSI no YUUZYOO wa || ítu made mo | tuzukimásu.

97. kimi g̃a | sonna ni KANAsisóo na | HYOOZYÓO o suru to || bóku mo | KANAsiku náru.

98. EIG̃O wa || dóo mo | NIG̃ATE désu.

99. SÁMUsa wa | tittó mo | KÚ ni | narimasén.

100. KUG̃ÁKUSEI wa || ZIBUN de | HATARAita o-KANE de | BENKYOO suru.

101. mukoo no <u>tíimu</u> g̃a | TÚYOkute || nakanaka KUSEN désita.

102. <u>koohíi</u> wa || NIG̃Ái kara | kirai désu.

103. NAG̃Ái AIDA || BYÓOKU ni | KURUsimeráreta.

DÁI | ZYUU NÍ-KA

1. GÉNKI na | OTOKÓ-no-KO desu.

2. NIHÓN de wa | GANZITU ni || dónna koto o | simásu ka.

3. MOTODE g̃a NÁi kara || OOkíi SIG̃OTO wa | dekimasén.

4. NING̃EN wa || GÁNRAI | SYAKAI-TEKI na DOOBUTU désu.

5. YUUMEI na ONG̃AKKA.

6. TANOsíi | <u>píkunikku</u>.

7. ANRAKÚisu ni | kosikakéru.

8. sekinin g̃a NÁi kara || KIRAKU désu.

9. dóozo || o-RAKU ni nasátte kudasai.

10. o-ME ni kakáru no o | TANOsími ni site imasu.

11. ÁME g̃a | hútta no de || SYUUZITU | IÉ de | <u>rekoodo</u>ÓNG̃AKU o | TANOsínda.

12. SYUUG̃YOO wa || GÓG̃O | GO-ZI-HÁN desu.

13. syukudai o Oeté kara || ASObu.

14. syukudai g̃a OWAtté kara || ASObu.

15. syukudai o | OWAri máde | sité kara || ASObu.

16. KOOBÁ de || SYUUZITU hataraité kara || YAḠAKU e mairimásu.

17. KYUUYOO ḡa dékita no de || ISÓide | KAEránakereba | narimasén.

18. kono SIḠOTO wa || OOÍSOḡi de | site kudasái.

19. TOKKYUU wa || ITIBAN hayái KYUUKOO de || ZYUNKYUU wa || KYUUKOO yóri | osoi.

20. KYUU ni | amerika e Iku kotó ni | narimásita.

21. ATÚi SYOTYUU wa || ÚMI e Ikimasu.

22. kono heyá wa | mádo ḡa | TIIsái no de || YÓRU de mo | ATUKURUsíi.

23. ano TIHÓO wa || KÁNSYO || dotira mo hidói.

24. SYOTYUU ó-mimai | MOOsiaḡemásu.

25. ZYUUḠO YA no TUKÍ wa | marúi.

26. YÓRU no GAKKOO o | YAḠAKU to iu.

27. YONAKÁ made | SÓTO de | ASOnde ité wa | ikemasén yo.

28. NIHÓN wa | SÍKI ḡa | hakkíri site iru.

29. NIHON no ÚKI wa | ROKUḠATÚ desu.

30. KISÉTU no | kudámono wa | oisíi.

31. DÁI IS-SETU o | YÓnde kudasai.

32. dónna HUSI no | ÓNḠAKU desu ka.

33. yubi no HUSI ḡa HUTÓi.

34. kinoo | omoi nímotu o | HAKOndá no de || kyóo wa | karada no HUSÍBUSI ḡa | itamimásu.

35. KÓN'YA wa | HÚUU ḡa | hídoku | náru desyoo.

36. HÚUSYA wa || móo || hotóndo | TUKAwaremasén.

37. KANPUU no NÁKA ni | TÁtte | itá no de || BYOOKI ni nátta.

38. hidói KAZE desu.

39. anó HITO wa | IPPUU KAwatte imásu.

40. TOOKYOO no KAMIKAZE-tákusii ni | SUKÓsi wa | naremásita ka.

41. háwai wa || TAIHÉIYOO ni | áru.

42. yóku | HUTÓtta | ÁKAtyan desu ne.

43. SAMÚi no wa | HEIKI désu ḡa || ATÚi to | súḡu | BYOOKI ni narimásu.

44. SUIHEI na TOKORÓ nara || MIZU wa | naḡarénai hazu desu.

45. dótira no | HANASÍ mo | KOOHEI ni KIite moraitái.

46. BYOODOO ni WAkemasyóo.

47. TAIRA na yóo ni | MIemásu ḡa || SUIHEI zya arimasén.

48. HIRAtai ISÍ ni | kosikákete || YASÚnda.

49. SÉIYOO to | TÓOYOO de wa || KANG̃AeKÁTA g̃a | tig̃aú desyoo.

50. ano résutoran no YOOSYOKU wa | umái.

51. nyuuyóoku kara || TAISÉIYOO o | HÉte || róndon e Itta.

52. pári ni iru AIDA ni || YOOSYO o takusan KAiatúmeta.

53. KAISUI wa | karái.

54. KAIG̃AI-RYÓKOO wa || ITI-DO | háwai e | Itta kotó g̃a aru | daké desu.

55. ÚMI g̃a | MIéru.

56. ÚN yoku || suita DÉNSYA g̃a | súg̃u | KImásita.

57. ÚN no | WARÚi | TOKÍ ni wa || NÁNI o | sité mo || úmaku | dekimasén.

58. ÚNMEI desu kara || SIKATA g̃a arimasén.

59. torákku de || nímotu o HAKObu.

60. KION wa TAKÁi g̃a || musiÁTUku | nái.

61. ONSUI-púuru de | oyóg̃u.

62. ÍMA || kono heya no ÓNDO wa || ROKUZYUU SITÍ-DO desu.

63. BEIKOKU no NOOMÍN wa | taitei HIRÓi | NÓOTI o | MÓtte | irú no de || NIHON no NÓOG̃YOO to wa || yariKATA g̃a tig̃au.

64. kotosi no BEISAKU wa || hidói | HUSAKU dá kara || hyakusyóo de mo | KOMÉ g̃a | TAberarénai ka mo sirenai.

65. buraziru || aruzéntin || tíri || péruu nado wa || mina | NANBEI ni áru.

66. kono HÁKUMAI wa | tóreta | bákari no | SINMAI desu.

67. watakusi wa || SINMAI désu kara || dóozo | iroiro | OSIete kudasái.

68. HITUYOO na monó g̃a | áttara || Iinasái.

69. kore wa | KOOKÓOSEI HITUDOKU no | SYÓMOTU desu.

70. KANARAzu | HATÍ-ZI made ni | KIté kudasai.

71. kono SIG̃OTO ní wa || TYÚUI o | YOOsúru.

72. kono KÓOZI ni | YÓOsita | NObe-NISSÚU wa | SAN BYAKÚ-NITI desita.

73. káre wa || SEIKAI no | YOOZIN désu.

74. I g̃a WARÚi kara || sake wa | nomemasén.

75. TYOO-kátaru no tame || KON'YA | ITYOO-BYÓOIN ni | NYUUIN simásu.

76. SITAsíi TOMOdati to | RYOKOO surú no wa || TANOsíi | monó desu.

77. MURAYAMA-KUN wa || bóku no | SIN'YUU désu.

78. yóku nite iru | ÓYAKO desu ne.

79. anó KO wa || TIIsái TOKI kara || umá ya | USI ni | SITAsínde | irú kara || tittó mo | osoremasén.

80. RÚI no | nái | UTUKÚsisa.

81. TOOKYOO ní wa | SINRUI g̃a ÓOi.

82. OOkisa ni yotte || BUNRUI site kudasái.

83. ZINRUIĜAKU-TEKI ni MÍta | BÚNKA.

84. HATYOO no OOkíi | ÓNPA wa || hikúi | OTÓ o DAsu.

85. ATUsuĝirú no de || BYOONIN ĝa | ZOKUSYUTU site | komátta.

86. kono KÁI wa || IS-SYÚUKAN || ZOKKOO simásu.

87. tuyu wa || IK-kaĜETU ĝúrai TUZUku.

88. moo ITÍ-NEN | BENKYOO o TUZUkeru tumori désu.

89. KAIĜAI-RYÓKOO no | TETÚZUki ĝa | yatto OWArimásita.

90. kono SYOOSETU no TUZUki wa || RÁIĜETU | DEmásu.

91. SIKAKUi teeburu o KAtta.

92. kono SANKAKÚKEI no | MI-Ttú no KAKU no | KÁKUDO o | hakátte kudasai.

93. USI no TUNO.

94. TANAKA-KUN || KIMI wa || DAIĜAKU de || NÁNI o | BENKYOO sitá n desu ka.

95. anó HITO wa || sake mo | tabako mo | kirai de || zyoodán mo Iwazu || KÚNSI no | yóo desu.

DÁI | ZYUU SÁN-KA

1. HATUON ni TYÚUI sinasai.

2. kono HÓN no HAKKOOZYO wa || KYÓOTO ni aru.

3. anó HITO wa | pisutoru no MEIZÍN de || HYAPPATU-HYAKUTYUU da sóo desu.

4. GÓĜO | YO-ZI-HÁN no | KISYÁ de || sikágo kara SYUPPATU simasu.

5. GAKKAI de || ATARAsíi GAKUSETU no | HAPPYOO ĝa átta.

6. kono TEĜAMI wa | SINTEN dá kara || HONNIN ÍĜAI | YÓnde wa | ikenai.

7. TENBÓOSYA kara | késiki o | TANOsímu.

8. koko wa || ÓOki na | KOOZYÓO ĝa | TÁtte kara || KYUU ni HATTEN sita.

9. ZYUUYOO na HANASÍ ĝa aru.

10. kono sakura wa | YÁE desu.   HANAbíra ĝa | takusan KASAnatte imásu.

11. OMOi nímotu o HAKOnda.

12. IKKOKU no DAIHYÓOSYA wa || ZITYOO sinákereba | naránai.

13. HÁRA-san wa || BOOEKÍSYOO de || NANBEI no KAISYA to | TOríHIki o site imasu.

14. BOOEKI tó wa || GAIKOKU ÁITE ni | YUSYUTU ya | YUNYUU o | suru kotó desu.

15. HEII na SYÓMOTU nara | YOmemásu.

16. EKISYA wa | EKI ni yotte || ÚNMEI o | MÍru HITO desu.

17. SITÚREI desu ḡa || go-SYÓOBAI wa?

18. yasai ya kudámono o | AKINÁu | TIIsái | SYÓONIN desu.

19. IN'YÓOBUN ni wa || "kaḡi-kákko" o | tukéru.

20. TUKI no ÍNRYOKU ni yotte || ÚMI no MIZU ḡa | mítitari | hiitári suru.

21. sono dóa wa | HIite kudasái.

22. depáato de || MANBIki ḡa tukamatta.

23. NIHÓN de KAKOO suru to | YASÚi ḡa || tooí kara || UN'YU ni KANE ḡa kakáru.

24. ONAzi HOOKOO ni SUSUmu.

25. NINḠEN wa || KOOZYOO sinákereba | naránai.

26. SITA o MUku.

27. MUkatte MIḠI no HITO.

28. MINAMIMUki no IE.

29. MÉNKA wa || momen no GENRYÓO de aru.

30. huton no NÁKA ni || atui WATÁ o Ireru.

31. ORIMONO-KÓOZYOO no | SYOKKOO ní wa || ZYOKOO ḡa ÓOi.

32. kínu no | TEOrí wa | KÓOKA desu.

33. BUKKA ḡa Aḡaru.

34. TÓKKA de | Uru.

35. íi HON da kara || ITIDOKU ni ATAIsuru.

36. GOSEN-EN no ATAI ḡa áru.

37. ZATUON ḡa ÓOi kara || rázio o kesite.

38. ZAKKITYOO ḡa NÍ-satu | hosíi.

39. ZOOKI no hayasi.

40. ZATUYOO ḡa ÓOkute || SIḠOTO ḡa SUSUmanai.

41. NIHON no KÍNKA o | MÍta koto ḡa | arimásu ka.

42. komakái | KATEI-YÓOHIN nado o | ZAKKA to iimásu.

43. amerika no HUNAḠÁISYA no KAMOTUSEN de || NIHÓN e | KImásita.

44. rosuanzérusu o | HUNADE sité kara || honóruru de | GESEN surú made | TANOsíi | HÚNE no TABI o | TUZUkemásita.

45. SÉNTYOO wa || SYÓKOKU o | RYOKOO sita HITÓ de || iroiro | omosirói | HANASÍ o | KIkasete kuremásita.

46. mukasi wa || watasiBÚNE de || KAWAMÚkoo e | Itta monó da.

47. TOOKYOO no ZINKOO wa || dóndon | ZOOKA site iru.

48. OOÁME de || IKE no MIZU ḡa MAsita.

49. KUMIAI ni KANYUU suru.

50. KUMIAI ni KUWAwáru.

51. míruku o | SYÓOSYOO | KUWAete kudasái.

52. GÉNKA ḡa | TAKÁi kara || TÁKAku Uru.

53. kororadoKÓOGEN wa || NATÚ de mo | suzusíi.

54. HIRÓi | HÁRA.

55. kore wa || GENBUN no mamá desu.

56. SIYOO no DENWA o káketara || RYÓOKIN o | harátte kudasai.

57. NYUUZYOO | MURYOO.

58. RYÓORI no | zyoozú na | ókusan.

59. SYOKURYOOHIN'YA de | báta o KAu.

60. BAKUḠA o Irete || bíiru o | TUKÚru.

61. KOMÚḠI wa || pán no | GENRYÓO desu.

62. MUGIwara-bóosi o | kabúru.

63. SOOTOO umái EIḠO o | HANÁsu.

64. KOdomo ní mo || KOdomo ni SOOTOO sita SIḠOTO ḡa | áru hazu desu.

65. ÍMA || ITÍ-doru no | kawase-SÓOBA wa|SÁNBYAKU|ROKUZYÚU-EN desu ka.

66. SOOBA de sippai sita.

67. anó HITO wa || o-KANEMOti no IÉ no | SOOZOKÚNIN desu.

68. SÉKAI SAIDAI no | depáato.

69. SAIZYOO no okurimono.

70. MOTTÓmo | ATARAsíi | KIKÁI.

71. SAIKIN no syasin.

72. kore ḡa SÁIḠO no | o-wakare désu.

73. TÍI no aru HITO.

74. eeru-DÁIḠAKU de || GÁKUI o | tótta.

75. AÍHARA-san no | HÓO ḡa || KURAI ḡa UE désu.

76. ano apáato wa || ÍTI ḡa | WARÚi.

77. sore ni túite wa || SYOSETU ḡa átte || máda | kimatta GAKUSETU ḡa | NÁi.

78. dónna SIḠOTO ḡa | o-NOZOmi désu ka.

79. SIBÓOSYA ḡa | ÓOi no de || sikén o simasu.

80. ano OTOKÓ ni wa | SITUBOO sita.

81. TAIMOO o toḡéru koto ḡa | dékizu || SÍTUI no uti ni | sinimásita.

82. HIRÓi |SIKAI de || KANḠÁeru koto ḡa | NOZOmasíi.

83. KI-no-dóku de || SEISI dekimasén desita.

84. KOKUMIN no ÍSI o | MUSI sita SEIZI o sita.

DÁI |ZYUU YÓN-KA

1. DAIḠAKU o SOTUḠYOO site || BOOEKI-ḠÁISYA ni | SYUUSYOKU sita.

2. KYOSYUU ni mayótte iru.

3. SYOKÚḠYOO wa | ISYA désu.

4. KOOBA no SYOKKOO.

5. TANOsíi SYOKUBA de || HATARAite iru.

6. TOMOdati no IÉ ni | DOOKYO site iru.

7. kono apáato no | KYOZYÚUSYA wa || OTOKO bákari desu.

8. IMA ni Imásu.

9. bóku no | ZIMÚSYO wa || SAN-ḠAI ni arimásu.

10. depáato no TIKAI ní wa || taitei | TOKUBAIZYOO ḡa áru.

11. ONKAI o naráu.

12. NIḠÁi KUSURI o | nónda.

13. KUSURIYA de || MEḠÚSURI o KAtta.

14. KAYAKU dá kara || TYÚUI site kudasai.

15. kono RYÓORI ni wa || dónna YAKUMI o | TUKAimásu ka.

16. TYOKUSETU ni KIita HANASÍ desu.

17. TYOKKAKU wa || KYUUZYÚU-DO desu.

18. KÓN'YA wa | TOOTYOKU dá kara || IÉ e | KAErénai.

19. SYOOZÍKI na | HITÓ wa || úso o | tukánai.

20. HATUON o NAÓsite kudasai.

21. kono KISYÁ wa || TOOKYOO de | AOMORI-YUKI ni | SETUZOKU suru.

22. TYOKUSETU ní wa | HANAsi-nikúi kara || KANSETU ni tanómu.

23. o-TYA no SÉTTAI o suru.

24. go-SÍNSETU | aríḡatoo.

25. náihu de || TÉ o KItta.

26. huutoo ni | KITTE o haru.

27. TOKUBAIHIN wa || UriKIre désu.

28. RAINEN no púran wa || máda | KImarimasén.

29. RAINEN no púran o | KImeta.

30. sonna mondai wa || móo | KAIKETU simásita.

31. TUḠÍ no yoo na | TOriKIme o sita.

32. NI-DO to KESsíte | nusumí wa | itasimasén kara || YURÚsite kudasai.

33. TUKIḠIme ni site || apaató-DAI o | harátte imasu.

34. TANÍ e KUDAru.

35. TANIḠAWA de | TÉ o arau.

36. ZYÚUSYO to NAmae o | KANARAzu KÁku koto.

37. SÚMAI to | TAbéMONO to | KIru MONÓ wa || SEIKATU ni | TAISETU na monó desu.

38. dóko ni | SÚnde imasu ka.

39. TOOKYOO no ZYUUMÍN ni wa || ZÉNKOKU | KÁKUTI kara | KItá MONO ḡa | ÓOi.

40. inakaZÚmai wa | sukí zya | nái.

41. BETU ni | nyúusu wa | arimasén.

42. BETU ni tutúnde kudasai.

43. BETU na HITÓ desu.

44. ókusan to BEKKYO site iru.

45. ókusan to | WAKÁrete | kurasite iru.

46. TOKUBETU na ÍMI wa | arimasén.

47. KODOMO o nakusité kara || BETUZIN no yóo ni | nátta.

48. watasiBÚNE no HATTYAKUZYO wa || dóko desu ka.

49. kono KISYÁ wa || SITÍ-HUN | ENTYAKU sita.

50. UTUKUsíi KIMONO.

51. kyóo TUita | bákari desu.

52. íyoiyo | sono DAI-KÉNtiku ni | TYÁKUSYU suru koto ni | nátta.

53. UWAḠI to SITAḠI wa || BETU ni site | araimásu.

54. HOKKYOKU mo | NANKYOKU mo || SUmi-nikúi | TOKORÓ da.

55. NIHÓN wa | KYOKUTOO no IK-KOKU de áru.

56. koko wa || TIZYOO no GOKURAKU désu yo.

57. GOKKAN no KISÉTU ni | nátta.

58. BÁSYA de | nímotu o HAKObu.

59. BÁBA de | UMÁ ni noru.

60. kono TATÉMONO wa || móto wa | UMAḠOYA désita.

61. BANKEN ḡa iru.

62. INÚ ḡa | sukí de || NIHONKEN ya | YOOKEN ya | KOINU o | takusan kátte iru.

63. kono KANZI wa || TUKAu KAISÚU ḡa | SUKUnái.

64. KÓNKAI no | KAIGOO wa || KYÓOTO de OKOnawareru.

65. IKE no MAWAri o MAWAru.

66. tooMAWAsi ni | MONÓ o | Iwanái de kudasai.

67. KANEMAWAri ga WARÚi.

68. moo IK-KAI site miyóo.

69. kóma o MAWAsu.

70. KIMONO o KIte || ÓBI o | siméru.

71. pisutoru o Óbita | zyúnsa.

72. kono apáato ni wa || ZYUU GO-SYÓTAI | SÚnde iru.

73. ONNÁ ni | TEKÍsita SIGOTO.

74. TEKITOO na IÉ ga | nái no de || komátte iru.

75. TÉKIDO ni | TAbéru.

76. SÍZAI de || GAKKOO o TÁteta.

77. ZÁISAN wa | NANI mo nái.

78. KUNI no ZAISEI ga | KURÚsiku | nátta.

79. KOdomo o Umu.

80. o-SAN o suru.

81. ano KOOBÁ de || SEISAN suru MEN'ÓRIMONO wa || mina | YUSYUTU-YOO
no SINAMONO désu.

82. TOOKYOO no MEISAN wa || "norí" desu.

83. o-KANE o Otósita.

84. WATAKUSI no TEOtí desita.   sumimasén.

85. ÁKI ni | náru to || KÍ no ha ga | Otíru.

86. BENKYOO sinákatta no de || RAKUDAI sita.

87. UTUKUsíi RAKUZITU!

88. nóoto ni | RAKUGAki o sita.

89. ZIPPU wa || WATAKUSI ga Umareru MÁE ni | nakunarimásita.

90. YAKUSYÓ de HATARAite iru | YAKUNIN désu.

91. táipu o | útu no ga || watasi no YAKÚ desu.

92. EIGO ga YAKÚ ni tatte || BOOEKI-GÁISYA ni | SYUUSYOKU suru kotó ga |
dekimásita.

93. turai SÍEKI ni | taerarézu || taórete simatta.

94. dónna SIGOTO ni | ZYÚUZI site imasu ka.

95. ZYÚURAI no|KANGAeKÁTA de wa || RIKAI dekínai desyoo.

96. KÉRAI o | takusan SITAGÁeta | DAIMYÓO.

DÁI | ZYUU GÓ-KA

1. ÚMI to RIKU.

2. NINḠEN wa ‖ RIKUTI ni SÚnde iru.

3. yooroppaTÁIRIKU ni wa ‖ takusán no | KUNI ḡa áru.

4. zyettóKI ḡa ‖ BUZI ni TYAKURIKU sita.

5. itaríi wa ‖ HᴀNTÓOKOKU de aru.

6. ano SIMÁ wa ‖ MUZINTOO désu yo.

7. NIHÓN wa ‖ SIMÁḠUNI de ‖ KOZIMA ḡa ÓOi.

8. kono HUKÍN de ‖ ASOndé wa | ikenai.

9. TEḠAMI ní wa ‖ HIZUKE o | KANARAzu KÁite kudasai.

10. tyuuíngamu ḡa | TÚite | komátta.

11. TÉ o | KÍttara ‖ súḡu | KUSURI o TUkenasái.

12. YOHAKU no ÓOi TEḠAMI.

13. YOBUN ni KAtte okimasyóo.

14. SEN YO-NEN MÁE no | TATÉMONO desu.

15. AMÁtta | TAbéMONO wa ‖ sutete kudasái.

16. kono GAKKOO ní wa ‖ HYAKU-NIN ÁMAri no | SÉITO ḡa iru.

17. KOdomo no SEITYOO wa | hayái.

18. KEIZAI-HÁKUSYO o | SAKUSEI suru.

19. kono KUSURI no | SÉIBUN wa ‖ NÁN desu ka.

20. NIHÓN wa | DÁISYOO no | SIMÁZIMA kara | NÁru.

21. ZIMÚSYO de | MENKAI suru.

22. MIZU no HYOOMÉN ni ‖ abura ḡa uite iru.

23. AKKAN ni | SYOOMÉN kara ‖ KÍtte | kakaráreta.

24. MEN o kabútte | odoru.

25. OMOTÉ o aḡeru.

26. OMONAḠA na BIZIN.

27. MENBOKU arimasén.   WATAKUSI no TEOtí desu.

28. SAN ni | SAN o | kakéru to ‖ sono SÉKI wa | KYÚU ni naru.

29. kono TOTI no MÉNSEKI wa ‖ dono ḡurai arimásu ka.

30. SEKKYOKUTEKI na SEISITU désu.

31. SANZYOO wa ‖ SEKISETU SAN-méetoru ni | oyónda.

32. YUKÍ ḡa | TUmóru.

33. ATARAsíi | káaten o | TUketái no desu ḡa ‖ ikura ḡúrai | kakáru ka | MITUmori o dásite kudasai.

34. HÓN o │ YAMA no yóo ni TUmu.

35. YÁKU │ IK-káḠETU │ RYOKOO simásu.

36. MIZU o SETUYAKU site kudasái.

37. gwamuTOO wa ‖ BEIKOKU no RYÓODO de aru.

38. ano KATÁ wa ‖ amerika no RYÓOZI desu.

39. UKETOri to │ RYOOSYUUSYO wa │ ONAzi désu.

40. ATARAsíi │ SIḠOTO dá kara ‖ YOORYÓO o │ OSIete kudasái.

41. aitu wa │ YOORYÓO no │ íi │ OTOKÓ da.

42. YOORYÓO no │ WARÚi HITO wa ‖ SIPPAI bákari suru.

43. NIHÓN wa ‖ DAI NI-ZI TAISEN ni │ HAIBOKU site ‖ HAISÉNKOKU to │ nátta.

44. géemu ni ZENPAI sita.

45. géemu ni │ YABÚreta.

46. sikén no KEKKA wa ‖ dóo desu ka.

47. HUTA-tú no KUMIAI ḡa │ KETUḠOO site ‖ ATARAsíi KUMIAI o │ SÓSIKI sita.

48. nékutai o MUSUbu.

49. MUSUbiME ḡa kátakute ‖ tokemasén.

50. MUSUbi no kotobá.

51. KÁZITU wa ‖ karada ni íi.

52. SIḠOTO o │ HATÁsita.

53. HÉI o │ HIKIíru.

54. HEIEKI no GÍMU wa │ NÁi.

55. SÚIHEI desita.

56. HÍ o │ mitomenái.

57. ZÉNPI o │ kúite ‖ mazime ni náru │ tumori désu.

58. HIZYOO no BAAI ní wa ‖ kono béru o │ osite kudasái.

59. HIZYOO ni ÓOki na │ MONDAI désu.

60. HIBÁIHIN desu kara │ Uremasén.

61. NITIZYOO-SÉIKATU ni │ HITUYOO na KAIWA o naráu.

62. anó HITO no OKOnai wa ‖ SEIZYOO zya arimasén ne.

63. TÚNE ni │ KOdomo no OKOnai ni │ TYÚUI site iru.

64. RÍTU ḡa │ íi.

65. HYAKUBÚNRITU wa │ paasentéezi to mo iu.

66. SOTTYOKU ni HANÁsu.

67. HITO ni SOSSEN site ‖ dóndon SIḠOTO o suru.

68. HYAKU-MÁN wa ‖ ITÍ-OKU no │ HYAKU-BUN no ITÍ desu.

69. SOOBA de │ móokete ‖ OKUMAN-TYÓOZYA ni │ nátta.

70. SENSÉI ḡa │ SÉITO o │ HIKÍite ‖ ENSOKU ni Iku.

71. ENPOO kara │ TOMOdati ḡa KIté kureta.

72. KOOZI-TYUU dá kara ‖ TOOMÁWAri o │ sinákereba │ naránai.

73. TOOMAWAsi ni Iwazu ni ‖ SOTTYOKU ni HANÁsite kudasai.

74. "KUON" to iu kotobá wa ‖ KOOḠO dé wa │ hotóndo │ TUKAwanai.

75. YO-nó-NAKA no TAISEI o │ KANḠÁeru beki da.

76. TAZEI ni │ BÚZEI de │ MAkemásita.

77. SUIDOO kara │ MIZU ḡa │ IKIOi yóku │ déru.

78. SINBUN o ITÍ-BU KAtta.

79. UTUsí o │ NÍ-BU │ táipu site kudasai.

80. DAIḠAKU-ZÍDAI wa ‖ ONḠÁKU-BU no │ ménbaa desita.

81. kono TATÉMONO wa ‖ ITI-BÚBUN │ ATARÁsiku │ TAteMAsita tokoró ḡa arimasu.

82. KUMIAI HÓNBU.

83. KÓOTI o │ TAḠAYÁsite ‖ MÚḠI o maku.

84. KOOSAKU-YOO no UMÁ ḡa iru.

85. GENZITU-TEKI na KANḠÁe.

86. GENZYÚUSYO wa ‖ dótira desu ka.

87. ZIBUN no KANḠÁe ḡa │ arimásu ḡa ‖ úmaku │ HYOOḠEN dekimasén.

88. ZIBUN no KANḠÁe ḡa │ arimásu ḡa ‖ úmaku IiARAwasemasén.

89. kirisuto no SYUTUḠEN.

90. TUKÍ ḡa │ kúmo no AIDA kara │ ARAwáreta.

91. GÉNZAI │ kono GAKKOO no ZAIḠÁKUSEI wa ‖ NI SEN-MEI désu.

92. KÓOZI no GENBA o │ MÍ ni Itta.

93. tadá-IMA ‖ TITÍ wa │ HUZAI désu.

94. ZISSI ḡa NÁkatta no de ‖ YOOSI o moraimásita.

95. ano KATÁ wa ‖ TAKÁi KYOOYOO ḡa │ oari ni narimásu.

96. HATARAite ‖ KOdomo ya kánai o │ YASINÁu.

97. HÁHA wa ‖ BYOOḠO no YOOZYÓO o site imasu.

98. yóku │ BENKYOO sitá no de ‖ íi TEN o moratta.

99. kono TEN o │ mótto │ KENKYUU site kudasái.

100. HIRÓi │ HÁRA ni │ NÓOKA ḡa │ TENZAI site iru.

101. sikén no │ TENSÚU ḡa │ WÁRUkatta.

102. MÉ ḡa | MIénai HITO no | tamé ni || TENZI no HÓN o | TUKÚru.

103. gasu-sutóobu ni | TENKA suru.

104. SITUMON ḡa arimásu.

105. GAKÚMON wa || GAKKOO de nákute mo | dekimásu.

106. TOI ni kotaéru.

107. TOéba | kotaéru.

108. HÓN no | DÁI.

109. kyóo no WADAI wa || NÁN desyoo ka.

110. komátta MONDAI ḡa | arimásu.

DÁI | ZYUU RÓK-KA

1. SENSÉI o KAKOnde | HANAsiÁu.

2. HITÓBITO no KAKOmi kara | nukeDÁsu.

3. hazime ni YOORYÓO o || áto de || SÁIBU ni | túite | oHANAsi itasimásu.

4. kono yubiwa no SAIKÚ wa | míḡoto desu ne.

5. HOSÓi MITI.

6. HOSONAḠÁi teeburu.

7. KOMAkái o-KANE ḡa | arimásu ka.

8. KOMAkái TEN wa || áto de | HANAsimásu.

9. BYOOKI dá kara || MYAKÚ ḡa | hayái.

10. kono HANASÍ wa || MYAKÚ ḡa aru.

11. kororadoSÁNMYAKU.

12. DOOMYAKU o KÍru to || sinde simau.

13. NIHÓN ni wa || NAḠÁi | KÁSEN ḡa | SUKUnái.

14. suezuÚNḠA.

15. súisu de || HYÓOḠA o | MImásita.

16. TÁIḠA no | KAKOO ní wa || taitei | MINATO ḡa áru.

17. RYUUKOO wa || pári kara hazimaru.

18. RYUUKOO no KIMONO.

19. TUYÓi DENRYUU ḡa | TÓOtte iru kara || KI o tukéte kudasai.

20. ITIRYUU no depáato nara || SIN'YOO dekimásu.

21. kono HUKÍN o | NAḠAréru KAIRYUU wa || KANRYUU désu.

22. kono KAWÁ wa || NAḠAré ḡa | KYUU désu.

23. KAWAKAMI kara | KAWASIMO e | KÍ o | NAḠÁsu.

24. DÉNKI ni wa ‖ KOORYUU to │ TYOKURYUU g̃a áru.

25. mukasi ‖ WARÚi koto o sita │ MONÓ o │ TOOku no SIMÁ e │ yatte simau kotó o │ "ONRU" to itta.

26. YÁG̃AI no │ ONG̃ÁKKAI e Iku.

27. YAKEN désu kara ‖ abunái desu yo.

28. amerika ní wa ‖ KOODAI na HEIYA g̃a áru.

29. NÓ no HANA.

30. NÓHARA de ‖ booruNÁg̃e o site │ ASObu.

31. MONDAI no │ ZYUUYOO na TEN o │ RIKISETU suru.

32. ano SYOOSETU wa ‖ SAIKIN no │ RIKISAKU désu.

33. GENSÍRYOKU KENKYUUZYO.

34. TIKARA-SÍG̃OTO wa ‖ dekimasén.

35. TIKARÁ g̃a │ TUYÓi.

36. básu no │ BÉN g̃a │ íi.

37. DANSI-YOO BENZYO.

38. BÉNRI na │ apáato.

39. HUNABIN nára ‖ YASÚi desu g̃a ‖ NISSÚU g̃a kakarimasu.

40. asoko de ‖ o-KANE o kariru to ‖ RÍSI g̃a │ TAKÁi.

41. KÓORI no KANE o │ kariru.

42. KOOKUUBIN o RIYOO suru.

43. kono KUSURI wa ‖ anmari TUZUkete nómu to │ GÁI g̃a aru.

44. SUKÓsi nara ‖ SAKE mo │ MÚG̃AI da.

45. HUHEI g̃a áru.

46. HÚBEN na │ IÉ ni │ SÚnde iru.

47. HUSEI na kotó o │ sité wa │ ikenái.

48. HÚZIYUU na SEIKATU.

49. ZIBUN ni HÚRI na koto wa ‖ KESsite sinai HITÓ da.

50. HUSOKÚBUN wa ‖ áto de haraimasu.

51. KOOTUU-KIKÁN to │ sité wa ‖ HÚNE ‖ KOOKÚUKI ‖ ZIDÓOSYA g̃a │ áru.

52. KOOBAN ni Iru zyúnsa ni ‖ MITI o KIku.

53. GAIKOO-TEKI na kotobá o │ sono mama SÍNzite wa │ ikenái.

54. NITI-BÉI-KAN no │ GAIKOO-MÓNDAI ni tuite │ HANAsiÁtta.

55. tukáreta kara ¦│ KOOTAI site kudasái.

56. íi MONO mo │ WARÚi MONO mo │ MAzítte imasu.

57. GAIKOKÚZIN to │ MAZIwátte │ GAIKOKUG̃O o naráu.

58. úuru wa | HOON no TEN dé wa || ITIBAN íi.

59. TÚNE ni | ONAzi ÓNDO o | TAMÓtu | HITUYOO g̃a áru.

60. KOKUMIN no tamé ni || KOMÉ o | KÁKUHO | sinákereba | naránai.

61. HANKYOO | SINBEI no HITO.

62. "TAKÁi" no HANTAI wa || "YASÚi" de || "OOkíi" no HANTAI wa || "TIIsái" desu.

63. kono pisutoru wa || HANDOO g̃a SUKUnái.

64. ano gurúupu wa || HANDOO-TEKI da.

65. TÁ o | GÓ-TAN | MÓtte iru.

66. KIMONO no tamé ni || ITI, NI-TAN | eránde kudasai.

67. NING̃EN mo | HIRÓi | ÍMI de || DOOBUTU désu.

68. DÓORYOKU o TUKAtte || KIKÁI o | UG̃Okásu.

69. UG̃Óite wa | ikemasén.

70. HIZYOO no BAAI ni | KESsite DOOzinai OTOKÓ da.

71. ZIDÓOSYA wa | ZITÚ ni | BÉNRI da.

72. UTUKUsíi DOOSA.

73. nyuuyóoku ni wa || ÓOki na KUUKOO g̃a | HUTA-tu áru.

74. HÚNE g̃a | MINATO ni TÚku.

75. YASUmí ni wa || KOSUI no sóba no | hóteru e Iku.

76. MIZUÚMI de || turi o suru.

77. KAKÓOKO wa || TIIsákute mo || hukái mono g̃a | ÓOi.

78. ÁME g̃a | SUKUnái no de || SANRIN no KÁZI g̃a | ÓOi.

79. NING̃EN no SUménai | SINRIN.

80. IÉ wa || HAYASI no NÁKA ni aru.

81. NÓOG̃YOO ya | RING̃YOO o | MANÁbu tame ni || NOORIN-GÁKKOO g̃a | áru.

82. mezurasíi | SYOKÚBUTU g̃a | Uete áru.

83. INSATU no AYAMÁri o | GOSYOKU to iimasu.

84. UEKIYA ni | UEKI no TEIré o saseru.

85. TAUé wa || tuyu no MÁE ni suru.

86. ázia ya | ahurika ní wa || SYOKUMÍNTI g̃a | ÓOkatta.

87. sakura ní wa || iroiro na HINSYU g̃a arimásu.

88. amerika-NÁNBU ni wa || máda | ZINSYU-MÓNDAI g̃a | nokótte iru.

89. MÚG̃I no | TÁNE o maku.

90. depáato ni wa || arayúru | SYÚRUI no | SINA g̃a áru.

91. KIKOO g̃a yói.

92. GENSÍRYOKU no | HEIWA-TEKI RIYOO.

93. WAHUU no IÉ g̃a | íi.

94. GOKAI g̃a tókete || WAKAI sita.

95. SÁMUsa g̃a | YAWAróg̃u.

96. WAEI to | EIWA no | ZIBIKÍ g̃a | hosíi.

97. TOOKYÓO-TO ni wa || NÍZYUU | SÁN-KU ari || sorézore ni | KUYÁKUSYO g̃a | áru.

98. yóku | nite irú kara || KÚBETU g̃a | dekínai.

99. KÓOSI o | KÚBETU suru.

100. TOOKYÓO-TO o | NÍZYUU SAN ni | KÚBUN sita.

101. NIHON-KÓOKUU no | zyettóKI de || RAINITI sita.

102. TANOsíi | KÓOKAI o TUZUketa.

103. KÚUKI g̃a | WARÚi kara || mádo o | akenasái.

104. KÚUKI g̃a | YAWAróg̃u.

105. SÓRA g̃a | kumóru.

106. SEIZI no KUUHAKU o | mitásu.

107. KUUHAKU no BÚBUN ni || KINYUU site kudasái.

108. SINKUU dá kara || KÚUKI g̃a | NÁi.

109. MOKUTEKI ni TASsuru máde || yamenai.

110. MOKUTEKI o TASSEI suru máde || yamenai.

111. BUTURÍG̃AKU no HATTATU wa | subarasíi.

112. yóku | BENKYOO sitá no de || taihen ZYOOTATU simásita.

DÁI |ZYUU SITÍ-KA

1. KYAKU o | KYAKUMA e TÓOsu.

2. RAIKYAKU g̃a átta no de || GAISYUTU dekínakatta.

3. RYOKÁKKI no HATTATU wa || SÉKAI o | TIKAzúketa.

4. GYOKUSEKI o KÚBETU suru.

5. sono YUBIWA no TAMÁ wa || mezurasíi mono desu ne.

6. MIZUTAMA-móyoo no | sukáato.

7. HAKUTYÓO o hazime || MIZUTORI no takusan iru IKE.

8. TYÓORUI no KENKYUUKA to site || YUUMEI na GAKUSYA désu.

9. TAIHÉIYOO o | MUTYÁKURIKU de || tonda TYOOZIN.

10. TORI g̃a naku.

11. ZÍNZYA no | AKAi TORII ḡa | MIéru.

12. sonna muzukasíi SIḠOTO wa || ITTYOO-ISSEKI ní wa | dekimasén.

13. YUUḠATA GO-ZI góro || ASObi ni Ikimásu.

14. GIKAI-SÉIZI no OKOnawarete iru KUNI.

15. KAIḠITYUU désu kara || SYÓOSYOO | oMAti kudasái.

16. MONḠÁMAe no | rippa na IÉ ni | SÚnde iru.

17. SÁKI no | TOKORÓ ni | SÍNKYO o | KAMAemásita.

18. SYÁKAI wa || HITÓBITO ḡa | atumátte || KOOSEI sita monó desu.

19. kono SYOOSETU wa || KOOSEI ḡa omosirói.

20. KÍNḠYO o | káu.

21. NETTÁIḠYO o | káu no ḡa || RYUUKOO désu.

22. UOÍTIBA de || sakana no BÁIBAI o suru.

23. TOOKYOO || KYÓOTO wa || DAITÓSI desu.

24. SÍ no SEIZI wa || SITYÓO no | sekinin désu.

25. TOONANázia wa || NIHON-SÉIHIN no | íi SIZYOO da.

26. AOMONÓITI wa || YASAI to KÁZITU no | ITIBA de áru.

27. ITIRITU no DAIḠAKU.

28. ÁME ni | hurárete || ZENSIN nurete simatta.

29. SINTYOO wa || ITI-méetoru | NANAZYUS-sénti desu.

30. máda | DOKUSIN désu.

31. MÍBUN no | TAKÁi KATA.

32. MI ni TUkéru mono wa || ítu mo | kírei ni | site oku yóo ni.

33. teeburu no UÉ ni | SYOKÚEN o | dásu.

34. NIHÓN wa || ÚMI ni | KAKOmarete irú kara || KAISUI kara | SIÓ o | tóru | SEIENZYO ḡa | takusan arimásu.

35. ÚN | WÁRUku || SÚMAI ḡa | RUISYOO sita.

36. YUUMEI na TERÁ ḡa | SIKKA de | SYOOSITU sita.

37. pán o YAku.

38. pán ḡa YAketa.

39. UTUKUsíi | YUUYAke no SÓRA o | goran nasái.

40. SAISYOKU bákari de || nikú ya sakana wa | TAbemasén.

41. yaoYA de | AONA o KAu.

42. kore wa || INRYÓOSUI zya | arimasén kara || NOmemasén.

43. SAKENÓmi desu ḡa || yopparai zya arimasén.

44. NIHONSYU wa || KOMÉ kara | TUKÚtta | SAKE désu.

45. SAKABA dé no | ÍNSYOKU wa || TÁKAku tuku.

46. SAKAYA dé wa || taitei | SAKE ÍĠAI ni || SIÓ ya | kanzúme nado no | SYOKURYOOHIN o Utte iru.

47. BYOOKI dá kara || SYOKUYOKU ḡa nái.

48. SEIZIKA to sité wa || mezurásiku | MÚYOKU na | HITÓ desu.

49. oboeyóo to suru | ÍYOKU ḡa | nákereba || GAKKOO e Itté mo | muda désu.

50. KOKUMIN no HOSsúru HEIWA.

51. REISUI o | MI ni abiru.

52. kotosi no HOKKÁIDOO no REIĠAI wa | hídokatta.

53. RYÓORI ḡa | HIénai uti ni || háyaku | TÁbete kudasai.

54. TUMEtai bíiru ḡa | NOmitái kara || HIyásite oite.

55. sonna SÉTU ni wa | SANSEI dekínai.

56. KÁMI o | SÁNBI suru.

57. takusán no | KATÁĠATA no | go-SANDOO o itadakimásita no de || kono TÓOri || ZIKKOO suru kotó ni itasimasu.

58. ameriká̲Z̲I̲N̲ de mo || NÁMA no | KÁI wa | TAbéru yoo desu.

59. YUUHAN ní wa | YAkiMESI o TUKUrimasyóo.

60. MUĠIMESI de SITÚREI desu ḡa || issyo ni góHAN o | TÁbete kudasai.

61. MÁIASA || ROKÚ-ZI made ni | HANBA ni Iku.

62. "MITUmori o dásite kudasai."
    "háa || SYOOTI itasimásita."

63. kotira de | go-TYUUMON o UKETAMAWArimásu.

64. NETÚ ḡa | aru rásiku || karada ḡa ATÚi kara || HAKÁtte mite kudasai.

65. h̲u̲t̲t̲o̲b̲ó̲o̲r̲u̲ ni NETTYUU site || tittó mo | BENKYOO simasén.

66. tetu o | NESsuru to || AKAku náru.

67. kono TOKEI wa | okurete iru.

68. GOOKEI | íkura ni | narimásu ka.

69. KEIRYAKU ni kakátte || SIPPAI sita.

70. ITÍ-NEN no | KÉI wa || GANZITU ni áru.

71. ITI-MÁN | NI SEN-EN.

72. ENKEI no TATÉMONO.

73. ÉN o | káku.

74. YOKIN ḡa SOOTOO áru.

75. o-KANE o AZÚke ni Iku.

76. ó̲o̲b̲a̲a̲ ya o-bóosi wa || kotira de || oAZUkari itasimásu.

77. s̲u̲u̲t̲u̲k̲é̲e̲s̲u̲ o | ITIZI-AZUkariZYO ni | AZUkéru.

DÁI | ZYUU HÁK-KA

1. SINSEIHIN g̃a NYUUKA simásita.

2. RYOOTE de | NÍMOTU o | MÓtu.

3. HATAKE kara || AONA o | NIG̃ÚRUMA de HAKObu.

4. KOdomo ni | sonna SIG̃OTO wa | OMONI desyóo.

5. ITIRYÓOZITU no uti ni | ukag̃aimásu.

6. RYÓOSIN wa | inaka ni SÚnde iru.

7. RYOOHOO | ITI-DÓ ni wa | dekimasén.

8. DAIHYOO o SIMEI suru.

9. TÉ no | YUBÍ ni wa || sorézore || OYAYUBI || HITOsásiYUBI ||
   NAKÁYUBI || KUSURÍYUBI || KOYUBI to iu | NAmae g̃a áru.

10. NIHON no SYÚTO wa | TOOKYOO de áru.

11. HITO o KOROsité kara || KOOBAN ni ZISYU sita.

12. tyáatiru wa | NAG̃Ái AIDA || EIKOKU no SYUSYOO dátta.

13. KUBI o KÍru.

14. SYÚI o | arasóu.

15. taitei | HIDARI no TÉKUBI ni | TOKEI o hameru.

16. BÉNRI na DOOG̃U.

17. kono ZIDÓOSYA wa || buréeki no GUAI g̃a | WARÚi kara || garéezi e |
    motte ikanákereba | naránai.

18. HUKADE o Otte || HÚG̃U ni | nátta.

19. ATARAsíi | NÓOG̃U o TUKAtte | KOOSAKU suru.

20. ÁSA | HÁYAku kara | TÁHATA de HATARAku.

21. BEIKOKU no | KOODAI na MUG̃IBÁTAKE o | MÍte || odoróita.

22. NIHON no KÓKKA o | KIita kotó g̃a | arimásu ka.

23. ano KÁSYU no | UTAu UTÁ wa | HUNÁUTA g̃a | ÓOi.

24. SUIEI wa dekimasén.

25. GUAI g̃a WÁRUkatta no ni || yóku RIKIEI site || ITÍ-I ni | nátta.

26. HUKÁi | TOKORÓ de | OYÓg̃u no wa | kowái.

27. SÍNKAI ni | SÚmu | sakana.

28. isog̃asíi no de || SÍN'YA made HATARAku.

29. ano TIHÓO no | SÍNZAN ni wa || dónna DOOBUTU g̃a | imásu ka.

30. KAWA no HUKÁsa o | HAKÁru.

31. ÁKAtyan o senaka ni Otta | okáasan g̃a | KAIMONO o site iru.

32. bóku no | MAke désu.

33. zéro yori | TIIsái | ZISSÚU o | HUSÚU to iu.

34. KOOEN de ASObu.

35. UTUKUsíi | HANAZÓNO.

36. TOOKYOO ní wa || YUUMEI na DOOBÚTUEN mo | SYOKUBÚTUEN mo | arimásu.

37. SÍZI ni SITAḠAtte || KOODOO suru.

38. SENSÉI ḡa | TEHÓN o SIMEsita.

39. yóku | ZYÚNBI site kara || SIḠOTO o HAZImeru.

40. KÁḠU o | SONÁeta apáato ḡa | hosíi.

41. SONAé ḡa | NÁkereba || HUAN da.

42. OOSETUMA de || KYAKU ni ÓOTAI suru.

43. IḠAI na HANNOO o SIMEsita.

44. HITUYOO ni ÓOzite || HÓN o KAu.

45. GAKURI dake obóete mo || OOYOO ḡa dekínakereba || NAN ni mo narimasén.

46. SIḠYOO wa || GÓZEN | KÚ-ZI desu.

47. SYÚUSI KAwaranai YUUZYOO o MOtiTUZUketa.

48. sáa || BENKYOO HAZImemasyóo.

49. huttobooru-síizun ḡa HAZImatta.

50. KYUUYOO ḡa dékita no de || DADEN sita.

51. kyóo no | géemu de wa || ANDA ḡa | NÁN-BON | arimásita ka.

52. SITÚREI na koto o | Ittá no de || HIRATE de Útte yatta.

53. SISSAKU ḡa ÓOi no de || KUBI o KÍtta.

54. TAIBEI-GAIKOO-SÉISAKU o | tatéru.

55. DAIZÍKEN ḡa | okótta no de || súḡu ni | TAISAKU o KANḠÁenakereba | naránai.

56. kono KÉN ni | túite wa || kore ÍZYOO wa | MOOsemasén.

57. KÁKARI no | MONÓ ḡa | go-YOOKEN o UKETAMAWArimásu.

58. WATAKUSI wa | kono MONDAI tó wa | ZENZEN KANKEI arimasén.

59. RYOKYAKU-ḠÁKARI ḡa | RYOKYAKU no ÓOTAI o suru.

60. SÁIḠO no | DÁN o kudasu.

61. DOKUDAN de sita kotó desu kara || sekinin wa | ZÉNBU | ZIBUN de motimásu.

62. KANKEI o TÁtu.

63. tabako o TÁtta.

64. KAKUSIN o mótte | DANḠÉN simasu.

65. sonna kotó wa | dekimasén kara || sumimasén ḡa | oKOTOWAri simásu.

66. tanónda koto o | KOTOWAráreta.

67. KOTOWAri nási ni || BIHIN o | MOtiDÁsu yoo na OKOnai wa || DÁNzite | YURUsimasén.

68. SATUZIN-ZÍKEN ḡa | átta.

69. SEINEN no ZISATU ḡa | kánari | ÓOi.

70. HITOḠÓROsi ya | HOOKA no ÓOi | HUAN na SYÁKAI.

71. KAIZYOO wa SAKKIdátta.

72. INÚ o | NOBÁNAsi ni | site óite wa | ikenai.

73. TORI o | SÓRA ni | HANÁsu.

74. tumaránai koto o | HOOḠEN sité wa | ikenai.   yóku | KANḠÁete kara || HANÁsu yoo ni.

75. BÚNSYOO o | KÁku.

76. DÁI | ÍS-SYOO kara || YÓnde kudasai.

77. GINKOO ni YOKIN surú no ni wa || INSYOO ḡa HITUYOO da.

78. SYUUNYUU ḡa SUKUnái no de || NAISYOKU o site iru.

79. kono HÓN no | DÁI wa | omosirói ḡa || NAIYOO wa tumaránai.

80. MIUTI no MONÓ wa || ONAzi SYOKUBA de HATARAkanai hóo ḡa | íi.

81. NÁIḠAI no ZIZYOO o | yóku | KANḠÁete kara | KImeru.

82. YÓOSEKI wa KYUU-RIPPOO-méetoru | de áru.

83. ano BIYÓOIN de | paamanénto o | káketa.

84. OMONI o Otte || SAKÁMITI o | NOBOrú no wa || YOOI zya arimasén.

85. KOKKAI wa | RIPPOO no KIKÁN de aru.

86. HOO wa | mamoránakereba | naránai.

87. NIHONḠO no BUNPOO o | BENKYOO suru.

88. kore ÍḠAI ni | SIKATA ḡa NÁi.

89. TOODAI-HOOḠÁKUBU no | GAKUSEI désu.

90. kono HUKUSEI wa | taihen yóku | dékite ite || HONMONO no yóo da.

91. kono TEḠAMI o | HUKUSYA site kudasái.

92. HUKUZATU na MONDAI.

93. kono SIḠOTO wa | HUKUZATU désu kara || HITÓ-KUTI ni | SETUMEI suru kotó wa | dekimasén.

DÁI | ZYUU KYÚU-KA

1. amerika no DAITÓORYOO wa || howaito-háusu ni | SÚmi || GASSYÚUKOKU o | SUbéru | TÍI ni aru.

2. TOOKEI o tóru to || ONNA no hóo ḡa | NAḠAÍki da | sóo desu.

3. kanazúkai o | TOOITI suru kotó wa | nakanaka muzukasíi.

4. DENTOO o MUSI sita KOODOO.

5. NIHÓN wa | NI SEN-NEN no DENTOO o YUUsúru | KUNI de áru.

6. SYÚU o | HIKIíru DAISEIZIKA.

7. TAISYUU o baka ni sité wa | ikenai.

8. KOOEN no NÁKA no | KOOSYUU-DÉNWA kara | DENWA site imásu.

9. yóku NIte iru | ÓYAKO desu ne.

10. RUIZI no MONÓ no | NÁKA ni wa || SITU no WARÚi MONO mo | áru kara | KI o tukéte kudasai.

11. GÓGATU | ITUKA ní wa | MUSYA-NÍNGYOO o kazaru.

12. BÚRYOKU o | HITUYOO to sinai | HEIWA na SÉKAI o NOZOnde iru.

13. BUSÍDOO to wa || BÚSI ga | mamoru béki MITI to iu | ÍMI de aru.

14. piano || orugan || baiorin nádo wa || GAKKI to iimásu.

15. uti dé wa || YOOSYÓKKI mo | WASYÓKKI mo | dotira mo TUKAimásu.

16. MIZU wa || UTUWA ni SITAGAu.

17. ISYA ga TUKAu KIKÁI no SEISAKU o | site iru.

18. ano KÁSYU wa || KÓSEI ga | áru.

19. ÍK-KO | GOZYÚU-EN no ringo.

20. KÓZIN no SEIKATU o | TAISETU ni suru.

21. HAYASI-san to | syoogi o sitá ga || SYÓOBU ga | tukánakatta.

22. SYÓORI no SIRUSI no | KINmédaru.

23. MEISYOO o otozuréru.

24. dótti no | tíimu ga | KÁtu ka.

25. KATTE na HITÓ desu ne.

26. KATTÉGUTI kara | háiru.

27. kono SYOOSETU no KOOSEI wa || RUIKEI-TEKI de || ATARÁsisa ga | NÁi.

28. are wa || BÚSI no | TENKEI dátta.

29. KATÁ ni hamete | tukútta | garasuZÁIKU desu.

30. OOGATA no ZIDÓOSYA.

31. NÁNI o KIZYUN ni site || GAKUSEI o erabimásu ka.

32. KOOTUU-HÓOKI o | SIranákereba || ZIDÓOSYA o | UNTEN suru kotó wa | dekimasén.

33. KISÓKU wa || KANARAzu mamótte kudasai.

34. MIZU wa || SIZEN no HOOSOKU ni SITAGÁtte || TAKÁi TOKORO kara || hikúi TOKORO e MUKAtte | NAGAréru.

35. GAIKOKÚZIN ni | NIHONGO o OSIeru HOOHOO to sité wa || GENSOKU to site || NIHONGO dake TUKAu.

36. mukasi wa || SÍ-NOO-KOO-SYOO no BETU ḡa | átte || BÚSI no | MÍBUN
    ḡa | ITIBAN TÁKAkatta.

37. NIHON-GÚN no | SÍKI wa | sakan dátta.

38. DAIḠÍSI wa || KOKKAI de HATARAku.

39. kono SYASIN wa || ZÚIBUN | SYUUSEI site áru.

40. ZIDÓOSYA no | SYUURI-KÓOZYOO.

41. SENSÉI ni | INSOTU sarete || SYUUḠAKU-RYÓKOO o sita.

42. SÍNPU ni | náru tame no SYUḠYOO wa || kibisíi soo desu.

43. YO-NÉNKAN no | GAKUḠYOO o | OSÁmete || DAIḠAKU o SOTUḠYOO sita.

44. SYÓOBU ḡa Owatte || TEKI mo | MIKATA mo | TÉ o | TOriÁtta.

45. anó HITO wa || MORI-san ni TÁIsite || TÉKII o | MÓtte iru | yóo desu.

46. NAḠÁi AIDA || ÁME ḡa | huránai kara || SANRIN no BOOKA ni | TYÚUI
    site kudasai.

47. BOOKÁNḠU o | YÓOI site || sukii-RYÓKOO ni DEkakeru.

48. GAITEKI o HUSÉḡu.

49. TOOYOO-BÍZYUTU o | KENKYUU site iru.

50. GAKUZYUTU-KÁIḠI ni | DÉru.

51. BYOOIN de || SYÚZITU o | Úketa.

52. góruhu no RENSYUU o | si ni Iku.

53. OTOKO no GAKUSEI wa || DAIḠAKU de || KYÓOREN o | Ukesaseráreta |
    monó desu.

54. GUN'YOOKEN o KÚNREN suru.

55. TÓNAI o | NÉtte aruku | GAKUSEI no démo ḡa | átta.

56. TEKIKOKU no KOKUḠO o NARÁu.

57. pen-SYÚUZI o suru.

58. HATUON no RENSYUU o suru.

59. GAKUSYUU ni HITUYOO na HÓN nara || KAtte aḡemásu.

60. piano to IkéBANA o | NARÁtte iru.

61. DOOBUTU no SYUUSEI.

62. NARAwasi ni sitaḡáu.

63. RYOORÍNIN no MINARAi o site iru.

64. ZYUNKIN no SAIKU.

65. ZYUNPAKU no séetaa.

66. ZYUN-NIHON-HUU no SEIKATU o suru.

67. KOdomo wa | ZYUNSIN désu.

68. GUNZIN wa || GUNTOO o | TAISETU ni suru.

69. BOKUTOO de || Utáreta.

70. KOḠATÁNA de | enpitu o kezuru.

71. KATANÁ o | NÍ-HON | sásita | BÚSI.

72. amerika de || TAKE o MÍta koto wa | arimasén ḡa || yooróppa ni mo | arimasén ka.

73. TANAKA-KUN wa || TÍKUBA no | TÓMO da.

74. TAKE-ZÁIKU no kaḡo o KAtta.

75. anó HITO wa || DAI-NI-ZI-TÁISEN no | YÚUSI de || taihen ISAmásiku | TATAKAttá no da | sóo desu.

76. KANARAzu KÁtte | KÁEru to || ISAmitátte | DÉte Itta.

77. sonna kotó o suru | YÚUKI wa | arimasén.

78. BUZI ni TUkimásita kara || ANSIN site kudasái.

79. MAḠÓKORO o | kómeta okurimono.

80. SÍNZIN no | atúi | ONNÁ da.

81. anó HITO wa || KUTI to | KOKORÓ ḡa | tiḡaú kara || SIN'YOO dekimasén.

82. ÓNḠAKU ni | KANSIN o MÓtte imasu.

83. yóku | HATARAku HITÓ desu ne.   KANSIN simásita.

84. KEIBA ni kótte || MOTÓ mo | KO mo | nakusita.

85. KYÓOḠI ni | KÁtta.

86. "sumoo" wa || NIHON no KÓKUḠI de aru.

87. KÍN || SAN-EN || oAZUkari itasimásita.

88. NIHONḠO no SANKOOSYO o YÓmu.

89. go-SANKOO máde ni || o-HANAsi simásu.

90. orinpikku-TÁIKAI ni | SANKA suru.

91. GANZITU ní wa || KÁKKOKU | TÁISI mo | SANDAI suru.

92. SINZANMONO de ḡozaimásu kara || dóozo yorosiku.

93. oTERAMÁIri ni Iku.

DÁI | NÍZYUK-KA

1. TYÚUḠAKU no | KYÓOSI desu.

2. WATAKUSI no SYOKÚḠYOO wa || ÍSI desu.

3. DENKI-ḠÁISYA no | GÍSI o site imasu.

4. kono KATÁ wa || DAIḠAKU-KYÓOZYU desu.

5. NIHONḠO no KYOOZYUHOO ní wa || iroiro arimásu.

6. DOYÓO ni wa || ZYÚḠYOO wa | arimasén.

7. MEIZÍN ḡa | ITIBAN TAISETU na himitu o | DÉNZYU suru.

8. KÁMI-sama kara | SAZUkátta mono.

9. GAKUI o SAZUkeraréru.

10. GÍN no naihu.

11. GINKOO ni | YOKIN ḡa áru.

12. SÓRA ni | UTUKUsíi | GÍNḠA ḡa | MIéru.

13. SUIḠIN o RIYOO sita ONDOKEI ḡa áru.

14. KINBEN na GINKÓOIN desu.

15. DÉNSYA de | TUUKIN site imásu.

16. KUYÁKUSYO ni | TUTÓmete imasu.

17. ÁSA || SITÍ-ZI no | básu de | TUTOmé ni | DÉru.

18. SYOKÚIN no | tamé no | kafetériya ḡa | arimaśu.

19. ZIMÚIN wa || ZIMÚSYO de HATARAku.

20. TITÍ wa || GINKÓOIN desita.

21. YÓRU || ZYÚU-ZI made EIḠYOO site iru | SYÓOTEN ḡa | ÓOi.

22. SAKABA no KEIEI wa || muzukasíi soo desu.

23. KUMIAI no UN'EI ḡa umái.

24. TÍIsa na | HÓN'YA o | ITONÁnde orimasu.

25. kono MATI no TYÓOTYOO no NAmae o | SItte imásu ka.

26. SITAMATI e KAIMONO ni Iku.

27. maruséeyu wa || huransu no | ÓOki na | MINATÓMATI desu.

28. ano MISÉ no | TEN'IN wa || ONNA bákari desu.

29. GAKKOO no BAITEN de || nóoto ya | HÓN o KAimasu.

30. MITI ni | YOMISE ḡa narande iru.

31. INSYÓKUTEN de | HATARAite imásu.

32. NIKÚ ḡa | TAbetái kara || NIKÚYA e | DENWA o kákete || GYUUNIKU o
    TYUUMON simasyóo.

33. rázio ya | rekóodo de || anó HITO no | UTÁ o | KIita kotó ḡa | arimásu
    ḡa || NIKUSEI o KIitá no wa || hazímete desu.

34. NIKÚRUI wa || SEITYOO ni HITUYOO désu.

35. SUMIBI de YAita NIKÚ wa | oisíi desu yo.

36. SEKITÁN no | HÓO ḡa | MOKUTÁN yori | KARYOKU ḡa TUYÓi.

37. NIHÓN ni wa | TANDEN ḡa takusan áru.

38. HUKÚ o KIru.

39. YOOHUKU no HITÓ mo | WAHUKU no HITÓ mo | imasu.

40. ZYUU-NÉNKAN | siberiya de | HUKUEKI sita.

41. OYÁ ni HUKUZYUU suru.

42. bitámin o | HUKUYOO site imásu.

43. ZAIRYÓO o | ZYÚNBI suru.

44. IÉ o | TAtéru tame ni | ZAIMOKU o KAu.

45. SEIZAIZYO de | ZAIMOKU o TUKÚru.

46. íi KYOOZAI ḡa | mitukarimasén.

47. SÉKAI | IS-SYUU-RYÓKOO ḡa | sitai.

48. kore wa | BANNIN-SYÚUTI no | ZÍZITU da.

49. kono MIZUÚMI no | SYÚUI wa | ZYÚK-kiro arimasu.

50. ENSYÚURITU wa || SÁN ten || ITI || YÓN || ITI || GO | KYÓO de aru.

51. DAI-NI-ZI-TÁISEN no | TOKÍ wa || KÁIḠUN de | GÚN'I o | site imásita.

52. HÉIRYOKU wa || RIKU || KÁI || KUUḠUN | awásete || HYAKU-MÁN desu.

53. ZYUUḠUN-KÍSYA to site || MINAMI-TAIHÉIYOO e Itta.

54. GUNPUKU o KIrú to || rippa ni MIemásu ne.

55. NIHÓN ni wa || ÍT-TO || NÍ-HU ari || KYOOTÓ-HU ḡa | sono hitó-tu de aru.

56. TOOKYOO wa || NIHON no SYÚHU desu.

57. EIKOKU-SÉIHU no | GAIKOO-SÉISAKU ni | túite || HANAsiÁtta.

58. BEIKOKU no KOKUMU-TYÓOKAN ḡa | NIHÓN e Iku.

59. TAISÍKAN ni wa || BUNKAN daké de | náku || BUKAN mo TUTÓmete iru.

60. zyúuDOO wa || ÍS-SYU no | GOSÍNZYUTU desu.

61. KANEMÓti ḡa | GEIZYUTUKA o HÓḠO suru.

62. BENḠÓSI wa || HOORITU o BENKYOO sinákereba | naránai.

63. KOKUMIN o HÓḠO suru | tamé ni || HOORITU ḡa áru.

64. KIRITU TADAsíi SEIKATU o suru.

65. KÁKU-GINKOO no|RÍSI o | ZÉNKOKU | ITIRITU ni suru kotó wa | dekimasén ka.

66. dare de mo SItte iru HUBÚNRITU desu.

67. ZANKÍN wa | SANZEN-EN désu.

68. UreNOKOri no SINAMONO no | TOKUBAI désu.

69. NOKÓtta | NIKÚ wa || INÚ ni | yarimasyóo.

70. TAbeNOKOsita NIKÚ wa || INÚ ni | yarimasyóo.

71. HÁ o miḡaku.

72. ano HÁISYA wa || GÍZYUTU ḡa | íi.

73. kono KIKÁI no | HAGÚRUMA o | ITI-BÚBUN | SYÚURI suru | HITUYOO ḡa arimásu.

74. MUSIBA o nuite moraimásita.

75. TITÍ wa || IreBA o site imásu.

76. ZITÉNSYA no | NÁi | NÓOKA wa | arumái.

77. ZIDÓOSYA o UNTEN suru.

78. atikoti | TENTÉN to sita.

79. TOOKYOO e TENKIN ni narimásita.

80. WÁKA to | iú no wa || NIHON no DENTOO-TEKI na | SI no ÍS-SYU desu ḡa || WÁKA o | TUKÚru HITO wa || KÁZIN to itte | SIZIN tó wa | iimasén.

81. KANḠAKU o MANÁnda | NIHONZÍN wa || yóku | KANSI o TUKÚru.

82. SIZIN || GAKA || ONḠAKKA nádo wa || GEIZYUTUKA to iu.

83. ano GAKA wa || YOOḠA o yarimásu.

84. RAINEN no KEIKAKU o tatemásita.

85. iwáyuru GEIZYUTUKA wa || KAKUITU-TEKI na SEIKATU ḡa | dekínai.

86. TOTI o | KUKAKU site | Uru.

87. róoma wa || ATARAsíi KENTIKU ni ⏋ mazítte || KÓDAI no | KENTIKU no áto ḡa | NOKÓtte iru | omosirói | TÓSI desu.

88. ZIMÚSYO o SINTIKU sita.

89. DOKUḠAKU de || rippa na TÍI o | KIZÚita HITO desu.

90. NIHÓN wa || ÚMI ni KAKOmareta | KUNI dá kara || GYÓḠYOO ḡa | sakan désu.

91. TÍIsa na GYOSON kara HATTEN site || ÓOki na | MINATO ni nátta.

92. RYÓOSI ḡa | sakana o tóru.

93. TAIRYOO de | GYOSON ḡa niḡíyaka desu.

94. anó HITO wa || SINRUI zya arimasén. KANKEI no nái | TANIN désu.

95. yooróppa ni wa || róndon || pári || berurín || róoma || sonó TA no | DAITÓKAI ḡa | áru.

96. tóotoo | TAKAI saremásita.

97. kessite TAḠON sité wa | narimasén.

98. SYÚZIN wa || ZIDÓOSYA | SYUURI-KÓOZYOO ni | KÍNMU site imasu.

99. BEIKOKU wa || MINSYU-SYUḠI-KÓKKA de aru.

100. NÚSI no | nái | OtosiMÓNO.

101. uti no YÁNUSI wa || IÉ dake de | náku || HIRÓi | TOTI mo Áru | OOZÍNUSI desu.

DÁI | NÍZYUU | ÍK-KA

1. kotti no hóo ḡa | TIKÁMITI da kara || TOKU désu yo.

2. "ÍMA || TOKUTÉN wa | dóo natte | imásu ka."
   "NÍ | TAI | NÍ de || DOOTEN désu yo.　dotti mo TUYÓi kara || kono géemu no | SYÓOBU wa | SÁIḠO made | wakarimasén ne."

3. kono MONDAI no TOKUSITU ni túite || moo ITI-DO | yóku | KANGÁete | miyóo.

4. anó HITO wa || SUUḠAKU ḡa TOKÚI da.

5. o-TOKUI-san désu kara || o-YASUku simásu.

6. GAKUSEI no KOKORÓE ni | túite no | INSATÚBUTU desu.

7. ETEGÁTTE na | kotó o | Iu HITÓ desu ne.

8. KUSEN no NOTÍ ni | SYÓORI o | Éta.

9. OOSETUMA ni | UTUKUsíi | GAKU ḡa | kakátte iru.

10. dono ḡurai no KÍNḠAKU ḡa | HITUYOO désu ka.

11. SOOBA ḡa | GAKUMEN ÍKA ni | Ótita.

12. NETÚ ḡa | TÁKAkute || HITAI ḡa | HÍ no | yóo da.

13. TEITI ni IÉ o | TAtéru no wa | yóku | nái.

14. SYUSSÁNRITU ḡa TEIKA sita.

15. HIKÚi teeburu ḡa | yói.

16. MAITUKI | ITI-DO | SYUUKAI ḡa áru.

17. DENKI-RYÓOKIN no | SYUUKIN ni KImásita.

18. HITO o ATÚmete | HANASÍ o KIkaseru.

19. HITO ḡa ATUmátte | imásu ḡa || NÁNI ka | okótta n desyoo ka.

20. KÓNDO || ZENSYUU ḡa DÉru no da | sóo desu.

21. SYUUTYUU-TEKI ni | BENKYOO site imásu.

22. go-KÚROO-sama desita.

23. SIḠOTO ḡa TOROO ni OWAtta.

24. ROODÓOSYA wa || taitei | ROODOO-KÚMIAI ni | KAÑYUU-site iru.

25. KAḠAKU-HÍRYOO de || YASAI o tukúru.

26. MUḠIBÁTAKE ni | KINPI o yaru.

27. kono USI wa | yóku | KÓete iru.

28. SYAKUYA ni SÚnde | irú kara || MAITUKI || YÁTIN o | harátte iru.

29. KYÓOTO made no | KISYÁTIN wa || NITOO dé mo | SEN-EN ÍZYOO | suru desyóo.

30. kono NÍMOTU no | ÚNTIN wa || íkura desu ka.

31. yatto | RÓOTIN ḡa | Aḡarimásita.

32. SYAKKÍN o | sinai yóo ni.

33. pén o KArita.

34. HITO no MONÓ o | damátte SYAKUYOO sita.

35. ano MISÉ ni wa || KAri ḡa áru.

36. DOKUSIN de || MAḠAri o site imásu.

37. HINMIN o TASUkéru no ḡa | MOKUTEKI désu.

38. HINZYAKU na NAIYOO dá kara || MONDAI ni naránai.

39. MAZUsíi SEIKATU o site iru.

40. HÍNSOO na | narí o sita | OTOKÓ ḡa | yatté KIta.

41. KOKUREN-HÓNBU wa || nyuuyóoku ni áru.

42. RENZITU no ÁME de || MIZU ḡa MAsita.

43. toréeraa o RENKETU sita | ZIDÓOSYA.

44. KOdomo o TUrete | KOOEN e Iku.

45. kyóo mo | RENZYUU to | bíiru o | NÓmi ni Iku.

46. kono RYOKOO wa || íi TUre ḡa | áru kara || sabísiku | nái desyoo.

47. SANMYAKU ḡa TUranátte iru.

48. RENMEI de || SÉIHU ni | TEḠAMI o | KÁita.

49. RIPPOO || SIHOO || GYOOSEI wa || SEIZI no MOTÓI de aru.

50. KUUḠUN no | SAIKOO-SIRÉIKAN desu.

51. kono KÁI no | SIKÁISYA wa || MORÍKAWA-san desu.

52. SIRÉIKAN no MEIREI desu.

53. GOOREI o kakéru.

54. HOOREI ni yori || TAtiIri o tomerarete áru.

55. SÉIHU no KANKOKU ni yori || YUSYUTU o | ZISYU-KÍSEI sita.

56. KANḠYOO-GÍNKOO ni | TUTOméru.

57. TOMOdati ni SUSUmerarete | KAIMEI sita.

58. HOOREI o KAISEI suru.

59. kore o KIKÁI ni | KAISIN site || kore kará wa | móo | WARÚi koto wa | itasimasén.

60. ano hóteru wa || ZYÚN-YOOHUU ni | KAITIKU sita.

61. ARATÁmete | KAkinaosita HÓN desu.

62. ARATAmátta TEḠAMI o UkeTOtta.

63. KYOOIKU-SÉIDO o KAIKAKU suru.

64. TÓOZI | HITÓBITO wa || KAKUSIN no ÍKI ḡa | sakan désita.

65. SANḠYOO-KÁKUMEI wa || SYÁKAI o KAeta.

66. ano GINKOO to │ TAISYAKU-KÁNKEI wa │ arimasén.

67. HÓN o │ KAsite kudasái.

68. KAsíTIN wa ‖ íkura desu ka.

69. KASIYA ḡa SUKUnái.

70. KAsi mo │ KAri mo │ arimasén.

71. KEISOTU ni KOODOO sézu ni ‖ yóku │ KANḠÁete kara ‖ site kudasái.

72. KEISYOO de gozaimásu ḡa ‖ o-REI no SIRUSI de gozaimásu.

73. KARUi kaban.

74. KARÚKUTI ḡa │ úmakute ‖ yóku │ HITO o warawaseru OTOKÓ da.

75. KIḠARU ni │ ASObi ni irassyái.

76. SANZEN-EN no GENSYUU désu.

77. SYOKUYOKU ḡa HEtte ‖ komátte iru.

78. SYUUNYUU no GENSYOO ni yori ‖ SEIKATU o ARATAméru │ HITUYOO ḡa áru.

79. o-KAḠEN wa ‖ ikáḡa desu ka.

80. ii-KAḠEN de ‖ yamete kudasái.

81. ÍḠAKU no HATTATU de ‖ BYOOKI ḡa HEtta.

82. KEIZAI-TEKI na MONDAI ḡa áru no de ‖ ROODÓOSYA o │ HErasimásita.

83. tóreta │ KOMÉ ya │ MÚḠI o │ NÁYA ni Ireru.

84. ano OTOKÓ o │ NATTOKU saserú no wa │ muzukasíi.

85. GINKOO de │ GENKÍN no │ SUITOOGÁKARI o site imasu.

86. RYÓOKIN o │ OSAméru.

87. YOWAKI ḡa sásite │ yamemásita.

88. ano kóro wa ‖ ZYAKUNIKU KYOOSYOKU no ZIDAI dátta.

89. NÁN da ka │ YOWAYOWAsíi │ OTOKÓ da.

90. ZENNIN dá ḡa │ ÍSI no │ YOWÁi no ḡa ‖ ano OTOKÓ no │ ZYAKUTÉN da.

91. hidói BYOOKI de ‖ HI-ḡoto ni │ karada ḡa YOWÁtte iku.

92. TYÚUḠOKU no │ áru GAKUSYA wa ‖ NINḠEN no HÓNSEI wa ‖ ZÉN da to itta.

93. NOOSON no SEIKATU o │ KAIZEN suru.

94. anó HITO no │ KANGÁe wa ‖ DOKUZEN-TEKI de ‖ SÍYA ḡa │ semái.

95. HINMÍN o │ KYUUSAI suru tamé ni ‖ SÍZAI o │ ZÉNBU TUKAtte simatta.

96. keḡaNIN o KYÚUZYO suru │ tamé ni ‖ KYUUKYÚUSYA ḡa │ tonde Ítta.

97. MÉII ni │ ITIMEI o SUKUwaremásita.

98. KÁMI ni │ SUKUi o motoméru.

99. SEIBUTÚGAKU no KYOOZYU no | ZYOSYU o site imásu.

100. KENKYUU no tamé ni | ZYOGEN o site morau.

101. TASUkéte kudasai.

102. go-ZYÓRYOKU|itadakimásite || arígatoo gozaimasu.

103. okage de | ÍNOTI ga | TASUkarimásita.

104. TOMOdati no TASUké o KAriru.

105. NOmíSUKE wa | DÁIkirai desu.

106. NIHONGO no | KIHON-TEKI na BUNPOO ni túite | KAISETU sita HÓN
      desu.

107. ROODOOHOO de || KIZYUN-TÍNGIN ga | KImátte imasu.

108. KÓOGYOO wa || kono TÓSI no | HATTEN no MOTOÍ desu.

109. GOKAI ni MOTOzúite || okótta | HÚWA desu.

110. KINBEN wa || SEIKOO no MOTÓI desu.

111. SYÓONIN to site || SEIKOO simásita.

112. EIKOKU no | bénsamu ya | míru wa || KOORI-SYUGÍSYA to site ||
      YUUMEI désu.

113. KÁKO no koto | bákari | KANGÁete'ité wa || SÍNPO|simasén yo.

114. KYUUKOO désu kara || TIIsái | éki wa | TUUKA simasu.

115. KASITU o YURÚsu.

116. KÁZITU no | SITÚREI || oYURUsi kudasái.

117. móo | YO-ZI SUgí desu yo.

118. KABUN no o-REI o itadaite || itami irimásu.

119. TANÓsiku | YASUmí o | SUgosimásita.

DÁI | NÍZYUU | NÍ-KA

1. MÁIASA | SITI-ZI-HÁN ni Okimasu.

2. TOKIDOKI | ZYOTYUU ni Okósite moraimasu.

3. ZYUUDAI na MONDAI ga Okótta.

4. OMOi MONÓ o | KIZYÚUKI de | HIkiAgéru.

5. KÓKKA o | UTAu TOKÍ ni wa || KIRITU simásu.

6. SIKYUU sinákereba | naránai | YOOZI ga áru.

7. kono mamá de wa || TATAKAi ni ITÁru | osoré ga | áru.

8. TOOKYOO kara || ODAWARA e ITÁru MITI.

9. KOKKAI no KAISAN wa || HISSI da.

10. ONAzi KYÓKU desu ga || KÁSI ga | tigaimásu.

11. NIHONḠO no MEISI to | EIḠO no MEISI wa || SEISITU ḡa tiḡaimásu.

12. dónata no | SAKKYOKU désu ka.

13. KÓN'YA no | ONḠÁKKAI no KYOKUMOKU wa || NÁN desu ka.

14. KOOSÍNKYOKU ni | Awásete || KOOSIN suru.

15. kosi no MAḠatta tosiyóri.

16. TAKE o MAḠete ánda | basukétto desu.

17. ano kádo o | MIḠI e MAḠatte kudasái.

18. MANNÉNHITU de | KÁite mo || HUDE de KÁite mo || kamaimasén.

19. SENSÉI no|o-HANASI o | HIKKI suru.

20. HIKOOBIN de dásu.

21. HIKOOZYOO ní wa || OOḠATA no HIKÓOKI mo | KOḠATA nó mo | takusan áru.

22. SÓRA o TObu TORI.

23. DENSINBÁSIRA ni | kaminári ḡa | Ótite || HIBÁSIRA ḡa | TÁtta.

24. DENTYUU o | TIKÁ ni | utúsu.

25. kono IE no HASIRÁ wa || HUTÓkute | rippa désu.

26. HASIRA-DÓKEI ḡa | ZYÚU-ZI o | Útta.

27. ÁME ḡa | húttara || píkunikku wa | TYUUSI simásu.

28. tukáreta kara || KOOSIN o | KYUUSI simasyóo.

29. TOKEI ḡa TOmatte iru.

30. kono MITI wa || KOOZITYUU désu kara || TUUKOODOme désu.

31. kono DAIḠAKU wa || TÉIDO ḡa | TAKÁi.

32. KANSAI-RYÓKOO no | NITTEI o TUKÚru.

33. SIPPAI ni ITÁtta | KATEI ni túite || KENKYUU suru.

34. KÚUKI ḡa | NÁkereba || NINḠEN wa | SEIZON dekimasén.

35. YUUMEI na HITO no TEḠAMI o | TAISETU ni HOZON suru.

36. KÁMI no SONZAI o | SINzimásu ka.

37. sonna kotó wa | ZONzimasén.

38. GANMEN no SYÚZYUTU o | Úketa.

39. dónna | GÁNRYOO o TUKAtte || someta monó desu ka.

40. KAO o arau.

41. KAOIRO ḡa WARÚi | yóo desu ḡa || dóo ka | simásita ka.

42. KONZIKI ni kaḡayáku | RAKUZITU o MÍta.

43. TENNÉNSYOKU no SYASIN.

44. TEKITOO na ZYOSYU o | BUSSYOKU site imásu.

45. SAN-GÉNSYOKU wa ‖ ÁKA to │ kiiro to │ ÁO desu.

46. WATAKUSI wa ‖ ano KATÁ no │ KANGÁe ni │ KYOOMEI site imásu.

47. TORI ga NAku.

48. USI no NAkigóe ga KIkoeru.

49. SYUUGYOO no béru ga NAtta.

50. ano GINKOO no RÍSI wa │ YASÚi.

51. SIGOTO o yamete ‖ KYUUSOKU suru.

52. anó HITO kara wa ‖ tittó mo │ SYOOSOKU ga arimasén.

53. HANA de │ ÍKI o suru.

54. komátte ‖ tameÍKI o │ túku.

55. NÍ-TYOO │ SAKI ni áru GINKOO e Iku.

56. kono HÓN ni wa ‖ RAKUTYOO ga áru kara ‖ TOrikaete kudasái.

57. BATEI ga │ UMA no SEWÁ o suru.

58. NIWA no TEIré o suru ENTEI o │ yatótte aru.

59. marason no SÓOSYA ga │ HASÍtte iru.

60. KOMUGÍKO no │ SEIHUN-KÓOZYOO o │ KEIEI suru.

61. SÚIYAKU (MIZUGÚSURI) wa ‖ SYOKUZEN de ‖ KONAGÚSURI wa ‖
     SYOKUGO ni NÓnde kudasai.

62. GYUUNIKU wa ‖ SYOOKA ga WARÚi │ monó desu ka.

63. yakusoku o KAISYOO suru.

64. SYOOBÓOSYA wa ‖ taitei │ AKAku nutte áru.

65. YUKÍ ga KIeru.

66. KEsigomu de ‖ GOZI o KEsite kudasái.

67. yakusoku o TOriKÉsita.

68. SÁNGATU TOOKA no │ KESIIN ga áru TEGAMI.

69. KÓGAI de ‖ UNDOO suru.

70. kono MATI no KOSÚU wa ‖ NI SEN TÁrazu desu.

71. TO o akeru.

72. AMÁDO o │ siméru.

73. TÉNKI ga │ íi kara ‖ KOOEN e SANPO ni Iku.

74. ÁKI ni │ náru to ‖ KÍ no ha ga TIru.

75. ano GAKUSEI wa ‖ ATAMÁ ga │ íi.

76. ZU no TAKÁi │ HITÓ desu ne.

77. KOOSIN no SENTOO ni TÁtte │ irú no wa ‖ dáre desyoo.

78. KOOTOO no sikén o │ Úketa.

79. KUYÁKUSYO ni | SYUTTOO sinákereba | naránai.

80. MEKATA o KURAberu.

81. <u>arasuka</u> no SÁMUsa wa || <u>kánada</u> no | HÍ de wa | nái.

82. SITI SAN no HIRITU de || WAkéru.

83. SUIḠIN no HIZYUU wa || ZYUUSÁN ten || GÓ | GÓ de aru.

DÁI | NÍZYUU | SÁN-KA

1. HÁRU to | NATÚ ni wa || KANKÓOKYAKU ḡa | ÓOi.

2. KANKYAKU no| SUKUnái sibai.

3. sikén ni RAKUDAI site || HIKAN site iru.

4. amari ní mo | RAKKAN-TEKI na KANḠAeKATÁ de aru.

5. KOKUSAI-KÁNKEI ḡa HUKUZATU da.

6. ZISSAI no BAAI ni YAKÚ ni TAtu BENKYOO o suru.

7. TAIRIKU-OODAN-HÍKOO o sita.

8. TANIN no ZÁISAN o | OORYOO sita.

9. YOKO o MUita mama || HITO-KOTO mo HANAsánakatta.

10. YOKOḠAO ḡa UTUKUsíi.

11. ZYUU ROKU-SÉIKI no | NIHON-BÚNḠAKU o | KENKYUU site iru.

12. HUUKI no WARÚi | MINATÓMATI.

13. <u>yooroppa</u>-RYÓKOO no | KIKÓOBUN desu.

14. OORAI de ASOndé wa | ikemasén.

15. ZIDÓOSYA no OORAI ḡa | haḡesíi.

16. EIḠO no SETUMEI o KIita.

17. DENWA o HATUMEI sitá no wa || dáre desu ka.

18. MYOONEN wa || TAIRIKU-RYÓKOO o | sitái.

19. DÓKUSYO site iru AIDA ni || YÓ ḡa Aketa.

20. IMA no hóo ḡa | AKArúi kara || MI-yasúi desyoo.

21. AKÍraka na | AYAMÁri desu.

22. OTÓ yori | HAYÁi | <u>zyettóKI</u> ni | notte mitái desu.

23. SÓKUDO wa || ITI-ZÍKAN | ROKUZYUU-<u>máiru</u> desu.

24. SOKUTATU da to || NAN-ZIKAN ḡúrai de | TUkimásu ka.

25. kono HÚNE wa || HURÚi kara || amari SOKÚRYOKU wa | arimasén.

26. ATARAsíi | <u>hóteru</u> o | KENSETU-TYUU désu.

27. kono IÉ wa || ZIBUN de SEKKEI simásita.

28. GAIKOKÚZIN no | tamé no | GAKKOO o MOOkéru.

29. KENKYUU no KEKKÀ o | SÉIRI suru.

30. HIKÓOKI o | SÉIBI suru.

31. teeburu o TOTONÓeru.

32. SEKIYU wa || ABURA no ÍSSYU desu.

33. ABURÁGAMI ni | nureta MONÓ o | tutúmu.

34. YUDAN surú to || matigaéru.

35. KÓN'YA | KÚ-ZI ni | SYUSYOO no HOOSOO ga áru.

36. KOdomo ni SOOKIN suru.

37. SÓORYOO wa | BETU désu.

38. HUNABIN de || GAIKOKU ni Iru YUUZIN ni | HÓN o OKUru.

39. amerika e Iku TOMOdati o | MIOKUri ni Iku.

40. hóteru yori | RYOKAN no hóo ga | íi.

41. wasínton no | NIHON-TAISÍKAN ni | TUTOméru.

42. go-KÁZOKU wa || NÁN-NIN desu ka.

43. SÍNZOKU no | SUKUnái HITO.

44. anguro-sakuson-MÍNZOKU.

45. SÍNSETU na KUTYOO de || HANÁsite kureta.

46. IRO no TYOOWA ga UTUKUsíi.

47. bótan de || heya no ÓNDO o | TYOOSETU suru.

48. DÉNPA no HATYOO o | SIRAbéru.

49. ayasii OTOKÓ o | SIRAbéru.

50. ZÉI o | OSAméru | kotó o | NOOZEI to iu.

51. SYOTOKÚ-ZEI o HIita SYUUNYUU.

52. ZEIKAN de || RYOKAKU no NÍMOTU o | SIRAbéru.

53. YUNYUUHIN ni | KANZEI o kakéru.

54. SÓOKO no | NÁKA ni | NÍMOTU o Ireru.

55. SENSOO ni | NÍMOTU o oku.

56. KURÁ ga | takusan áru | KANEMÓti no IE.

57. KOMEGURA ni | ippai | KOMÉ ga | áru.

58. KURUMA o | SYÁKO ni simau.

59. TAISETU na SYORUI ya KANE wa || KÍNKO ni Irete oku.

60. apáato no KANRININ wa || dónata.

61. gásu no gomuKAN ga | HÚRUku | nátta.

62. gómu no | KÚDA yori | purasutíkku no | KÚDA no hoo ga | NAGAMÓti suru.

63. ZÁISAN o | KÁNRI suru.

64. NITI-BÉI-KAN de || ZYOOYAKU o MUSUnda.

65. ZYOOKEN no WARÚi ZYOOYAKU o MUSUnda SYUSYOO ni | TÁIsite || KOKUMIN g̅a | SÁIGO made | HANTAI sita.

66. ZYOOYAKU no ZYOOBUN o | yóku | YÓmu.

67. kono SEIHIN wa || HURYOOHIN désu kara || Utté wa | ikenái.

68. HURYOO-GÁKUSEI no | ÓOi | GAKKOO da sóo desu.

69. RYÓOSIN g̅a | áttara || sonna kotó wa | dekínai hazu desu.

70. ZYOOKEN g̅a YÓkereba || SYUUSYOKU simasu.

71. MITI o KAIRYOO site || ZIDOOSYA-YOO no | HIRÓi KOKUDOO o | tukúru | HITUYOO g̅a áru.

72. hikidasi no SOKO ni || NÁNI ka | áru.

73. anó HITO wa || SOKOZIKARA g̅a áru kara || KÁtu ka mo | sirenái.

74. HUNAZOKO wa || KÚUKI no RYUUTUU g̅a | WÁRUkute || ATÚi.

75. KAITEI-RYÓKOO g̅a | dékitara || omosirói daroo.

76. SENG̅AKU de gozaimásu kara || dóo ka | oOSIE kudasái.

77. MIZUÚMI no SINSEN o | HAKÁru.

78. ASAi TOKORÓ de | OYÓg̅u.

79. kono hen wa || TOOASA dá kara || KOdomo dé mo | OYOg̅éru.

80. SENZEN || ZISAKÚNOO to | KOSAKÚNOO to de wa || SYUUNYUU ni | hidói | SA g̅a átta.

81. TOOKYOO to róndon no AIDA no | ZÍSA wa || KU-ZIKAN g̅úrai desyoo.

82. kamí ni | HANÁ o SAsu.

83. KAIHI wa | HUYOO désu.

84. kono KENKYUU ní wa || NAGÁi ZIKAN o | TUIYÁsita.

85. kono DAIG̅AKU ni | háiru to || ITI-NÉNKAN ni | dono g̅urai | HÍYOO g̅a | kakáru desyoo ka.

86. RYOHI g̅a NÁi kara || YUkitákute (Ikitákute) mo || YUku (Iku) kotó wa | dekimasén.

*

1. ÚMI ni | hairázu ni || HAMÁ de ASObu.

2. KAIHIN no hóteru de | YASÚmu.

3. TOOKYOO to YOKOHAMÁ-KAN no | KOOZYOO-TÍTAI o | KEIHIN-KOOG̅YOO-TÍTAI to iu.

DÁI | NÍZYUU | YÓN-KA

1. SYUKUZITU ní wa ‖ o-IWAi o site ‖ HATARAkanai kotó ni | nátte imasu.

2. SOTUG̃YOO no HÍ ni | KOOTYOO-SENSÉI kara | SYUKUZI o itadakimásita.

3. ÍKKA | sorótte | SÍNNEN o | IWÁu.

4. ZÍNZYA no SAIREI no | HÍ ni wa ‖ iroiro na GYÓOZI g̃a | áru.

5. SAIZITU to NITIYÓOBI g̃a | TUZUkú kara ‖ dóko ka e | RYOKOO ni Ikimasyóo.

6. kono ZÍNZYA ni wa ‖ dónata o | MATUtte arimásu ka.

7. o-MATUri wa | KOdomo no | ITIBAN TANOsími ni site iru | HÍ desu.

8. kono HÓN no TEIKA wa ‖ GOHYAKU GOZYÚU-EN desu.

9. erebéetaa no TEIIN wa ‖ ZYÚU-MEI desu kara ‖ TUG̃Í no o | oMAti kudasái.

10. TUG̃Í no | BEIKOKU-DAITÓORYOO g̃a | KETTEI sita.

11. KOKKAI KAISAN wa | HITUZYOO da.

12. SOOZOKÚNIN o | SADÁmeta.

13. kono KUMÍ wa | SYÓHO desu kara ‖ KANZI wa OSIezu ‖ KAIWA bákari | site imásu.

14. SAISYO g̃a TAISETU désu kara ‖ yasasíkute mo | YUDAN sinái de ‖ yóku | BENKYOO site kudasái.

15. ZYUUG̃ATÚ ni | HATUYUKI g̃a hútta.

16. HAZIme wa hetá de mo ‖ dandan úmaku | narimásu yo.

17. OBOe no WARÚi HITO.

18. TANAKA | ÁIITI-san o | OBÓete imasu ka.

19. ZIBUN no ZYAKUTÉN wa ‖ ZIKAKU site orimásu.

20. ÁKUZI g̃a | HAKKAKU sita.

21. KANKAKU g̃a surudói.

22. KOdomo ní wa ‖ HAHAOYA no AIZYOO g̃a | HITUYOO désu.

23. SIZEN o AIsúru.

24. AIYOO no kámera de ‖ SYASIN o tóru.

25. AIKOKÚSIN no | TUYÓi | KOKUMIN désu.

26. AIZIN g̃a áru soo da.

27. TÉN made | todóku hodo | TAKÁi KI.

28. íi|o-TÉNKI desu ne.

29. koko wa ‖ TIZYOO no TÉNG̃OKU desu.

30. AMA-nó-GAWA wa ‖ GÍNG̃A to mo iimasu.

31. ÁME-tuti ni | táda | hitóri no | HÁHA o | nakusimásita.

32. KOOTÁISI wa || TUǦÍ no | TENNÓO ni | náru KATA desu.

33. mukasi wa || TENNOO-HÉIKA wa | KÁMI-sama da to | OMOwárete | imásita.

34. KÉNPOO o | YÓNda koto no | nái KOKUMIN wa || íi KOKUMIN | tó wa | ienái desyoo.

35. GÉNZAI | NIHÓN ni | KÉNPEI wa || inái.

36. KOKUREN-KÉNSYOO wa || SÉN | KYÚUHYAKU | YÓNZYUU GO-NEN ni | SEITEI sareta.

37. kawaisóo de || DOOZYOO no NÉN o | osaéru koto ǧa | dekínakatta.

38. KANARAzu || asitá made ni || káesu yoo ni | NEN o osite || o-KANE o KAsimásita.

39. amerika dé mo || KENPOO-KINÉNBI wa || SAIZITU ni nátte imasu ka.

40. ÁME de || géemu ǧa | TYUUSI ni nári || ZANNÉN desita.

41. anó HITO wa || ZIKAN no | KÁNNEN ǧa | tittó mo | NÁi.

42. NIHONǦO wa || SÉKAI de || MÓTTOmo | muzukasíi to iu | AYAMÁtta | KÁNNEN o | MÓtte iru | HITÓ mo | áru yoo da.

43. móo | SÁIǦO da to KÁNNEN sita | TOKÍ ni || TASUkeráreta.

44. ITI-ǦAKÚNEN o | NI-GÁKKI ni | WÁkete || KÁKU-GAKKI | góto ni | sikén o | Ukesaséru.

45. anó HITO wa || KANARAzu | ITIRYUU no GAKUSYA ni náru to || KITAI sarete imásu.

46. ZYOKYÓOZYU kara || KYOOZYU e | KAKU ǧa Aǧatta.

47. ano KATÁ no | ZINKAKU o | SONKEI site orimásu.

48. KAKAKU o hakkíri | SIMEsite kudasái.

49. ano hutarí wa || SIN'YUU désu ǧa || SEIKAKU wa | ZENZEN tiǧaimásu.

50. kotosi wa || KOOUN ǧa TUZUkimásita.

51. HUKÓO na | HITÓ ni | DOOZYOO suru.

52. SAIWAi | KÁZOKU wa || mina GÉNKI desu.

53. "HUKÚ wa UTI || oní wa SOTO"

54. KOOHUKU na KATEI désu.

55. KÁMI no SYUKUHUKU o | inorimásu.

56. MITI ǧa wakaránai kara || TÍZU o | KÁite kudasai.

57. ÁIZU suru made | MÁtte kudasai.

58. TOSYÓKAN kara | HÓN o KAriru.

59. ZISATU o HAKÁtta.

60. ÍKUZI ni SENNEN suru.

61. DÁNZI SYUSSYOO.

62. ano ISYA wa || SYOONI-SENMÓN'I desu.

63. ZÍDOO no | tamé no | yói | YOmíMONO ḡa | hosíi.

64. MÁINITI || DOOWA o HITO-tu zútu | YÓnde yaru.

65. SYUSYOO no KANḠÁe wa || HOSYU-TEKI désu.

66. SYÚBI ḡa | hetá na | tíimu.

67. GAKUDOO o MAMÓru | tamé ni || zyúnsa ḡa | OODAN-HÓDOO de |
    KOOTUU-SÉIRI o site iru.

68. BÓKOKU no | tamé ni | TATAKAtta.

69. HÚBO wa || NIHÓN ni orimasu.

70. NIHONḠO no || a || i || u || e || o wa || mina BOIN désu.

71. SÍNSETU o | SYÁsite | SÁtta.

72. GESSYA ḡa Aḡaru.

73. RYÓOSIN ni | KÁNSYA suru.

74. SÉNZO wa || BÚSI desita.

75. SÓKOKU no | tamé ni | TATAkau.

76. kono MISÉ ḡa | kasutera no GÁNSO desu.

77. ZYOOKAN ni | KEIREI suru.

78. MEUE no HITÓ ni wa || UYAMÁtte || KEIḠO o TUKAu.

79. ano KATÁ no SIḠOTO ni | KEIHUKU site imásu.

80. RIYUU o SETUMEI suru.

81. KÓZIN no | ZIYÚU o | SONTYOO suru.

82. miná-SAMA | o-GÉNKI no YOSI || ANSIN itasimásita.

83. NAMAE no YÚRAI o KIita.

84. NINḠEN no SÉIMEI wa || TATTÓi.

85. amerika wa ZIYÚU o | TATTÓbu | KUNI de áru.

DÁI | NÍZYUU | GÓ-KA

1. KYOKUSETU no ÓOi MITI.

2. SYUUNYUU o SÉPPAN suru.

3. OriḠAMI-ZÁIKU o site | ASObu.

4. RENSYUU-TYUU ni | udé o | Ótta.

5. IWA no ÓOi | KAIGAN désu kara || OYOḡi-nikúi desu.

6. NIHÓN de wa || GAN'EN wa | SANSYUTU sinai.

7. TITYUU no HUKÁi | TOKORÓ de || NESseráreta | GÁNSEKI ḡa | tókete ||
   ZIHYOO ni NAḠAre-DÉte || KYUU ni | HÍete | katamatta monó ḡa |
   KAZÁNḠAN de aru.

8. NENMATU ní wa | OOÚriDAsi g̃a | áru.

9. GETUMATU ni naránai to || SYUUNYUU g̃a NÁi.

10. SYUUMATU ní wa || inaka no IÉ e Iku.

11. UE wa || OTOKÓ-no-KO de || AIDA ni | ONNÁ-no-KO g̃a | hutari ári || SUE wa | mata | OTOKÓ-no-KO desu.

12. SUEkKO désu kara || ANE ya | ÁNI g̃a | kawaig̃átte kuremaşu.

13. TYÓOSI wa || GAIKOKU ni Iru.

14. KOKUZIN-MÓNDAI wa || máda | KAIKETU sarete nái.

15. KOKUBYAKU o | hakkíri | sasemasyóo.

16. KOKUBAN ni | tyóoku de | KANZI o KÁita.

17. HARUYÁSUmi ni || IS-SYÚUKAN || sukíi ni | Itte itára || KAO g̃a makKÚRO ni | nátta.

18. ZIBUN g̃a TADAsíi | kotó o | SYUTYOO sita.

19. KYÓOTO ni | SYUTTYOO site iru.

20. MÓN ni | MIHAri g̃a TÁtte iru.

21. ZÍKO o | HUSÉg̃u tame || róopu o HAru.

22. ÁME ya | YUKÍ g̃a | húru to || ZIDOOSYA-ZÍKO g̃a | ÓOi.

23. móo | KÓZIN ni | nátta | KATÁ desu.

24. GAIKOKU ni NÁG̃Aku | SÚnde | irú kara || KÓKOKU g̃a | natukasíi.

25. ITIBAN SEISEKI no yói MONO ni || KIN-médaru o | ag̃emasyóo.

26. KYOOIKU ni | TISEKI o ag̃eta HITÓ desu.

27. dámu no KENSETU ni | HIZYOO ni KOOSEKI no átta | HITÓ desu.

28. SINBUN o HAITATU suru.

29. HITÓsiku BUNPAI suru.

30. OTOOTÓ g̃a BYOOKI de || SINPAI site imásu.

31. GAKUSEI ni | KAMÍ o | KUBÁtte | sikén o suru.

32. NOOMIN g̃a | KOMÉ o | SÉIHU ni KYOOSYUTU-site || SÉIHU g̃a | KOKUMIN ni Uru.

33. SINZEN ni | KÚMOTU o | SONAéru.

34. ZYOTYUU o o-TÓMO ni site || KAIMONO ni Iku.

35. ÓtiBA o | NAG̃Ái AIDA || MIZU no NÁKA ni | tukete oku to || YOOMYAKU daké g̃a | NOKÓru.

36. TOOKYOO kara | TIBÁ-SI made no | ATARAsíi MITI o | KEIYOO-KÓKUDOO to iu.

37. KAWAG̃ISI ni | TÁtte || TAIG̃AN o nag̃améru.

38. ANPO-ZYÓOYAKU | KAITEI no TÓKI || KÍSI-san g̃a | SYUSYOO dátta.

39. ITÍ-RI wa │ YÁKU │ NI-mairu-HÁN de aru.

40. RITEI o hakáru.

41. YAMÁ kara │ SATO e │ KUDAru.

42. SATOOYA to SATOḠO désu ḡa ‖ hontoo no ÓYAKO no │ yóo desu.

43. nite imasén ḡa ‖ ZITUMAI désu.

44. IMOOTÓ ḡa │ tonari no KODOMO to │ NIWA de ASOnde iru.

45. TÉIMAI ḡa │ ÓOi no de ‖ RYÓOSIN o │ TASUkéte │ yóku HATARAite iru.

46. KYÓODAI wa arimasén. hitoríkKO desu.

47. MAINEN │ KÚḠATU hazime │ ní wa ‖ TAIHÚU ḡa │ kúru.

48. YATAI no susíYA de │ TÁbeta.

49. DÁI no │ UÉ ni NOtte ‖ TAKÁi │ TOKORÓ kara │ MONÓ o │ TÓru.

50. DAIDOKORO de │ RYÓORI suru.

51. ZYÓOBA to │ iú no wa ‖ UMÁ ni │ NOru kotó desu.

52. básu mo │ DÉNSYA mo │ TOOKYOO no NOriMONO wa │ ítu mo │
    ZYOOKYAKU ḡa ÓOi.

53. TOMOdati no KURUMA ni BINZYOO site ‖ KUUKOO ni MUkatta.

54. kono BYOOIN wa ‖ áru HITO no │ KÍHU de │ TÁteta │ monó desu.

55. kono HÚNE wa ‖ mánira ni KIKOO suru.

56. GAKKOO no KAErí ni │ TOSYÓKAN ni YOtte ‖ HÓN o KAriru tumori da.

57. sutóobu no │ sóba ni ‖ isu o YOseru.

58. TYÚUYA no │ KÚBETU │ náku ‖ NÍZYUU │ YO-ZÍKAN │ EIḠYOO site iru.

59. HAKUTYUU ‖ SATUZIN ḡa átta.

60. HIRU-YÁSUmi wa │ ZYUU NI-ZI-HÁN kara ‖ SANZIP-PÚNKAN desu.

61. kono SYASIN wa │ MEIAN ḡa hakkírí site iru.

62. ANḠOO de │ TUUSIN suru.

63. NIHONḠO no │ BÚNSYOO o │ ANKI suru.

64. KURAi MITI o ARÚku.

65. NAḠAréBOSI to │ RYUUSEI wa ‖ ONAzi monó desu.

66. SÓRA ITIMEN ni │ HOSI ḡa DÉte iru.

67. MYOOZYOO to iú no wa ‖ KINSEI no BETUMEI de áru.

68. SATUZIN no YOOḠÍSYA to site ‖ SIRAberárete iru.

69. HITO o KOROsita UTAḠAi ḡa áru no de ‖ SIRÁbete imasu.

70. kono MONDAI ni túite ‖ GIMON ḡa áttara ‖ NAN de mo oKIki kudasái.

71. anó HITO no │ ÍKEN ḡa │ TADAsíi to iu │ kotó o │ UTAḠAu MONÓ wa │
    hitori mo NÁi.

72. SAMÚi kara || MÓOHU ḡa iru.

73. MOOHITU de KÁita TEḠAMI.

74. NIHONZÍN no | kami-nó-KE wa | KURÓi.

75. KEITO no séetaa o KIru.

76. MÉNPU o | Óru | KOOZYÓO.

77. SUIḠAI o Úketa | HITÓBITO ni || NUNOZI o HÁIHU suru.

78. KÍITO no | SEISI-KÓOZYOO de | HATARAku.

DÁI | NÍZYUU | RÓK-KA

1. I-SYOKÚ-ZYUU wa || NINḠEN-SÉIKATU ni | MOTTÓmo | HITUYOO na monó desu.

2. hutuu || ÍRUI to wa || KIru MONO || ÍRYOO to wa || ÍTO || NUNO nádo no | KIru MONÓ no | ZAIRYÓO no | kotó desu.

3. ISYA wa || SIḠOTO-TYUU | HÁKUI o KIru.

4. KOROMÓḡae no KISÉTU wa || ROKUḠATÚ de aru.

5. SENSOO-TYUU wa || GUNZYU-KÓOZYOO de | HATARAite ita.

6. HITUZYUHIN wa || súbete | TOTONÓtte imasu.

7. KÍNU no | kutúsita to | náiron no to || dótti ḡa | zyoobu désu ka.

8. ZINKEN wa || ÍRYOO no HUSOKU o | OḠINÁu | tamé ni | KANḠAeDAsáreta.

9. SENḠO || NIHON no KINU-ÓRIMONO no YUSYUTU wa || GENSYOO sita.

10. sonna HINIKU o | Iwanái de kudasai.

11. KEḠAWA no kóoto wa || TÁKAkute | KAemasén.

12. HIKAKU-SÉIHIN wa || SAIKIN | YÁSUku natte | kimásita.

13. BAke no KAWÁ o | haḡáreta.

14. anáta no SAIYOO ḡa | KETTEI simásita.

15. SAIKETU o tótta tokoro || HANTÁISYA wa | ITI-MEI mo arimasén desita.

16. MYÓONITI | SAITEN sité kara || SEISEKI o HAPPYOO simásu.

17. ATARAsíi | KANḠÁe o | ToriIréru.

18. RIKIRYOO o tamésu tame || sikén o | Úketa.

19. kinoo no ÚRYOO wa || NIZYÚU-miri desita.

20. TAIRYOO-SÉISAN o suru to || BUKKA wa | SAḡáru hazu desu.

21. SAKE o | masú de | HAKÁtte | Uru.

22. uínzaaKOO wa || AIsúru HITO no tame || ÓOI o suteta.

23. erizabesuZYÓOO ni wa || SAN-NÍN no | ÓOZI ḡa arimasu.

24. HOOÓO wa || katorikku-KYÓOTO ni | TITÍ to | SYOO sárete iru.

25. KYOOTO-DÁIĜAKU de | GÁKUSI no | SYOOĜÓO o | torimásita.

26. YAMAMOTO-san no KOODOO wa || SYOOSAN ni ATAIsuru.

27. DAIĜAKU o DÉta to | ZISYOO site imásu ĝa ..

28. kore wa || SITAĜAki désu kara || SEISYO site kudasái.

29. ATARAsíi | KAObure ní wa || SEISIN no KÍ ĝa | mítite iru.

30. karada o KIYÓmete kara || ZÍNZYA e Iku.

31. sono OTOKÓ wa || kono ZÍKEN ni | TÁIsite || ZIBUN wa | KEPPAKU de áru to | IiHÁtta.

32. HUKETU na KANzi no suru OTOKÓ da.

33. YAMANAKA-san wa || KOOKETU na ZÍNBUTU de aru.

34. uti no KODOMO wa || YOWÁMUSI de | komarimásu.

35. MUSI no IDOKORO ĝa WARÚi ñ desyoo.

36. GAITYUU dá kara || KOROsité mo | íi desu.

37. MUĜI-BÁTAKE wa || ÓOki na | TYUUĜAI o Úketa.

38. SÉITO no | SYUKKETU o tóru.

39. dare ni de mo || TYÓOSYO to | KETTÉN ĝa | áru.

40. KETUIN o OĜINÁu tame ni || SAIYOO-sikén o | sinákereba | naránai.

41. kono TYAwan wa || KAkete irú kara | suteyóo.

42. NÁNI ka | REIBUN o TUKÚtte kudasai.

43. REIĜAI no NÁi | KISÓKU wa | NÁi.

44. sonna KOTÓ o suru to || AKUREI o NOKÓsu | kotó ni narimasu.

45. RÉI o | aĝete kudasái.

46. NIHÓN de wa || kono GO,ROKU-NEN || KOMÉ wa | HOOSAKU TÚZUki de aru.

47. SAKÚMOTU no | yóku | dékita | TOSÍ o | HOONÉN to iu.

48. YÚTAka na | SYÁKAI o | KENSETU suru tamé ni | DÓRYOKU suru.

49. SYUUNYUU ĝa huéreba || sore dake | SEIKATU ĝa YÚTAka ni naru.

50. HOKKÁIDOO wa || BOKUSOO no SEIIKU ni TEKÍsite iru si || TOTI ĝa HIRÓi no de || BOKUZYOO ĝa ÓOi.

51. BOKUZYOO wa || KUN'YOmi ni site || MAKIBÁ to mo iu.

52. BOKUSI ni nátte || NIHÓN de | DENDOO no SIĜOTO ĝa sitái no desu.

53. BÓKKA wa || BOKUZIN | matá wa | NÓOHU no SEIKATU o UTAtta | SI désu.

54. kono TEĜAMI wa || SOOSYO de KÁite | áru kara || YOmemasén.

55. YAMADA-san wa || kono MURÁ no | KUSAWAke no HITÓ desu.

56. ZASSOO no yóo ni | TÚYOku | Ikíru.

57. KUSABUKÁi inaka ni | SÚnde iru.

58. SENZEN || YOOSÁNḠYOO ḡa | sakan dátta | TOKÍ ni || KÁIKO wa || "o-KÁIKO-san" to yobare || TAISETU ni atukawarete ita.

59. SAIKIN | KINU-ITO no ZYUYOO ḡa MAsú ni turete || YOOSÁNḠYOO ḡa | ÍKI o | hukikáesite kita | yóo da.

60. HUKU-DAITÓORYOO wa || BEIKOKU-ZYOOIN ni | HUKÁi | KANKEI ḡa áru.

61. kono KUSURI wa || HUKUSÁYOO wa | arimasén.

62. SÉI-HUKU NI-TUU no SYORUI o | DÁsite kudasai.

63. SINBUN déwa || TOKUBETU na BAAI no hoka || KANZI no SIYOO wa | TOOYOO-KÁNZI | daké ni | SEIḠÉN sarete imasu.

64. soo iu húu ni | GENTEI suru kotó wa || dekínai to | OMÓu.

65. MONÓḠOTO ni wa || taitei | GÉNDO ḡa | áru.

66. kono HUUSYUU wa || TYUUḠOKU-TÍHOO ni | KAḠIrárete imasu.

67. OYÁ kara | SEIKÁTUHI no | HÓZYO o | Úkete imasu.

68. moo SUKÓsi | SETUMEI o HOSOKU itasimásu to . .

69. SYUUNYUU no HUSOKU o OGINÁu tame ni || arubáito o|sinákereba | naránai.

70. KETUIN o OḠINÁu tame || ATARAsîi | SYÁIN o | SAIYOO suru.

71. TOOKYOO wa || YOKOHAMA no KYUU-BAI ÍZYOO no | ZINKOO ḡa áru.

72. BAIKYUU no o-HÍkiTÁte o | oneḡai itasimásu.

73. anó HITO no | KEIZAI-SÉISAKU de wa || SYOTOKU-BAIZOO-KÉIKAKU ḡa | HITÓ-tu no | HASIRÁ tò | nátte iru.

74. KOOTÚU-RYOO no | BAIKA ni SONÁete || TAISAKU o taténakereba | naránai.

75. SÁNRUI to wa || ENSAN || TANSAN nádo no | kotó desu.

76. SANKA o HUSÉḡu | tamé ni || penki o nuttári simasu.

77. SIZEN-KÁḠAKU to | SYAKAI-KÁḠAKU to de wa || KENKYUU-HÓOHOO ḡa tiḡaimasu.

78. NI-GÁKKI ni wa || YON-KÁMOKU | tóru tumori desu.

79. KONḠÁKKI kara || kono KYOOKÁSYO o TUKAimasu.

80. SENḠO || NIHÓN de wa || SYAKAI-KA no KYOOIKU ḡa | ZYUUYÓOSI sarete imasu.

81. "SENSOO to HEIWA" to iu HÓN o | YÓnda koto ḡa | arimásu ka.

82. NIHON no ROODOO-SÓOḠI ni wa || KEIZAI-MÓNDAI | daké de | náku || SEIZI-MÓNDAI ḡa karánde iru BAAI ḡa | ÓOi.

83. KYOOSOO to | KYOOSOO wa || HATUON wa ONAzi dé mo || ÍMI wa | tiḡaimásu.

84. HITÓ-tu no | TÍI o | SAN-NÍN de | ARASÓu.

85. ikura ATAMÁ ḡa | YÓkute mo || DÓRYOKU|sinákereba || damé da.

86. OOHASI-san wa || DORYOKUKA désu.

87. kono HUKUZATU na MONDAI o TOkóo to | TUTÓmeta.

88. RENSYUU-ZÍKAN ḡa | SUKUnákatta kara || SIAI ni KAtéru ka | dóo ka | HUAN désu.

89. SIÚNTEN no KEKKA || SEISEKI wa | ZYOOZYOO de átta.

90. NÁN-DO mo | KOKORÓmita ḡa | SIPPAI sita.

91. ATARAsíi | KOKORÓmi desu kara || SEIKOO surú ka | dóo ka | wakarimasén.

DÁI | NÍZYUU | SITÍ-KA

1. KIMI no ÍKEN ni wa | ZETTAI-HÁNTAI da.

2. sono KEIKAKU o | ZIKKOO surú no ni | GÉNḠO ni ZESsuru | KURUsími o KASAneta.

3. SAMÚi kara || HÍ o | TAyasánai | yóo ni | site kudasái.

4. anó HITO wa || TÁezu | HUHEI o Itte iru.

5. SÉKAI wa || KENRYOKU-SÉIZI ni yotte | SÍHAI sarete iru.

6. GAIKÓOKAN ni wa || SYÚZYU no | TOKKEN ḡa áru.

7. RIKEN o Éru | tamé ni || iroiro UNDOO suru.

8. GONḠEN-SÁMA e | o-MAIri ni Iku.

9. SISYUTU ḡa | SYUUNYUU ÍZYOO ni | náreba || KAKEI wa | AKAZI dá to iu.

10. TOKÚḠAWA-san ni SInarete || TAISETU na SITYUU o USINAtta yóo na KI ḡa suru.

11. HONTEN kara | TIHÓO no SITEN e | TENKIN ni nátta.

12. SÉKAI wa || HUTA-tú no | SYÚḠI ni yotte | SÍHAI sarete iru.

13. "SININ ni KUTI NÁsi"

14. kore wa || SÉISI ni | KAKAwáru MONDAI desu.

15. KÁZAN ni wa || KATU-KÁZAN || KYUU-KÁZAN || SI-KÁZAN no | SAN-SYÚRUI ḡa | áru.

16. BUSÍDOO to wa || SInu kotó de aru to iu | KANḠÁe ḡa | SIHAI-TEKI dátta.

17. áto | NI-SYUUKAN ḡúrai de || TAIIN dekimásu.

18. MÓKKA || ÍSSIN-ITTAI no | ZYOOTAI désu.

19. DAIḠAKU o TYUUTAI site || SYÓOBAI o HAZImeta.

20. ano OTOKÓ wa || SUSUmu kotó wa | SItte irú ḡa || SIRIZÓku | kotó wa | SIranai.

21. SEKINÍN-KAN no | TUYÓi | HITÓ desu.

22. ZISEKI no NÉN ni | karárete || YÓRU mo | nerarenai.

23. anna MU-SÉKININ na | OTOKÓ o | SÉmete mo | syoo ḡa nái.

24. DAITÓORYOO no NINKI wa || YO-NEN désu.

25. OOTA-san no KOONIN wa || dáre desu ka.

26. sono KUNI no TÁISI ni | NINMEI saremásita ḡa || NÍNTI ni | omomúku no
    wa | IK-káḠETU | áto desyoo.

27. kono SIḠOTO wa || TANIN ni MAKAserarénai.

28. sono HÓN ni wa || NÉMOTO-SENSEI no | ZYOBUN ga áru.

29. ZYÚNZYO | yóku | HANÁsite kudasai.

30. ópera no | ZYÓKYOKU no | NÁKA de || dóre ḡa | ITIBAN suki desu ka.

31. NIHON-RÉTTOO wa || KITA wa | HOOKÁIDOO kara || MINAMI wa |
    KYÚUSYUU made | HASÍtte iru.

32. KYUUKOO-RÉSSYA desu kara || soko ní wa | TOmarimasén.

33. ZIDOOSYA-ZÍKO de || DÉNSYA ḡa || NÁN-DAI mo | GYOORETU site |
    TOmatta.

34. ano RÉTU no | MÁE kara | NI-BAN-MÉ no | HITÓ ḡa | TOKÚḠAWA-san
    no | o-MAḠO-san désu.

35. GENSEI-TYÚURITU o | MAMÓru koto wa | muzukasíi.

36. mótto | GENZYUU ni | SIRÁbete kudasai.

37. ZIKAN-GENSYU désu yo.

38. KAIḠI no SEKIZYOO || BÉI-DAIHYOO wa || TUḠÍ no | yóo ni | SETUMEI
    sita.

39. BYOOKI ḡa RYUUKOO site || KESSÉKISYA ḡa | ZOKUSYUTU sita.

40. SYUSSÉKISYA wa || SANZYÚU-MEI desita.

41. SYUUMATU ní wa || KAISÚIYOKU ni | Iku tumori désu.

42. huroba no kotó o | YOKUZYOO tó mo iimasu.

43. ÁTUkatta no de || uti e KÁEtte || MIZU o Abimásita.

44. o-SAKE o | Abiru hodo NÓmu.

45. SIAI wa || ZYUNTOO na KEKKA ni Owarimásita.

46. ROOZÍN wa || ATARAsíi ZIDAI ni | ZYUNNOO sinikúi.

47. SENTYAKU-ZYUN ni KUBArimásu.

48. dotira mo SEISEKI ḡa íi no de || ZYÚN'I o | tukéru no ḡa | muzukasíi.

49. SÍNPU wa | YAMADA-KE kara KImásita.

50. SENḠO | NIHÓN de wa || HUZIN no TÍI wa | KOOZYOO sita sóo desu.

51. náka no | íi | HÚUHU desu ne.

52. YAMANE-HÚSAI ni | SYÓOTAI saremasita.

53. SÁISI o │ YASINAu tamé ni │ HATARAku.

54. TÚMA ni │ SAKIDAtáreta.

55. ÍKKA no │ SYÚHU wa │ KAKEI o AZUkátte iru.

56. kono KATÁ wa ‖ TIBA-HÚZIN no │ SINRUI ni Atarimásu.

57. BENKYOO-HÓOHOO o │ iroiro KUHUU simásita.

58. OTTO wa ‖ ÍMA │ KYÓOTO e │ SYUTTYOO-TYUU désu.

59. DOOTOKU-KYÓOIKU no HITUYOO-SEI g̃a │ sakebárete iru.

60. TOKUG̃AWA-ZÍDAI wa ‖ YÁKU │ SANBYAKÚ-NEN no │ TAIHEI o
    TAMÓtta.

61. ano OTOKÓ wa ‖ AKUTOKU no KAG̃Irí o │ tukúsita.

62. kono hóo g̃a │ o-TOKUYOOHIN de gozaimásu.

63. mótto ‖ KEITOO-TEKI ni │ KENKYUU sitára ‖ íi to OMOimasu.

64. KAKÉIZU ni yoru to ‖ SÓSEN wa │ HÉIKE da │ sóo desu.

65. NIKKEI-BEIZIN tó wa ‖ BEIKOKU no SIMÍNKEN o │ MÓtte iru │ NIHONZÍN
    no │ kotó desu.

66. TYOKKEI no SÍSON de │ áru ka │ dóo ka │ UTAG̃Awasíi.

67. kono ZÍKEN ni │ túite ‖ SÉIHU kara ‖ KOOSIKI no KENKAI wa ‖ máda │
    HAPPYOO sarete inái.

68. nánra ka no KEISIKI de ‖ KOOHYOO sarerú to OMOimasu.

69. ano KOOBÁ de wa ‖ KYUUSIKI no │ KIKÁI o │ TUKAtte imasu.

70. SEISIKI no TUUTI g̃a ‖ NI,SAN-NITI-TYUU ni │ áru hazu desu.

71. ii-KAG̃EN ni│ HÁKUZYOO sinasai.

72. NIHON no KEIZÁIKAI no │ GENZYOO ni túite ‖ HANÁsite kudasai.

73. ZYOOSÁsi wa ‖ TEG̃AMI o Irete oku MONÓ desu.

74. kono MONDAI ni TÁIsite ‖ TÁIDO o │ AKÍraka ni │ sinákereba │ naránai.

75. YÓRU ni │ nátte ‖ YÓODAI g̃a AKKA sita.

76. TAISEI o TOTONÓete kara ‖ DENAOsu.

77. SENG̃O │ ZYUU SITÍ-NEN │ tátte ‖ NIHON no SYÁKAI wa ‖ ZYOOTAI ni
    hukúsita │ yóo de aru.

78. TENNÓo no │ SÍSON o ‖ KOOSON to iimásu.

79. HÉIKE no │ SÍSON de aru to │ SYÓOsite │ imásu g̃a .

80. ROKUZYÚU no TOKI ‖ TYOONÁN ni│ HAZÍmete no │ MAG̃Ó g̃a Umareta.

81. anáta no │ KANG̃Áe wa ‖ KONPON kara │ matig̃átte iru.

82. KONKI g̃a NÁkereba ‖ GÓG̃AKU wa │ ZYOOTATU sinai.

83. ano OTOKÓ no │ KÓNZYOO wa ‖ MAg̃atte iru.

84. KÍ no NE o │ horiokósu.

85. ÍMA kara || ROOGO no SINPAI o surú no wa || HAYA-SUgimásu.

86. YOORÓOIN wa | Óita | SAKI no MIZIKÁi | HITÓBITO no | SEIKATU no BA désu.

87. UEDA-san wa || OSIeru kotó ni | kákete wa || ROOREN désu.

88. SISOO no ZIYÚU no | nái | KUNI dé wa || SEIKATU sitaku arimasén.

89. TAKÁi RISOO o | MOtiTUZUkeru kotó ga | HITUYOO da.

90. veruréenu no | KUUSOO no SÉKAI ga | ÍMA ya | GENZITU to nátte | kité iru.

91. NIHÓN wa || huransu to | BUNKA-KYÓOTEI o MUSUnda.

92. kono MONDAI ni KÁNsite wa || MÓKKA | KYOOGI-TYUU désu.

93. KYOOKAI SETURITU no ZYÚNBI o | site imasu.

94. sono AIDA || HUKÁI na | OMÓi o | sita kotó wa || ITI-DO mo arimasén desita.

95. dare de mo | KAITEKI na SEIKATU o OKUritái to | OMÓtte iru.

96. KUMIAI no tamé ni || KEIÉISYA wa || KOKOROYÓku | TIN'Age ni OOzita.

DÁI | NÍZYUU | HÁK-KA

1. NIHÓN de wa || NIGATÚ kara | SÁNGATU ni | kákete || SOTUGYOO-SIKÉN no | KISÉTU desu.

2. RÓO-SI tomo | KEIKEN ga ASÁi kara || kono SÓOGI wa | NAGABIki-sóo da.

3. KÁGAKU no ZIKKEN o | SUU ZYUK-KAI KASAneru.

4. dóko no | KUNI dé mo || ZIKYUU-ZISOKU no KÉIZAI o | ITONÁmu koto wa | muzukasíi.

5. anáta no yoo na | KOOKYÚU-TOri nara || SEIKATU wa | RAKÚ desyoo.

6. NIHÓN de wa || KOMÉ wa | HAIKYUU-SÉIDO desu.

7. ZYUYOO to | KYOOKYUU tó no | KANKEI o SIRAbéru.

8. YUUHAN-MÁE ni | SYUKUDAI o site simau tumori désu.

9. sono RYOKAN wa || WATAKUSI ga | KYÓOTO e | Itta TÓKI no | ZYOOYADO désu.

10. AMAYÁDOri ni | sono MISÉ e | kakekónda.

11. NAGANEN no SYUKUBOO de átta | KAIGAI-RYÓKOO ga | ZITUGEN sita.

12. KISYÁ de RYOKOO suru | TANOsími no | HITÓ-tu wa || EKIBEN o TAbéru koto desu.

13. EKÍIN ni | RESSYA no TÚku ZIKAN o kiku.

14. ÍP-PUN wa | ROKUZYÚU-BYOO desu.

15. MORÍSITA-san no EIGO wa || GÚN o nuite iru.

16. BEIKOKU wa || KOKUREN kara | maasyaruGÚNTOO no | TÓOTI o | MAKAsárete iru.

17. kono sáwaḡi wa | GUNSYUU-SÍNRI ni | MOTOzúite iru.

18. ÚMI no | ITIMEN ni MURAḡáru | TORI no MUré kara || GYOḠUN o HAKKEN suru kotó ḡa | dekíru.

19. sono SIKÉN de || MANTÉN o | tóru koto wa || nakanaka muzukasíi.

20. kyóo wa | MÁNḠETU da kara || MITI ḡa | AKArúi desyoo.

21. kono sutoráiki o | ENMAN ni KAIKETU suru HOOHOO wa | nái desyoo ka.

22. NINKI ḡa Mítite || KAISYA o yameta.

23. SYOKUYOKU o Mításu tame ni || SYOKUZI o suru.

24. GUNZÍ-HI | ZOODAI ni tomonátte || TUIKA-YÓSAN o | KÚmu.

25. BYOOKI de | SIKÉN o | Ukerarénakatta no de || TUI-SÍKEN o site moratta.

26. SIḠOTO ni Owarete || ASObu hima ḡa arimasén.

27. HIBIYA-KOOKAIDOO yóri || UENO no | BUNKA-KÁIKAN no hoo ḡa || zutto SÉTUBI ḡa | íi.

28. SYOKUDOO wa || ZYUU NÍ-ZI kara | ITÍ-ZI made || aite imásu.

29. gúntai ḡa | OODÓOri o | DOODÓO to | KOOSIN suru.

30. go-SYUSSEKI itadakeréba || KOOEI ni ZONzimásu.

31. KYOOTO-SITÉNTYOO wa || KÓNDO || TOOKYOO no | HÓNSYA no hoo e | EITEN ni náru soo da.

32. KUNI ḡa SAKÁe || KOKUMIN no SEIKATU ḡa | YÚTAka ni | náru yoo ni | DÓRYOKU suru.

33. NÁN-DO | KEISAN sité mo || GOOKEI ḡa | Awánakatta.

34. SYOOḠÁKKOO no | SANSUU dé wa || TAsíZAN || HIkíZAN nado o | OSIeru.

35. SAISAN ḡa toréru yoo na KEIEI o | sinákereba | naránai.

36. ÚMI wa || TIKYUU no MÉNSEKI no | SAN-BUN no NÍ o | símete iru.

37. DENKYUU ḡa Kíreta kara || ATARAsíi no o | KAtté kite kudasai.

38. íi | TAMÁ o | NÁḡeta ḡa || báttaa ni | Utáreta.

39. DOKUSYÓOSYA wa | SINZIN désu.

40. DOOTOKU-KYÓOIKU no HITUYOO ḡa | TONAerárete imasu.

41. KAWAKAMI-san no SYOODOO sita SINSETU o | KENKYUU suru.

42. DANTAI de RYOKOO suréba || YÁSUku narimasu.

43. GAIKOKU-ZÍZYOO o | SIRAbéru tame ni || SISETÚDAN o OKUru.

44. ROOKUMÍ-IN ni | ITIBAN HITUYOO na monó wa || DANKETÚSIN de aru.

45. tyótto | SOODAN sitai kotó ḡa | arimásu ḡa . . .

46. ZATUDAN bákari site || SUKOsi mo BENKYOO sinákatta.

47. sono hutarí no | KUmiAwase ḡa | TAIDAN to site | ITIBAN omosirói desyoo.

48. GAISYOO wa || KAKKOKU-TÁISI to | KAIDAN sita.

49. anáta no | go-KÓOI o | HUKÁku | KÁNSYA itasimasu.

50. TÓBITA-san wa || ONKOO na KATÁ desu.

51. tukue no UÉ no | AKAi | ATUi HÓN o | TÓtte kudasai.

52. KISYUKÚSYA ḡa | MAN'IN ná no de || DAIḠAKU no TIKÁku no | IÉ ni | GESYUKU sita.

53. UNDOOZYOO wa || KÓOSYA ni | KAKOmarete imásu.

54. koko wa || mukasi || RIKÚḠUN no | HÉISYA ḡa | átta | TOKORÓ desu.

55. NIHÓN wa || SIZYUU NÍ-KEN ni | WAkárete iru.

56. YAMAMURA-san wa || KENKAI-GÍIN desu.

57. KEN-TÍZI no NINKI wa || YO-NEN de áru.

58. HOKENZYO wa || MATI no EISEI ya | BYOOKI no YOBOO nádo no | SIḠOTO o suru ZIMÚSYO desu.

59. karada o KYOOKEN ni suru tamé ni || supóotu o suru.

60. TANAKA-san wa || KENZEN na SISOO no MOtíNUSI desu.

61. KODOMO o | SUKÓyaka ni | SODAtéru.

62. BYOOKI wa || ITÍZI | SYOOKOO o TAMOtte iru.

63. KENKOO o TAMÓtu tame ni || EIYOO no áru | TABÉMONO o | TAbéru.

64. HIḠASI-yooróppa no KUNI wa || hotóndo | sóREN no | EISÉIKOKU de aru.

65. BOOÉIRYOKU ZOOKYOO no tame || YÓSAN ḡa | ZOODAI suru.

66. IRIḠUTI ni IRU SYUEI ni | KIite kudasái.

67. HÓN o | YOYAKU-TYUUMON suru.

68. sono tíimu wa || YOSOOdóori | TAISYOO sita.

69. kúrasu no | MÁE ni || YOSYUU o simásu.

70. anó HITO no YOḠEN wa || SINzirarénai.

71. GÁISI | DOONYUU no tamé ni wa || KOKUNAI-KÉIZAI ḡa | ANTEI site inákereba | naránai.

72. KUMIAI-KÁNBU no | SIDÓORYOKU ḡa | YOWAmátte kita.

73. AKUNIN o | ZÉN no MITI e | MITIBÍku koto wa || taihen na SIḠOTO désu.

74. maasyaruGÚNTOO wa || BEIKOKU no ININ-TOOTÍ-KA ni aru.

75. SYUUIN no YOSAN-Í de || TÓOḠI ḡa sarete iru.

76. zéhi || IÍNKAI ni | go-SYUSSEKI kudasái.

77. kono KÁI no | KÁNZI wa || TADA-san désu.

78. KÍ no | MÍKI ni || turú ḡa | makitúku.

79. KÁNBU ḡa | ATUMÁtte || sono MONDAI o TÓOḠI sita.

80. mukasi wa || tabitabi | adaÚti ḡa | OKOnawareta.

81. SIHON-SYÚḠI to | SYAKAI-SYÚḠI no | HUTA-tú no | SÉKAI ḡa | TAIRITU site iru.

82. KYÓOSI no SIKAKU o | TÓru tame ni || DAIḠAKU de | BENKYOO suru.

83. sono KAISYA no SIHÓNKIN wa || dono ḡurai désu ka.

84. SÍRYOO ḡa | NÁi kara || SETUMEI dekimasén.

DÁI | NÍZYUU | KYÚU-KA

1. SYOOWA GÁN-NEN wa || SÉN | KYÚUHYAKU | NÍZYUU | GO-NEN ni Atarimásu.

2. ÁSA | HÁYAku | Ókite || BENKYOO suru hóo ḡa || KÓOKA ḡa Aḡarimasu.

3. kono kippu no YUUKOO-KÍKAN wa || IK-káḠETU desu.

4. kono ZYOOYAKU wa || GÍKAI no | SYOONIN o Éte || HAZÍmete | KÓORYOKU o | SYOOzúru.

5. sono BYOOKI ní wa || máda | TOKKÓOYAKU wa | arimasén.

6. AKÍYAMA-san wa || HEIAN-ZÍDAI no | BÚNḠAKU ni | SEITUU site imásu.

7. kono HÓN wa || ATÚi kara || SEIDOKU sitára || ZIKAN ḡa kakarimásu.

8. SYOOZIN-RYÓORI ni wa || NIKÚ-RUI wa || ÍSSAI | TUKAimasén.

9. YAMADA-san wa || HUDE-BÚSYOO na | OTOKÓ de || TEḠAMI o | hotóndo | KAkimasén.

10. BÚNSYOO o | KANZEN ni ANKI suru.

11. sono TATÉMONO ḡa | KANSEI suru máde || SUU ZYÚU-NEN no | TUKÍHI o | YÓOsita.

12. AÍKAWA-san wa || kono MONDAI ni KÁNsite || HITEI-TEKI na KENKAI o NÓbeta.

13. SAISYO no AIDA wa | HININ site itá ḡa || tóotoo ZIHAKU sita.

14. HÁHA kara | ÁNPI o | KIzukáu | NAḠÁi TEḠAMI o moratta.

15. ano OTOKÓ ḡa | ÍNA to | Iéba || doo suru koto mo dekimasén.

16. NÓORYOKU o | tamésu tame ni || SIKÉN o suru.

17. mótto | NOORITU ḡa Aḡaru yóo na | BENKYOO-HOO wa | arimasén ka.

18. DOOBUTU wa || súbete | HÓNNOO ni yotte || KOODOO suru.

19. anna MUNOO na OTOKÓ wa || yamesaseta hóo ḡa | íi.

20. SÉISYO no | YOOḠO ni túite | KENKYUU site imásu.

21. orinpíkku no | SÉIKA o | gírisya kara | HAKObu kotó wa || berurinTÁIKAI kara HAZImatta.

22. GAKUSEI to Iéba || súgu | beetóoben o | OMOiDAsimásu.

23. KOOḠÓO-SAMA wa || KANSAI-RYÓKOO ni | oDEkake ni narimásita.

24. ano OTOKÓ no | SIḠOTO-buri wa || nakanaka SEIZITU de áru.

25. SÉII o | mótte | MONDAI no KAIKETU ni | DÓRYOKU suru.

26. NIHON no GÚNTAI wa || TENNÓO ni | TYUUSEI o tikatta monó da.

27. MAKOTO no áru HITO ka | NÁi HITO ka | MIWAkerú no wa || muzukasíi.

28. anáta no KIBOO ni | OOziru kotó wa | dekimasén.

29. aitu wa || KÍDAI no AKUNIN to | mirárete iru.

30. KYUUZIN | KYUUSYOKU no KOOKOKU wa || taitei | SINBUN no | DÁI | ZYÚU-MEN ni | notte imásu.

31. ROOKUMI wa | KESsite HUTOO na YOOKYUU dé wa | nái to | SYUTYOO sita.

32. KANE o MÉAte ni || KYUUkon sita wáke de wa | arimasén.

33. hitori daké no | KANGÁe de wa | KImerarenái no de || UEDA-san ni ÍKEN o | MOTÓmeta.

34. GAIKOKU ni EIZYUU suru tumori de || KUNI o DÉta.

35. súisu wa || TYUURITU o | EIKYUU ni MAMÓru koto ḡa | dekíru desyoo ka.

36. EIZOKU-SEI no áru SIḠOTO o | saḡasite imásu.

37. KÁKKOKU wa || EIEN no HEIWA o MOTÓmete | DÓRYOKU site iru.

38. ZIKYÚU-RYOKU ḡa | NÁkereba || sono SIḠOTO o KANSEI suru kotó wa | dekínai.

39. KUON no RISOO o MOTÓmete || GAKÚMON ni | haḡému.

40. kinoo | MATÍ de | HISAsiburi ni | YAMADA-san ni Átta.

41. NIHÓN de wa || GÚNTAI to iu | KOTOBÁ o | TUKAwázu ni || ZIEITAI to iu.

42. ÁNI wa | HEITAI ni toráre || TYÚUḠOKU de | SENSI simásita.

43. BÚTAI wa || ZENSIN ni ZENSIN o TUZUketa.

44. TYUUKYOO SYOONIN wa || TOKI no MONDAI de áru.

45. SINḠOO o KAKUNIN sité kara || HASSYA suru.

46. WATAKUSI ḡa WÁRUkatta to | MITOmemásu.

47. sezánnu no | é ḡa || SÉKEN ni | MITOmeraretá no wa || SÍḠO no | kotó de aru.

48. HUKOKU KYOOHEI wa || MEIZI-SÉIHU no | KIHON-SÉISAKU de atta.

49. HÁRU ni | nátte || TENTOO ni | YASAI ḡa | HOOHU ni DEMAWAru yóo ni | nátta.

50. TÉNKI no | íi HI ni wa || TOOKYOO kará de mo || HÚZISAN ḡa | MIemásu.

51. EIYOO ni TÓnda | TABEMONO bákari | TÁbete iru.

52. INÚ wa || SYÚZIN ni | TYUUZITU na DOOBUTU de áru to | iwarete iru.

53. SENḠO | TYUUKUN-ÁIKOKU to iu | KANGÁe wa || sutarete simatta.

54. SYUKÚN ni | TYUUSETU o tukúsu no ḡa || BÚSI no | DOOTOKU de átta.

55. OYA-KÓOKOO to wa || HÚBO ni | yóku | TUKÁe || HÚBO o | TAISETU ni suru kotó de aru.

56. ÍZYUTU wa | ZÍNZYUTU de aru to iwarete iru.

57. DAIḠAKÚIN de | HAKUSI-KÁTEI no BENKYOO o | site imásu.

58. KODOMO no TÓKI || yóku | KAḠAKU-HAKUBUTÚKAN e Itta.

59. HAKUḠAKU na OTOKÓ da ḡa || KENKYUU-HÁPPYOO wa | ITI-DO mo sita
    kotó wa | nái.

60. HITO no WARÚḠUTI o | Itté mo || nan no RÍEKI ni mo | naránai.

61. gásu || DÉNKI nado no | KOOKYOO-ZÍḠYOO de wa || ROOKUMI no SOOḠÍ-
    KEN wa | SEIḠÉN sarete iru.

62. taihen YUUEKI na o-HANASI o ukaḡaimásite || aríḡatoo gozaimasita.

63. SYOKÚBUTU no GAITYUU o | TÁbete || ZÍNRUI ni | RÍEKI o ataeru MUSI
    o | EKITYUU to iu.

64. ROO-TÁIKA no KOOZYUTU o HIKKI si || HÓN ni matomeru.

65. kono MONDAI ni KÁNsite wa || KOOZYUTU no YOTEI de áru.

66. MÁE ni mo | NÓbeta to | OMOimásu ḡa . .

67. NATTOKU saseru tame || RIYUU o NObénakereba | naránai.

68. KITYOOHIN wa || TYOOBA no hóo e | oAZUke kudasái.

69. KIKÉI no | ÍKEN o | UKETAMAWAritái to OMOimasu.

70. GÉNZAI no | SANḠÍIN wa || mukasi | KIZOKÚIN to | SYOOsárete ita.

71. MÓKKA | ZINSEN-TYUU désu ḡa || nakanaka | TEKITOO na HITÓ ga |
    MItukarimasén.

72. zyúudoo no | SEKAI-SENSYUKEN-TÁIKAI ḡa || pári de OKOnawareta.

73. TÚNODA-san wa || TOOSEN KAKUZITU to iwarete imásita ḡa || SÉNKYO
    no KEKKA || ZITEN to nátte simatta.

74. ANZEN na MITI bákari | ERÁnde ite wa || GENDAI-SYÁKAI de wa |
    SEIKOO sinai.

75. GENSOKU to site || hátati ni | náru to || dare de mo | SENKYÓ-KEN o |
    Éru.

76. SENSYOO o KINEN site || SIKITEN o KYOKOO suru.

77. tatta hitóri de no | yótto ni yoru | TAIHEIYOO-ÓODAN wa || KÍNRAI no |
    KÁIKYO de atta.

78. YUUMÉIZIN no | ÍKKYO | ITIDOO wa || SYÁKAI no TYUUMOKU o Abiru.

DÁI | SANZYÚK-KA

1. KITA-KYÚUSYUU o nozoite || HOKKÁIDOO || KÁNTOO || TYUUḠOKU-
   TÍHOO no TANKOO wa || MEIZI ÍḠO || SANḠYOO no KINDAI-KA to tómo
   ni || KAIHATU ḡa | SUSUmerareta monó de aru.

2. NIHÓN de wa || TEKKOO no SANSYUTU ḡa SUKUnái no de || DAIBÚBUN |
   GAIKOKU kara || YUNYUU site iru.

3. ZYUUKYUU-SÉIKI-MATU kara || NIZYUS-SÉIKI ni | kákete || DÉNKI no RIYOO ḡa | KÓOḠYOO ZENTAI ni | KAKUSIN no MITI o HIRÁita.

4. SITÚNAI no | ÓNDO ḡa | TAKÁi no de || SÓTO no | SÁMUsa ḡa | wakari-masén.

5. AKÁISI-san wa || SYASIN-kítiḡai de || ZIBUN no IÉ ni | ANSITU máde | MÓtte imasu.

6. KYOOSITU no NÁKA de || tabako o nónde wa | ikemasén.

7. áru | TIHÓO de wa || MIZUÚMI no KOORI o | KIritótte || MURÓ ni Irete oki || NÁTU ni | nátte || TUKAimásu.

8. NIHÓN de wa || DÁI | ITÍ-ZI | SEKAI-TAISEN ḡóro made wa || DÓO wa | ZYUUYOO YUSITUHIN de átta.

9. MITI ḡa | kónde iru kara || KURUMA de Iku yóri || TIKATETU de Itta hóo ḡa | HAYÁi desyoo.

10. NIHON no TETUDOO wa || HATTYAKU-ZÍKAN ḡa | SEIKAKU na kotó de || YUUMEI de áru.

11. KENKOO o TAMÓtu ⌋ tamé ni wa || KOOBUTÚSITU o | tóru koto ḡa | HITUYOO da. sono ÍMI de || TETÚBUN no | ÓOi | gyuunyuu o NÓmu koto wa || ROOZÍN ni wa | íi koto da.

12. sóREN wa || BEIKOKU no | kyúuba ni | TAIsúru KOODOO o | haḡésiku | HÍNAN sita.

13. kono HÓN wa || NANKAI na BÚNSYOO ḡa | ÓOkute || YÓmu no ni || KÚROO suru.

14. KYÓNEN wa || MATTAku | TÁZI | TANAN no | TOSÍ desita.

15. NIHÓN no | KEIZAI-SEITYÓO-RITU hodo || YOSOO si-NIKÚi mono wa | nái.

16. KITAI wa || EKI-KA suréba || HAKObú no ni | BÉNRI da.

17. KETÚEKI no | NÁKA ni wa || HAKKÉKKYUU || SEKKÉKKYUU ḡa | áru.

18. SENḠO || NIHON no SEINEN-DÁNZYO ZENTAI no | TAIKAKU ḡa | KOOZYOO sita.

19. KOKUMIN-TAIIKU-TÁIKAI ni wa || TENNÓO | KOOḠÓO ḡa | go-SYUSSEKI nasaimásu.

20. NÁNI ka | TÉI yoku | KOTOwáru HOOHOO wa | nái desyoo ka.

21. KÁKKOKU de || GENSÍRYOKU o | NENRYÓO to site | RIYOO suru tame || KAIHATU ḡa OKOnawarete iru.

22. kore wa || KANEN-SEI-BÚSSITU da kara || TYÚUI suru koto.

23. sutóobu no | HÍ ḡa | AKAku | MOeAḡátta.

24. HURÚi TEḠAMI o | YOmi-náḡara || IT-TUU zútu | MOyasite ítta.

25. HÚNE wa || TOODAI no Akari o táyori ni || KOOKOO suru.

26. heyá ḡa | KURÁi no de || HIRUMÁ de mo || DENTOO o tukénakereba | naránai.

27. SENḠO || NIHON no ZOOSÉN-ḠYOO wa || YUSITU no | HANAḠATA-SÁNḠYOO ni | nátta.

28. HURÚi | MOKUZOO-KÉNTIKU no | HOZON ní wa || iroiro KUSÍN ḡa iru.

29. <u>damu</u>-KÉNSETU ni yotte || NIHON no atíkoti ni | ZINZÓO-KO ḡa | dékita.

30. GAIKOKU e OKUru BAAI wa || NIZÚKUri o | GENZYUU ni sinákereba | naránai.

31. KAIḠÍ wa | ITÍZI | TYUUDAN sarete imásita ḡa || MYÓONITI kara | mata | HIRAkaremásu.

32. KAITEN sita bákari no | MISÉ desu kara || YASUÚri o site imasu.

33. TEI-KAIHATÚ-KOKU no | KAIHATU ní wa || SENSÍNKOKU no | SIHON to | GÍZYUTU ḡa | HITUYOO de áru.

34. KYÓOTO de || NIHON-KINDAI-BUNḠAKÚ-KAI ḡa | HIRAkáreta.

35. ítu ni | náttara || ÚN ḡa | HIRAkéru desyoo | née.

36. DAI-TÓKAI de || SEIKATU si || UNDOO mo sinai to || KESSYOKU ḡa WÁRUku narimasu.

37. YAMÁKAWA-san wa || BYOOKI-áḡari na no de || TI no KE no nái KAO o site imasu.

38. SYUKKETU | TARYOO no tame || ZETUMEI sita.

39. KINḠAN ná no ni || HÓN o | YÓmu toki | ÍḠAI wa || méḡane o | TUKAimasén.

40. hutarí wa || TANIN no SONZAI nádo | MATTAku | GÁNTYUU ni | nákatta.

41. HAHAOYA wa || TIMANAKO ni nátte || KODOMO o saḡasiMAWÁtta.

42. SYUUḠÍIN wa || GENSOKU to site || YO-NEN ni ITI-DO || SOO-SÉNKYO | suru kotó ni | nátte iru.

43. ITÍ-NEN ni ITI-DO || SOOKAI o HIRÁku.

44. NIHON no YUSYUTU-SÓOḠAKU no | SANZYUP-<u>paasénto</u> wa || TAI-BEI-YÚSITU de aru.

45. sono HIKOOKI-ZÍKO no GEN'IN wa || HUMEI de áru.

46. SIAI no HAIIN ni túite || NANI mo KATAranákatta.

47. sonna ÍNḠOO na | kotó o | Iwanái de kudasai.

48. KANOO-SEI ḡa NÁi to wa | Ienai.

49. kono KEIKAKU wa || SYATYOO no KYÓKA ḡa | Nákereba || ZIKKOO dekínai.

50. ZETTAI TASÚU de || KAKETU sareta.

51. SEIKEI-HUKÁBUN to | iú no ḡa | TYÚUḠOKU no | SEISAKU de áru.

52. NAḠÁi AIDA | RENSYUU site imásu ḡa || GARYUU désu kara || SUKOsi mo ZYOOTATU simasén.

53. TOKÚḠAWA-san wa || ítu mo | GA o HAtte || TANIN no ÍKEN o | KIkóo to mo | simasén.

54. WÁRE to | OMÓu MONO wa || SANKA site kudasái.

55. KANKYAKU wa || WAREḠAti ni | SÓTO e | DEyóo to sita.

56. konna KOTÓ wa || ZYOOSIKI désu yo.

57. sonó HITO to wa || ITI-MÉNSIKI mo | arimasén.

58. sibáraku no AIDA || ÍSIKI o USINAtte ita.

59. YAMAMOTO-san wa || nakanaka | KENSIKI no áru HITO desu.

60. SIZYOO no KAKUTYOO o HAKÁru tame || KEIZAI-SISETÚDAN o |
    KÁKKOKU e OKUru.

61. DÁI | NÍ-ZI | SEKAI-TÁISEN made wa || KÁKKOKU tomo | GUNKAKU-
    KYÓOSOO ni NETTYUU sita.

DÁI | SÁNZYUU | ÍK-KA

1. MURAYAMA-san ḡa KUWAwátta no de || páat^ei wa | KYUU ni YOOKI ni
   nátta.

2. YOOSYUN no KÓO || miná-SAMA ni wa | o-KAwari | náku | oSUḠOsi no
   kotó to | ZONzimásu.

3. SÓNTOKU o | KANḠÁezu ni | SYÓOBAI suru | kotó wa | dekínai.

4. ZÍḠYOO no SIPPAI ni yotte || ÓOkina SONSITU o | Úketa.

5. kono SYÓOBAI de || daibu SÓN o | simásita kara || hoka no SYÓOBAI o |
   HAZImeyóo to | OMÓtte imasu.

6. DAI-ITI-ÍNSYOO ḡa | WÁRUkatta no de || ITI-NEN ÍZYOO | SÚnde ite mo |
   máda | kono KUNI ḡa | sukí ni | naremasén.

7. KANZI wa | SYOOKEI-MÓZI to iimasu.

8. TUTOmeNIN o TAISYOO ni site || KOOZYÓO (KOOBÁ) no | sóba ni | MISÉ
   o | HIRÁku.

9. SYUZYU no | SIZEN-GÉNSYOO no | NÁKA de || TAIHÚU ni yoru | SONḠAI
   ḡa | ITIBAN OOkíi.

10. ZÓO wa | HANA o TUKAtte | esá o HIROu.

11. ano ONNÁ wa | KYOODAI no MÁE ni | suwaru to || ITI-ZIKAN ḡúrai |
    UḠOkánai.

12. BOOENKYOO de | YÓZORA no HOSI o | KANSOKU suru.

13. KAḠAMÍ ni MUkatte | serihu no RENSYUU o suru.

14. SYUSYOO wa | MÓKKA | SEIYOO-TYUU désu.

15. SYUKKETU ḡa haḡésiku || ZETTAI-ÁNSEI ni | site inákereba | naránai.

16. SEIBUTUḠA dáttara || burákku no | É ḡa | sukí desu ne.

17. KEKKAN ní wa || DOOMYAKU to | ZYOOMYAKU tó ḡa | áru.

18. moo SUKÓsi | SÍZUka ni | HANÁsite kudasai.

19. ano hutarí wa | omosirói | TAISYOO désu ne.

20. SYOOMEI ḡa KURASÚḡite ‖ KÓOKA ḡa | aḡaranákatta.

21. HIDEri-TÚZUki de | MIZU-BÚSOKU ni | nayánde imasu.

22. ÁME ḡa yande ‖ HI ḡa TEriDÁsita.

23. HUUUN | KYUU o TUḡeru.

24. AMAḠÚMO ḡa | HIKÚku | tarekómete ‖ ÍMA ni mo | ÁME ḡa | hurisóo na | SÓRA datta.

25. dandan | KUMOYUki ḡa ayasiku nátte kita.

26. HANSEIHU-BÓODOO ḡa | KÁKUTI ni | Okótta.

27. dónna BAAI | dé mo ‖ BÓORYOKU o | hurutté wa | naránai.

28. UWAYAKU ni TÁIsite | HIZYOO ni OOBOO na TÁIDO o | tótta no de ‖ KUBI ni nátta.

29. NITIYÓOBI datta no de ‖ KODOMO no tamé ni | EHÓN o | YÓnde yatta.

30. SEIYOO-KÁIḠA ‖ TÓKU ni ‖ ZYUUKYUU-SÉIKI ZENPAN no | huransu no ABURÁE ni | túite | KENKYUU site imásu.

31. IMOOTÓ kara | UTUKUsíi KAIḠAN no | KÉSIKI no | Eháḡaki o moratta.

32. KYÓNEN wa | HUKÉIKI datta kara ‖ kotosi wa | KEIKI ḡa YÓku natte | moraitai.

33. nyuuyóoku no YAKEI wa | UTUKUsíi.

34. SAPPÚUKEI na | apáato ni | SÚnde iru.

35. móto wa | ÉKI to iwazu ‖ TEISYABA to itta.

36. TEIDEN dá kara ‖ roosóku o | tukéte.

37. ano SÓOḠI wa ‖ ROOSÍ-KAN ni | TYOOTEI ni tátu HITO ḡa ite ‖ yatto RAKUTYAKU sita.

38. ZYÓOḠI o TUKAtte ‖ TYOKUSEN o HIku.

39. TÁIYOO wa ‖ AKAÁKA to MOete ‖ SUIHÉISEN ni | sizunde ítta.

40. KOKUTETU no | TOOKAIDOO-HÓNSEN wa | KUROZI désu ḡa ‖ TIHÓO no | SISEN wa | hotóndo | AKAZI désu.

41. DENSEN no UÉ ni | TORI ḡa | MUré o nasite | TOmatte iru.

42. TOOKYOO no yóo na | DAITÓKAI de mo ‖ DÓORO ḡa | WARÚi n desu kara ‖ TIHÓO e | Ittára ‖ mótto | hidói desyoo.

43. sono RÓZI no tukiatari ḡa | AKAḠI-san no IÉ desu.

44. KOOKÚUKI no HATTATU ni yotte ‖ TAISEIYOO-KÓORO no | KYAKUSEN no ZYOOKYAKU wa | GENSYOO si-tútu aru.

45. ITI-NITÍ no | TUTOmé o Oe ‖ IEZI ni ISÓḡu | HITÓBITO ḡa | TOOriSÚḡite ‖ MITI wa mata | SÍZUka ni | nátta.

46. TENSAI wa | wasurerareta kóro | yatte KÚru.

47. SENSAI o Ukénakatta | KYÓOTO wa | SEN-YÓ-NEN no | DENTOO o TAMÓtte iru.

48. MOKUZOO-KÉNTIKU ḡa | ÓOi TOKAI wa || KASAI ni yoru SONḠAI ḡa | HIZYOO ni OOkíi.

49. WAZAWAi o TÉNzite || HUKÚ to suru.

50. anáta wa | NINḠEN no | MÍRAI o | SINzimásu ka.

51. MISEINÉNSYA wa | NYUUZYOO dekimasén.

52. anó HITO no IkiSAKI wa | MITEI désu.

53. MÍTI no | TAIRIKU o MOTÓmete | KÓOKAI ni | DÉru.

54. syuubéruto no | 'MIKÁNSEI' wa | NIHÓN de | NINKI no áru | ÓNḠAKU no | hitótu desu.

55. NÁNI ka | íi IiWAKE o | KANḠÁete kudasai.

56. YÁKUSYA wa | ITIRYUU no HITÓ desu ḡa || amari íi· | YÁKU to wa | Iemasén.

57. bóku ni wa | WABUN-ÉIYAKU yori || EIBUN-WAYAKU no hóo ḡa | zutto yasasíi.

58. TYOKUYAKU siSUḡíru to YAKUBUN ḡa hakkíri | sinái si || IYAKU siSUḡíru to | GENBUN kara hanárete simau.

59. KOKUREN de | TÚUYAKU no SIḠOTO o | site imásu.

60. MYOOTYOO SITÍ-ZI ni | TÚku to iu | DENPOO o Útta.

61. SEIKAKU na ZYOOHOO o Éta to | Itte itá ḡa || TATAKAi wa | DAITÓORYOO no | KITAI dóori ni wa | SINTEN sinákatta.

62. kono ZÍKEN ni | KANsúru | kuwasíi HOOKOKU wa | máda | UkeTOtte nái.

63. KYÓOSI wa | BUSSITU-TEKI ní wa | MUKUiraréru koto no | SUKUnái | SEIKATU de áru.

64. GÁIBU kara no | ATÚRYOKU ni yotte || SEIZI ḡa SÁYUU sareru.

65. TAIHÚU wa | NETTAISEI-TEIKÍATU no | ÍSSYU de aru.

66. KETUATU ḡa TAKÁi kara || SAKÉ-RUI wa | NOmánai yoo ni site iru.

67. KOKUÓO no|ASSEI ni | KURUsínda KOKUMIN wa | KÁKUTI de | BOODOO o Okósita.

68. KENSÉTU-SYOO wa | SAIḠÁITI SISATU ni | DEkaketa.

69. ano OTOKÓ wa | SASsi no WARÚi | yátu da.

70. anáta no o-KIMOTI | ZYUUBÚN | oSASsi itasimásu.

71. kono SIAI wa | SÉIU ni | kakawárazu || OKOnawaremásu.

72. TAIHÚU wa | SUḡiSÁtte || MATTAku no KAISEI to nátta.

73. kyóo no | yóo na | AKIBAre no HÍ wa | KIMOTI ḡa íi | monó da.

74. KIMI no ITI ḠON (HITÓ-KOTO) de || UTAḠAi ḡa HÁreta yo.

75. KISYOO-ZYÓOKEN ḡa | íi no de || SEKAI-KÍROKU ḡa | UMarerú ka mo | siremasén.

76. ROKUON-ZYÓOTAI ḡa | WÁRUkute || yóku | KIkitoremasén.

77. KODOMO wa │ HUROKU no takusan áru zassi o │ KAitagáru │ monó da.

78. HÓNSYUU no │ TYUUÓO de wa ‖ SANMYAKU ḡa │ HÓNSYUU to │ TYOKKAKU ni HASÍtte iru.

79. TYUUOO-SYUUKEN-KA o HUSÉḡu │ ÍMI de ‖ KÁKUKEN no │ ZÍTI o │ KYOORYOKU ni SUSUmenákereba │ naránai.

80. ATARAsíi TOTI o │ MOTÓmete ‖ buraziru ni IMIN suru.

81. KÓNDO ‖ SÁKI no │ TOKORÓ e │ ITEN simásita.

82. UTUriḠI na OTOKÓ desu kara ‖ KI o tukenasái.

DÁI │ SÁNZYUU │ NÍ-KA

1. kono HOOTYOO wa │ KIreAZI ḡa │ íi.

2. TEKI no TAIḠUN ni │ HÓOI sareta.

3. KAMÍ ni │ TUTÚnde │ hukuró ni │ Irete kudasái.

4. GAIKOKU e │ KOZÚTUMI o OKUru BAAI wa ‖ NIZÚKUri o │ yóku │ sinákereba │ damé da.

5. sono HÓN ḡa │ KANKOO sareta no wa ‖ SANZYÚU-NEN mo │ MÁE no │ kotó desu.

6. NIHON no TYUUÓOSI wa ‖ TYOOKAN mo │ YUUKAN mo │ HAKKOO site iru.

7. sono HÓN wa ‖ KONSYUU no SINKANSYO no NÁKA de ‖ ITIBAN │ UreYUki ḡa íi soo desu.

8. KÓNNITI no │ yóo ni │ HUTA-tú no │ SÉIRYOKU ḡa │ ÁI-TAIRITU suru │ SÉKAI de ‖ KYOKUḠAI-TYÚURITU o │ TAMÓtu no wa ‖ ÍNDO no │ RÉI o │ míru made mo │ náku ‖ nakanaka muzukasíi.

9. GÉNZAI no KYOKUMEN o │ DAKAI surú ni wa ‖ yori KYOORYOKU na SEISAKU o toránakereba │ naránai.

10. dótti no MITI o │ TÓOtte mo ‖ KEKKYOKU ONAzi TOKORÓ e │ DÉru n desu ḡa ‖ kotira no hóo ḡa │ KOOTÚU-RYOO ḡa │ SUKUnái to OMOimasu.

11. SENKYOKU ḡa │ AKKA sita.

12. sono MONDAI no ZÉHI o │ hakkíri to │ sasenákereba │ naránai.

13. kono yóo na AKUSYUU wa ‖ ZÉHI ‖ ARATAméru HITUYOO ḡa │ áru.

14. ISYOKU áru │ SINZIN da.

15. anáta no │ go-IKEN ni │ IZON wa gozaimasén.

16. anó HITO no KOODOO wa │ kánari IZYOO da.

17. SEKÁI-KAN o │ KOTÓ ni suru │ HITÓBITO ḡa │ KYOORYOKU surú no wa │ muzukasíi.

18. ÓNSI no │ GAKUSETU tó wa │ KOTOnáru SINSETU o │ HAPPYOO surú ni wa ‖ YÚUKI ḡa │ irimásu ne.

19. NIHON-RÉKISI wa | NIHÓN-SI to mo iu.

20. ano KATÁ wa | YUUMEI na DAIGAKU o | REKININ sita KYOOZYU désu
    ḡa || MÓKKA | SEIKOO-ÚDOKU no | MÁINITI o OKUtte iru.

21. TYUUḠÁKKOO | SOTUḠYOO daké no | GAKUREKI dé wa | SAIYOO
    dekimasén.

22. dóo iu KEIREKI no | HITÓ ka | SIranái ḡa || SOOTOO ZITURYOKU no áru
    HITO da.

23. SYOKUREKI o | NENDAI-ZYUN ni KÁite kudasai.

24. mukasi wa || SEIYÓO-SI to | TOOYÓO-SI to o | WÁkete | OSIete itá ḡa ||
    SAIKIN | KOOTOO-GÁKKOO de wa | kore o matomete SEKÁI-SI to site |
    OSIete iru.

25. anó HITO wa | SIZITU ni kuwasíi.

26. SANḠOKU-DÓOMEI ni | TYOOIN sita kotó wa | NIHÓN o | HAISEN e
    TIKAzúketa | yóo na | monó desu.

27. DÁI | ITÍZI TAISEN-ḠO | dékita¦KOKUSAI-RÉNMEI to | SENḠO no
    KOKUSAI-RÉNḠOO to wa || sono SEIKAKU ḡa | itizirúsiku | KOTOnátte iru.

28. "TYÚUḠOKU no | KOKUREN KAMEI wa | ZIKAN no MONDAI de áru" to
    Itta.

29. HEIKÍN-TEN | ÍKA o | tóru to || RAKUDAI simásu yo.

30. MÓNKO-KAIHOO || KIKÁI-KINTOO to | iú no ḡa || seodoa·ruuzubéruto no |
    TAI-TYUUḠOKU-SÉISAKU datta.

31. HYAKU-EN-KÍN'ITU no | OOÚriDAsi o site imasu.

32. démo o OKOnatte || KÉNKYO sareta.

33. KENTEI-SIKÉN o | Úkete || ÍSI ni | nátta.

34. yóku | KENTOO sité kara de | nái to || ÍKEN o | HAPPYOO dekimasén.

35. TIKÁḡoro | TIIsái KATUZI ḡa | yóku | YOménaku | nátta no de || MÉ-ISYA
    e Itte || KENḠAN site moraóo to | OMÓtte imasu.

36. KUNI ni yotte || SASYOO o | HITUYOO to sinai TOKORÓ mo arimasu.

37. TYÓOSA no UE || go-HENZI itasimásu.

38. aizenháawaa wa | GUNZI-KÍTI no | KUUTYUU-SÁSATU o | sóREN ni |
    MOOsikónda.

39. sono hutarí ḡa | SAIKAI sitá no wa | SENḠO ZYÚU-NEN | tátte kara de aru.

40. BYOOKI ḡa SAIHATU si || NYUUIN-TYUU désu.

41. SAI-GÚNBI HANTAI no demoTAI ḡa | KOKKAÍ no SYÚUI ni | ATUmátta.

42. NIHON-KÓKUMIN wa || SENḠO || KÉIZAI-SAIKEN no tame ||DÓRYOKU site
    iru.

43. móo | HUTATAbi KÚru koto wa | aru mái to || sono TAIRIKU o | SENZYOO
    kara | zit to naḡámeta.

44. NENMATU wa | taihen KÓNZATU simasu kara || NENḠÁZYOO wa |
    NÍZYUU | SAN-NITÍ made ni | oDAsi kudasái.

45. SENSYOO o KINEN suru SYUKUĞÁKAI ğa | HIRAkáreta.

46. ITIĞATU HUTUKA wa | SÁNĞA no | HITÓBITO de || KOOKYO-MÁE wa | KÓNZATU simasu.

47. anó HITO wa | WATAKUSI o | TANAKA-san to | KONDOO site iru rasíi.

48. HANASÍ ğa | KONSEN site simattá kara || moo ITI-DO | HAZIme kara | HANÁsite kudasai.

49. anó HITO wa | KONKETUZI-MÓNDAI KAIKETU ni | ISSYOO o sasáğete imasu.

50. RINZI-KÓKKAI wa | SÁNĞATU SUE no | YOTEI désu.

51. RINKAI-ÓNDO to wa | KITAI ni | ATÚRYOKU o | KUWAeté mo | EKIKA sinai GENKAI no ÓNDO no | kotó desu.

52. TOKUBETU-KÓKKAI ni NOZOmu | SYUSYOO no TÁIDO ni | túite | KÍZI o | KÁku.

53. TYOKIN sitái n desu ğa || KÁZOKU ğa | ÓOkute || nakanaka dekimasén.

54. HIDEri-TÚZUki de || TYOSÚITI no SUIRYOO ğa | dóndon | HEtte imásu.

55. SEKITÁN no UreYUki ğa | WÁRUku || TYOTAN-ZYO wa | SEKITÁN no | YAMÁ da.

56. kono KATÁ wa | WATAKUSI no SYOONEN-ZÍDAI no | ONZÍN desu.

57. moo ITÍ-NEN | TUTOméreba | ONKYUU ğa tukimásu.

58. anáta no | go-ÓN wa | ISSYOO wasuremasén.

59. anna HITÓ kara | o-KANE o KAritára || ISSYOO | ÓN ni | kiseraremásu yo.

60. RYÓOKOKU no KANKEI wa | MÓKKA | KEN'AKU na ZYOOTAI ni arimásu.

61. HOKENKIN MÉAte ni | ZIBUN no IÉ ni | HÍ o | TUkéta.

62. KEWAsíi | YAMÁMITI o | noború no ğa | dóo site | TANOsími na n desyoo ka ne.

63. BYOOKI no BAAI wa | KESSEKI-TÓDOKE o | DÁsite kudasai.

64. TÉ ğa | TArimasén no de || NANI tozo HUyukiTÓDOki no TEN wa | oYURUsi kudasái.

65. KONSYUU-TYUU ni | IÉ e | TODÓkete kudasai.

66. NIHÓN-GUN wa | HAZIme no AIDA wa | HATIKU no IKIÓi datta.

67. KAISYA no | KEIEI-HÓOHOO ğa | WÁRUkute || HASAN sita.

68. RYÓOKE no | SYAKAI-TEKI TÍI no MONDAI kara || kono KEKkon no HANASÍ wa | HADAN to nátta.

69. HURÚi TEĞAMI o | YABÚtte | MOyasu.

70. TATAKAi ni YABÚreta | naporéon wa | erubaTOO e NAĞAsáreta.

71. BEIKOKU e RYUUĞAKU site || NÁNI o | BENKYOO sitái n desu ka.

72. o-RÚSU no AIDA ni | o-KYAKU-SÁMA ğa | irassyaimásita.

73. MI-ttu-MÉ no TEIRYUUZYO de | GESYA no koto.

74. keisatu de || YOOG̃ÍSYA nado o | ITÍZI | TOmete oku TOKORÓ o | RYUUTIZYOO to iimásu.

75. KOONAN o osórete || dare mo | SYÓONIN ni | naránakatta.

76. TAIKIN o KAsu TOKÍ ni wa | SYOOMON o KAkáseta hoo g̃a | íi.

77. YAMÁSITA-san no SYOOG̃EN ni yotte || ZÍKEN wa OtiTUita.

78. HÓNNIN de | áru koto o | SYOOMEI suru tame || SYORUI ni | SYASIN o TUkéte kudasai.

79. HOSYÓONIN wa | NÍ-MEI HITUYOO desu.

80. NI,SÁN-NITI no uti || go-HENZI itasimásu.

81. SYAKKÍN o | HENSAI surú no ni || ROK-káG̃ETU mo | kakátta.

82. TOSYÓKAN e | HÓN o | KÁesi ni | Iku tokoró desu.

83. KAsita KANE wa | ZÉNBU | KÁEtte | kimásita ka.

84. go-ON-G̃ÁEsi mo | sinai uti ni || nakunararete || KOKORO-NÓKOri de | narimasén.

85. KENSÉTU-SYOO wa | SAIG̃ÁITI HUKKYUU ni | ZENRYOKU o ag̃eta.

86. YOSYUU mo TAISETU désu g̃a || HUKUSYUU mo TAISETU désu yo.

87. koko kara TÓSIN made || OOHUKU | ITI-ZÍKAN kakarimasu.

88. íisutaa wa | kirisuto no HUKKATU o KINEN suru | MATUri désu.

89. YOOZYÓO g̃a | yókatta no de || móto no | KENKOO-ZYÓOTAI ni | KAIHUKU sita.

DÁI | SÁNZYUU | SÁN-KA

1. anáta g̃a | soo suréba || WARÚi KANREI o | NOKÓsu | kotó ni narimasu.

2. GAIKOKU e Ittára || sono KUNI no SYUUKAN ni | HÁYAku | NAréru koto g̃a | HITUYOO da.

3. áru SYOOSETU g̃a | GEIZYUTU-TEKI de áru ka || TUUZOKU-TEKI de áru ka o | KImeru KIZYUN wa | NÁN desyoo ka.

4. MÁINITI | ZÓKUZI ni Owarete || BENKYOO no hima g̃a | arimasén.

5. KANKÓOKYAKU g̃a | huéreba | huéru hodo || MEISYÓOTI wa | ZOKKA suru monó da.

6. anó HITO wa | MATÍ de | ZOKUG̃O bákari | OBÓete kimasu.

7. tyótto | ZIBIKÍ o | HAISYAKU itasimásu.

8. HAIKÁN-RYOO wa | SYÁZI ni yotte | KOTOnáru.

9. TÉ o | Awásete | OG̃Ámu.

10. UZIG̃ÁMI-SAMA no o-MATUri wa || MURABITO ni tótte || MOTTÓmo | TANOsíi | G̃YÓOZI de aru.

11. MÍZUTA-SI wa │ TOOSEN KAKUZITU to │ mirárete iru.

12. "ÚZI yori SODAti"

13. KYUUTYUU-SÁNGA no │ HITÓBITO de ‖ KOOKYO-MÁE wa │ KÓNZATU site imasu.

14. MEIZI-ZINGÚU wa ‖ MEIZI-TENNÓO o o-MATUri sita │ ZÍNZYA desu.

15. kono ZÍKEN wa ‖ MEIKYUU-Iri ni náru │ osoré ga │ áru.

16. ZÍNZYA wa │ o-MIYA tó mo iu.

17. kono HEN ni │ KOOBAN wa arimasén ka.

18. KOKKAI SYUUHEN ni │ demo-TAI ga ATUmátta.

19. MAN'YÓOSYUU no │ NÁKA de wa ‖ HENKYOO no MAMOri ni túku │ "sakímori" tati no │ UTÁ ga │ ITIBAN sukí desu.

20. SI-SYÓOSETU wa ‖ ZIBUN no SÍNPEN ni │ Okótta │ ZÍKEN o │ sono mama KÁita │ monó de aru.

21. WATAKUSI no sukíi wa │ ZIKO-RYUU désu kara ‖ nakanaka ZYOOTATU simasén.

22. anna RIKO-SYÚGI na │ OTOKÓ wa │ MÍta koto ga │ arimasén.

23. TÍKI ‖ TÍZIN ‖ SIriAi wa │ hotóndo │ ONAzi ÍMI desu.

24. kono MONDAI ni KAN súru │ NÍTI-BEI │ KYOODOO-SÉIMEI ga │ HAPPYOO sareta.

25. URIro no SÉKI no │ HITÓ ga ‖ yóku │ KIkoenái desyoo kara ‖ moo SUKÓsi │ ÓOkina │ KÓE de │ HANÁsite kudasai.

26. HAZIme wa │ SÍZUka ni │ HANÁsite ita ga ‖ dandan KOWADAKA ni nátte kita.

27. DAITOORYOO-HÚSAI no │ KOWAIRO o maneta rekóodo ga │ UriDAsáreta.

28. taitei no BUSSITU wa ‖ ÓNDO ni yotte ‖ KOTAI ‖ EKITAI ‖ KITAI to │ HÉNKA suru.

29. TOTI ‖ KÁOKU o │ KOTEI-SÍSAN to iu.

30. TOSÍ o │ tóru to ‖ HITÓ-tu no │ KANGÁe ni │ KATAmatte simatte ‖ ATARAsii │ KANGÁe wa │ nakanaka TOriIre-níkuku │ náru mono da.

31. sórosoro │ MI o KATAmetára ‖ dóo desu ka.

32. BUKKYÓO kara │ kirisutoKYOO ni KAISYUU sita.

33. anó HITO wa │ MATTAku SYUUKYÓO-SIN no │ NÁi │ OTOKÓ da.

34. GEIDOO o Uketúida │ IÉ no │ TÓOSYU o ‖ IEMOTO │ matá wa │ SÓOKE to iu.

35. sono BÓTI ni wa ‖ YUUMEI na HITÓBITO no │ o-HAKA ga arimásu.

36. BUKKYÓO ga │ NIHÓN ni │ DENRAI sitá no wa ‖ ROKU-SÉIKI no │ NAKÁgoro de aru.

37. NENBUTU sáe │ TONÁete │ itára ‖ GOKURAKU-ÓOZYOO suru to │ iú no ga ‖ BUKKYÓO no │ KANGÁe desu ka.

38. "HOTOKE TUKÚtte ‖ támasii Irezu"

39. ano OTOKÓ wa ‖ NÉNzyuu │ MÓNKU o Itte iru.

40. kono BÚNSYOO ni wa || NANKAI na GÓKU ḡa | ÓOi.

41. koohíi ḡa | NOmitái kara || o-YU o wakasite kudasái.

42. NATÚ wa | MAÍNITI | SÉNTOO e Ikimasu.

43. o-húro no | YU-KÁḠEN wa | ikáḡa desu ka.

44. anó HITO to wa || KINSEN-ZYOO no KANKEI wa nái.

45. SINBUN o KAitái ḡa || KOZENI ḡa NÁi.

46. "AKUSEN | MI ni túkazu"

47. ÍNDO to | TYÚUḠOKU to no AIDA no | KOKKYOO-MÓNDAI wa || KAIKETU
ni | ZIKAN ḡa kakáru daroo.

48. o-MATUri no HÍ ni wa || ZÍNZYA no | KÉIDAI ni wa || iroiro na YÁTAI ya |
MISÉ ḡa narabu.

49. TANAKÁ-SI wa | GÉNZAI no | SINKYOO ni túite || KISYÁ ni KATAtta.

50. TOOKYOO kara | YOKOHAMA máde || KOOZYOO-TÍTAI ḡa | TUZUite irú
no de || SÍ to | SÍ no | SAKÁI ḡa || dóko ni | áru no ka | wakari-nikúi.

51. supein wa || torafárugaa no KAISEN ni | YABÚre || sono OOḠON-ZÍDAI ḡa
OWAtta.

52. SÉKAI ni wa || OOSYOKU || HAKUSYOKU || KOKUSYOKU || SEKISYOKU no |
YON-ZÍNSYU ḡa | SÚnde iru.

53. KIIRO no TUKAiKATA ḡa umái no wa | góhho de aru.

54. tamáḡo no | KIMI to SÍROMI o | WAkéru.

55. koko wa || SINRYOKU no KISÉTU ni wa | KANKÓO-KYAKU ḡa | ÓOi.

56. DOO-SÉIHIN wa || HOZON ni KI o TUkénai to | ROKUSYÓO ḡa | déru.

57. kono HEN wa | RYOKUTI-TAI ni SITEI sarete irú kara || TATÉMONO o |
TAtéru koto wa | dekimasén.

58. NÓ mo | YAMÁ mo | ITIMEN no MÍDORI desu.

59. SYUKU-SÁI-ZITU ni wa || KATEI ya | ZIMÚSYO de || KOKKI o kakaḡéru
koto ni | nátte imasu.

60. YAMADA-san wa || HATAIRO ḡa WÁRUku | nátta no de || heyá kara |
DÉte Itta.

61. NIHON no HATÁ wa | NISSYÓOKI to iimasu.

62. KEIBA || KEIRIN nádo no | kakéḡoto wa | sinai hóo ḡa | íi desu.

63. anó HITO wa || dáiya no YUBIWA o | site imásu.

64. KÍ no | NENRIN o SIRAbéreba || sono HÚRUsa ḡa | wakarimásu.

65. BEIBAKU (KOME-MÚḠI) nádo o | KOKÚMOTU to iimasu.

66. KANTOO-HÉIYA wa || NIHON no ITIBAN ÓOkina | KOKUSOO-TÍTAI desu.

67. MIYAKAWÁ-SI (MIYAḠAWÁ-SI) wa | KO-ḠÁISYA no YAKUSYOKU mo |
KENNIN site imásu.

68. orinpíkku made ni | KANSEI suru kotó o | MEzásite || TYÚUYA KENKOO
no | DOORO-KÓOZI g̃a OKOnawareta.

69. YOOZI to ASObi tó o | KÁnete | KYÓOTO e Iku.

70. anó HITO wa || dare ni mo KIG̃Ane sézu || ZIBUN no OMÓu | tóori
yarimásu.

71. koko de | SYASIN o tóru koto wa | KINSI sarete imásu.

72. IMA-máde | ITI-DO mo SIPPAI sinákatta to | itté mo || YUDAN wa KINMOTU
désu yo.

73. YÚKAWA-san no KINSYU wa || IS-SYÚUKAN to | TUZUita kotó wa | nái.

74. IMA máde | MEISÍN da to | OMOwárete kita | kotó de mo || KAG̃AKU-TEKI
na KENKYUU no KEKKA || SÍNZITU g̃a | SYOOMEI sareta BAAI g̃a áru.

75. MITI ni MAYÓtte || TUUKOO-NIN ni | HOOG̃AKU o tazúneta.

76. HITO no KOKORÓ o | MAYOwásu yoo na | HOOSOO o sité wa | ikenai.

77. anó HITO wa || ÍSYO mo | NOKÓsazu || ZISATU sita.

78. ÍZOKU no | HITÓBITO no | MÁE de || YUIG̃ON-ZYOO o HIRÁku.

79. KOOTUU-ZÍZYOO g̃a | AKKA sita KÓNNITI || ROMEN-DÉNSYA wa |
MATTAku | ZEN-SÉIKI no | IBUTU de áru.

DÁI | SÁNZYUU | YÓN-KA

1. ZIBUN no HÁNDAN de | KImete kudasái.

2. anó HITO no | ATARAsíi SYOOSETU wa || amari | HYOOBAN g̃a YÓku |
arimasén.

3. sono ZÍKEN no SINSOO wa || ZYUU-NEN-G̃Ó ni HANMEI sita.

4. HANKETU no KEKKA || ZEN'IN MÚZAI to | nátta.

5. DAIG̃AKU no HUZOKU-BYÓOIN ni | KÍNMU site imasu.

6. SENZI-TYÚU wa || GÚNZOKU to site || MINAMI-TAIHÉIYOO no | KOZIMA
ni Imásita.

7. KÍN || GÍN || DÓO || TETU nádo o | KÍNZOKU to iu.

8. dóno | SEITOO ní mo | ZOKUsánai | GÍIN o | MU-SYOZOKU-GÍIN to iimasu.

9. KÁKU-SYOO ni wa | DÁIZIN no SITA ni | hutarí no | SEIMU-ZÍKAN g̃a Iru.

10. KYUU-KÉNPOO de wa || SINMÍN to iu | KOTOBÁ g̃a | TUKAwarete itá g̃a ||
SIN-KÉNPOO de wa || KOKUMIN to iu KOTOBÁ g̃a | TUKAwarete iru.

11. KAIHYOO no KEKKA || SÉN-BYOO no SA de || TÁG̃AWA-SI no TOOSEN g̃a |
KImatta.

12. TOOHYOO ni yotte KETTEI suru kotó o | HYOOKETU to iu.

13. DENSI-KEISÁNKI o TUKAtte || HYOO-SÚU o KEISAN suru.

14. GOG̃AKU-TEKI-SAINÓO g̃a | NÁi kara || GAIKOKUG̃O wa | damé desu.

15. YAMAMURÁ-SI wa || GÓGAKU no TENSAI de || ROK-kaKOKUGO ni TUUzite iru.

16. zyoruzyu· sándo wa || SAI-SYOKU-KÉNBI no | ZYOSEI de átta.

17. KAWAKAMI-san wa || BUNSAI ga áru no de || SYOOSETUKA o | SIBOO site iru.

18. SÍ wa | torókkisuto (torotúkisuto) to iu MEIMOKU de || TÓO kara | ZYOMEI sareta.

19. YAMADA-san o NOZOite || ZEN'IN ga | SANKA simásita.

20. ZYOSETU-SÁGYOO no tame || ZIEITAI ga SYUTUDOO sita.

21. TYUUKYOO o ZYOGAI sité wa || SÉKAI no HEIWA o | RONzúru koto wa || dekinai soo da.

22. TOKUGAWA-ZÍDAI ni wa || SÍ|| NÓO || KÓO || SYÓO no|YON-KÁIKYUU ga | KIBÍsiku | WAkárete ita.

23. ano MISÉ de wa || KOOKYUUHIN bákari atukatte imasu.

24. ZYOOKYÚUSEI mo | KAKYÚUSEI mo | issyo ni | RYOKOO ni Iku.

25. HINSITU ni yotte || TOOKYUU o KImeru.

26. NIHÓN de wa || HOSYUTOO to sité wa || ZIMINTOO || KAKUSIN-SÉITOO to | sité wa || SYAKAITOO || MINSYATOO || KYOOSANTOO nádo ga | áru.

27. TOOHA BETU ni MÍreba || SYUUGÍIN de mo || SANGÍIN de mo || ZIMINTOO ga | DÁI | ITTOO de áru.

28. sobiéto wa || SYAKAISYUGÍ-KÓKKA de | áru ga || súbete no | HITÓ ga | KYOOSANTÓO-IN to iu | wáke de wa | nái.

29. SÍ wa || ZIMINTOO no NÁKA de mo || dotira ka to Iéba || SINPO-HA ni ZOKUsúru.

30. NIHON KÓRAI kara no | GEIZYUTU ní wa || iroiro RYUUHA ga áru.

31. KAWAMURA-san wa || "ÁSAHI" no | TOKUHÁIN to site || nyuuyóoku ni Itte imasu.

32. IN'YOO ga NÁGAku | narimásu no de || ÍKA | SYOORYAKU simásu.

33. ZIBUN no sita kotó ni | túite || HUKÁku | HANSEI site imásu.

34. KANKEI KÁKU-SYOO no | ZÍKAN ga | ATUmátte || UtiAwase o suru.

35. kono BÚNSYOO wa || SAN-GYOO-MÉ kara || GO-GYOO-ME máde | HABÚitara | dóo desu ka.

36. anó HITO wa || ZIBUN no GENDOO o KAERImízu || TANIN no WARÚKUTI (WARÚGUTI) | bákari Itte imasu.

37. SÍ no ZOOSYO wa || YUIGON ni yori || súbete | TOSYÓKAN ni | KÍHU sita.

38. REIZÓOKO kara | bíiru o | NÍ-HON | DÁsite kudasai.

39. OOKURA-DÁIZIN wa || SIN-YÓSAN ni | túite | KISYÁDAN ni | SETUMEI sita.

40. ano | DOZOO no áru | ÓOkina | IÉ ga || HONMA-san no o-SÚMAi desu.

41. iranai MONÓ o | SYÓBUN site || MIGARU ni nátte | RYOKOO ni DÉru.

42. KÉNZI no | SITUMON ni TÁIsite || YOOG̃ÍSYA wa || KANE no DEDOKORO
ni túite wa || KATAku KUTI o tug̃únda.

43. kono MONDAI ni KÁNsite || TÓOKYOKU g̃a | TEKISETU na SYÓTI o | TÓru
desyoo.

44. "ANzuru yori || Umú g̃a|yásusi"

45. YAMAMOTO-san ni | MATÍ o | ANNÁI site moratta.

46. SIKÉN no SEISEKI wa | ÁNG̃AI | YÓkatta.

47. NÁNI ka | kono NAN-MÓNDAI KAIKETU no | MEIAN wa | NÁi desyoo ka.

48. NAKADA-san no TEIAN ní wa || hitori no SANSÉISYA mo | NÁkatta.

49. RONBUN no TEISYUTU-KÍZITU wa | KONG̃ETU-MATU (SUE) máde desu.

50. KIMI no GÍRON wa || ZENTEI kara matig̃átte imasu yo.

51. SÍ no TEISYOO sita SINSETU wa || GAKKAI kara | MUSI sareta.

52. KOBAYASÍ-SI wa || BUNG̃EI-HYOORON-KA to site | YUUMEI de áru.

53. sono "sibai" wa | ÁNG̃AI | HYOOBAN g̃a íi no de || SÁKUSYA wa |
YOROKÓnde imasu.

54. KYÓOSI no KINMU-HYÓOZYOO o meg̃utte | NIK-KYÓO-SO to | MONBÚ-
SYOO g̃a | TAIRITU sita.

55. MATUMOTÓ-SI wa | SUIRI-SYÓOSETU no SAKKA to site || TEIHYOO g̃a
áru.

56. GAIMU-DÁIZIN wa || kono ZÍKEN no | SEKININ o tótte || ZIHYOO o
TEISYUTU sita.

57. kono ZÍSYO ni wa | kuwásiku | SETUMEI sarete arimasén.

58. sobiéto no | DAI-ITINÍNSYA g̃a | MÍZUKAra | ZÍI o | HYOOMEI sitá no wa ||
HAZÍmete no | kotó de aru.

59. HYAKKA-ZÍTEN de | SIRAbemásita.

60. TÓOKYOKU no | SUITEI dé wa || KOTOSI mo | KOMÉ wa | HOOSAKU da
sóo da.

61. kono KEIKAKU o SUISIN surú ni wa || kánari | SIKÍN o | HITUYOO to simásu.

62. SÍ o | KAITYOO ni Osu kotó ni wa || IRON g̃a arimásu.

63. "GÚN" wa || GYOOSEI-TEKI KUKAKU dé wa | nákute || TÁN ni | TIRI-TEKI
na KUKAKU de áru.

64. kono kóosu wa | NI-TÁN'I to site || KEISAN saremásu.

65. SÍ g̃a | TANDOKU de KOODOO sita kotó wa || KAIIN kara | hag̃ésiku |
HÍNAN sareta.

66. SEIKATU no TANTYOOsa o YABÚru tame ni || SYUUMATU ní wa | RYOKOO
ni Iku.

67. NARÁtta | TANG̃O no KÁZU wa | húeta keredomo || máda | zyoozú ni |
TUKAemasén.

68. "HANZAI no kág̃e ni || ONNA|ári"

69. YOOĜÍSYA wa | HANKOO o HININ sita.

70. sono HÁNNIN wa || KYOOHÁNSYA no NAmae o | ZIHAKU sita.

71. TÚMI o | OKÁsita HITO ĝa | súbete | AKUNIN tó wa | KAĜIránai.

72. MÚZAI no SENKOKU o | Úke || HÁrete | ZIYÚU no | MI ni nátta.

73. NIHÓN de wa || SYUSEKI-HÁNZI ĝa | YUUZAI ka | MÚZAI ka no | HANKETU o KUDAsu.

74. anáta ĝa | TÚMI o | hitóri de Ou HITUYOO wa | arimasén.

75. híttoraa no KUZAI wa || KÓOSEI no REKISIKA ni yotte | KImerareru.

76. GÍRON | bákari site ite || KETURON wa || NANI mo DÉnakatta.

77. DAIĜAKU de | RONRÍĜAKU to | SINRÍGAKU o | BENKYOO site imásu.

78. RIRON wa TADÁsikute mo || ZISSAI ni TEKIYOO dekínai BAAI mo | arimásu.

79. KANEMÓti na no ni || SÍSSO na SEIKATU o site imasu.

80. YOOĜÍSYA wa || SÚNAO ni | HANKOO o MITOmeta.

81. MIZU wa || SÚISO to | SÁNSO no | NI-GÉNSO kara | náru.

82. BEIKOKU wa || SÉN | NANÁHYAKU | NANÁZYUU | ROKÚ-NEN || SITIĜATU | DOKURITU o SENĜÉN sita.

83. NIHÓN wa || SYOOWA ZYUU ROKÚ-NEN || ZYUU NIĜATU || BEI-ÉI ni | SENSEN-HUKOKU sita.

84. SENKYÓOSI ni | nátte || HUKYOO no SIĜOTO ni ZYÚUZI suru | tumori désu.

DÁI | SÁNZYUU | GÓ-KA

1. NIHON-BÚNĜAKU ni | HIZYOO ni KYOOMÍ o | MÓtte imasu.

2. SENĜO NIHON-KÉIZAI no | ITIZIRUsíi HUKKOO wa || NIHONZÍN no KINBENsa ni Ou tokoro | DÁI de aru.

3. MÉIZI ni | nátte | OKÓtta | NIHON no SANĜYÓO wa || KOKURYOKU no ZOODAI to tómo ni | HATTATU sita.

4. amari KOOHUN surú to || KETUATU ĝa Aĝarimásu.

5. KAITOO wa || kono HÓN no | ITIBAN Owari no peezi ni | KÁite arimasu.

6. BENKYOO site kónakatta no de || TOOAN o | HAKUSI no mama TEISYUTU sita.

7. DÁIZIN no | TÓOBEN ni wa || nanra SINMI wa nákatta.

8. KOTÁE wa | BETU no KAMÍ ni | KÁite kudasai.

9. SITIĜATU TUITATI no | YAMA-BÍRAki no | HÍ ni wa || TOZÁNSYA de | KÓNZATU simasu.

10. TOOROKU-SYÓOHYOO to | iú no wa || TOOROKU no TETÚZUki o | site óite || hoka no monó no | SIYOO o YURUsánai | SYOOHYOO de áru.

11. YAMÁ ni | NOBOru kotó ḡa | dóo site | sonna ni TANOsíi n desu ka.

12. SÍ wa | ZIBUN no KOODOO ni túite || KISYÁDAN ni | SYAKUMEI sita.

13. kono HÓN wa | TYUUSYAKU ḡa SUKUnái kara || ZIBUN de BENKYOO suru kotó wa | dekimasén.

14. SYÚZIN ḡa | MÚZAI | SYAKUHOO ni náru no o | SÍNzite orimasu.

15. ZYOOBUN no KÁISYAKU no sikata ni | GOKAI ḡa átte wa | ikenái kara || NÍTI-EI RYOOBUN o | SEISIKI-ZYÓOBUN to suru.

16. baanaado·syóo wa | DOKUZETUKA to site | SIrarete iru.

17. sonna kotó o | sité mo || DOKÚ ni mo | KUSURI ní mo | naránai.

18. NATÚ ni wa | NAMA-zákana wa | kusari-yasúi kara || TAbéru TOKI | TYÚUDOKU | sinai yóo ni | KI o tukénakereba | naránai.

19. moo SEN-EN HUNPATU sitára || íi MONO ḡa KAemasu.

20. WARE-WARE no tíimu wa | SÍKI | HURÚwazu | TAIHAI sita.

21. KOOHUN sita GUNSYUU wa || tóotoo | BOODOO o Okósita.

22. HITÓ-KABU de mo | KABUKEN o MÓtte | iréba || KABUNUSI de áru.

23. SAIKIN no SIZYOO ni óite wa || KABUSIKI-SYÓYUU no | BUNSAN-KA ḡa MEdátu.

24. ano KIriKÁBU ni | kosikákete || YASUmimasyóo.

25. SYOOKEN-SÍZYOO de wa || KOKU-NÁI,ḠAI no | SEIZI no UḠOkí ḡa | súḡu | KABUKA ni hibíku.

26. NYUUKOKU no tamé ni | RYOKEN daké de | SASYOO no iranai KUNI mo arimásu.

27. HITO o MIOKUru tamé ni | NYUUZYÓO-KEN o KÁtte | hóomu e Iku.

28. ZYUUHAS-SAI ÍKA no | HÁNNIN wa | SINBUN dé wa | KAMEI o TUKÁtte KÁku koto ni | nátte imasu.

29. KATEI-TEKI na SITUMON ní wa | KOTAemasén.

30. neboo sitá no de || KEBYOO o tukatte || KAISYA o YASÚnde simatta.

31. KARI ni | WATAKUSI ḡa | anáta no | TATIBÁ ni | Iréba || sonna kotó wa | simasén ḡa . . .

32. SYUSYOO no SOKKIN ní wa || YUUNOO na GAKUSYA ḡa Iru.

33. MONÓḠOTO no | SOKUMEN bákari o | MÍzu || SYOOMÉN o | MÍnakereba | ikenai.

34. NIHON no KOOTUU-HÓOKI de wa || SASOKU-TÚUKOO ḡa | SADAmerárete iru.

35. MITI no RYOOḠAWA ní wa | OOzéi no HITO ḡa | TÁtte || sono GYOORETU o naḡámeta.

36. DAIḠAKU to site || ITIBAN SOORITU no HURÚi no wa || dóno | DAIḠAKU désu ka.

37. SÍ wa || GAKKAI de | DOKUSOO-TEKI na KANḠÁe o | HAPPYOO sita.

38. SOOKA-GÁKKAI no | ITIZIRUsíi KOKKAI SINSYUTU wa || NÁNI o | MONOĞATÁru mono de | aróo ka.

39. SOOSAKÚ-RYOKU no | nái NINĞEN ni | SYOOSETU ğa KAkéru wake ğa | nái.

40. SAKUNEN no HATIĞATU || NIHÓN e | Ikimásita.

41. SAKKON no KOKUSAI-ZYÓOSEI ni | túite | dóo OMOimasu ka.

42. KUNI no tamé ni | KOOSEKI no átta HITO no | DOOZOO o TAtéru.

43. mótto | TOSIYÓri da to | SOOZOO site imásita.

44. TENPYOO-ZÍDAI no | BUTUZOO ní wa || ZENTAI to site | yawarakami ğa áru.

45. uti ní wa | ANSITU ğa áru kara || sono SYASIN o | GENZOO site ağemasyóo.

46. NIHÓN de wa || SYOOSETU no TYOSAKÚ-KEN wa | SÍ-GO | SANZYÚU-NEN made | áru.

47. kono HÓN no | TYÓSYA wa | TYOMEI na SEIZI-KA désu.

48. SÍ wa | SENMON ÍĞAI no | kotó ni | túite mo || iroiro na HÓN o | ARAwásite imasu.

49. sono hutarí no | RÓORYOKU o KURAberu to | ITIZIRUsíi SA ğa | áru to OMOimasu.

50. DOHYOO no | súğu | TIKÁku de || "sumoo" o MÍru.

51. SÓOKO ni wa || KOME-DÁWARA ğa | YAMA no yóo ni | TUnde arimásu.

52. terebíKYOKU de || BANĞUMI HENSEI no SIĞOTO o | site imásu.

53. kurásikku no MEIKYOKU o zyázu ni HENKYOKU suru.

54. SINBÚNSYA no | HENSYÚU-BU wa | ZYUUDAI-nyúusu ğa | háitte || SENZYOO no yóo datta.

55. SÍ no SAKUHIN wa || hotóndo | TANPEN de || TYOOHEN-SYÓOSETU wa | wázuka ni | hitó-tu sika | nái.

56. TÉNKI ğa | íi no de || HI ni Atari-náğara || AmíMONO o simasu.

57. DAIĞAKU de || KÓOSI o | site imásu.

58. KOODOO wa || SÍ no KOOEN o KIku | HITÓBITO de | MAN'IN dátta.

59. ano SENSÉI no | KOOĞÍ o | RIKAI suru tamé ni wa || iroiro na HÓN o | YÓmu | HITUYOO ğa áru.

60. TAINITI-KOOWA-KÁIĞI wa || sanhuransísuko de | HIRAkáreta.

61. íkura | ÉNĞI ğa | úmakute mo || sutáa ni | naréru to wa || KAĞIránai.

62. WATAKUSI wa || ENZETU ní wa | NÁrete | nái kara || SINPAI désu.

63. YUUMEI ni náru ni turete || térebi nado no | SYUTUÉN-RYOO mo | TÁKAku naru.

64. ano OTOKÓ wa || UWAYAKU no KANSIN o KÁu koto | bákari | KANĞÁete iru.

65. NÍTI-BEI KOOKAN | SUIEI-TÁIKAI ḡa | NÍ-NEN ni | ITI-DO zútu |
HIRAkárete iru.

66. rindobáaku no | HIKÓOKI ḡa || párii ZYOOKUU ni | ARAwaréru to ||
SÍMIN wa | KANSEI o aḡeta.

67. ano HÓN wa || HYOOBAN ḡa YÓkute || SAIHAN ni | SAIHAN o |
KASAneta.

68. WATAKUSI wa || SÉKAI no HANḠA o | ATÚmete imasu.

69. ano TOSYÓKAN ni wa || iroiro na | mezurasíi | SYOHAN-BON ḡa arimásu.

70. nooberú-SYOO no | ZYUSYÓO-SIKI ni | SYUSSEKI suru.

71. kono géemu ni wa || IT-TOO kara | ROKU-TOO máde no SYOOHIN ḡa |
YÓOI sarete arimasu.

72. BIZYUTÚKAN e Itte || MÉIḠA o | KANSYOO suru.

Part VI

ENGLISH TRANSLATIONS OF THE DRILL SENTENCES

LESSON 1

1. Since the most important thing is to read until we thoroughly understand, today we have read only from Lesson One to Lesson Three.

2. Would you care for a cigarette?

3. "Please give me one of the small pieces of paper on the table." "Oh, those white ones? Please take some. I will give you [= You may have] as many as you want."

4. How much is that blue suit, both jacket and trousers together?

5. I am glad that you came. [Or: How nice to see you!] Please come in.

6. The price of food has gone up.

7. I have three questions.

8. Who is the actress (standing) third from the left on the stage?

9. The next train in-bound to Tōkyō leaves at 3:02. The next train out-bound from Tōkyō leaves at four o'clock sharp.

10. At that store they sell various memo books, large and small.

11. Do you have a telephone directory?

12. Which (do you think) is better, the big one or the small one?

13. I bought two bunches of red flowers.

14. There are five people working in my section.

15. I would like to wash my hands.

16. There was a letter underneath the book.

17. I troubled my teacher to write a copy-book of the kana for me.

18. I studied under Mr. Smith.

19. (I guess) I will buy it if the price goes down.

20. There are four or five dollars in the blue wallet.

21. I climbed the mountain in the morning and came down it early in the evening.

22. I want four or five small cardboard boxes.

23. There are four pencils on the table.

24. My room is on the fourth floor.

25. I turned in the paper blank as it was, because I did not understand the questions.

271

26. That teacher went to Europe five years ago.

27. I understand that he intends to stay in America all his life.

28. That baby was born in February.

29. Have you ever eaten raw fish?

30. This fish is alive.

31. He drinks his whisky straight.

32. Excuse me for going first.

33. The point of the pen has become thick [= blunt].

34. I have to go to a town two kilometers from here.

LESSON 2

1. This book contains Lessons One through Thirty-five. Altogether there are thirty-five lessons.

2. It rained all day yesterday, so I did not go out but watched television (instead).

3. The British teacher of English who comes here every day can speak various foreign languages, such as French, Spanish, Italian, etc., in addition to English.

4. After studying the Japanese language, I mean to study the languages of other countries.

5. Who wrote this Japanese (-language) book?

6. The word "kataru" is hardly ever used in the spoken language.

7. Man has a mouth and a nose, two eyes and two ears, and two hands and two legs.

8. What (kind of things) do you do on a vacation?

9. "What date is it today?"

    "Why, it's the sixth."

10. Life is a matter of having both happy experiences and bitter experiences.

11. In New York there are many foreigners.

12. Please speak politely to your elders. You do not have to speak so politely to your juniors.

13. Enclosed with this letter is sample medicine.

14. This morning's news surprised the public.

15. How large is the population of Japan?

16. The entrance is this way.

17. This building needs repairing because it is (so) old.

18. "I would like to have two pairs of white shoes."

   "Can't you make do with one?"

19. I wrote so many letters that I ran out of paper.

20. The paper is in the second drawer from the top.

21. It is (only) a light rain, so I do not need an umbrella.

22. "Cold, isn't it?"

   "This, being midwinter, is the coldest time."

23. He went to Africa to study the life of the natives.

24. I hear that you hardly ever see the (naked) ground if you live in New York.

25. In Japan there are nine national holidays a year.

26. I would like to learn Chinese and (then) speak in Chinese with Chinese people.

27. I am learning the semi-cursive writing style with brush and Chinese ink.

28. All of sixty or seventy people gathered and held a party.

29. Please read (the text) from the third line on page five.

30. Watch your step.

31. The person who wrote this letter (is someone who) has good handwriting.

LESSON 3

1. It was very cold in February last year.

2. With the departure of the typhoon, the rain stopped falling, the wind died down, and the weather cleared.

3. There is a vacation in August every year.

4. That young man studies hard.

5. "How old are you?"

   "Nine."

6. I lost my father the year I came here from England.

7. The fourth from the right is Mr. Yamada.

8. Every week I work six days and rest one.

9. I plan to go see a play next Friday with my friends.

10. It is cold so please put more burning charcoal in the brazier.

11. In [When it gets to be] summer, we often go to see fireworks.

12. Let's read (our books) under the tree.

13. There are many big trees in that forest.

14. What is that white stone building over there?

15. Rice was counted by koku's.

16. River water flows downstream from upstream.

17. There are many trees on the bank of that river.

18. I will come again on the tenth of next month.

19. The twentieth of April is Tuesday.

20. The moon is out, so it is bright outside, too.

21. The Japanese people love viewing (cherry) blossoms and gazing at the full moon (of August).

22. They lost both their house and their rice field in last year's flood.

23. They draw water from the river to the rice paddy and plant rice.

24. A girl is wrapping red flowers in white paper.

25. I drank some water from a blue glass.

26. One cannot live without money.

27. These earrings are made of genuine gold.

28. The two big powers today are America and the Soviet Union.

29. I cannot drink such strong whisky.

30. That team is so strong that they always win.

31. I will call on you in the near future.

32. Mr. Ueda lives near Ōmori station.

33. That maid works hard.

34. The women's entrance is on the left-hand side of the building.

35. Over New Year's, we stay closed until the seventh.

36. That answer is correct.

37. Please cross the railway crossing after carefully looking right and left. [=Please look carefully to either side before crossing the tracks.]

38. Most people write with their right hands.

39. Japan is a mountainous country and has many forests and volcanoes.

40. I hear that Mr. Moriyama is a close friend of Mr. Tanaka.

41. Let me introduce my friend, Miss Honda.

42. Since Mr. Ōishi has studied many foreign languages, I expect he can write both English and French.

LESSON 4

1. That college student entered Tōkyō University last year and is now studying English.

2. "Study hard and play well."

3. I went to see a grade school in a little village in the Kantō District.

4. Who proofread this book?

5. There is a gathering of alumni [= an alumni reunion] every year.

6. In that part of the country, it is rainy in spring, sultry in summer, and it snows heavily in winter. Why don't you take your trip in autumn?

7. There are seven days in a week and thirty days in a month.

8. The width of that entrance is about a <u>ken</u>. One <u>ken</u> is about six feet.

9. The person between Toshiko and Haruko is Hanako.

10. Mr. Murata lives near the school in an apartment of only two rooms.

11. From this train we will soon be able to see Mt. Fuji.

12. In Japan, the four seasons are distinct.

13. I like traveling very much.

14. I am traveling alone, but I am not at all lonesome.

15. The moon rises in the east and sets in the west.

16. This is a poor village of few people, with mountains on every side.

17. Houses facing north are cold in winter.

18. That building has eight stories aboveground and two underground.

19. Please weigh this package.

20. His feet are sore. That's why he walks in a funny way.

21. The severeness of winter varies with the district.

22. It is icy, so walk carefully watching every step.

23. Vehicles keep to the right, so (people) please walk on the left.

24. "Who is he?"

   "I've met him before, but I can't recall his name."

25. I suppose people have to live in the midst of snow about four months (of the year) in some parts of the Tōhoku area.

26. The top of the mountain is all white with fresh snow.

27. If you go to Alaska, you can see icebergs.

28. I understand that the principal of this school has made many trips to foreign countries.

29. They say that man will live a longer and longer life span.

30. What is the longest river in Japan?

31. My eldest daughter is now studying French in Paris.

32. I (will) carry the luggage on a handcart.

33. Mr. Nagata's new car is a blue Chevrolet.

34. Could I make a stopover with this ticket?

35. I went to Kansai on a school excursion with my teachers and friends when I was in the ninth grade.

36. In older times, there were barriers here and there, where travelers were inspected.

37. He left for the west on the nine o'clock train from Tōkyō.

38. This room is hot from the afternoon sun, so let's move to a room facing south.

39. Brazil is a country in South America.

40. When it gets to be spring, the buds of trees and grass appear.

41. Happy New Year.

42. I bought this new book last week.

43. He is the newly elected mayor of this village.

44. They say that there are bears that eat men.

45. During the rainy season, it rains steadily day after day for a long period, and food spoils easily.

LESSON 5

1. I read an English-language newspaper every day.

2. You may write either in Chinese characters and kana or in roman letters.

3. In this region, there are a great number of villages of under two thousand population.

4. Please count the number of people who are now in this room.

5. Mathematics is the study of number(s).

6. Among the students who participated in the demonstration, eight hundred were freshmen, and three hundred were co-eds.

7. Please take this medicine before meals.

8. I learned kana a long time ago.

9. There is a little memo book in front of the telephone.

10. The school is this side of the station.

11. We say "Let us begin" before eating.

12. He went to London to study English literature.

13. He is studying the differences between all cultures, ancient and modern, Eastern and Western.

14. If you want to read the classics, you must study (additional) Chinese characters outside the Tōyō-kanji and also (study) the old kana spelling.

15. This area is very snowy.

16. I got hold of a rare old book the other day.

17. They deal not only in new cars but also in secondhand cars.

18. I think it will be all right, but if anything should happen I will let you know at once.

19. Leaves of trees from many thousand years ago have remained as fossils.

20. If all countries had the same language, we would be able to understand each other, and wouldn't that be nice?

21. The champions of all countries gather together at the Olympics.

22. He is an old acquaintance of mine, who has been teaching English at a junior high school for over ten years.

23. I am at home only on Saturdays and Sundays.

24. Since it is a small college, I guess that the number of the students enrolled in it is less than one thousand.

25. He is an acquaintance of mine.

26. This new doll can even walk.

27. The actor who takes the role of a woman in Kabuki is called onnagata.

28. That land has a long shape extending from north to south.

29. This dictionary is a memento of my deceased uncle.

30. I like reading, so even on the train I usually read.

31. My friend studied for a long time at a Japanese university, so he can read both Japanese classics and Chinese classics.

32. I have forgotten how to read this Chinese character.

33. I have read about snow country in the reader.

34. I met an unexpected person in an unexpected place.

35. Please let me hear your opinion.

36. What does that mean?

37. Both enemy and ally fought well.

38. How does it taste?

39. I heard a strange sound.

40. I can hear the beautiful sounds of a piano.

41. He has at last spit out the truth.

42. I know the on reading of this character, but I can't recall the kun reading.

43. "Cheerful, strong, and righteous" was the motto of my elementary school.

44. Nylon, dacron, and the like are new fabrics brought into being by chemistry.

45. There are no such things as ghosts.

46. We dance in couples.

47. In my class there is not a single girl student.

48. Nowadays, there are unions of workers in all sorts of companies.

49. He crossed his arms and sank into deep thought.

50. That gentleman (is a teacher and) teaches chemistry and is also engaged in alloy research.

51. The date of Mr. Nishimura's death is the fourth of September.

52. Man can live only about a hundred years at most.

53. I fled desperately.

54. I cannot make out what it means.

55. A pistol bullet had hit him in the leg, so we treated him immediately.

56. I have something to do; excuse me for leaving first.

57. That's no trouble at all.

58. Please get the meal ready.

59. The newspapers of today do not use the literary style as much as before.

60. There is a special form; please fill it out.

61. I hear that people in the old days studied by the light from the snow and the glow of fireflies.

62. It will be scandalous if you are heard by other people, so please do not quarrel so loud.

LESSON 6

1. If you are building a house, first you must choose a good location.

2. The landlord of that two-story house is an authority on Japanese classical literature.

3. The name of Don Quixote's retainer is Sancho Panza.

4. Is the light brown stone building over there a school?

5. He summoned the child with a wave of his hand.

6. I have been invited by an American university to study linguistics for a year there.

7. Thank you for inviting me to your delightful party.

8. Wait a minute.

9. I will be waiting for you in the waiting room at the station.

10. Let me have a word to say, too.

11. Would birds and beasts also have language?

12. Nylon is much more durable than silk. So it is practical.

13. Easier said than done.

14. It was only an excuse that he said he was sick; the truth of the matter, as I understand it, is that he cut school because he did not want to study.

15. About what month does the rice ripen?

16. I am very fond of cakes with nuts in them.

17. The Japanese drink tea a lot.

18. The Japanese living room is a place where the family gather to chat, eat, and so on.

19. Birds and beasts and trees and grass all are living things.

20. Mr. Imanishi is a biologist.

21. Without food, man cannot survive.

22. "The Tale of Genji" is a Japanese classic. It is very long so it is hard to finish (reading) it.

23. Please walk quietly. There is a sick person (here).

24. "We dig our graves with our teeth." (= Immoderate eating leads to illness.)

25. He is suffering from tuberculosis of the lungs.

26. From a slight cold he turned seriously ill.

27. That chemistry teacher is very popular with the students.

28. This fruit is nice and juicy.

29. His weakness is that he has a short temper and angers easily.

30. Everybody has strong points and weak points. [. . . mono da 'It is only natural that . . .']

31. An impatient man cannot do this kind of work.

32. My name is Yoshiko Yamada.

33. We have agreed to talk in Japanese as much as possible.

34. The book I ordered has arrived.

35. If you pour oil into the fire, it will flare up all the more.

36. It is a small house, so if you do not watch for it, you will miss it.

37. The "ga" in "hon ga aru [there is a book]" is nasal.

38. The elephant has a long trunk.

39. We're out of Kleenex.

40. He looks like his father around the eyebrows and nostrils.

41. Please place this ornament in the alcove.

42. Let's keep things we have no use for in the storage room.

43. You shouldn't stick out your tongue.

44. My child is still lisping. Especially the lingual sounds seem to be difficult for him.

45. Tōkyō-born people trill their R's.

46. This is a true story that really happened.

47. A good listener listens to the end of what the speaker has to tell.

48. I heard an old story from my grandmother.

49. "A good talker, a poor listener."

50. I hasten to inquire after your health.

51. This Chinese character is a simplified [abbreviated] one.

52. Some people abbreviate the "University of Pennsylvania" to "Penn."

53. There is a newspaper for boys and girls.

54. This is too little. Please give me some more.

55. Please push in a little closer.

56. I had lost my money and was in trouble.

57. The richer one becomes, the less rich one behaves.

58. That little girl has a doll in her hand.

59. My friend never gets over his chronic complaint, no matter how much he sees the doctor. I feel sorry for him.

60. This is such a small place that there is no room even for oneself.

61. In what cases do you use the word "okonau" instead of the word "suru?"

62. There must be a golf course around here open to everybody.

63. The letter I got from England today has the correct address, but my family name and personal name are reversed.

64. I understand he had an abstract painting hung upside down for a long time.

65. He is short-tempered and loses his head easily, so be especially careful not to offend him.

66. The cookies and cakes (sold) at that bakery are good.

67. Mt. Fuji can be seen from the roof of the school.

68. These days both land and houses keep rising in price.

69. That doctor is famous also as a literary man.

70. Medical science has improved to the point where most diseases can be cured.

71. My aunt is a woman doctor. Recently, quite a few women are studying medicine.

72. "Time" and the "Life" have lots of readers.

73. The number of those who travel abroad has increased.

LESSON 7

1. He is a bit odd, but not a bad person.

2. I hear that there is no change of seasons in Hawaii.

3. "I heard a strange noise; go and see (what it is)."

   "There is no sign of anything (unusual)."

4. Choose merchandise of a good quality.

5. That young lady is graceful.

6. The elder sister is graceful. The younger sister lacks grace.

7. He looks like a refined person in appearance, but I was quite surprised to hear him speak only about unrefined things once he started talking.

8. It is natural for things of good quality to be expensive.

9. If you do not like it at all, I will exchange it for this article.

10. I have seen some Chinese jugglery.

11. These rice-bowls come in a pair.

12. There was a pair of vases in the parlor.

13. I heard a dialogue in the Tōhoku dialect. I understood almost nothing.

14. The dialogue between Goethe and Eckermann is often read in colleges along with "Faust."

15. I will lose, if it is a fight between two persons.

16. I do not know of such a thing at all.

17. Wherever you go in Japan there is no place you will not find radios and newspapers.

18. That is a problem common to the whole nation.

19. Esperanto was created with the aim of a common language for the world.

20. There is no telling when we will be able to go to Communist China.

21. There are many nonresident students who commute by train.

22. I went to a coeducational junior high school.

23. Go on this street straight to the end, then turn right and it will take you to the main street. Get a policeman to show you the way from there.

24. Just when I was figuring my elder child was at last recovered after his lengthy doctoring, my younger child in turn fell ill.

25. To withdraw money, you need your name seal and your bankbook.

26. Tsūchō is also called kayoichō.

27. When you teach Japanese, you should let the students use English and think in English as little as possible.

28. I am going on a little errand; please wait.

29. In many cases, those old people who have never been taught the new kana spelling still use the older kana spelling.

30. Nobody but doctors can use this medicine.

31. The American Ambassador has arrived.

32. During the summer vacation, children make albums of dragonflies and butterflies.

33. What did you aim at when you shot the pistol?

34. "Study hard and play well" is the motto of the students here.

35. This baby weighs less than the average.

36. America is a country with a high standard of living.

37. This applies correspondingly to the following cases.

38. I suffered from a dreadful illness, and I am alive only thanks to a good doctor.

39. I went to the seashore and picked up some seashells.

40. I studied at a Christian college in Japan.

41. It is hard to learn, but it is harder to teach.

42. This failure was a good lesson for me.

43. I was born in California.

44. I have traveled in Kyūshū and Shikoku, to say nothing of Honshū.

45. There is a small shoal in the middle of the river.

46. I forgot to bring my lunch.

47. There are five petals on a cherry blossom.

48. You need not explain. Be careful from now on.

49. How many weeks are there in a year?

50. I went into detail so there would be no misunderstanding.

51. This letter is full of misspelling(s).

52. Please correct any mistakes you may find.

53. A child slipped and fell in the river.

54. I have been making him study the same lesson for a number of weeks, but, fool that he is, he never learns anything. If I have him write, he misspells; if I have him read, he misreads.

55. As scholars we differ in view, but we are good friends.

56. I hear that winter in Tōhoku is long and that they feel impatient waiting for the season when the snow melts.

57. I untied my tie.

58. What is the aim of archeology research?

59. I mean to fight for my life as far as this is concerned.

60. He is a person who never speaks ill of others.

61. He is not a person of ill will but he is sometimes misunderstood, as he speaks about anything without considering the place (where he may be).

62. Nazi Germany abused medical science to kill people.

63. Each person has a different personality.

64. I traveled through various countries in Europe and visited the biological research laboratories.

65. I am making a study of dialects, visiting around all parts of the country.

66. For a woman, she has an intense temper.

67. I will pawn some things and borrow money from the pawnbroker.

68. Stores that sell goods of bad quality will soon fail.

69. It is important to grasp the essentials of the matter.

70. The more I think of it, the more difficult it becomes.

71. I am not yet familiar with this area, so please show me around.

72. Some students are quick to comprehend but quick to forget, too.

LESSON 8

1. This is a reservoir for the Tōkyō water system.

2. The battery went dead, so I bought a new one.

3. "My name is Masako Koike. Nice to meet you."

   "I am Michiko Morita. How do you do."

4. They keep two cows.

5. "How about having beef sukiyaki?"

   "Wouldn't you rather have veal cutlet?"

6. Buffaloes are creatures of southern countries.

7. Whose turn is it next?

8. There are two guards at the entrance.

9. What is your house number? While I'm at it, please give me your phone number, too.

10. Though it is just the beginning of December, they are already selling January issues of magazines at the bookstores.

11. The newspapers carry the daily television and radio programs every day.

12. I am on duty tomorrow. I have to go to the office early in the morning.

13. My father is a Chinese calligrapher. His name as a calligrapher is Yūzan.

14. As it was big news, they printed an extra (edition).

15. "Taishō" is the name of the era between 1912 and 1926.

16. The impatient man is apt to lose his reason.

17. Excuse me.

18. This is a very impolite way of talking, don't you agree?

19. It was a slip of the tongue. Forgive me.

20. I bowed to the teacher and stepped out of the room.

21. He greeted the teacher with his eyes and made room for him.

22. I got a policeman to tell me the way.

23. The hanamichi [raised runway leading to the stage] is something indispensable in kabuki.

24. I cannot talk with a person who does not understand the reasons for things.

25. "I hear that he studied at an American college."

    "No wonder he speaks such good English."

26. I have something to do. Excuse me for leaving first.

27. We most fear fires. Please be careful with the fire of matches and cigarettes.

28. It is said that this fire started from carelessness (with fire).

29. What do you do at your office?

30. You should not loaf around neglecting your work.

31. Let's talk about it in a businesslike manner.

32. A long time ago, naturalized Chinese introduced Chinese culture to Japan.

33. I intend to go home by autumn or winter of next year.

34. I will stop by at Mr. Moriyama's place in Akasaka on my way home, for it is near where I get off the train.

35. From time to time, I take a one-day trip to Tōkyō to enjoy myself.

36. I hear your father is ill. How is he?

37. However much of a shortcut it may be, let's not drive up a hill like this.

38. It is said that life is like climbing a hill pulling a cart. If one relaxes the tiniest bit, the cart goes back down the hill one has gone to the trouble of climbing.

39. One day has twenty-four hours.

40. Usually I have a break from twelve-thirty to one-thirty for lunch, but occasionally I take an hour's rest at one o'clock.

41. It takes me an hour and a half to go home. But I commute every day by train.

42. It gets cold in the middle of October.

43. What you need to learn Chinese calligraphy is calligraphy paper, brushes, an ink-slab, and an ink-stick.

44. I want to enter that college. So I sent my application in.

45. My wish is to study at an American college.

46. Hello, please connect me with Mr. Hashimoto in (room number) 301.

47. Turn on the light.

48. What time is it now? I have to go to the transformer substation at four o'clock, so please let me know (when it is four).

49. As soon as the sun rises, I get up and quickly prepare breakfast.

50. What are you fussing about so early in the morning?

51. I came to Tōkyō from Kyōto last year. I am at Tōkyō University now.

52. For certain reasons, I take the liberty of excusing the morning class on Monday.

53. Kyōto is the old capital (of the Emperor).

54. I heard the noon siren.

55. Please call me at the office between 9:00 a.m. and 5:00 p.m.

56. Is this medicine to be taken before or after meals?

57. The last half of this book is uninteresting.

58. See you later.

59. A truck is coming up from behind.

60. Maids and servants are eating on the wooden floor.

61. They will put a pane of glass in the window frame.

62. The garage is on the other side of the big bridge.

63. Where(abouts) is Nihombashi?

64. Mr. Tamura wrote on the bulletin board of the R. R. station what he wanted to have his friends know.

65. Ill report [evil-speaking] spreads fast.

66. When convenient, please come see me.

67. He is traveling abroad at the moment.

LESSON 9

1. He deals in houses and land.

2. Christmas and New Year's sales have started. [Note: Kurisumasu to oshōgatsu-yōhin can be regarded as an abbreviation of Kurisumasu (-yōhin) to oshōgatsu-yōhin or as an anomalous formation to take the place of the expected *Kurisumasu to oshōgatsu no yōhin. It is possible to replace the expression with one large compound: Kurisumasu-oshōgatsu-yōhin.]

3. Teenagers love jazz.

4. As times change, ways of thinking also change.

5. If you do not like this article, I will refund your money.

6. It was inconvenient for me, so I had somebody go in my place.

7. I am supposed to go to Kyōto on behalf of my father.

8. If you get tired, I will take your place.

9. You will not be understood if you speak in such an old-fashioned manner in this age.

10. This is a house rebuilt in my father's generation.

11. Tōkyō and Kyōto are representative Japanese cities.

12. If you have a timetable, please let me have a look at it. I would like to know when the next train leaves.

13. Isn't this a pretty (book) cover?

14. I have written a chart of the new Chinese characters. [Or: I have written a new chart of Chinese characters.]

15. I will be waiting for you outside.

16. Which side of this cloth is the outside?

17. The Japanese people do not express their feelings as much as foreigners.

18. Miss Hirota is out.

19. You need a passport and a visa for leaving and entering a country.

20. Shukke means a Buddhist priest.

21. I hear that the daughter of that house has run away from home.

22. The moon has come out [or: up].

23. This is the entrance. Please drive your car out through the exit over there.

24. I told them recollections of my student days.

25. Today, there was an interview between the American Ambassador and reporters.

26. I keep my diary up faithfully every day.

27. I am reading the biography of a doctor who is spreading Christianity in Africa.

28. I am a reporter from the Yomiuri (Newspaper).

29. What kind of signs do you use to indicate the accent?

30. Please fill it in accurately.

31. I would like to know the exact number.

32. It is certain that he is coming home, but it is not yet definite in what month.

33. Please ascertain by phone whether he will come or not.

34. There is a big flower-shop behind my house. You will find my house easily if you use that as a landmark when you come.

35. I have always read only printed books. So I cannot read old manuscripts copied by hand.

36. I am correcting the proofs of a book.

37. Let us make sure once more whether there are any mistakes before we send it to be printed.

38. The proof-sheets have come. As might be expected from a reliable printing house, they are quite accurately done.

39. How many copies does the Asahi (Newspaper) print each day?

40. I believe in Christianity. [I am a Christian.]

41. You will lose people's confidence if you tell lies.

42. It may sound hard to believe, but I hear it is a true story.

43. Watch the signals.

44. I cannot say because I have no confidence (in the story).

45. I learned from the paper about the return of a friend I had not heard from for ten years, so I went to see him.

46. Opinion on political matters is called seiken [political views].

47. Women predominate among students who study home economy.

48. "Matsurigoto [governance]" is an archaic word.

49. That illness will probably take about a month to cure.

50. I would like to become a politician and rule the nation.

51. Police exist for the maintenance of peace in the country.

52. America is a land of credit (economy).

53. Have you ever listened to a Buddhist sutra?

54. This train goes to Aomori by way of Tōkyō.

55. I (will) play after finishing my homework.

56. I have to pay back the money I borrowed by the first of next month.

57. Mr. Furuta is the president of a big company, but he is also known as a sociologist.

58. Where there is a village, there is a shrine.

59. Since I go to church on Sunday, let's meet there.

60. He is studying English conversation.

61. The hall was too large for the people in back to hear.

62. The geisha is an entertainer peculiar to Japan: a woman who is engaged out to perform songs and dances.

63. Are the cultures of Japan and Europe fundamentally different?

64. It is a quarter past four now.

65. "Half" and "one half" are the same.

66. Do they teach fractions in elementary school?

67. Three percent of a hundred Yen is three Yen.

68. They divided the first-graders into two classes.

69. The first-graders are divided into two classes.

70. An editorial is the view of a newspaper (company).

71. There are many interesting tales among the old legends.

72. I have read a new theory advanced by a certain economist.

73. Most politicians go on a campaign tour when an election is approaching.

74. If I listen to a sermon on Christianity, being no Christian, I cannot understand it, no matter how much it is explained.

75. According to him, this montage is very well done.

· 76. I love to contribute to newspapers and magazines.

77. That team will lose because it lacks a good pitcher.

78. Don't throw things out the window.

79. I prefer nature sketching in person to taking photographs.

80. I can understand realistic paintings that are like photographs, but . . .

81. Please make an exact copy of this letter.

82. There is only one truth.

83. I have bought a coat with a deep red flower on it.

84. It is not so cold even in midwinter.

85. If the advertisement is clever, the demand for merchandise spreads.

86. I was surprised to see the vast lands of America.

87. A Father [priest] must not divulge a confession heard at church.

88. Every year we have to report our incomes.

89. He spoke his business hurriedly and left.

90. Safety first. Please take care.

91. There is no such thing as a completely safe vehicle.

92. Most cheap things are of bad quality.

93. They have sales all through the year, don't they?

94. This article is so expensive that there are no buyers.

95. I mean to go downtown to do some shopping in the afternoon.

96. The income for the month is called monthly revenue.

97. They give a receipt after receiving money.

98. A politician who has bribed people to get elected is no good.

LESSON 10

1. Let us begin reading with the page after the table of contents.

2. My second daughter is a high school student.

3. London is the second biggest city next to Tōkyō.

4. It dawns upon one gradually. [=One gradually comes to understand.]

5. Let us write the program of the meeting down in big letters and paste it up in some conspicuous place.

6. Losing comrades one after another on the battlefield, I kept thinking that it would be my turn next.

7. At the Olympics, the representatives from each country fought hard.

8. Every citizen has a duty to get an education.

9. She will bring up the baby.

10. The baby will be brought up.

11. A rational person can control his feelings.

12. The social systems are different, so we cannot adopt all the various American systems without modification.

13. Please say it again.

14. I drink a glass of water in one gulp.

15. In this part of the country, it is about seventy degrees even in summer.

16. I met an old friend in an unexpected place.

17. The university that I graduated from was under the old system.

18. Happy New Year. Please favor us with your patronage as you did last year.

19. I received a beautiful picture of the Swiss Alps.

20. He is a man of very high social standing, but he is not at all arrogant.

21. I hear that there are still men walking around with bowlers on in London. [Note: <u>Rondon ni</u> . . . <u>aruite iru</u> exceptionally has particle <u>ni</u> with action verb, which is here treated as if descriptive of a state.]

22. Japan had enjoyed a high culture from of old, but economically she was still an underdeveloped country even in the eighteenth century.

23. I ride second class when I travel by train. First class is too expensive.

24. If you travel by first-class trains and stay only at expensive hotels, it can not be said that you have seen the country.

25. In their eyes, obligation and duty are equivalent.

26. Unless your goods are of better quality, you won't be able to sell them.

27. One half of six and one third of nine are equal.

28. He has two sons. The elder is a grade-school teacher and the younger is a student.

29. He is very masculine.

30. Junior high school students go on a walking tour from time to time.

31. He has progressive ideas.

32. It would be distressing if the progress of physics led to the destruction of human life.

33. Red students marched on May Day.

34. If you do not quite understand, please review instead of going on.

35. I majored in economics at college.

36. This swimming pool is for women only.

37. Cigarettes are a monopoly; patented public companies produce and sell them.

38. There are few houses in America with gates.

39. I got the porter to unlock the gate.

40. I will get somebody to mail the letter in the mailbox at the gate.

41. That teacher is a specialist in Chinese calligraphy. He has lots of disciples.

42. I am a layman when it comes to Chinese calligraphy.

43. Without permission, I cannot go out on personal business while on duty.

44. A man of strong will does not change his mind in adversity.

45. As there are too many applicants, you are asked to take an examination.

46. I am studying with the aim to be a doctor.

47. I thank you for your good intention, but I cannot take the money. [-i-kaneru = -(r)u koto ga dekinai]

48. The representatives of the nation work in the Diet.

49. Let's all discuss it and then decide democratically.

50. I was taught the beauty of Japanese folk arts by a foreigner.

51. "The hearth of the people" means the national economy.

52. That statesman is popular among the people.

53. Do you mean that you can print in the morning paper the news you receive (by teletype) at 3:00 a.m.?

54. "Government of the people, by the people, and for the people."

55. Righteousness is naturally strong.

56. You ought not forget old obligations.

57. Lead a meaningful life!

58. I entered this company upon graduating from college.

59. I am traveling alone with no companions.

60. Several students did their research jointly.

61. I think we ought to get the cheaper one if both are of the same quality.

62. I have postponed my return home for a year, as I have not yet finished my work.

63. The picnic is to be postponed in case of rain.

64. A hundred scholars in all worked on this study.

65. Wanting to stay here a little longer, I got my visa extended.

66. I will give my opinion after listening to both parties impartially.

67. I am supposed to go to America on official business.

68. Please distinguish clearly between public and private matters in your thinking.

69. This holds nine cubic meters of water.

70. Let us consider it from the opposite standpoint, too.

71. Switzerland is a neutral country.

72. Risshun is the first day of spring.

73. It is etiquette for a man to stand up when a woman enters the room.

74. We rested a while in the shade of a summer grove.

75. "To raise one's bile" means "to run out of patience." [Note: The verb niyasu is little used except in this expression.]

76. I am head of the business department of the company.

77. He was admitted to the University Hospital.

78. In America they have the bicameral system of Senate and House of Representatives.

79. When I graduate from college next spring I plan to go to graduate school and study Japanese economics.

LESSON 11

1. I do not want to undertake such a job because I have no confidence I can do it.

2. I have confidence in myself as far as physics goes.

3. He has finally confessed his evil deeds.

4. Do things for yourself. (= Do not rely on others.)

5. He goes to work in his own car.

6. If you talk with Japanese only in Japanese every day, you will naturally become proficient in it.

7. Bi [beauty] and utsukushisa [beauty] mean almost the same thing.

8. She is no belle but there is something of intellectual beauty about her.

9. Gourmets get fat.

10. Lack of sunshine leads to illness.

11. I saw the news in electric lights on the newspaper building.

12. I brushed my shoes until they were shiny.

13. The contrast of light and darkness is beautiful.

14. He graduated from an American seminary [or: divinity school].

15. There are many beautiful buildings among the old shrines and temples.

16. "Danger past, God forgotten."

17. There are many shrines and temples in Kyōto.

18. November the fifteenth is the gala day for children of seven, five, and three years of age. Girls aged seven and three and boys aged five go with their mothers to pay homage at the shrines.

19. That is an old temple and nobody lives there now.

20. "The Canterbury Tales" are in the form of written versions of tales narrated one after another by the pilgrims to the Cathedral of Canterbury to amuse themselves on their way.

21. In the gardens of famous temples, there are well-tended trees, stones, and ponds.

22. I play at the schoolground.

23. I was brought up in a strict family.

24. Not only school education but also home education is important.

25. My father loves gardening. He works on his trees and flowers whenever he has a spare minute.

26. This road is under repair. You can't get through on it.

27. It is noisy near a factory.

28. We will have a carpenter build us a house.

29. What is the highest building in the world?

30. He has had no more than compulsory education but he has risen high in the world.

31. He is young and does not know the world.

32. He is young and does not know about the world.

33. In pre-modern Japanese literature, the puppet-show is an important genre.

34. There are both pains and sorrows on this earth.

35. This land is government property.

36. In Japan, there was a time in the eighth century when all land in the country was put under state ownership after the example of China.

37. Sholokhov is an internationally known author.

38. He forced her into it willy-nilly.

39. I investigated whether or not each family has a television set.

40. Some people have lots of money, but others have only a little.

41. Who is the owner of this article?

42. There are many famous sights in Kyōto.

43. He is a master of Japanese chess.

44. There are some diseases which even the best doctors cannot cure.

45. Please write down your name.

46. He is living like a daimyō [Japanese feudal lord].

47. We have selected two people as our representatives.

48. Mit-chan is her nickname. Her real name is Michiko.

49. The Italian Renaissance gave birth to many famous works.

50. The noted product of this area is soba [noodles].

51. I have to write a composition in Japanese every week.

52. This medicine brings on no bad side effects.

53. Please teach me how to make it.

54. This piece of sculpture is attributed to Michelangelo.

55. Who is the author of this novel?

56. The crop was good last year, but this year we had a poor harvest and got but few crops.

57. Both of them were sitting in silence.

58. He got home safely.

59. It is annoying of you to insist on such an impossibility.

60. He is usually taciturn, but he talks a lot when he drinks beer or the like.

61. He is a rude guy.

62. Is Tibet an independent country?

63. He became a famous scholar, educating himself.

64. I am studying German at the Japano-German Institute for Conversation.

65. That is a good university; they are especially noted for medicine.

66. The advantage of that machine is that you just push the button and need no man power.

67. Sliced raw fish is a dish peculiar to Japan, I guess.

68. Today I went to work at a discount section as an Arbeit student [= a student working his way through school].

69. This article is patented. No one can produce a copy without permission.

70. It cannot be helped.

71. That woman served God and never got married.

72. This radio receiver is wonderful. I wonder what kind of rig it has inside?

73. How many hours does it take a jet to fly from Tōkyō to New York?

74. The children waved to the locomotive engineer.

75. A train will not run without a locomotive.

76. I hear that women of old mostly wove and sewed their clothes themselves.

77. I would like to meet him if there is an opportunity.

78. I will see to it when the time comes.

79. They are waiting fully prepared.

80. The newspapers are printed by machine.

81. Wherever you go in the world, you come across goods made in Japan.

82. You can rely on the products of this company.

83. It is expensive because it is a special make.

84. I am working in a factory.

85. Among the eight hours' work, the hours I am actually at work are seven.

86. Thank you for your invitation. I will be very happy to come.

87. This factory deals with that company.

88. A man of progressive spirit is not afraid to take up new things one after another.

89. I have a dictation test tomorrow, so I have to study.

90. If you do any shopping, please get a receipt.

91. This radio is highly sensitive, and the sound is clear.

92. He is such a nice person!

93. He did evil under the influence of his evil friend.

94. The stubborn person will not easily say, "I have lost."

95. He is a wretched fellow without a bit of confidence.

96. The friendships born among those who have fought together on the battlefield last forever.

97. When you put on such a sad look, I grow sad, too.

98. I am ever so poor in English.

99. The cold does not cause me any distress.

100. Self-supporting students study with money they have worked for themselves.

101. The opposing team was strong and the game was close.

102. I do not like coffee because it is bitter.

103. I suffered from illness for a long time.

LESSON 12

1. He is a (high-) spirited lad.

2. What do they do in Japan on New Year's Day?

3. I can't do anything big because I lack capital.

4. Man is by nature a social animal.

5. A famous musician.

6. A pleasant picnic.

7. I will sit in the easy-chair.

8. I have no responsibility, I feel at ease.

9. Please feel at home.

10. I am looking forward to meeting you.

11. As it rained, I amused myself with music on records all day long at home.

12. The closing hour is 5:30 p.m.

13. I (will) play after I finish my homework.

14. I (will) play after my homework is done.

15. I (will) play after I do my homework all the way through.

16. After working all day at a factory I go to a night-school.

17. Something urgent has come up. I have to go home in a hurry.

18. Please finish this work in a hurry.

19. The special express is the fastest express train. The semi-express is slower than the express.

20. It's been suddenly decided that I should go to America. [= All of a sudden I'm supposed to go to America.]

21. I go to the seashore during the hot season.

22. This room has small windows. So it is sultry in here even at night.

23. In that part of the country, both hot and cold seasons are extreme.

24. I am concerned for your health in this hot season.

25. The moon on the fifteenth night [= the full moon] is round.

26. School (held) at night is called night-school.

27. Do not stay out till midnight.

28. In Japan, the four seasons are distinct.

29. The rainy season in Japan is in June.

30. Fruits in season are delicious.

31. Please read Section I.

32. How does the melody go?

33. His fingers have large joints.

34. I carried such heavy luggage yesterday that all the joints in my body are sore today.

35. Tonight the rain and the wind will be raging.

36. Nowadays windmills are seldom used.

37. I got ill from standing in the cold wind.

38. It is awfully windy.

39. He is an eccentric.

40. Have you become somewhat used to Tōkyō's kamikaze taxies?

41. Hawaii is in the Pacific Ocean.

42. She's a nice plump baby, isn't she?

43. I am all right when it is cold, but I get sick as soon as it is hot.

44. You can't expect water to flow in a level place.

45. I would like you to listen to both parties impartially.

46. Let's share it equally.

47. It looks flat, but it is not level.

48. I sat down on a flat stone and rested.

49. I think the ways of thinking must be different in the West and the East.

50. They serve good Western food at that restaurant.

51. I went from New York across the Atlantic Ocean to London.

52. While I was in Paris, I bought myself many Western books.

53. Seawater is salty.

54. As far as travel abroad goes, I have been to Hawaii once and that is all.

55. The sea is in view. [= You can see the sea.]

56. Fortunately, a train with plenty of room came along right away.

57. There are those unfortunate moments when you just can't get anything done successfully.

58. This is my destiny. It cannot be helped.

59. They will carry the luggage on a truck.

60. The temperature is high, but it is not sultry.

61. We swim in a heated pool.

62. Right now the temperature of this room is 67 degrees.

63. American farmers generally have large farmlands. So their way of doing things is different from Japanese farming.

64. This year's rice crop is extremely poor. Even the farmers may not be able to eat rice.

65. Brazil, Argentina, Chili, Peru, etc. are all in South America.

66. This cleaned rice is some of the first crop of the year which has just been harvested.

67. I am but a beginner. Please teach me everything.

68. Speak up if there is anything you need.

69. This book is something every high school student should be sure to read.

70. Please be sure to come by eight o'clock.

71. This job requires careful attention.

72. The total number of days required for this job was three hundred.

73. He is a key figure in the political world.

74. I cannot drink, because I have a bad stomach.

75. Tonight I am going into a hospital which specializes in alimentary disorders for my gastroenteritis.

76. It is pleasant to travel with good friends.

77. Mr. Murayama is a good friend of mine.

78. There's quite a likeness between that man and his child, isn't there?

79. That girl has been accustomed to horses and cows from childhood; she is not at all afraid of them.

80. Unparalleled beauty.

81. I have many relatives in Tōkyō.

82. Please sort them by size.

83. Culture looked at from the standpoint of anthropology.

84. Sound waves with a long wave length produce low sounds.

85. It was too hot, and we fell sick one after another, to our distress.

86. This meeting goes on for a week.

87. The rainy season lasts about a month.

88. I plan to continue my studies [= to stay in school] for another year.

89. I have finally finished the red tape to travel abroad.

90. A continuation [= The next installment] of this novel will be published next month.

91. I bought a square table.

92. Please measure (the degree of) the three angles of this triangle.

93. The horns of a bull.

94. (Mr.) Tanaka, what did you study at college?

95. He dislikes liquor and tobacco, he never jokes: he is like a Confucian gentleman (= a saint).

LESSON 13

1. Be careful about pronunciation.

2. The publishers of this book are in Kyōto.

3. He is an expert pistol shot. I hear he never misses.

4. I am leaving from Chicago by the 4:30 p.m. train.

5. A new theory was presented at the conference.

6. This letter is confidential. No one but the person addressed should read it.

7. You (will) enjoy the landscape from your observation car.

8. This place has developed rapidly since the big factory was built.

9. I have something important to tell you.

10. These are double cherry-blossoms; they have lots of petals.

11. He carried a heavy load.

12. The representative of a nation should behave himself.

13. Mr. Hara is (a merchant) in foreign trade. He deals with companies in South America.

14. Foreign trade means exporting and importing with foreign countries.

15. I can read easy books.

16. An Eki-diviner is a person who tells fortune by the Book of Changes.

17. Pardon my asking, but what business are you in?

18. I am a small (-scale) merchant who sells vegetables and fruits.

19. Kagi-kakko ["Key" brackets] set off quotations.

20. The water of the sea ebbs and flows by the pull of the moon.

21. Please pull that door.

22. A pickpocket was caught in a department store.

23. It is cheap to process things in Japan but transportation costs a lot because of the distance.

24. I (will) advance in the same direction.

25. Man should improve himself.

26. I (will) look down.

27. The person on the right as you face them.

28. A house facing south.

29. Cotton wool is the raw material of cotton fabric.

30. I (will) put thick wadding in the mattress.

31. There are many women among the weavers at the textile factory.

32. Handwoven silk is expensive.

33. The price goes up.

34. He sells it at a special price.

35. It is a good book; it deserves a reading.

36. It is worth five thousand Yen.

37. Turn off the radio. There is too much static.

38. I want two miscellanea [= all-purpose] notebooks.

39. A forest of various trees.

40. I have too many miscellaneous chores to get ahead with my job.

41. Have you ever seen a Japanese gold coin?

42. Small household goods are called notions.

43. I came to Japan on a freighter of an American ship company.

44. I had a continuously pleasant voyage from the time I boarded at Los Angeles till I got off at Honolulu.

45. The captain, being a man who had traveled in many countries, told us many interesting stories.

46. In older times, people crossed rivers by ferryboat.

47. The population of Tōkyō is increasing rapidly.

48. With the heavy rain, the water in the pond increased.

49. We (will) join the labor union.

50. We (will) join the labor union.

51. Please add a little milk.

52. The original cost is high. So we (will) sell it at a high price.

53. The Colorado plateau is cool even in summer.

54. (It is) a vast field.

55. This is just as it is in the original text.

56. If you make a private phone-call, please pay the cost.

57. Admission (is) free.

58. (She is) a wife who cooks well.

59. I will buy butter at the grocery store.

60. They brew beer with malt.

61. Wheat is the material for bread.

62. I (will) wear a straw hat.

63. He speaks fairly good English.

64. There must be some job for a child that is suitable for a child.

65. Is the exchange rate for a dollar currently 360 Yen?

66. He suffered a loss on the stock market.

67. He is an heir of a rich family.

68. The biggest department store in the world.

69. The best present.

70. The newest machine.

71. A recent photograph.

72. This is our last meeting. [I'm afraid we will not be able to see you again.]

73. A man of position.

74. He took a degree at Yale University.

75. Mr. Aihara is higher in position.

76. That apartment is poorly located.

77. There are various opinions about it, but no fixed theory yet.

78. What sort of work would you like to do?

79. As there are too many applicants, an examination will be given.

80. I was disappointed in that man.

81. He died in disappointment, unable to attain his ambition.

82. It is desirable to have broad vision.

83. He was so wretched, I could not look at him directly.

84. He ruled in disregard of the feelings of the people.

LESSON 14

1. I graduated from college and joined an export-import business.

2. I am hesitating what to do.

3. My occupation is physician.

4. A factory worker.

5. He is working at a pleasant post.

6. He is living with his friend.

7. The residents of this apartment are all men.

8. He is in the living room.

9. My office is on the third floor.

10. Department stores usually have a bargain basement.

11. We (will) learn the musical scales.

12. He took bitter medicine. [He swallowed a bitter pill.]

13. I bought some eyedrops [eye lotion] at a drugstore.

14. This is gunpowder. Please be careful.

15. What kind of seasonings do you use in this dish?

16. ˙I heard it from a direct source. [This is straight from the horse's mouth.]

17. A right angle is ninety degrees.

18. I cannot go home tonight because I am on duty.

19. Honest people do not tell lies.

20. Please correct my pronunciation.

21. This train will connect at Tōkyō with the one bound for Aomori.

22. I will make my request through a third person, as it is embarrassing to speak (to him) directly.

23. They will serve tea.

24. Thank you for your kindness.

25. I've cut my hand with a knife.

26. I (will) stick a stamp on the envelope.

27. The bargain goods are all gone.

28. Next year's plan has not been settled.

29. I have decided next year's plan.

30. Problems of that sort have already been solved.

31. We have come to the following conclusion.

32. Forgive me, please, for I will never steal again.

33. I'm paying rent for the apartment on a monthly basis.

34. I (will) go down to the valley.

35. I (will) wash my hands in the mountain stream.

36. Be sure to write address and name.

37. Housing, food, and clothing are important to life.

38. Where do you live?

39. Among the residents of Tōkyō there are many from places all over the country.

40. I am not fond of living in the country(side).

41. There's no special news.

42. Please wrap it separately.

43. It is a different person.

44. He is separated from his wife.

45. He lives apart from his wife.

46. It has no special meaning.

47. Since he lost his child he has become like a different person.

48. Where is the wharf for the ferry?

49. This train was seven minutes late.

50. A beautiful dress.

51. I just arrived today.

52. At last they have started to build the great building.

53. We wash the outer garments and the underwear separately.

54. Both the North Pole and the South Pole are places hard to live at.

55. Japan is a country in the Far East.

56. This is a paradise on earth.

57. The coldest season is upon us.

58. They (will) carry the luggage on a horse cart.

59. They ride horses at a riding stable.

60. This building was originally a stable.

61. There is [or: They have] a watchdog.

62. He is fond of dogs. He keeps many of them—Japanese dogs, European dogs, puppies, etc.

63. This Chinese character has a low frequency of use.

64. The next meeting will be held in Kyōto.

65. We (will) go around the pond.

66. Please do not say things in a roundabout way.

67. I'm hard up for money.

68. Let's try again.

69. I (will) spin the top.

70. I will wear a kimono and an obi.

71. A policeman wearing a pistol.

72. Fifteen families live in this apartment building.

73. A job fit for a woman.

74. I am hard put to it to find a suitable house.

75. They eat moderately.

76. He built a school with his own money.

77. He has no property.

78. National finances have grown stringent.

79. I (will) bear a child.

80. I (will) bear a child.

81. The cotton textiles produced in that factory are all goods meant for export.

82. The local specialty of Tōkyō is dried seaweed.

83. I lost my money.

84. It was a slip on my part. I apologize.

85. In autumn the leaves fall.

86. He flunked because he did not study.

87. A beautiful sunset.

88. I scribbled in my notebook.

89. My real father died before I was born.

90. He is an official in a government office.

91. It is my job to type.

92. My English proved useful in getting a job with an export-import firm.

93. Not being able to stand the hard work any longer, he collapsed [got sick].

94. What kind of job do you have?

95. You cannot understand it if you think in the old manner.

96. A daimyō [feudal lord] attended by many retainers.

LESSON 15

1. The sea and the land.

2. Man lives on land.

3. There are many countries on the European Continent.

4. The jet landed safely.

5. Italy is a peninsular country.

6. That island is uninhabited.

7. Japan is an insular country with many little islands.

8. You must not play around here.

9. Be sure to date your letters.

10. It was annoying to have the chewing gum stuck on.

11. If you cut your finger, apply some medicine at once.

12. A letter full of blank spaces.

13. Let's buy more than just what we need.

14. It is a building more than a thousand years old.

15. Please throw away the leftover food.

16. There are over a hundred students in this school.

17. Children grow fast.

18. They (will) compose an economic "white paper."

19. What are the ingredients of this medicine?

20. Japan is comprised of islands of various sizes.

21. I see people at the office.

22. Oil is floating on the surface of the water.

23. I was attacked and slashed from the front by a hoodlum.

24. I (will) dance with a mask on.

25. I (will) rise in men's eyes. [Or: I (will) raise my eyes.]

26. A beautiful woman with an oval face.

27. I am ashamed. I am to blame for it. [It was negligence on my part.]

28. When you multiply three by three, the product is nine.

29. How much area does this land comprise?

30. He is progressive by nature.

31. The snow has reached a three-meter depth on top of the mountain.

32. The snow accumulates.

33. I want to put up new curtains. Please give me an estimate of the cost.

34. They pile books up in a great heap.

35. I'll be traveling about a month.

36. Please use water sparingly.

37. (The island of) Guam is American territory.

38. He is the American Consul.

39. Uketori [receipt] and ryōshūsho are the same thing.

40. This is a new job for me; please teach me what I need to know.

41. He is a pretty sharp fellow.

42. A man lacking quick wits keeps failing.

43. Japan lost World War II and became a defeated country.

44. I was totally defeated in the game.

45. I lost the game.

46. How were the results of the examination? [= How did the exam turn out?]

47. Two unions combined to form a new union.

48. I (will) put on a tie.

49. I can't get it untied; the knot is too tight.

50. Conclusion. [= Concluding remarks.]

51. Fruit is good for you [= for one's health].

52. He has done his duty. [He has successfully completed his work.]

53. I (will) command a force.

54. There is no obligation of military service.

55. He was a (Naval) seaman.

56. I find nothing to blame.

57. I regret my former misconduct and intend to go straight.

58. In case of emergency, please push this bell.

59. This is a very big problem.

60. This is non-merchandise; we cannot sell it.

61. We learn conversation necessary for everyday life.

62. His conduct is not normal, is it?

63. We are always watchful about the children's behavior.

64. The percentage is high. [= It is very profitable.]

65. Hyakubun-ritsu [percentage] is also called pāsentēji.

66. I will speak frankly.

67. He takes the leadership of other people in dispatching work.

68. One million is a hundredth of one hundred million.

69. He made money in the stock market and became a billionaire.

70. A teacher takes his pupils for an outing [= picnic or hike].

71. A friend came to see me from afar.

72. The road is under repair. We have to make a detour.

73. Please don't beat around the bush but speak frankly.

74. The word "kuon" is seldom used in spoken (Japanese).

75. You ought to think of the world situation.

76. We lost because the odds were against us.

77. Water gushes out from the faucet.

78. I bought a copy of the newspaper.

79. Please type three copies. [Please make two carbon copies.]

80. He was a member of the music club while at college.

81. A part of this building was added afterwards.

82. Union headquarters.

83. They cultivate the farmland and sow wheat.

84. There are horses for farming.

85. A realistic idea.

86. What is your present address?

87. I have my own idea, but I cannot express it well.

88. I have my own idea, but I cannot express it well [or: I can't put it in the right words].

89. The appearance [= coming] of Christ.

90. The moon appeared from behind the clouds.

91. At present the students of this school are two thousand (in number).

92. I went to see the construction site.

93. My father is away at the moment.

94. As I had no children of my own, I adopted a son.

95. He is a highly cultured gentleman.

96. I work to support my children and wife.

97. My mother is convalescing from her illness.

98. As I studied hard, I got good marks.

99. Please study this point some more.

100. Farmhouses lie scattered on the vast field.

101. The examination grades were poor.

102. They make books in braille for the blind.

103. I will light the gas stove.

104. I have a question.

105. School is not the only place one can acquire learning.

106. I will answer the question.

107. I will answer if asked.

108. The title of a book.

109. What is today's topic?

110. I have a problem bothering me.

LESSON 16

1. We gather around the teacher and talk together.

2. I will slip out of the circle of people.

3. I will explain first the main points and then the details.

4. Isn't the work(manship) of this ring marvellous?

5. A narrow road.

6. An oblong table.

7. Do you have any (small) change?

8. I will tell you the details later.

9. He is sick, so his pulse is fast.

10. There is hope in this talk.

11. The mountain ranges of Colorado.

12. The cutting of an artery can cause death.

13. There are few long rivers in Japan.

14. The Suez Canal.

15. I saw a glacier in Switzerland.

16. Generally there is a harbor near the mouth of a big river.

17. Fashions originate in Paris.

18. Fashionable dresses.

19. Please be careful of [because there is] the strong electric current.

20. You can trust (it if it's one of) the better department stores.

21. The tide that flows around here is a cold current.

22. This is a fast-running river.

23. They float wood downstream from upstream.

24. Electricity includes alternating current and direct current.

25. In older times exiling a person who committed an evil act to a far-away island was called onru [banishment].

26. We (will) go to an outdoor concert.

27. This is a wild dog; it is dangerous.

28. There are vast prairies in America.

29. Wild flowers.

30. We (will) play catch(-ball) in the field.

31. I (will) stress the main points of the problem.

32. That novel is a recent effort.

33. An atomic energy research center.

34. I cannot do heavy work.

35. He is physically strong.

36. The bus service is good.

37. Men's Room.

38. A convenient [= well-located] apartment house.

39. You can send it by boat cheaper but it takes time.

40. If you borrow money there, the interest is high.

41. They borrow money at usurious rates.

42. I (will) use airmail.

43. This medicine is injurious under prolonged use.

44. Alcohol is harmless if taken in moderation.

45. I have a complaint.

46. He lives in an inconvenient house.

47. You must not act unjustly.

48. A restricted [= hampered, inconvenient] life.

49. He is a person who never does anything unfavorable to himself.

50. I will pay the remainder [= unpaid balance] later.

51. As means of transportation, there are boats, airplanes, and automobiles.

52. I will ask the policeman at the police-box for the way.

53. You should not take diplomatic language at face value.

54. They talked about the diplomatic problems between Japan and America.

55. I am tired. Please take my place.

56. Good things and bad things are mixed together.

57. We learn foreign languages by associating with foreigners.

58. Wool is best as far as warmth goes.

59. It is necessary to keep a constant temperature at all times.

60. It is necessary to secure rice for the nation.

61. An anti-Communist and pro-American man.

62. The opposite of "expensive" is "cheap," and the opposite of "big" is "small."

63. This pistol has little recoil.

64. That group is reactionary.

65. He has five tan of riceland. [One tan = .245 acres.]

66. Please choose a tan or two (of cloth) for a kimono. [One tan = about twelve yards, one roll of cloth.]

67. Man, too, is an animal in the larger sense.

68. They use power to run machines.

69. You must not move.

70. He is a person who faces emergencies calmly.

71. Automobiles are really convenient.

72. A beautiful movement.

73. There are two big airports in New York.

74. The ship arrives at the port.

75. He goes to a lakeside hotel for his vacation.

76. He fishes in the lake.

77. Many volcanic lakes are deep though small.

78. There are many fires in the mountain forests from the shortage of rain.

79. Forests where no human can live.

80. The house is in the forest.

81. There are agriculture and forestry schools for learning agriculture and forestry.

82. Rare plants are grown.

83. Errors in printing are called misprints.

84. We have the gardener work on the plants.

85. Rice transplanting is done before the rainy season.

86. There were many colonies in Asia and Africa.

87. There are many kinds of cherry blossoms.

88. There still remain racial problems in the American South(land).

89. They sow wheat.

90. There are all sorts of articles in department stores.

91. The weather [= climate] is fine.

92. The peaceful use of atomic energy.

93. I prefer a Japanese-style house.

94. The misunderstanding was cleared up and they made peace.

95. The cold eases.

96. I want to get Japanese-English and English-Japanese dictionaries.

97. There are twenty-three wards in Tōkyō. Each has its ward office.

98. You can't tell them apart, they look so much alike.

99. We distinguish between public and private.

100. They divided Tōkyō into twenty-three wards.

101. He came to Japan on a JAL [Japan Air Line] jet.

102. They continued a pleasant voyage.

103. The air is stuffy. Open a window.

104. The air turns mild.

105. The sky clouds up.

106. He will fill a political gap.

107. Please fill in the blanks.

108. It is a vacuum so there is no air.

109. We will not stop before achieving our aim.

110. He will not stop until he achieves his goal.

111. Physics has made splendid progress.

112. He studied hard and made great progress.

LESSON 17

1. I (will) show the guest into the parlor.

2. A visitor came so I could not go out.

3. The development of the passenger plane has brought the world closer [together].

4. They distinguish precious gems from worthless stones.

5. The stone in that ring is a rare one, isn't it?

6. A polka-dot skirt.

7. A pond where there are swans and many other aquatic birds.

8. He is famous as an ornithologist.

9. An aviator who flew nonstop across the Pacific Ocean.

10. Birds sing.

11. You can see the red gateway of the shrine.

12. Such a difficult job can't be done in a single day.

13. I'm going visiting at about five o'clock in the early evening.

14. A country where parliamentary government is in force.

15. He is in conference, so please wait a moment.

16. He lives in a fine house with a gate.

17. I have set up a new residence at the following address.

18. Society is comprised of people gathered together.

19. This novel has an interesting plot.

20. I keep [or: raise] goldfish.

21. It is in fashion to keep tropical fish.

22. At the fish market, they deal in fish.

23. Tōkyō and Kyōto are major cities.

24. Municipal government is the responsibility of the mayor.

25. Southeast Asia is a good market for goods made in Japan.

26. The greengrocer's market is the marketplace for vegetables and fruits.

27. A municipal college.

28. I was caught in the rain and got drenched all over.

29. His height is one meter and seventy centimeters.

30. He is still single.

31. A person of high social position.

32. See that what you wear is always clean.

33. I will put (table-)salt on the table.

34. Japan is surrounded by sea, so that there are many saltworks which extract salt from the seawater.

35. As luck would have it, my house burned to the ground by a (spreading) fire.

36. A famous temple was destroyed in a careless fire.

37. I (will) bake bread.

38. The bread has been baked.

39. Look at the beautiful sunset sky.

40. He eats only vegetables and no meat or fish.

41. We buy greens at the grocer's.

42. This is not drinking water; you can't drink it.

43. He is a (sake) drinker, but he is not a drunkard.

44. Sake is a wine made from rice.

45. It is expensive to drink and eat at bars.

46. At wineshops they usually sell salt, canned goods, and the like, as well as liquors.

47. I am sick and have no appetite.

48. For a politician he is a person curiously free of avarice.

49. It will be useless to go to school if you have no will to learn.

50. Peace which the nation desires.

51. I bathe myself in cold water.

52. This year's frost damage in Hokkaidō was terrible.

53. Eat quickly before your food gets cold.

54. I want to drink some cold beer, so put some on ice.

55. I cannot subscribe to such a theory.

56. I praise God.

57. As I have received the approval of many people, I have decided to go at it in this manner.

58. Even Americans seem to eat raw shellfish.

59. Let's make fried rice for supper.

60. I apologize that it is only boiled wheat and rice, but please eat with me.

61. Every morning I go to the workers' mess-hall by six o'clock.

62. "Please give me an estimate."
    "Yes, I will."

63. I will take your orders.

64. His body is hot with what seems to be a fever, so please take his temperature.

65. He is so wrapped up [= completely absorbed] in football that he doesn't study at all.

66. When you heat iron it gets red.

67. This watch is slow.

68. How much is the total?

69. I was trapped and I lost [or: failed].

70. One's plans for the year should be made on New Year's Day.

71. Twelve thousand-yen.

72. A circular building.

73. I will draw a circle.

74. He has fairly large savings.

75. I will go deposit the money.

76. I will take care of your coat and hat.

77. I will check my suitcase for a while at the checkroom.

LESSON 18

1. I have received a fresh supply of goods.

2. I carry the baggage in both hands.

3. I (will) take the green vegetables from the field by wagon.

4. That kind of work is a heavy load for a child, isn't it?

5. I'll call on you in a day or two.

6. My parents live in the country.

7. I cannot do both at once.

8. We name [= designate] a representative.

9. The fingers of the hand have names: thumb, index finger, middle finger, ring [medicine] finger, and little finger.

10. The capital of Japan is Tōkyō.

11. After killing a man he surrendered himself to the police.

12. Churchill was for a long time England's Prime Minister.

13. I will fire him.

14. We will compete for first place.

15. Watches are usually worn on the left wrist.

16. A handy tool.

17. The brakes on this car aren't working right, so I must take it to a garage.

18. I suffered a severe wound and became disabled.

19. I (will) use new farm equipment to plow the soil.

20. I work in the fields from early morning.

21. I was surprised when I saw America's huge wheat fields.

22. Have you ever heard the Japanese national anthem?

23. The songs that singer sings are mostly boatmen's songs.

24. I can't swim.

25. In spite of being in poor condition, he swam hard and won first place.

26. I am scared to swim where it is deep.

27. Deep-sea fish.

28. I am busy so I work late into the night.

29. What kind of animals are there deep in the mountains of that part of the country?

30. I (will) measure the depth of the river.

31. The mother with the baby on her back is shopping.

32. It is my loss. [= It is a loss for me.]

33. We call a number smaller than zero a negative number.

34. We (will) play in the park.

35. A beautiful flower garden.

36. Tōkyō has both a famous zoo and a famous botanical garden.

37. I (will) act according to directions.

38. The teacher set the example.

39. I (will) begin my work after careful preparation.

40. I want a furnished apartment.

41. I am ill at ease unless there are preparations.

42. We receive guests in the reception room.

43. He showed an unexpected reaction.

44. I buy books according to the need.

45. Mere learning of theory is no use to you unless you can put it to practical application.

46. Work begins at 9:00 a.m.

47. We maintained a steady friendship.

48. Well, let's start studying.

49. The football season has begun.

50. Urgent business came up so I sent a telegram.

51. How many hits were there in today's game?

52. He said something impolite so I gave him a slap.

53. He made a lot of mistakes so I fired him.

54. They (will) set up a foreign policy with respect to the United States.

55. A big incident has come up so we must think out a counterplan at once.

56. On this matter I can say no more than this.

57. The person in charge will hear your business.

58. I have absolutely no connection with this matter.

59. The travel leader deals with the travelers.

60. I (will) hand down the final decision.

61. Since I alone made the decision, I will bear the full responsibility.

62. We (will) sever relations.

63. I have given up smoking.

64. I assert it with firm conviction.

65. I cannot do such a thing; I am sorry, but I refuse.

66. I was refused my request.

67. You cannot remove the furnishings without notice.

68. There was a homicide.

69. Suicides among young people are quite numerous.

70. A disturbed society where killings and arson are frequent.

71. A stormy atmosphere fell on the assembly hall.

72. You should not let the dog loose (in the fields).

73. I release birds into the sky.

74. You must not blurt out stupid things; think before you speak.

75. We write sentences.

76. Please start reading from the first chapter.

77. A (personal) seal is necessary in order to deposit money in a bank.

78. Since my income is small I do side jobs.

79. This book has an interesting title, but the content is dull.

80. It is better if one does not have a relative working at the same place with one.

81. I will decide after taking various factors into consideration.

82. The volume is nine cubic meters.

83. I got a permanent at that beauty parlor.

84. It is not easy to climb a hill with a heavy burden.

85. The National Diet is a legislative organ.

86. We must observe the law.

87. I study Japanese grammar.

88. There is no other way than this.

89. He is a student at the Tōkyō University Law School.

90. This replica is very well done, just like the real thing.

91. Please make a copy of this letter.

92. A complex problem.

93. This job is so complicated I cannot explain it briefly.

LESSON 19

1. The American President lives in the White House, and he is in a position to exercise general control over the United States.

2. From (taking) statistics, they say that women have longer lives.

3. It is very difficult to unify kana spelling.

4. An action which ignored tradition.

5. Japan possesses two thousand years of tradition.

6. (He is) a great statesman who leads the people.

7. One must not make fools of the masses.

8. I am telephoning from a public telephone in the park.

9. Looking at them it is easy to tell they are parent and child [or: father and son], isn't it?

10. Among items which are similar to one another there are some which are of poor quality, so be careful.

11. We display warrior dolls on May fifth.

12. I am hoping for a peaceful world where military power is not thought necessary.

13. Bushidō is the way a warrior must follow.

14. We call pianos, organs, violins, etc., musical instruments.

15. At home we use both Western and Japanese tableware.

16. Water conforms to the shape of its container.

17. We manufacture instruments which doctors use.

18. That singer has personality.

19. Apples at fifty yen apiece.

20. We place great importance on the life of an individual.

21. I played shōgi with Mr. Hayashi, but neither of us won.

22. A gold medal is an emblem of victory.

23. I (will) visit scenic spots.

24. Which team will win?

25. He is a selfish person, isn't he?

26. We (will) enter by the kitchen entrance.

27. The plot of this novel is stereotyped and lacks novelty.

28. That [= He] was a model of a warrior.

29. It is glassware made in a mold. [= It is molded glass.]

30. A large-size car.

31. On what basis do you select students?

32. If you do not know the traffic regulations, you cannot drive a car.

33. Please obey the rules without fail.

34. Water, following the laws of nature, flows from high places to low places.

35. As a basic rule in teaching Japanese to foreigners, we use Japanese only.

36. Long ago there was class distinction between warriors, farmers, artisans, and merchants, and the warrior's social status was the highest.

37. The Japanese Army's morale was excellent.

38. Diet members work at the National Diet.

39. This photograph has been considerably retouched.

40. An automobile repair shop.

41. We took a school excursion under the leadership of the teacher.

42. I understand that the training to become a Catholic priest is strict.

43. I pursued four years of study and graduated from college.

44. The contest over, both friends and enemies joined hands.

45. He seems to hold a grudge against Mr. Mori.

46. Rain has not fallen for a long time, so please pay attention to fire prevention in the forests.

47. We (will) get our winter clothing [or: cold-weather gear] ready and go off on a ski trip.

48. We defend ourselves against a foreign enemy.

49. I'm studying Oriental art.

50. I will attend an academic conference.

51. I was operated on at the hospital.

52. I'm off to practice my golf.

53. The men students were regularly obliged to receive military training at college.

54. We train military dogs.

55. There was a student demonstration which filed through the city of Tōkyō.

56. We learn the language of an enemy nation.

57. I practice writing with a pen.

58. We practice pronunciation.

59. If it is a book necessary for your studies I will buy it for you.

60. I am studying piano (playing) and flower arranging.

61. Animal habits.

62. I follow convention.

63. I am apprenticed to a cook.

64. Workmanship in pure gold.

65. A spotless white sweater.

66. I lead a purely Japanese-style life.

67. Children are unsophisticated.

68. The military man takes good care of his sabre.

69. I was struck by a wooden sword.

70. I will sharpen the pencil with my penknife.

71. A warrior wearing two swords.

72. I have seen no bamboo in America, but is there none in Europe either?

73. I have known Mr. Tanaka since we were kids together.

74. I bought a bamboo workbasket.

75. He is a hero of the Second World War; I hear that he fought very bravely.

76. Saying he would definitely win and return home, he departed in high spirits.

77. I lack the courage to do such a thing.

78. I arrived safely so please do not worry.

79. A gift given in all sincerity.

80. She is a very pious woman.

81. I have no confidence in him because what he says and what he thinks are not the same.

82. I am interested in music.

83. He is a hard-working man, isn't he? I admire him.

84. I was so absorbed in horse racing that I lost both the stake I had started with and the winnings I had made.

85. We won the game.

86. Sumō [Japanese wrestling] is considered to be the national sport of Japan.

87. I have your three yen.

88. We read reference books (written) in Japanese.

89. I will tell you for your information.

90. We participate in the Olympic Games.

91. On New Year's Day the various ambassadors also go to the Imperial Palace.

92. I am a newcomer; how do you do.

93. I go to a (Buddhist) temple to worship.

LESSON 20

1. I am a junior high school teacher.

2. My occupation is that of a physician.

3. I am a technician for the electric company.

4. This gentleman is a university professor.

5. There are a variety of ways of teaching Japanese.

6. There are no classes on Saturdays.

7. The expert transmits the most important secret.

8. A blessing from God.

9. I am awarded an academic degree.

10. A silver knife.

11. I have savings at the bank.

12. One can see the beautiful Milky Way in the sky.

13. There are thermometers which use mercury.

14. He is an industrious bank clerk.

15. I commute to work by the electric train.

16. I am employed at the ward office.

17. I go to work on the 7:00 a.m. bus.

18. There is a cafeteria for employees.

19. A clerk works in an office.

20. My father was a bank clerk.

21. There are many shops which are open until ten at night.

22. I understand that operating a tavern is difficult.

23. He is good at running the union.

24. I run a small bookshop.

25. Do you know the name of the mayor of this town?

26. I go downtown for shopping.

27. Marseilles is a large port city in France.

28. The clerks in that shop are all women.

29. I bought a notebook at the school store.

30. Night-stalls line the street.

31. I am working at a restaurant.

32. I want to eat meat, so, I think I will call the butcher shop and order some.

33. I have heard her songs on records and the radio, but this is the first time I have heard her sing in person.

34. Meats are necessary for growth.

35. Meat broiled over a charcoal fire is delicious.

36. The heating power of coal is stronger than that of charcoal.

37. There are many coal mines in Japan.

38. We wear clothes.

39. There are people dressed in both Western and Japanese clothes.

40. I served a term of ten years in Siberia.

41. They obey their parents.

42. I am taking vitamins.

43. We prepare the raw materials.

44. I will purchase lumber to build a house.

45. A lumber mill makes lumber.

46. I cannot find any good teaching materials.

47. I would like to take a trip around the world.

48. This is a widely known fact.

49. The circumference of this lake is ten kilometers.

50. Pi is 3.1415-plus.

51. I was a navy doctor during World War II.

52. The combined army, navy, and air force number one million.

53. I went to the South Pacific as a war correspondent.

54. He looks splendid when he puts on his military uniform, doesn't he?

55. Japan contains of one To [metropolis] and two Fu [urban prefectures], one of which is Kyōto-Fu.

56. Tōkyō is the capital of Japan.

57. We talked together about the British government's foreign policy.

58. The American Secretary of State will visit Japan.

59. At the embassy are employed not only civil service officials but also military officials.

60. Jūdō is one of the arts of self-defense.

61. The rich man patronizes the artist.

62. Lawyers must study laws.

63. We have laws to protect the people.

64. I carry on a regular life.

65. Can't we make bank interest uniform throughout the country?

66. It is an unwritten law that everyone knows.

67. The remaining sum is three thousand yen.

68. It's a special sale of unsold goods.

69. Let's give the remaining meat to the dog.

70. Let's give the leftover meat to the dog.

71. I brush my teeth.

72. That dentist has a fine technique.

73. A part of the gears on this machine must be repaired.

74. I had a decayed tooth pulled.

75. My father wears false teeth.

76. It is unlikely that there exists a farmhouse without a bicycle. [aru mai = nai darō]

77. I drive an automobile.

78. I wandered here and there from place to place.

79. I was transferred to Tōkyō.

80. The waka is one type of traditional Japanese poem, but we call the composer of a waka a kajin; we do not call him shijin.

81. Japanese who have studied the Chinese classics often compose Chinese poems.

82. Poets, painters, and musicians are called artists.

83. That painter paints Western-style paintings.

84. I made plans for next year.

85. Those who are known as "artists" cannot lead uniform lives.

86. I will mark off the lots and sell them.

87. In Rome the remaining traces of ancient architecture mingle with new architecture to make it an interesting city.

88. We built a new office.

89. He is a man who raised himself to an excellent position through home study.

90. Since Japan is surrounded by the sea it has a flourishing fishing industry.

91. Developing from a small fishing village it became a great port.

92. The fisherman catches fish.

93. The fishing village is all a-bustle over the big catch.

94. He is not a relative. He is an unrelated stranger.

95. In Europe there are London, Paris, Berlin, Rome, and other great cities.

96. He finally passed away.

97. You must never tell anyone else.

98. My husband works for an auto repair shop.

99. America is a democratic nation.

100. An unclaimed lost-and-found article.

101. The owner of my house is a great landlord who owns not only houses but also large land holdings.

LESSON 21

1. This is a shortcut, so we will be better off (taking it).

2. "What's the score now?"
"It's a tie at two to two. They're both strong, so we won't know the outcome of this game until the end."

3. I will give careful thought once more to the relative merits of this matter.

4. His specialty is mathematics. [= He is especially good at mathematics.]

5. Since you are a customer of long standing, I'll make it cheaper.

6. It is a publication on what students ought to know.

7. He is a person who says things just to suit his own purpose.

8. After hard fighting we were victorious.

9. There is a lovely picture hanging in the parlor.

10. How much money is needed?

11. The market fell below par.

12. The fever is so high that my forehead feels on fire.

13. It is not good to build a house on low ground.

14. The birthrate declined.

15. A low table will be fine.

16. There is a meeting once a month.

17. I came to collect the electric bill.

18. I will gather the people together and have them listen to the story.

19. People are gathering; did something happen?

20. I hear that his "Complete Works" will come out soon.

21. I am studying intensively.

22. Thank you for your trouble.

23. The work ended as wasted effort.

24. The workers mostly belong to labor unions.

25. We grow vegetables with chemical fertilizers.

26. We will put chemical fertilizer on the wheat field.

27. This cow is fattening up well.

28. We live in a rented house, so every month we pay the rent.

29. The train fare to Kyōto even second class must cost over a thousand yen.

30. How much is the freight charge for this baggage?

31. Wages have finally gone up.

32. Don't go into debt.

33. I borrowed a pen.

34. I borrowed something belonging to somebody without asking.

35. I'm in debt to that shop.

36. I'm single and I'm renting a room.

37. The aim is to help the poor.

38. It is so meager in content it doesn't enter the picture.

39. He is living a life of poverty.

40. A shabbily clad man came by.

41. The United Nations headquarters are in New York.

42. The water rose due to a succession of rainy days.

43. An automobile with a trailer attached.

44. I will take the children to the park.

45. I'm going beer-drinking with the gang today (again).

46. I've got fine companions on this trip, so I don't think I'll be lonely.

47. The mountain ranges are linked together.

48. We wrote a joint letter to the government.

49. The legislature, the judicature, and the administration are the basis of government.

50. He is the commander-in-chief of the Air Force.

51. The chairman of this meeting is Mr. Morikawa.

52. It is the commander's order.

53. I will give the command.

54. Entrance is prohibited by ordinance.

55. In accordance with the government's recommendation, exports are independently regulated.

56. I will work at the Kangyō Bank.

57. I changed my name on the advice of a friend.

58. We will revise the law.

59. I will take this opportunity to mend my ways and from now on I will do evil things no more.

60. That hotel was remodeled in purely Western style.

61. It is a book which has been rewritten.

62. I received a very formal letter.

63. They reform the educational system.

64. Among the people of that time the spirit of reform was at its highest.

65. The industrial revolution altered society.

66. We have no accounts with that bank.

67. Lend me a book, please.

68. How much is the rental fee?

69. There aren't many houses for rent.

70. I have neither loans nor debts.

71. Don't act rashly; think it over carefully before you do it.

72. It's only a trifle, just a token of my gratitude.

73. A lightweight briefcase.

74. He is a man who is good at jokes and often makes people laugh.

75. Please come over for a visit any time you wish.

76. There was a three thousand yen drop in income.

77. I'm troubled with a loss of appetite.

78. It is necessary to alter our way of life because of a decrease in income.

79. How do you feel today?

80. That's enough; please stop it.

81. With the progress of medicine, illness has diminished.

82. We laid off workers because of our economic problems.

83. We put the harvested rice and barley into the barn.

84. Persuading him is difficult.

85. I am a teller at the bank.

86. I will pay the fee.

87. Losing courage, I gave it up.

88. That period was a time when the strong devoured the weak.

89. He is a somewhat feeble-looking man.

90. He is a good man, but his shortcoming is a lack of willpower.

91. He grows weaker by the day with a grave ailment.

92. A certain Chinese scholar said that the fundamental nature of man is virtue.

93. We improve the life of the farm villages.

94. His ideas are dogmatic and his views narrow.

95. I used up all my own wealth in order to help the poor.

96. An ambulance went racing to assist the casualties.

97. My life was saved by a noted doctor.

98. I seek salvation in God.

99. I am an assistant to a biology professor.

100. I (will) get some suggestions for my research.

101. Help me please.

102. Thank you for giving me your assistance.

103. Thanks to you my life was saved.

104. I (will) get the help of a friend.

105. I hate heavy drinkers.

106. It is a book which explains the basic grammar of Japanese.

107. Standard wages are fixed by the labor laws.

108. The manufacturing industry is the basis of this city's development.

109. It is discord which arose out of a misunderstanding.

110. Diligence is the basis of achievement.

111. He was successful as a merchant.

112. England's Bentham and Mill are famous as advocates of utilitarianism.

113. If you think only of the past you will make no progress.

114. It's an express train so it passes up the smaller stations.

115. I will forgive the slip.

116. Please forgive me for my rudeness of the other day.

117. It's already past four o'clock.

118. I'm afraid I don't deserve such generous remuneration.

119. I spent the vacation pleasantly.

LESSON 22

1. I get up every morning at seven-thirty.

2. Sometimes I have the maid wake me up.

3. A serious problem has come up.

4. We lift heavy things with a crane.

5. We stand up when we sing the national anthem.

6. I have some business which I must attend to at once.

7. With things as they are, there is fear we will come to war.

8. The road going from Tōkyō to Odawara.

9. Dissolution of the Diet is unavoidable.

10. It's the same melody but the lyrics are different.

11. Japanese nouns and English nouns have different characteristics.

12. Whose composition is it?

13. What is the program for tonight's concert?

14. We march in step with the march music.

15. An old person all stooped over.

16. It is a basket woven of bent bamboo.

17. Turn right at that corner, please.

18. It makes no difference whether you write with fountain pen or brush.

19. We write down what the teacher says.

20. I will send it by airmail.

21. At the airport there are many airplanes both large and small.

22. A bird flying across [or: in] the sky.

23. Lightning struck a telephone pole and a column of fire shot up.

24. They will move the telephone poles underground.

25. The pillars of this house are thick and splendid.

26. The wall clock struck ten o'clock.

27. If it rains we will call off the picnic.

28. We are tired so let's stop marching.

29. The clock has stopped.

30. Since this street is under construction it is closed to traffic.

31. This college has high standards.

32. We will set an itinerary for our Kansai trip.

33. We will study the process by which we came to failure.

34. Without air, human beings cannot exist.

35. We carefully preserve letters of famous people.

36. Do you believe in the existence of God?

37. I don't know about such things as that.

38. I had some surgery performed on my face.

39. What pigments did you use to color it?

40. I wash my face.

41. You look pale; is there anything wrong?

42. I watched the setting sun shining golden.

43. A color photograph.

44. I'm looking for a suitable assistant.

45. The three primary colors are red, yellow, and blue.

46. I am in sympathy with that gentleman's ideas [or: opinions].

47. Birds sing.

48. I hear the mooing of a cow.

49. The bell sounded for the end of work.

50. That bank pays low interest.

51. I stop work and take a rest.

52. I have not received the slightest news from him.

53. We breathe through the nose.

54. I heave a sigh of distress.

55. We go to the bank which is two chō further on.

56. This book has a page [or: some pages] missing so will you exchange it, please.

57. Grooms take care of horses.

58. A gardener has been hired who will take care of the garden.

59. The marathon runner is running.

60. I operate a wheat flour mill.

61. Take the liquid medicine before meals and the powdered medicine after meals.

62. Does beef digest poorly?

63. I will cancel the appointment.

64. Fire engines are usually painted red.

65. Snow melts.

66. Please erase the wrong letters [= the mistake] with an eraser.

67. I withdrew my promise.

68. A letter with a March tenth cancellation mark.

69. I exercise outdoors.

70. The number of houses in this town is less than two thousand.

71. I (will) open the door.

72. I (will) close the amado [rain shutters].

73. The weather is so nice I will go for a stroll in the park.

74. In autumn the tree leaves scatter.

75. That student is smart.

76. He is a stuck-up person, isn't he?

77. Who is that walking at the head of the parade?

78. I took an oral exam.

79. I have to appear at the ward office.

80. We compare our weights.

81. The cold of Alaska is beyond comparing with any cold of Canada.

82. I will divide by a ratio of seven to three.

83. The specific gravity of mercury is 13.55.

LESSON 23

1. There are many tourists in spring and summer.

2. A play with a small audience.

3. I am distressed at failing the test.

4. It is too optimistic a view.

5. International relations are complicated.

6. I pursue studies which will be useful in actual situations.

7. I made a transcontinental flight.

8. He seized another man's property.

9. With his head turned aside, he spoke not a word.

10. She has a lovely profile.

11. I am doing a study of sixteenth-century Japanese literature.

12. An immoral port town.

13. It is a travel account of a European tour.

14. You must not play in the street.

15. The automobile traffic is heavy.

16. I heard the English explanation.

17. Who invented the telephone?

18. Next year I would like to take a continental trip.

19. The dawn broke while I was reading.

20. The light is better in the parlor; wouldn't it be easier to see in there?

21. It is an obvious error.

22. I would like to take a ride on a supersonic jet plane.

23. The speed is sixty miles per hour.

24. [In how many hours =] How soon will it arrive if you send it by special delivery?

25. This ship is old so it hasn't much speed.

26. A new hotel is under construction.

27. I designed this house myself.

28. We (will) establish a school for foreigners.

29. We (will) consolidate the results of our research.

30. We will service the airplane.

31. I (will) set the table.

32. Kerosene is a kind of oil.

33. I wrap wet things in waxed paper.

34. You may make a mistake if you are inattentive.

35. There will be a broadcast by the Prime Minister tonight at nine o'clock.

36. I (will) send money to the child.

37. Postage is extra.

38. I send a book by sea-mail to a friend abroad.

39. I'm on my way to see a friend off to America.

40. An inn is better than a hotel.

41. I work at the Japanese Embassy in Washington.

42. How many are there in your family?

43. A person with few relatives.

44. The Anglo-Saxon race.

45. He spoke to me in a kindly tone.

46. The harmony of color is beautiful.

47. You regulate the temperature of the room by button.

48. I will check the [wavelength =] frequency of the radio wave.

49. We investigate a suspicious man.

50. We call the payment of taxes nōzei.

51. Income with the income tax deducted.

52. I inspect travelers' baggage at the Customs.

53. We levy a customs duty on imported goods.

54. I will put the baggage into the storehouse.

55. I will place the baggage in the ship's hold.

56. A wealthy household with many storehouses.

57. The storehouse is filled with rice.

58. I will put the car away in the garage.

59. We keep important documents and money in the safe.

60. Who is the superintendent of the apartment building?

61. The rubber gas hose has gotten old.

62. Plastic hose lasts longer than rubber hose.

63. He administers the estate.

64. A treaty was concluded between Japan and America.

65. The people opposed to the end the Prime Minister, who concluded the treaty with its unfavorable terms.

66. I will read the text of the treaty carefully.

67. These products are of inferior quality so you must not sell them.

68. I hear that it is a school full of delinquent students.

69. If he had any conscience at all he ought to be unable to do such things.

70. If the terms are good I will take the job.

71. It is necessary to improve the roads and to build wide national highways for the use of automobiles.

72. There is something at the bottom of the drawer.

73. He is a powerful person so he may win.

74. The hold of the ship has poor air circulation and it is hot.

75. It would be fun to be able to make a journey to the bottom of the sea.

76. I have but little learning so please instruct me.

77. We will measure the depth of the lake.

78. I swim where it is shallow.

79. Since it is shoal water even children can swim here.

80. Before the war there was a tremendous difference in the income between the proprietary farmer and the tenant farmer.

81. The time difference between Tōkyō and London must be about nine hours.

82. I will put[or: wear]a flower in my hair.

83. No membership fee is required.

84. I have put a great deal of time into this research.

85. If I enter this college, about how much would the expense be for one year?

86. I have no travel money, so I cannot go even though I want to.

*

1. We play on the beach without[or: instead of] going into the water.

2. We relax at a beach hotel.

3. The industrial area between Tokyo and Yokohama is called the "Keihin [Tōkyō-Yokohama] Industrial District."

LESSON 24

1. On holidays we are supposed to celebrate and not work.

2. On graduation day we heard a congratulatory address by the principal.

3. The whole family celebrates the New Year together.

4. There are various events held on the day of the shrine festival.

5. Since the holiday and Sunday follow one another, let's take a trip somewhere.

6. Who is enshrined at this shrine?

7. Festivals are the days children enjoy most.

8. The list price of this book is 550 yen.

9. The capacity of this elevator is ten persons, so please wait for the next car.

10. The next American President was decided upon.

11. Dissolution of the National Diet is certain.

12. We decided on the heir.

13. This group is made up of beginners, so we do not teach kanji; we only do conversation.

14. Since beginnings are important, even though it is easy don't get careless but study hard.

15. The first snow fell in October.

16. Even though you are clumsy at first you will gradually become skillful.

17. A person with a poor memory.

18. Do you remember Aiichi Tanaka?

19. I am aware of my weak points.

20. An evil deed was brought to light.

21. He has keen senses.

22. A mother's love is indispensable for a child.

23. I love nature.

24. I (will) take pictures with my favorite camera.

25. They are a people with a strong sense of patriotism.

26. They say he's got a sweetheart.

27. A tree tall enough to reach to heaven.

28. Fine weather, isn't it?

29. This place is heaven on earth.

30. The "River of Heaven" is also called the "Milky Way."

31. I lost my only mother in all the world.

32. The Crown Prince is the one who will become the next Emperor.

33. Long ago His Imperial Majesty the Emperor was regarded as a god.

34. Citizens who have never read the Constitution cannot be called good citizens, can they?

35. At present there are no military police in Japan.

36. The United Nations Charter was enacted in 1945.

37. It was so pitiful I could not restrain a feeling of sympathy.

38. I lent him the money reminding him to be sure to return it by tomorrow.

39. In America, is Constitution Day also a national holiday?

40. Too bad, the game was called off on account of rain.

41. That person hasn't the slightest concept of time.

42. There seem to be some people who have the mistaken idea that Japanese is the most difficult language in the world.

43. Just when I had resigned myself that this was it [= the end], I was rescued.

44. The school year is divided into two semesters, and each semester we give them an examination.

45. It is expected that he will definitely become a first-rate scholar.

46. His rank rose from assistant professor to full professor.

47. I respect his character.

48. Please show me the price clearly.

49. Those two are close friends but they have completely different personalities.

50. Good fortune continued this year.

51. I sympathize with unfortunate people.

52. Fortunately, the whole family is well.

53. "Good fortune in, devils out!" [Said when throwing beans on the eve of the first day of spring.]

54. It is a happy family.

55. We pray for the blessing of God.

56. I don't know the way, so would you please draw me a map?

57. Wait till I signal you.

58. I borrow a book from the library.

59. He attempted suicide.

60. She devotes herself entirely to bringing up the child.

61. The birth of a son.

62. That doctor is a specialist in pediatrics.

63. I want some good reading material for the children.

64. I read them [or: him/her] one children's story every night.

65. The Prime Minister's ideas are conservative.

66. A team with a poor defense.

67. A policeman is directing traffic at the pedestrian crossing in order to protect the school children.

68. I fought for my home country.

69. My father and mother are in Japan.

70. The a, i, u, e, and o of Japanese are all vowels.

71. Expressing his thanks for the kindness, he left.

72. The monthly tuition fee rises.

73. I thank my parents.

74. My ancestors were warriors.

75. I fight for my fatherland.

76. This shop is the originator of Kasutera [Castella = spongecake].

77. We salute superior officers.

78. We respect our superiors and use honorific language to them.

79. I have great admiration for his work.

80. I will explain the reasons.

81. We respect the freedom of the individual.

82. I am relieved to hear that you are all well.

83. I asked about the origin of a name.

84. Human life is precious.

85. America is a country which holds freedom dear.

LESSON 25

1. A winding road.

2. We go fifty-fifty on the proceeds.

3. We amuse ourselves with paper-folding work.

4. I broke my arm during practice.

5. It is hard to swim because it is such a rocky coast.

6. Rock-salt is not produced in Japan.

7. Volcanic rock is rock which has been heated until it melts deep underground and flows out on the surface of the earth to cool and harden suddenly.

8. There are big sales at the end of the year.

9. We have no income until the end of the month.

10. At the end of the week I will go to a house in the country. [or: On weekends I go to my country house.]

11. The eldest is a boy, between there are two girls, and the youngest is another boy.

12. I am the youngest, so the older sisters and brothers make a great fuss over me.

13. My eldest sister is abroad.

14. The Negro problem has not yet been solved.

15. Let's make a clear distinction between right and wrong.

16. I wrote kanji with chalk on the blackboard.

17. I went skiing for a week during spring vacation and my face got dark with tan.

18. She asserted that she was right.

19. I am on an official trip to Kyōto.

20. A watchman is standing at the gate.

21. We string up a rope to prevent accidents.

22. When rain and snow falls there are many automobile accidents.

23. He has already died.

24. Because I have lived a long time in foreign countries, I long for my native land.

25. We'll give a gold medal to the person with the best records.

26. He is a person who has had success in educational administration.

27. He is a man who has been unusually successful in the construction of dams.

28. I deliver newspapers.

29. We (will) divide it equally.

30. I am worried that my younger brother is ill.

31. I distribute paper to the students and give them a test.

32. The farmers deliver rice to the government and the government sells it to the people.

33. We make our offerings before God.

34. I go shopping and take the maid along.

35. If you put fallen leaves into water for a long time only the lead veins will remain.

36. The new road from Tōkyō to Chiba City is called Keiyō [Tōkyō-Chiba] National Highway.

37. I stand on the river bank and gaze at the opposite shore.

38. Mr. Kishi was Prime Minister at the time of the revision of the Security Treaty.

39. One ri is about 2 1/2 miles.

40. I will measure the distance.

41. I come down from the mountain to the village.

42. They are foster parent and child, but they seem like true parent and child.

43. We do not resemble one another but she is my real younger sister.

44. My younger sister is playing in the yard with the child from next door.

45. Since he has many younger brothers and sisters he works hard and helps his parents out.

46. I have no brothers and sisters; I am an only child.

47. The typhoons come in early September every year.

48. I ate at an open sushi stall.

49. I (will) stand on the stool and take something from high up.

50. We cook in the kitchen.

51. Jōba means riding a horse.

52. There are always a lot of passengers on Tōkyō's public conveyances, both buses and trains.

53. I got a ride in my friend's car and headed for the airport.

54. This hospital was built through the contribution of a certain person.

55. This ship will stop at Manila.

56. On my way home from school I plan to stop by the library and borrow a book.

57. I will draw up a chair next to the stove.

58. We are open for business twenty-four hours, day and night.

59. There was a murder in broad daylight.

60. Lunch break lasts thirty minutes from [= starting at] eleven-thirty.

61. This photo has sharp contrasts of light and dark.

62. I will send a message by secret code.

63. I memorize Japanese sentences.

64. I walk along a dark street.

65. Shooting stars and meteors are the same thing.

66. The stars are out all over the sky.

67. Both Mars and Venus are planets.

68. He is being investigated as a murder suspect.

69. We are investigating him on a suspicion of murder.

70. If you have any questions whatsoever about this matter please ask me.

71. There is not a single person to doubt that his views are correct.

72. It is cold enough for a blanket.

73. A letter written with a brush.

74. The Japanese have black hair.

75. I wear a woolen sweater.

76. A factory that weaves cotton cloth.

77. We will distribute cloth to persons who suffered flood damage.

78. I work in a factory which makes silk thread from raw silk.

LESSON 26

1. Clothing, food, and shelter are the things most necessary for human life.

2. Generally speaking, _irui_ are the things we wear; _iryō_ are the materials of clothing such as thread, cloth, and the like.

3. Doctors wear white clothes while on duty.

4. The season for the changing of dress is June.

5. During the war I worked at a munition factory.

6. All the essentials are in order.

7. Which are stronger, silk or nylon stockings?

8. Rayon was devised in order to make up for the shortage of clothing materials.

9. After the war the export of Japanese silk goods diminished.

10. Please don't make such sarcastic remarks.

11. A fur coat is too expensive for me to buy.

12. Leather goods have grown cheaper lately.

13. He was discovered to be a fraud.

14. Your appointment was decided upon.

15. When we took a vote there was not a single opponent.

16. After I grade them tomorrow, I will announce the marks.

17. I accept a new idea.

18. I took an examination to test my ability.

19. Yesterday's rainfall was twenty millimeters.

20. With mass production, prices should drop.

21. They sell <u>sake</u> by the <u>masu</u> [a measuring box].

22. The Duke of Windsor cast aside the crown for the one he loved.

23. Queen Elizabeth has three princes (for sons).

24. Is the Pope called "Father" by Catholics?

25. I took my bachelor's degree at Kyōto University.

26. Mr. Yamamoto's actions deserve praise.

27. He claims to have graduated from college, but . . .

28. This is a rough draft, so please make me a fair copy.

29. The new personnel are filled with a fresh spirit.

30. After purifying ourselves we go to the shrine.

31. That man insisted that he was innocent with respect to this incident.

32. He's a man who gives you the feeling he is rather dirty[-minded].

33. Mr. Yamanaka is a high-minded person.

34. It distresses me for my child to be a cry-baby.

35. I guess he is in a bad mood.   [He must have gotten up on the wrong side of the bed.]

36. It's a harmful insect so you may kill it.

37. The barley field suffered terrible insect damage.

38. I will take the students' attendance.

39. Everybody has his strong points and his weak points.

40. We have to give an employment examination in order to fill a vacancy.

41. This teacup is chipped so let's throw it away.

42. Please write me some example sentences.

43. There are no rules without exceptions.

44. If you do that sort of thing, you'll set a bad example.

45. Give me an example.

46. In Japan these five or six years have seen continuous bumper crops of rice.

47. Years when the crops come in very well we call "rich years."

48. We strive to establish a wealthy society.

49. To the extent that income increases, our daily lives become (more) abundant.

50. Since Hokkaidō is suitable for the growth of pasturage and has vast lands, there are many ranches.

51. The word bokujō is also pronounced makiba in its Japanese reading.

52. I want to become a missionary and do missionary work in Japan.

53. Pastoral songs are poems which sing of the life of herdsmen or farmers.

54. I cannot read this letter because it is written in sōsho [cursive style].

55. Mr. Yamada is a pioneer in this village.

56. They thrive like weeds.

57. I live in the back woods.

58. Before the war when sericulture prospered, the silkworms were called (politely) okaiko-san and were treated with great care.

59. With the recent increase in the demand for silk thread, sericulture seems to have been given a new lease on life.

60. The Vice-President has a close relationship with the American Senate.

61. This medicine has no side effects.

62. Send the documents in duplicate, please.

63. In newspapers the use of Chinese characters is, except for special cases, restricted to the "standard characters" [tōyō kanji].

64. I don't think we can restrict it in that way.

65. Things usually have their limits.

66. This custom is restricted to the Chūgoku area of Japan.

67. I get some help in living expenses from my parents.

68. By way of supplementing the explanation a bit more . . .

69. I must take on side jobs to make up for the inadequacy of my income.

70. We hire a new employee to fill a vacancy.

71. Tōkyō has over nine times the population of Yokohama.

72. We request your increased patronage.

73. One of the pillars of his economic policy is the plan to double income.

74. We must prepare for the doubling of the volume of traffic and set up measures to cope with it.

75. By "acids" we mean such things as hydrochloric acid and carbonic acid.

76. One way to prevent oxidation is to paint things.

77. The methods of research differ for the natural sciences and the social sciences.

78. In the second semester I plan to take four courses.

79. We will start using this textbook this semester.

80. Since the war, education in social studies has been regarded as very important in Japan.

81. Have you ever read the book "War and Peace?"

82. In labor disputes in Japan there are many situations that involve not only economic problems but also political problems.

83. Kyōsō [competition] and kyōsō [footrace] have the same pronunciation, but the meanings are different.

84. Three persons compete for a single position.

85. No matter how smart a person may be, he will get nowhere if he puts in no effort.

86. Mr. Ōhashi is a hard worker.

87. I endeavored to solve this complex problem.

88. We've had little time for practice, so I'm worried whether or not we can win this game.

89. The result of the trial run was excellent.

90. I tried it many times but failed.

91. It is a new venture, so I don't know whether or not we will succeed.

LESSON 27

1. I am absolutely opposed to your view.

2. I suffered more hardship than words can express in putting that plan into operation.

3. It is cold, so don't let the fire go out.

4. He grumbles endlessly.

5. The world is controlled through power politics.

6. Foreign service officers have various privileges.

7. They carried on various activities in order to get concessions.

8. We (will) go on a pilgrimage to Tokugawa Ieyasu's tomb.

9. If expenditures exceed income we say that one's household economy is in the red.

10. We feel as though a great pillar of support has been lost with the death of Mr. Tokugawa.

11. I was transferred from the main store to a regional branch.

12. The world is controlled by two ideologies.

13. Dead men tell no tales.

14. This is a matter of life and death.

15. There are three kinds of volcanoes: active, dormant, and extinct.

16. The concept predominated that the Way of the Warrior was to die.

17. He will be able to leave the hospital in about two weeks.

18. At present it hangs in the balance.

19. I dropped out of college and went into business.

20. That man understands advance but not retreat.

21. He is a person with a strong sense of responsibility.

22. Suffering the pangs of conscience, he is unable to sleep even at night.

23. It will do no good to blame such an irresponsible man.

24. The President's term of office is four years.

25. Who is Mr. Ōta's successor?

26. He was appointed ambassador to that country, but it will probably be a month before he leaves for his post.

27. I cannot turn this work over to others.

28. That book contains a preface by Professor Nemoto.

29. Tell it to me in proper sequence.

30. Which is your favorite operatic overture?

31. The Japanese archipelago runs from Hokkaidō in the north to Kyūshū in the south.

32. It's an express train, so it does not stop there.

33. Quite a few trains were held up in line by an auto accident.

34. The person second from the front in that line is a grandchild of Mr. Tokugawa.

35. It is difficult to maintain strict neutrality.

36. Investigate it more intensively.

37. Be punctual!

38. At the conference the American representative made the following explanation.

39. The illness spread and absence followed one after another.

40. There were thirty persons present.

41. I plan to go for a dip in the sea on the weekend.

42. We call the _furoba_ [bathing room] also the "yokujō."

43. It was hot, so I went home and took a cold shower.

44. He drinks like a fish.

45. The game ended as expected.

46. Old people have difficulty in adapting to new times.

47. I'll distribute them on a first-come-first-served basis.

48. Since both have good marks it is difficult to rank them.

49. The bride is from the Yamada family.

50. I hear that the position of women has improved in postwar Japan.

51. They are a happy couple, aren't they?

52. We were invited by Mr. and Mrs. Yamane.

53. I work in order to support a wife and child.

54. My wife died before me.

55. The mistress of a family [= The lady of the house] has charge of the family budget.

56. This person is a relative of Mrs. Chiba.

57. I devised a variety of study techniques.

58. My husband is on a business trip to Kyōto at the moment.

59. The necessity of education in morals is being called for.

60. The Tokugawa Period maintained an era of some three hundred years of peace.

61. That man has exhausted the limits of depravity.

62. These are more economical items.

63. I think you had better study more systematically.

64. According to the family genealogy, the ancestors were of the Family of Taira.

65. "Japanese-Americans" means Japanese who hold American citizenship.

66. It is doubtful that he is a direct descendant.

67. No formal views on this incident have yet been announced by the government.

68. I think it will be announced through some kind of formalities.

69. They are using old-style machinery in that factory.

70. There should be a formal notice in two or three days.

71. Stop beating about the bush and tell me the whole story.

72. Tell me about the present state of the Japanese economic world.

73. A letter-file is something you put letters into.

74. We must make our attitude toward this matter clear.

75. As night came on, the patient's condition worsened.

76. I'll start again after I get things set up.

77. Seventeen years after the war, Japanese society seems to be back to normalcy.

78. The descendants of the Emperor are called "kōson."

79. They claim themselves to be descendants of the Family of Taira, but . . .

80. When he was sixty years old his first grandchild was born to his eldest son.

81. Your idea is thoroughly mistaken.

82. If you lack perseverance your language study will make no progress.

83. That man has a twisted disposition.

84. I will dig up the tree-root.

85. It is too early to be worrying about your old age now.

86. An old people's home is a place to live for those with but a few years left to them.

87. Mr. Ueda is quite experienced in teaching.

88. I don't want to live in a country with no freedom of thought.

89. One must continue to hold high ideals.

90. The world of Verlaine's dreams is now becoming a reality.

91. Japan concluded a cultural agreement with France.

92. They are deliberating on this problem at the moment.

93. I am making preparations for the establishment of an association.

94. During that time, I never once had occasion for an unpleasant feeling.

95. Everyone wants to live a comfortable life.

96. The management was happy to meet the union's request for a wage increase.

LESSON 28

1. From February through March is the period of graduation examinations in Japan.

2.   Both labor and capital are rather inexperienced, so it looks as though this dispute will last some time.

3.   He goes through a chemical experiment dozens of times.

4.   It is difficult for any country to carry on a self-sufficient economy.

5.   Life must be easy for anyone as high-salaried as you.

6.   We have a ration system for rice in Japan.

7.   We (will) investigate the relationship between supply and demand.

8.   I intend to finish my homework before supper.

9.   That inn is the one I stay at regularly when I go to Kyōto.

10. I dashed into that shop to take shelter from the rain.

11. The overseas trip that had been my dream for many years materialized.

12. One of the joys of traveling by train is eating the box lunches sold at the stations.

13. I will ask the station employee the [= what] time the train will arrive.

14. One minute is equal to sixty seconds.

15. Mr. Morishita's English is far better than that of the rest.

16. The administration of the Marshall Islands is left to the United States by the United Nations.

17. This disturbance is attributable to mob psychology.

18. From the flock of birds which hover over a stretch of ocean, one can find schools of fish.

19. It is very hard to make a perfect score on that test.

20. There is a full moon tonight, so it should be light on the road.

21. Isn't there some way of settling this strike amicably?

22. His term of service expired and he left the company.

23. We eat in order to satisfy our appetites.

24. To accompany the increase in military expenses we will draw up a supplementary budget.

25. As I was not able to take the test on account of illness, I was given a make-up test.

26. Harassed by work, I have no time for playing.

27. The Ueno Cultural Center has far better facilities than Hibiya Hall.

28. The dining hall is open from twelve to one.

29. The army marches magnificently up the main street.

30. I will deem it an honor if you will be present.

31. I hear the head of the Kyoto branch is to be promoted to the main office in Tokyo.

32. We work so that the country may flourish and the livelihood of the people will be enriched.

33. No matter how many times I computed it the totals did not tally.

34. They teach addition and subtraction in the elementary-school arithmetic course.

35. One must operate a business so that it makes a profit.

36. The sea occupies two-thirds of the earth's surface.

37. The light bulb has burned out so go buy me another one please.

38. He threw a good ball but it was hit by the batter.

39. The vocal soloist is a newcomer.

40. The necessity of education in morals is being advocated.

41. I will study the new theory advocated by Mr. Kawakami.

42. It is cheaper when you travel in a group.

43. They send out a mission to study conditions in foreign countries.

44. The most necessary thing for a union member is a spirit of unity.

45. There's something I'd like to discuss with you for a moment.

46. He did nothing but chatter; he didn't study a bit.

47. For a discussion, the combination of those two persons would be the most interesting.

48. The Foreign Minister held a conference with the ambassadors of various countries.

49. I am deeply grateful for your kindness.

50. Mr. Tobita is a gentle person.

51. Please get me the thick red book on the desk.

52. The dormitory was filled up so I boarded at a house near the university.

53. The athletic field is surrounded by school buildings.

54. This place is where long ago there were army barracks.

55. Japan is divided into forty-two prefectures.

56. Mr. Yamamura is a member of the Prefectural Assembly.

57. The term of office of a prefectural governor is four years.

58. The health center is the office for such tasks as town sanitation and the prevention of disease.

59. You play sports to put your body into shape.

60. Mr. Tanaka is a man of sound ideas.

61. We raise our children to be in perfect health.

62. There is a brief lull in his illness.

63. We eat nutritious food to maintain health.

64. Almost all the Eastern European countries are Russian satellites.

65. We will increase the budget to reinforce our defense strength.

66. Ask the doorman at the entrance, please.

67. I will order the book in advance.

68. As expected, that team scored a decisive victory.

69. I prepare lessons before class.

70. One cannot believe that man's predictions.

71. The domestic economy must be stabilized so that foreign capital will be brought in.

72. The leadership of the union officers has weakened.

73. Leading evil men to the paths of good is a tremendous task.

74. The Marshall Islands are under United States mandate.

75. There is a debate in the Budget Committee of the Lower House.

76. Please be sure to be present at the committee meeting.

77. The secretary of this meeting is Mr. Tada.

78. A vine winds itself about the trunk of a tree.

79. The executives got together and discussed the matter.

80. Long ago vendettas were frequently carried on.

81. The two worlds of capitalism and socialism confront [= oppose] one another.

82. He studies at college in order to get his teaching qualifications.

83. How much is the capital of that company?

84. I can give you no explanation because I have no sources here at hand.

LESSON 29

1. The first year of Showa is equivalent to the year 1925.

2. Rising early in the morning to study will bring better results.

3. This ticket is good [= valid] for one month.

4. This treaty will not come into force until it has gained the approval of the Diet.

5. There is still no specific remedy for that illness.

6. Mr. Akiyama is well versed on the literature of the Heian Period.

7. This book is thick, so it will take time to read it carefully.

8. Meats have no place in a vegetarian diet.

9. Mr. Yamada is a poor correspondent; he hardly ever writes letters.

10. We memorize sentences perfectly.

11. Several decades were required before that building was completed.

12. Mr. Aikawa expressed a negative opinion regarding this matter.

13. He denied it at first, but finally he confessed.

14. I received a long letter from my mother asking after my health.

15. If he says that he is unwilling then we can do nothing.

16. I give an examination to test one's ability.

17. Isn't there some more efficient method of study?

18. All animals act through instinct.

19. You'd better dismiss such an incompetent person as he is.

20. I am doing a study of biblical terms.

21. The bringing of the sacred fire of the Olympics from Greece began with the Berlin games.

22. If you say "master musician," we immediately think of Beethoven.

23. The Empress went on a trip to the Kansai area.

24. That man works in a thoroughly devoted way.

25. I will strive to solve the problem in all good faith.

26. The Japanese army would pledge their loyalty to the Emperor.

27. It is difficult to judge whether one is a sincere person or not.

28. I cannot comply with your desire.

29. That guy is regarded as a notorious scoundrel.

30. The help-wanted and situation-wanted ads usually appear on Page 10 in the paper.

31. The labor union asserted that they were by no means unreasonable demands.

32. It was not with money as my object that I proposed marriage.

33. Since I could not come to a decision on the basis of my opinion alone, I sought Ueda's views.

34. I left my country with the intention of taking up permanent residence abroad.

35. Can Switzerland maintain her neutrality indefinitely, I wonder?

36. I'm looking for a job which has permanence.

37. Each country is striving hard to seek an enduring peace.

38. If you do not have endurance you will not be able to complete that work.

39. In search of eternal ideals, I am devoting myself to learning.

40. I saw Mr. Yamada in town yesterday for the first time in ages.

41. In Japan we do not use the term "armed forces"; we say "self-defense forces."

42. My elder brother was taken by the army and he died in the war in China.

43. The (military) unit continued to advance.

44. Recognition of Red China is a matter of time.

45. After confirming the signal the train will depart.   [We will confirm the signal before departing.]

46. I recognized that I was at fault.

47. Recognition by the world of Cezanne's paintings came after his death.

48. "Wealthy country, strong army" was the fundamental government policy of the Meiji period.

49. Spring has come and vegetables have started to appear in abundance in front of the stores.

50. On clear days, Mount Fuji can be seen even from Tōkyō.

51. I eat only foods rich in nourishment.

52. Dogs are said to be animals faithful to their masters.

53. After the war the concept of loyalty to one's lord and patriotism to one's country was discarded.

54. Serving one's lord with the utmost loyalty was the morality of the samurai warriors.

55. Filial piety is [= means] serving one's father and mother and looking after them with great care.

56. The art of medicine is said to be the benevolent art.

57. I am studying the course for the doctorate at graduate school.

58. When I was a child I often went to the Science Museum.

59. He is a man of wide learning but he has not once published his research.

60. Speaking ill of others brings no gains.

61. In public utilities such as gas and electricity the right of unions to strike is restricted.

62. Thank you for a most instructive talk.

63. Insects beneficial to mankind which eat other insects harmful to plants are called beneficial insects.

64. We (will) write down the oral statements of a venerable authority and publish them in a book.

65. A later statement is expected with regard to this matter.

66. I believe I have stated it earlier, but . . .

67. In order to convince a person you must state your reasons.

68. Please check your valuables at the desk [or: counter].

69. I'd like to hear your opinion.

70. The present House of Councillors was once called the House of Peers.

71. We are currently looking for a candidate, but we just cannot find a suitable person.

72. The world championship jūdō matches were held in Paris.

73. Mr. Tsunoda was said to be assured of election, but in the polling he ended up a second-runner.

74. If one chooses only the safe way of doing something, he will not achieve success in modern society.

75. As a basic rule, anyone obtains the right to vote when he reaches the age of twenty.

76. We will hold a ceremony commemorating the war victory.

77. Crossing the Pacific Ocean alone on a small sailboat was the most brilliant feat of recent years.

78. Every movement of a famous person attracts the attention of society.

LESSON 30

1. Leaving aside Northern Kyushu, the modernization of industry since the Meiji period has promoted the exploitation of the coal fields in the Hokkaidō, Kantō, and Chūgoku regions.

2. Since there is little output of iron ore in Japan, the greater portion is imported from abroad.

3. The utilization of electricity from the end of the nineteenth century into the twentieth century has opened the way for reform in the whole mining industry.

4. Since the temperature inside the room is high, one is unaware of the cold outside.

5. Mr. Akashi is so crazy about photography that he even has a darkroom in his own house.

6. You must not smoke in the classroom.

7. In certain regions people cut the ice on lakes, put it away in ice-houses, and use it when summer comes.

8. Copper was an important export item in Japan up to the time of World War I.

9. The road is crowded, so it would probably be faster if we go by subway rather than car.

10. Japanese railroads are famous for their punctual arrivals and departures.

11. To maintain good health it is necessary to take (in) minerals. In that sense, it is good for older persons to drink milk, which is rich in iron.

12. Russia severely criticized the United States actions against Cuba.

13. This book has so many hard-to-understand passages, it is hard work to read it.

14. Last year was a very eventful one.

15. There is nothing so hard to predict as Japan's economic growth rate.

16. Gas is convenient to transport when liquefied.

17. In the blood there are white corpuscles and red corpuscles.

18. The physique of Japanese young men and women has improved tremendously since the war.

19. The Emperor and Empress attend national athletic meets.

20. Isn't there some way of giving a polite refusal?

21. In various countries developments are being carried on for utilizing atomic energy as fuel.

22. Caution! (In)flammable! [Need care (in handling) as this is inflammable.]

23. The fire in the stove blazed up bright red.

24. I burned the old letters up one by one as I read them.

25. Ships navigate by the light from the lighthouse.

26. The room is so dark that even in the daytime you have to turn on the light.

27. Since the war, Japanese shipbuilding has become the leading export industry.

28. All sorts of pains must be taken to preserve ancient wooden architecture.

29. In various parts of Japan man-made lakes have been formed by the construction of dams.

30. When sending things to foreign countries one must make the packing secure.

31. The conference was adjourned for a time, but it will be reconvened tomorrow.

32. It is a store that has just opened so it is selling things cheaply.

33. The capital and skills of advanced nations are necessary in the development of underdeveloped nations.

34. A scholarly meeting on modern Japanese literature was held in Kyōto.

35. When will my luck take a turn for the better, I wonder.

36. You will grow pale if you live in a big city and get no exercise.

37. Mr. Yamakawa is just getting over an illness so he still looks quite pale.

38. He died from an excessive loss of blood.

39. I am nearsighted, but I don't use glasses except when I'm reading (a book).

40. Those two were completely oblivious to the existence of others.

41. The mother went about frantically searching for her child.

42. As a basic rule, a general election for the House of Representatives is supposed to be held once every four years.

43. Once a year we hold a general meeting.

44. Thirty percent of Japan's total exports are to the United States.

45. The cause of the plane accident is unknown.

46. He told us nothing about the cause for the defeat in the game.

47. Please don't say such a heartless thing.

48. I cannot say that there is no possibility.

49. Without the permission of the head of the firm, we cannot put this plan into effect.

50. It was passed by an absolute majority.

51. China's policy is the indivisibility of politics and economics.

52. I have been practicing for a long time, but since I go my own way [in doing things] I don't make the least progress.

53. Mr. Tokugawa always persists in his own opinion and never bothers to listen to the opinions of others.

54. If there is a man among you, then join up.

55. The audience scrambled to get out.

56. This thing is just common knowledge.

57. I don't have even a nodding acquaintance with him.

58. I lost consciousness for a while.

59. Mr. Yamamoto is a man of broad vision.

60. In order to plan for an expansion of markets we will send economic missions abroad.

61. Up to World War II each country was engrossed in the arms race.

LESSON 31

1. Because Mr. Murayama joined the party it suddenly livened up.

2. In this warm season of spring I hope you are all well as ever.

3. One cannot go into business without a thought to profit and loss.

4. He suffered great losses because of business failure.

5. I've taken considerable losses in this business, so I'm thinking of starting a different business.

6. My first impression was unfavorable, and though I have lived here over a year I still cannot come to like this country.

7. Chinese characters are called pictographs.

8. I will open a shop near the factory with the employees in mind (as customers).

9. Of the various natural phenomena, typhoons cause the greatest damage.

10. The elephant uses his trunk to pick up food.

11. Once seated in front of her dressing table, that woman doesn't move for an hour.

12. I observe the stars in the night sky through a telescope.

13. I practice my lines before a mirror.

14. The Prime Minister is at present convalescing.

15. The hemorrhaging is severe, and he must have absolute rest and quiet.

16. When it comes to still life, I like Braque's paintings.

17. We have arteries and veins as blood vessels.

18. Talk a bit more quietly, please.

19. That pair is an interesting contrast, you know.

20. The lighting was too dim to be effective.

21. We are suffering with a water shortage as a result of the continued dry spell.

22. The rain stopped and the sun came out.

23. The situation is critical.

24. The rain clouds hung low and the sky threatened to rain any moment.

25. Gradually the situation started to take on a suspicious character.

26. Anti-government riots broke out all over.

27. No matter what the occasion may be you must not employ violence.

28. He adopted an extremely high-handed attitude toward his superior, so he was fired.

29. Since it was Sunday, I read a picture book for the children.

30. I am doing research on Western painting, especially French oil painting of the first half of the nineteenth century.

31. I got a beautiful picture postcard of the seashore scenery from my younger sister.

32. Business conditions were bad last year; we hope that the market will pick up this year.

33. Night scenery in New York is beautiful.

34. I live in a drab apartment.

35. We used to say teishaba instead of eki [train station].

36. The power's gone off. Light the candle, will you?

37. That dispute was finally settled through the efforts of the arbitrator who brought labor and management together.

38. I will use a ruler to draw a straight line.

39. Burning brightly the sun sank below the horizon.

40. The main Tōkkaidō line of the national railways is in the black, but the branch lines in the countryside are almost all in the red.

41. Birds have perched on the telephone wires in a flock.

42. With the roads so poor even in a metropolis like Tōkyō, (you can imagine) how much worse they must be out in the country.

43. At the end of that narrow alley is Mr. Akagi's house.

44. With the development of aircraft, passengers on the liners of the Atlantic run are dwindling (in number).

45. The people who had ended the day's work and were hurrying on the road home have all passed by, and the street has again grown peaceful.

46. Natural disasters occur when one has just forgotten about them.

47. Kyoto, which escaped war disaster, has maintained traditions for over a thousand years.

48. Destruction from fires is tremendous in cities with a lot of wooden architecture.

49. I will turn misfortune into a blessing.

50. Do you believe in a life after death for human beings?

51. We cannot admit minors.

52. His destination is undecided.

53. We will set out on a voyage in search of an unknown continent.

54. Schubert's "Unfinished Symphony" is one of the popular works of music in Japan.

55. Think of some good excuse.

56. The translator is one of the first rank, but I cannot say that it is a very good translation.

57. For me, translation from English to Japanese is much easier than from Japanese to English.

58. If you translate too literally your translation will not be clear; if you translate too freely you get away [= stray] from the original.

59. I am working as an interpreter at the United Nations.

60. I sent a telegram saying I would arrive tomorrow morning at seven.

61. He said that he had obtained accurate intelligence, but the battle did not progress as the President had expected.

62. I have not yet received a detailed report on this incident.

63. A teacher's life is one of small material reward.

64. Politics are controlled by pressures from outside.

65. Typhoons are a type of tropical low pressure condition.

66. Since my blood pressure is high, I try not to drink alcoholic beverages.

67. The people, suffering under the tyranny of the king, started riots all over (the country).

68. The Minister of Construction set out upon an inspection of the disaster area.

69. He is a stupid jerk. [Or: He is an insensible guy.]

70. I sympathize fully with your feeling.

71. This game will be played rain or shine.

72. The typhoon passed and the weather became perfectly clear.

73. You're bound to feel good on such a fine autumn day as today.

74. Your words have dispelled my doubts.

75. The weather conditions are good, so a world's record may be made.

76. The recording conditions are bad and I cannot catch what is said.

77. Children like to buy magazines with lots of supplements.

78. In the central part of Honshū the mountain ranges run at a right angle to Honshū.

79. In the sense of preventing the centralization of power, we must strongly promote the autonomy of the (various) prefectures.

80. I will emigrate to Brazil to seek new land.

81. I have now moved my residence to the following address.

82. Watch out, for he is a capricious man.

LESSON 32

1. This knife has a fine edge.

2. We were encircled by the enemy's overwhelming number.

3. Wrap it in paper and put it in a bag please.

4. When sending a package overseas one must pack it well.

5. It was all of thirty years ago that the book was published.

6. The major newspapers of Japan publish both morning and evening editions.

7. They say that book is the best seller among the new books published this week.

8. Even if we do not take the example of India into account, [= We need not even look at India's example to realize that] it is very difficult to maintain neutrality in a world such as this of today when two powers are confronting one another.

9. We must adopt more forceful policies to break the deadlock of the present situation.

10. Whichever road we take we will eventually come out at the same place, but I think the traffic is lighter on this one.

11. The war situation took a turn for the worse.

12. We must make them clarify the rights and wrongs of the question.

13. You simply [= absolutely] must correct this bad habit.

14. She is a unique "new face."

15. I have no objection to your opinion.

16. His actions are rather extraordinary.

17. It is hard for persons with differing views of the world to cooperate.

18. It takes courage to publish a new theory which differs from the theory of one's teacher.

19. Nihon rekishi [Japanese history] is also called Nihon-shi.

20. He was a professor who held one post after another in famous universities and now he spends his time every day doing as he pleases   [working in the field on fine days and reading at home on rainy days].

21. We cannot employ a person with a school record of only graduating from junior high school.

22. I don't know what sort of a career he has had, but he is a man with considerable real ability.

23. Please write down in chronological order your record of employment.

24. At one time they used to teach Western history and Oriental history separately, but recently in high school they have put them together and teach them as world history.

25. He knows historical facts in detail.

26. The signing of the Triple Alliance was what brought Japan to defeat.

27. There is a marked difference in character between the League of Nations which was formed after World War I and the postwar United Nations.

28. He said, "China's UN membership is a matter of time."

29. You will fail if you get a below-average grade.

30. The policies of Theodore Roosevelt toward China were the "Open Door Policy" and "Equality Of Opportunity."

31. We are having a sale where everything goes for a hundred yen (apiece).

32. They were arrested for holding a demonstration.

33. He took an examination (for the license) and became a medical doctor.

34. One cannot publish one's views until after a careful examination (of them).

35. I've not been able to read small print very well lately, so I've been thinking of going to an eye doctor and having an eye examination.

36. There are some countries which do not require a visa.

37. I will make my reply on the basis of the survey.

38. Eisenhower proposed to Russia the aerial inspection of military bases.

39. The second meeting of those two was ten years after the end of the war.

40. The illness recurred and he is now in the hospital.

41. The anti-rearmament demonstration congregated about the Diet.

42. Since the War, the Japanese nation has been striving hard for the rebuilding of its economy.

43. From the deck of the vessel he gazed fixedly at the land thinking that he would not likely return there again.

44. At the end of the year things are very congested [= mail is heavy] so please send out your New Year's greeting cards by the twenty-third (of December).

45. A celebration was held to commemorate the military victory.

46. On the second of January the front of the Imperial Palace is thronged with people offering their greetings to the Imperial Court.

47. He seems to be confusing me with Mr. Tanaka.

48. The story has gotten mixed up, so please tell it to me again from the very beginning.

49. He is devoting his entire life to a solution of the problem of mixed-blood [= interracial] children.

50. It is expected that an extra session of the Diet will be called at the end of March.

51. Critical temperature is the temperature limit at which a gas will not liquefy under pressure.

52. I will write an article about the attitude of the Prime Minister, who is facing a special session of the Diet.

53. I'd like to save money but my family is so large it just cannot be done.

54. The water volume of the reservoir is rapidly diminishing because of the long dry spell.

55. The sales of coal have been poor and the coal yards are (loaded with) mountains of coal.

56. I owe this person a debt of gratitude from the time of my boyhood.

57. If I work one more year, I'll be entitled to a pension.

58. I shall never in my life forget what you have done for me.

59. If you borrow money from such a person as that you'll be imposed upon by him for the rest of your life.

60. The relations between the two countries are currently in a tense state.

61. He set fire to his own house with his eye on (getting) the insurance money.

62. How can climbing up a steep mountain path be any pleasure?

63. Please send in a written report of absence in case of illness.

64. We are short of personnel, so please forgive any inconvenience [lack of service].

65. Please deliver it to my house within the week.

66. The Japanese army was invincible at first.

67. The management methods of the company were so bad it went into bankruptcy.

68. The marriage talks were broken off due to the problem of the (differing) social positions of the two families.

69. Old letters I tear up and burn.

70. The defeated Napoleon was exiled to the Island of Elba.

71. What do you want to study as a foreign student in America?

72. A visitor came while you were out.

73. Get off at the third stop from here.

74. The place where suspects are temporarily detained at the police station is called the detention ward [house of detention].

75. Nobody would testify, fearing subsequent trouble.

76. When lending large sums of money, one had best have a note signed.

77. The incident came to an end with Mr. Yamashita's testimony.

78. Attach a photograph to the document to prove that you are the party in question.

79. Two guarantors are necessary.

80. You will have my reply in two or three days.

81. It took all of six months to repay the loan.

82. I am just on my way to return a book to the library.

83. Did you get back all the money you lent?

84. I regret that he died before I could repay his kindness.

85. The Minister of Construction put all his efforts into rehabilitation of the disaster area.

86. Preparation of lessons is important, but review is also important.

87. The round trip from here to the center of the city takes an hour.

88. Easter is the festival commemorating Christ's resurrection.

89. His recuperation was good, and he regained his former healthy condition.

LESSON 33

1. If you do that you will set a bad precedent.

2. If one goes to a foreign country, it is necessary to become quickly accustomed to that country's ways.

3. What is the standard [or: basis] for deciding whether a certain novel is artistic or merely popular?

4. Every day I am so pursued by petty things that I have not time for study.

5. The more tourists there are, the more vulgar the scenic spots become.

6. From somewhere (or other) he has learned nothing but slang.

7. Let me borrow the dictionary for just a moment, please.

8. Entrance fees differ depending on the shrine or temple.

9. We clasp our hands and worship.

10. The most happy event for the villagers is the festival of their tutelary god.

11. Mr. Mizuta is regarded as a sure election winner.

12. Upbringing is more important than pedigree.

13. The front of the Imperial Palace is thronged with people offering their greetings to the Imperial Court.

14. The Meiji Shrine is where the Emperor Meiji is enshrined.

15. There are fears that this incident will become a baffling mystery.

16. Jinja is also called (o)miya [shrine].

17. Isn't there a police box around here?

18. The demonstrators congregated around the Diet (building).

19. In the Man'yōshū I like best the songs of the "saki-mori" who belonged to the frontier guards.

20. The "I-novel" is writing about the events pertaining to oneself just as they occurred.

21. I ski after my own fashion, and so I make no progress at all.

22. I've never seen such an egotistical man.

23. Chiki, chijin and shiriai [acquaintance] are all almost the same in meaning.

24. A joint United States-Japanese declaration was announced regarding this problem.

25. The people in the back seats probably can't hear very well, so please speak a little louder.

26. He spoke quietly at first, but his voice gradually grew louder.

27. A record has become popular which imitates the voices of the President and his wife.

28. Most substances will change to a solid, a liquid, or a gas depending on the temperature.

29. Real estate, buildings, and machinery are known as fixed assets.

30. As one grows older, a single outlook is apt to get fixed so that it is very difficult to adopt new views.

31. How about settling down [getting married] pretty soon?

32. He was converted from Buddhism to Christianity.

33. He is a man with absolutely no religious sentiment.

34. The current head of a house with an inherited artistic skill we call the iemoto or the sōka.

35. There are graves of famous people in that cemetery.

36. It was around the middle of the sixth century that Buddhism was transmitted to Japan.

37. Is it the concept of Buddhism that one gains access to paradise if he just recites the nembutsu prayer?

38. Making a statue of Buddha without any soul.   [Stopping short of what is needed to give life to the form.]

39. He complains all the time.

40. This sentence has many difficult words and phrases in it.

41. I'd like to have some coffee, so please boil some water.

42. In the summer I go to the public bath every day.

43. How is the temperature of the bath water?

44. I have no financial relations with that man.

45. I'd like to buy a newspaper, but I haven't any change.

46. Ill-got, ill-spent.

47. It will probably take time to settle the boundary problem between India and China.

48. On festival days all sorts of stalls and shops are lined up on the grounds of the shrine.

49. Mr. Tanaka related to the reporters his present thinking.

50. An industrial belt runs continuously from Tōkyō to Yokohama so that it is hard to tell the boundaries between cities.

51. Spain was defeated at the sea battle of Trafalgar and her golden age was over.

52. Four races — yellow, white, black, and red — live in the world.

53. Van Gogh was an expert in the use of yellow.

54. You separate the yolk and the white of an egg.

55. Tourists come here in droves during the early spring leafing season.

56. If one is not careful in the preservation of copperware, a green rust will appear.

57. This area has been designated as green belt so buildings cannot be erected here.

58. Both the plains and the mountains are a sea of green.

59. We hang up the national flag at home and at the office on festival days.

60. Things looked bad for Mr. Yamada, so he left the room.

61. The Japanese flag is called nisshōki.

62. We'd better not have such gambling games as horse racing and bicycle racing.

63. That person is wearing a diamond ring.

64. If you count up the annual rings of a tree you can tell its age.

65. We call rice, barley, and the like cereals.

66. The Kantō Plain is Japan's largest grain district.

67. Mr. Miyakawa also holds the additional post of an official of a subsidiary company.

68. Night and day street construction work was carried on with the aim of completion by the time of the Olympics.

69. I am going to Kyōto both on business and for pleasure.

70. He has regard for the feelings of nobody; he does just as he pleases.

71. Taking photographs is prohibited here.

72. Even though up to now I've not had a single failure, negligence is something to be avoided.

73. Mr. Yukawa's giving up drinking has never lasted for a week.

74. There are cases where, as a result of scientific study, even things hitherto thought to be superstition were proven to be truth.

75. I lost my way and asked a pedestrian for directions.

76. One must not make broadcasts which mislead public sentiment.

77. He committed suicide without leaving a note.

78. We will open the will before the survivors of the deceased.

79. Today when the traffic situation has worsened, the streetcar is an utter relic of a bygone age.

LESSON 34

1. Use your own judgment to decide.

2. His new novel is not very popular.

3. The truth about that incident was ascertained ten years later.

4. All were acquitted as a result of judicial decision.

5. I am working in the university hospital.

6. I was on a small island in the South Pacific during the war as a civilian attached to the military.

7. Gold, silver, copper, iron, etc. are called metals.

8. Members of the Diet who are affiliated with no political party are called independents.

9. Under the minister of each ministry, there are two parliamentary vice ministers.

10. In the old constitution the word "subjects" was used, but in the new constitution the term "people" is used.

11. As a result of the official ballot count, Mr. Tagawa was elected by a margin of one thousand votes.

12. The making of a decision through balloting is called "voting."

13. We use an electronic computer to count the number of votes.

14. Since he has no linguistic talent, it would be futile for him to study foreign languages.

15. Mr. Yamamura is a genius at language learning; he has mastered the languages of six countries.

16. George Sand was a woman who combined both wit and beauty.

17. Mr. Kawakami has literary talents and aspires to be a novelist.

18. He was expelled from the party for allegedly being a Trotskyite.

19. With the exception of Mr. Yamada, everyone took part.

20. The Self-Defense Forces were sent out for snow removal work.

21. I understand that we cannot discuss world peace if Communist China is excluded.

22. In the Tokugawa period there was a strict division into the four classes of warrior, farmer, artisan, and merchant.

23. They handle only high-class goods at that store.

24. Both the upperclassmen and the underclassmen will go on a trip together.

25. The classification is set according to quality.

26. In Japan, as a conservative party, there is the Liberal Democratic party; and as reform political parties, there are the Socialist party, the Democratic Socialist party and the Communist party.

27. As parties go, the Liberal Democratic party is the leading one in both the House of Representatives and the House of Councillors.

28. The Soviet Union is a socialist state, but this does not mean that everyone there is a member of the Communist party.

29. Within the Liberal Democratic party itself he is, if anything, more a member of the progressive faction.

30. In the ancient Japanese arts there are various schools.

31. Mr. Kawamura has gone to New York as a special correspondent for the Asahi (Newspaper).

32. The quotation is long, so I will omit the rest.

33. I am reflecting deeply on what I did.

34. The vice-ministers of the affected ministries are gathered and are making arrangements.

35. How about omitting (from) line 3 to line 5 in this passage?

36. He does not reflect upon his own conduct; he does nothing but disparage others.

37. In accordance with his last wish, all his books were donated to the library.

38. Get two bottles of beer out of the refrigerator, please.

39. The Minister of Finance explained the new budget to the press.

40. That large mansion with its earthen-walled storehouse is Mr. Homma's residence.

41. I dispose of things I do not need and, thus lightened, set out upon a trip.

42. In response to the prosecutor's questions the suspect kept his mouth shut as to the source of the money.

43. The authorities will surely take appropriate measures regarding this affair.

44. Better to go ahead and do a thing than worry about it.

45. I had Mr. Yamamoto show me about the town.

46. The exam results were better than I expected.

47. Aren't there any good ideas for the solution of this difficult problem?

48. There was not a single person in favor of Mr. Nakada's proposal.

49. I have until the end of this month to hand in my thesis.

50. Your argument is wrong from the very premise.

51. The new theory that he put forth went unobserved by the scholarly world.

52. Mr. Kobayashi is famous as a literary critic.

53. Since the play was unexpectedly well received the author is delighted.

54. The Japan Teachers Union and the Ministry of Education are in opposition to one another over (the issue of) efficiency reports for teachers.

55. Mr. Matsumoto has an established reputation as a writer of mystery stories.

56. The Foreign Minister took responsibility for this incident and submitted his resignation.

57. In this dictionary it is not explained fully.

58. This is [or: was] the first time the number one man in the Soviet Union has himself announced the intention of resigning.

59. I looked it up in an encyclopedia.

60. The estimate of the authorities, I hear, is that this year too there will be a bumper rice crop.

61. It will demand a fair amount of capital to push this plan ahead.

62. There is an objection to his being recommended for chairman.

63. The gun is not an administrative division; it is simply a geographical division.

64. This course is counted as two credits.

65. He was severely criticized by the membership for acting independently.

66. To break the monotony of life, I take trips on weekends.

67. The number of words I have learned has increased, but I still cannot use them well.

68. "Behind every crime there is a woman."

69. The suspect denied the crime.

70. The criminal confessed the name of his accomplice.

71. It does not necessarily follow that those who have committed crimes are all evil persons.

72. He received the verdict of "not guilty" and he legally became a free man.

73. In Japan the chief justice hands down the judgment of guilty or not guilty.

74. You needn't bear the blame alone.

75. Hitler's merits and faults will be decided by the historians of a later time.

76. They did nothing but argue and produced no conclusion.

77. I am studying logic and psychology in college.

78. Though the theory is correct, there are occasions when it cannot be actually applied.

79. Although he is a rich man, he lives a simple life.

80. The suspect meekly acknowledged his guilt.

81. Water is formed from two elements, hydrogen and oxygen.

82. America proclaimed its independence in July 1776.

83. In December 1941 Japan declared war on America and England.

84. I intend to become a missionary and take part in missionary work.

LESSON 35

1. I have a great interest in Japanese literature.

2. The marked comeback made by Japan's economy since the end of the war is largely due to the industriousness of the Japanese people.

3. Japanese industry, which sprang up in the Meiji period, developed with the increase in national power.

4. If you get too excited your blood pressure will go up!

5. The solution is written on the very last page of this book.

6. I came without having studied, so I handed in a blank examination paper.

7. The minister's reply contained nothing new at all.

8. Write your answers on a separate sheet of paper.

9. When the mountains are opened for climbing on July first, the area is packed with mountain climbers.

10. A registered trademark is one which has gone through the process of registration and is not allowed to be used on other articles.

11. Why is climbing mountains so much fun?

12. He elucidated his actions to a group of reporters.

13. This book has few annotations, so you will not be able to study it on your own.

14. I believe my husband will be acquitted and set free.

15. Since there must not be any mistakes in the way one interprets the wording (of the treaty), we will consider both the Japanese and the English as official texts.

16. Bernard Shaw was known as a man with a vitriolic tongue.

17. Even if (you do) such things, that will neither mend nor mar matters.

18. Raw fish spoils easily in the summer, so one must take care not to be poisoned when eating it.

19. If you're willing to put out one thousand yen more you can buy something nice.

20. Our team suffered a crushing defeat from lack of spirit.

21. The excited crowd finally raised a riot.

22. If you have a stock certificate, even if it's for only one share, you are a stockholder.

23. There has been a noticeable dispersion of stock ownership in the recent market.

24. Let's sit down and rest on that stump.

25. On the securities market political activities inside and outside the country are quickly reflected in the price of stocks.

26. There are countries which do not require a visa but only a passport for entry (into the country).

27. One buys an entrance ticket and goes to the platform to see a person off.

28. Newspapers are supposed to use assumed names for criminal offenders eighteen years old and under (in writing about them).

29. I will not answer hypothetical questions.

30. I overslept, so I pretended I was ill and stayed away from the office.

31. If, for instance, I were in your position, I wouldn't do such a thing (but . . .).

32. There are competent scholars very close to the Prime Minister.

33. Don't look at things indirectly (from the side); you must look at them head-on.

34. Japan's traffic regulations prescribe that traffic move on the left-hand side.

35. On either side of the street a crowd of people stood and watched the procession.

36. Which school was the first to be established as a college?

37. He published original ideas in the scholarly world.

38. What does the rapid advance in the Diet of the Sōka-gakkai tell us?

39. A person lacking creativity cannot write a novel.

40. I went to Japan in August of last year.

41. What do you think about the recent international situation?

42. We erect bronze statues of men who have rendered meritorious services to the country.

43. I imagined him to be more of an old man.

44. There is in general a gentle softness to be seen in the Buddhist statuary of the Tempyō period.

45. Since I have a darkroom in my house, let me develop that film for you.

46. In Japan the copyright on a novel is valid for thirty years after death (of the author).

47. The author of this book is a prominent politician.

48. He writes all kinds of books even outside the area of his specialty.

49. I feel that there is a noticeable difference when one compares the effort [work] of those two.

50. We watch sumō wrestling from very close to the ring.

51. Bags of rice are piled up like a mountain in the storehouse.

52. I do programming at the television station.

53. He does jazz arrangements of well-known classical pieces.

54. Some important news came in and the editorial department of the newspaper was like a battle front.

55. His works are almost all short stories; he has only one full-size novel.

56. The weather is so nice that I will do my knitting out in the sunshine.

57. I am a lecturer at a university.

58. The lecture hall was filled to capacity with people listening to his talk.

59. In order to understand that teacher's lectures one must read all sorts of books.

60. The Japanese peace conference was held at San Francisco.

61. No matter how well one can act, one cannot always become a star.

62. I am not used to giving speeches, so I am nervous about it.

63. As one grows famous, the fees for such things as TV appearances go up.

64. That man thinks of nothing but currying favor with his superiors.

65. The United States-Japanese Exchange Swimming Meet is held once every other year.

66. When Lindberg's plane appeared in the sky above Paris the populace shouted for joy.

67. That book received critical acclaim and piled edition upon edition.

68. I collect block prints from all over the world.

69. There are all sorts of rare first editions in that library.

70. I will attend the Nobel Prize presentation ceremonies.

71. Prizes ranging from first place to sixth place are provided for this game.

72. I go to an art museum and enjoy the famous paintings there.

Part VII

KEY TO KANA PRACTICE

1. NAMES OF FOREIGN PLACES

1.	ázia	Asia	13.	nyuuyóoku	New York
2.	amerika	America	14.	hwiraderúhwia	Philadelphia
3.	igirisu	England	15.	hwirípin	Philippine
4.	kánada	Canada	16.	huransu	France
5.	karihworunia	California	17.	maruséiyu	Marseille
6.	kyúuba	Cuba	18.	bétonamu	Viet Nam
7.	sanhuransísuko	San Francisco	19.	bósuton	Boston
8.	zyóoziya	Georgia	20.	masatyuséttu	Massachusetts
9.	sobiéto	Soviet Union	21.	mekísiko	Mexico
10.	tyekosurobákiya	Czechoslovakia	22.	mosukuwa	Moscow (Moskva)
11.	tékisasu	Texas	23.	yooróppa	Europe
12.	dóitu	Germany (Deutschland)	24.	rosanzérusu	Los Angeles
			25.	wasínton	Washington

2. NAMES OF FOREIGN PERSONS

26.	adenáuaa	Adenauer	34.	turugénehu	Turgenev
27.	uinsuton tyáatiru	Winston Churchill	35.	dᵉyúpon	Du Pont
28.	syeekusupía	Shakespeare	36.	naporeon	Napoleon
29.	sutáarin	Stalin	37.	néeru	Nehru
30.	ruuzubéruto	Roosevelt	38.	pasutúuru	Pasteur
31.	sezánnu	Cézanne	39.	reonarudo da bínti	Leonardo da Vinci
32.	dáawin	Darwin			
33.	dagurasu makkáasaa	Douglas Mac-Arthur	40.	rokkuhwéraa	Rockefeller

3. LOANWORDS

41.	aisukuríimu	ice cream	55.	kokakóra	Coca Cola
42.	apáato	apartment house	56.	kókku	cook
43.	inku	ink	57.	góruhu	golf
44.	uísukii	whisky	58.	sararíiman	salaried man
45.	úuru	wool	59.	syaapu-pénsiru	ever-sharp pencil
46.	erebéetaa	elevator			
47.	énzin	engine	60.	sukáato	skirt
48.	óobaa	overcoat	61.	zubón	pants (jupon F)
49.	kámera	camera	62.	séetaa	sweater
50.	gasorin	gasoline	63.	sóhwaa	sofa
51.	garéezi	garage	64.	tákusii	taxi
52.	kyándee	candy	65.	taipuráitaa	typewriter
53.	kurisúmasu	Christmas	66.	dánsu	dance
54.	kéeki	cake	67.	tyuuíngamu	chewing gum

68.	tyokoréeto	chocolate	88.	purogúramu	program
69.	teeburu	table	89.	herikóputaa	helicoptor
70.	térebi	television	90.	pén	pen
71.	depáato	department store	91.	hóteru	hotel
72.	tóire (tóiretto)	toilet	92.	pokétto	pocket
73.	tóosuto	toast	93.	máiku	microphone
74.	náiron	nylon		(maikuróhon)	
75.	nyúusu	news	94.	míruku	milk
76.	nékutai	necktie	95.	mémo	memorandum
77.	nóoto	note	96.	yúumoa	humor
78.	hámu	ham	97.	yótto	yacht
79.	páate^eii	party	98.	rassyu-áwaa	rush hours
80.	pán	bread (pão P)	99.	résutoran	restaurant
81.	báta	butter	100.	waisyatu	dress shirt
82.	hankati	handkerchief			(white shirt)
83.	handobákku	handbag			
84.	híitaa	heater			
85.	bíiru	beer (bier N)	F:	French	
86.	bíru (bírudingu)	building	N:	Dutch	
87.	buréeki	brake	P:	Portuguese	

4. HIRAGANA EXERCISES

1.	(1) aói	is blue		(4) kaze	wind
	(2) íi	is good		(5) kázoku	family
	(3) ue	above	6.	(1) takái	is tall
	(4) iie	no		(2) tikái	is near
	(5) óoi	are many		(3) tukue	desk
	(6) iu (yuu)	says		(4) teikoku-	Imperial Hotel
2.	(1) akai	is red		hóteru	
	(2) éki	station		(5) tokei	clock
	(3) ookíi	is big			
	(4) iku	goes	7.	(1) dáiku	carpenter
	(5) iké	pond		(2) tikázika	soon
	(6) kóe	voice		(3) tuzuku	continues
3.	(1) éiḡa	movie		(4) déḡuti	exit
	(2) kaḡí	key		(5) tokidoki	sometimes
	(3) káḡu	furniture	8.	(1) asátte	day after tomor-
	(4) géki	a play			row
	(5) góḡo	afternoon		(2) attakái	is warm
				(3) gakkoo	school
4.	(1) sake	rice wine		(4) kottí	this side
	(2) sió	salt		(5) zassi	magazine
	(3) sukósi	a little			
	(4) sékai	world	9.	(1) sakana	fish
	(5) osoi	is late		(2) nikú	meat
	(6) asoko	over there		(3) inú	dog
				(4) néko	cat
5.	(1) zasikí	Japanese room		(5) isoḡasíi	is busy
	(2) kázi	a fire			
	(3) sízuka	quiet	10.	(1) haná	flower

(2)	hitótu	one thing
(3)	hutatú	two things
(4)	heitai	soldier
(5)	hosói	is thin
(6)	hóo	side

11.
(1)	sibai	a play
(2)	zibiki	dictionary
(3)	abunai	is dangerous
(4)	beikoku	the United States
(5)	boosi	hat

12.
(1)	suppái	is sour
(2)	ippai	full
(3)	happi	workman's coat
(4)	kippu	ticket
(5)	seppuku	hara-kiri
(6)	íppo	one step

13.
(1)	íma	now
(2)	miti	road
(3)	samúi	is cold
(4)	meisi	name card
(5)	kimono	kimono
(6)	musumé	daughter

14.
(1)	yamá	mountain
(2)	yasai	vegetable
(3)	huyú	winter
(4)	yói	is good
(5)	yokohama	Yokohama

15.
(1)	terá	temple
(2)	turi	fishing
(3)	rúsu	away from home
(4)	kore	this one
(5)	sore	that one
(6)	sirói	is white

16.
(1)	watakusi	I
(2)	warúi	is bad

17.
(1)	hón	book
(2)	ténki	weather
(3)	tanaka-san	Mr. Tanaka
(4)	senséi	teacher
(5)	enpitu	pencil
(6)	denpoo	telegram

18.
(1)	kyaku	guest
(2)	kyúuzi	waiter

(3)	kyuukoo	express
(4)	tookyoo	Tokyo
(5)	yuubínkyoku	post office

19.
(1)	gyaku	reverse
(2)	gyuuniku	beef
(3)	sotug̅yoo	graduation

20.
(1)	syasin	photograph
(2)	zidóosya	automobile
(3)	syúzin	husband
(4)	issyúukan	one week
(5)	syokudoo	dining room

21.
(1)	zyama	hindrance
(2)	zínzya	Shinto shrine
(3)	zyúudoo	judo
(4)	zyoozú	skillful
(5)	benzyó	toilet

22.
(1)	tyawan	teacup
(2)	omótya	toy
(3)	tyúug̅aku	Jr. High
(4)	tyoodo	exactly
(5)	tyótto	a bit

23.
(1)	koohii-zyáwan	coffee cup
(2)	odawara-zyóotin	Japanese lantern

24.
(1)	konnyaku	devil's tongue jelly
(2)	nyuug̅aku	entrance into a school
(3)	gyuunyuu	milk
(4)	ténnyo	celestial nymph

25.
(1)	hyakusyóo	farmer
(2)	hyooban	reputation

26.
(1)	sánbyaku	three hundred
(2)	byooki	sick
(3)	byooin	hospital

27.
(1)	roppyakú	six hundred
(2)	happyakú	eight hundred
(3)	happyoo	announcement

28.
(1)	sanmyaku	mountain range
(2)	myóozi	family name
(3)	myóoniti	tomorrow

29.
(1)	ryakuzi	simplified character
(2)	ryuukoo	fashion
(3)	ryokan	inn
(4)	ryoozíkan	consulate

5. KANA DRILL SENTENCES

1. Tanaka-san wa | nihonzín desu ḡa ‖ Zyóonzu-san wa | amerikázin desu.

2. Yamamoto-san wa ‖ kinoo ‖ Súmisu-san to issyo ni | résutoran de | bangóhan o | tabemásita.

3. Buráun-san wa ‖ gakkoo e iku tóki ‖ ítu mo ‖ nihon͞go no hón to | ookíi | zísyo o | hurosiki ni tutúnde | motte ikimásu.

4. Kinoo ‖ Amerika ni iru tomodati ni okuru tamé ni ‖ Sinzyuku no depáato e | Nihon no nin͞gyoo o mí ni | ittá ḡa ‖ íi no ḡa | nákatta kara ‖ kawanákatta.

5. "Anáta wa ‖ Kyooto-dái͞gaku de | ei͞go o osiete iru Tónpuson to iu | senséi ni | átta koto ḡa | arimásu ka."
   "Iie. Onamae wa sitte imásu ḡa ‖ máda ‖ ome ni kakátta koto wa | arimasén."

6. Suzuki-san ni ‖ Tookyóo-eki no | tikáku ni aru | Kootuu-Kóosya de ‖ Oosaka máde no | oohuku-kíppu o | katte moraimásita.

7. "Kore wa | huransu͞go de nán te | iimásu ka."
   "Sáa. Dóo iu ka | sirimasén | née. Zutto máe ni | huransu͞go o narátta koto wa | áru n desu keredo ‖ móo wasuretyaimásita yo."

8. "Dóo site | konna ni osoku nátta n desu ka."
   "Mótto | háyaku | koko ni túku hazu | désita ḡa ‖ Tamá͞gawa no | hasí o watatte | sú͞gu | panku sityatte ‖ taiya o torikaerú no ni | zúibun | zikan ḡa kakátta kara . . ."

9. Tookyoo no rassyu-áwaa wa | totemo taihen da. Dóno | toorí mo | zidóosya de | ippai dá si ‖ dénsya ya | tikatetu no éki mo ‖ básu no noriba mo ‖ kaisya e kayou hitó de | zúibun | kónde iru. Háyaku | uti o déte mo ‖ nakanaka dénsya ya | básu ni | norenái de ‖ kaisya ni okureru kotó mo | áru.

10. Rítyaadoson-san wa | sensyuu | Amerika kara | Nihón e | irassyatta bákari desu. ‖ Máda | nihon-ryóori o | mesia͞gatta kotó ḡa | nái to | ossyáru no de ‖ sakúban ‖ Sinbasí-eki no | sóba no | ryooríya e | oture simásita. Tatami ni suwatte ‖ o-hási de | tabéru no wa | hazímete de ‖ totemo omosirói to | ossyátte ‖ o-sake mo | suki-yaki mo ‖ takusan mesia͞garimásita.

6. ENGLISH TRANSLATIONS OF THE KANA DRILL SENTENCES

1. Mr. Tanaka is a Japanese while Mr. Jones is an American.

2. Mr. Yamamoto ate dinner with Mr. Smith yesterday (evening) at a restaurant.

3. When Mr. Brown goes to school, he always carries his Japanese books and his big dictionary wrapped up in a furoshiki.

4. I went to a department store in Shinjuku yesterday to look at Japanese dolls [and pick one] to send to a friend of mine in America, but there was none that [I thought] was good, so I didn't buy any.

5. "Have you ever met a teacher named Mr. Thompson who teaches English at Kyoto University?"

   "No, I have heard his name, but I haven't met him yet."

6. I had Mr. Suzuki buy me a round-trip ticket to Osaka at the Travel Bureau near Tokyo Station.

7. "How do you say this in French?"

    "I don't know how you say it. I once studied French a long time ago, but I've forgotten it all now."

8. "How come you're so late?"

    "We should have got here earlier, but we had a flat right after crossing the Tamagawa Bridge and it took quite a while to change the tire, that's why."

9. The rush hour in Tokyo is terrible. Every street is full of automobiles; streetcar stops, subway stations, and bus stops are (all) crowded with the people who commute to ("company[-offices]"=) work. There are times when I leave home early but am still late for ("the company[-office]"=)work because I can't board a streetcar or bus for a long time.

10. Mr. Richardson just came to Japan from America last week. He said that he had never eaten Japanese food, so last night I took him to a Japanese restaurant near Shimbashi Station. He said that it was the first time he had sat on tatami and eaten with chopsticks and [so] he found it very interesting. He had quite a bit of sake [to drink] and sukiyaki [to eat].